iMovie 2
THE MISSING MANUAL

*The book that
should have been
in the box*

Reviews of *iMovie: The Missing Manual*

With characteristic humility, author/publisher David Pogue describes this as "the book that should have been in the box"—and, well, yeah, he's right. To quote Dizzy Dean, it ain't braggin' if you done it.

If you're an iMovie novice, you need this book. If you're an iMovie intermediate, you'll want this book. If you're an iMovie expert—hey, you already have this book, and that's one of the reasons you're an expert. *iMovie: The Missing Manual* is the only iMovie book I rate as "Must Have."

—*Jamie McCornack, About This Particular Macintosh (atpm.com)*

Buy this book, study it, and apply what you've learned; your audience will be grateful.

—*Stephen Withers, Australian Personal Computer*

Striking out on his own with Pogue Press, David loses none of the sparkle and wit in his writing. Befitting his musical background, Pogue's prose is equal parts lyrical and percussive—with a sometimes wry, sometimes silly humor that never gets in the way of the point he is making...It's a style Pogue has honed to an art; no one can take a subject as dry as a computer operating system and make it seem so completely accessible, and even fun.

—*Chuck La Tournous, NJ MUG Reviews*

iMovie: The Missing Manual is actually not so much a manual as a junior college degree in television production—and all for $19.95. Emulating the style of publishing partner O'Reilly & Associates, this Pogue Press volume has packed every page with useful information...All in all, a wonderful book and highly recommended by The REVIEW ZONE.

—*The Review Zone*

I felt iMovie's help files were pretty darn good. But David Pogue's book is better. For users of Apple's free editing software, *iMovie: The Missing Manual* will quickly become an well-thumbed resource. It looks like the series is going to be a winner.

—*John Mello, Mass High Tech*

David Pogue's prose is straight to the point, and he isn't afraid to point out iMovie's faults and offer some workarounds...Pogue has written the de facto iMovie manual.

—*Computer Arts*

This is the finest of the iMovie guides and equal to Pogue's best past efforts. He's a master of technical explanations and has a deservedly large and grateful following. If you have ever thought about making a simple movie, this stimulating book would be an smart, inexpensive first step—even before forking over a dime on any software, hardware, or a DV cam.

—*Robin Simmons, Desert Hot Springs, CA*

Quite simply the best computer book I have ever purchased. It is a very straightforward, lucid, step-by-step explanation of how to get the most out of this program...Using this book is like having an iMovie guru sitting next to you, helping you along.

—*Stephen E. Rosenblum, Ann Arbor, MI*

iMovie 2
THE MISSING MANUAL

David Pogue

POGUE PRESS™
O'REILLY®

Beijing • Cambridge • Farnham • Köln • Paris • Sebastopol • Taipei • Tokyo

iMovie 2: The Missing Manual

by David Pogue

Copyright © 2001 Pogue Press, LLC. All rights reserved.
Printed in the United States of America.

Published by Pogue Press/O'Reilly & Associates, Inc., 101 Morris Street, Sebastopol, CA 95472.

January 2001:   First Edition.
February 2001:   Second Printing

ISBN: 0-596-00104-5   [2/01]
[M]

Table of Contents

Part Two: Editing in iMovie

The Missing Credits

About the Author

 David Pogue, personal-technology columnist for the *New York Times* and award-winning former *Macworld* columnist, is the creator of the Missing Manual series. He's the author or co-author of 17 computer, humor, and music books, including six books in the "...for Dummies" series *(Macs, The iMac, The iBook, Magic, Opera,* and *Classical Music); PalmPilot: The Ultimate Guide;* and three books in the Missing Manual series: *Mac OS 9, iMovie,* and *Windows Me.*

In his other life, David is a former Broadway show conductor, a magician, and an incorrigible pianist. He and his wife Jennifer live in Connecticut with their young son and daughter, as copiously photographed at *www.davidpogue.com.*

He welcomes feedback about this book and others in the Missing Manual series by email: *david@pogueman.com.* (If you're seeking technical help, however, please refer to the help sources listed in Appendix B.)

About the Creative Team

Nan Barber (copy editor, first edition) works as a freelance writer and editor from her home near Boston. She serves as managing editor for *Salamander,* a magazine for poetry, fiction, and memoirs, and is the coauthor of *Office 2001 for Macintosh: The Missing Manual.*

Rose Cassano (cover camcorder illustration) has worked as an independent designer and illustrator for 20 years. Assignments have spanned the nonprofit sector to corporate clientele. She is lives in beautiful Southern Oregon, grateful for the miracles of modern technology that make living and working there a reality. Email: *cassano@cdsnet.net.* Web: *www.rosecassano.com.*

Dennis Cohen (technical reviewer, first edition), a veteran of the Jet Propulsion Laboratory, Claris, Ashton-Tate, and Aladdin, has served as the technical reviewer for many bestselling Mac books, including several editions of *Macworld Mac Secrets* and the first three Missing Manual titles. He's the co-author of *AppleWorks 6 for Dummies.* Email: *drcohen@mac.com.*

Tim Geaney (photographer) has shot editorial photos for *Self, GQ, Glamour,* and *Mademoiselle* magazines, among others. His commercial-photography clients include Victoria's Secret, Nautica, J.Crew, Spiegel, Nordstrom's, Neiman Marcus, and Saks Fifth Avenue. The DV filmmaking bug has bit him—he recently completed an Avon TV commercial. Web: *www.timgeaney.com.*

Jim Kanter (technical editor, first edition) is an award-winning independent filmmaker and broadcast journalist. He's a USC film school graduate who has worked for over 24 years as a cameraman and 10 years as a film and video editor. He teaches DV filmmaking in Atlanta, where he's working on his Master's degree in Communication with an emphasis on Digital Filmmaking. Web: *www.dfilminst.com*.

Irene Lusztig (technical reviewer, first edition) is a Boston-based independent documentary filmmaker. Her film *For Beijing with Love and Squalor* (1997) has been shown at film festivals and broadcast on public television in the U.S., East Asia, and Europe. She currently works as a teaching assistant in the film and video department at Harvard.

Glenn Reid (technical editor, this edition) was the architect and lead engineer for iMovie 1 and iMovie 2. He's had a long career in graphics and multimedia software, beginning when Adobe Systems was a startup with only 25 people. He is a leading expert on PostScript, electronic publishing, and digital typography, and has written two books on PostScript (Adobe's "green book" and a followup called *Thinking in PostScript).*

Glenn also founded RightBrain Software in the late 1980s, which developed a page-layout program for NeXT computers that delivered functionality rivalling QuarkXPress, but with a much more intuitive interface. He became known for simple but effective user interface design, contributing to Adobe Illustrator, Fractal Design Painter, and numerous other applications before joining Apple to create the revolutionary iMovie. Glenn's personal consulting page is *at www.rightbrain.com.*

Maarten Reilingh (copy editor, this edition) is from Red Hook, NY. A former university theater professor, reference writer, and academic journal editor, Reilingh has edited nonfiction works of all kinds, including computer-related titles for IDG Books and McGraw-Hill. Besides his family, the theater, and clear expression, Maarty's passion extends to the martial art of Tang Soo Do.

Phil Simpson (book design and layout) has been involved with computer graphics since 1977, when he worked with one of the first graphics-generating computers— an offspring of flight-simulation technology. He now works out of his office in Stamford, CT *(pmsimpson@earthlink.net),* where he has had his graphic design business for 18 years. He is experienced in many facets of graphic design, including corporate identity, publication design, and corporate and medical communications.

Acknowledgments

The Missing Manual series is a joint venture between Pogue Press (the dream team introduced on these pages) and O'Reilly & Associates (a dream publishing partner). In particular, this book owes its existence to Tim O'Reilly, Cathy Record, Edie Freedman, Allen Noren, Laura Schmier, Glenn Harden, Sue Willing, Mark Brokering, Dana Furby, and Sara Winge.

A special group did great favors for this project: David Rogelberg, Arwen O'Reilly, Doug Graham, Charles Petzold, Phil Lefebvre, Michael Krein, Charles Wiltgen, the iMovie fans whose stories appear in this book as sidebars, and the members of the Mac DV discussion list (*www.themacintoshguy.com*). Jim Kanter drafted Chapter 15, many terrific sidebars, and hundreds of technical points. Tim Franklin expertly drafted Chapter 13. (He also created the iMovie film festival at *www.hoverground.com*, as described on page 307.) And a bright yellow scrolling credit goes to Elizabeth "Eagle Eye" Tonis, this book's beta reader, who once again pulled all-nighters in a superhuman effort to stomp every typo and "wordo" out of existence.

One of the most thrilling moments of working on this new edition was the day Glenn Reid, iMovie's lead programmer, agreed to serve as technical editor. As the creator of the software itself, he was able to shine bright, exciting light into corners of the program that few others even know about.

Finally, thanks to Kelly and Tia, my favorite iMovie stars, and my wife, Jennifer, who made this book—and everything else—possible.

The Missing Manual Series

Missing Manual books are designed to be authoritative, superbly written guides to popular computer products that don't come with printed manuals (which is just about all of them). Each book features a hand-crafted index; cross-references to specific page numbers (not just "See Chapter 14"); and RepKover, a detached-spine binding that lets the book lie perfectly flat without the assistance of weights or cinder blocks.

Other recent and upcoming Missing Manual titles include:

- *DreamWeaver 4: The Missing Manual* by David Sawyer McFarland
- *Mac OS 9: The Missing Manual* by David Pogue
- *AppleWorks 6: The Missing Manual* by Jim Elferdink and David Reynolds
- *Office 2001 for Macintosh: The Missing Manual* by Nan Barber and David Reynolds
- *Mac OS X: The Missing Manual* by David Pogue
- *Windows Me: The Missing Manual* by David Pogue
- *Windows 2000 Pro: The Missing Manual* by Sharon Crawford

Introduction

Camcorder video is striking back.

Over the years, it had developed a bad name. After all, what contact do most people have with camcorder footage? It usually comes in one of these two forms:

- **Watching someone else's home movies.** An excruciating experience. Oh, sure, the baby with the overturned spaghetti bowl is cute—but for 45 *seconds,* not 45 minutes.

  The truth is, even camcorder owners are probably aware that the showing-to-others experience could be improved if the footage were edited down to just the good parts. But how's that supposed to happen? Until iMovie came along, editing camcorder footage on the computer required several thousand dollars' worth of digitizing cards (which you had to install into your computer yourself), extremely complicated editing software, and the highest-horsepower computer equipment available.

  Some clever souls tried to edit their videos by buying two VCRs, wiring them together, and copying parts of one tape onto another. That worked great—if you didn't mind the bursts of distortion and static at each splice point and the massive generational quality loss.

  You know what? Unless there was a paycheck involved, editing footage under those circumstances just wasn't worth it. The Fast-Forward button on the remote was a lot easier.

• **Watching camcorder footage on TV.** Whether it's plane crashes on the news or America's silliest home videos, amateur video has made quite a dent on broadcast TV. You know it when you see it: It's the footage that's jerky, has an ugly-font date stamp in the corner, and has been copied so many times that the picture looks like it's in a dirty aquarium.

All of that changed when iMovie came along. It certainly wasn't the first digital video (DV) editing software. But it was the first DV editing software for *nonprofessionals,* people who have a life outside of video editing. Within six months of its release in October 1999, iMovie had become, in words of beaming iMovie papa (and Apple CEO) Steve Jobs, "the most popular video editing software in the world."

Apple only fanned the flames when, in April 2000, it made iMovie a free download (from *www.apple.com/imovie),* ending a bizarre era where iMovie CD-ROMs that once came only with iMac DV models were being sold on eBay.com for $100.

Then, in July 2000, Apple unveiled iMovie 2 (and removed the free version from its Web site, despite Steve Jobs' promise not to do so). iMovie 2 costs $50 (unless you get it with the purchase of a new Mac), but most people still find it a bargain.

Meet iMovie 2

iMovie, of course, is video-editing software for the Macintosh. Over a special wire (a FireWire cable), iMovie grabs itself a copy of the raw footage from your digital camcorder. (See Chapter 1 for more on these astonishingly high-quality cameras.) Then it lets you edit this video, easily, quickly, and creatively.

Put another way, iMovie is the world's least expensive version of what the Hollywood pros call *nonlinear editing* (NLE) software for video, just like the $600 program called EditDV, the $1,000 software called Final Cut Pro, or the $100,000 computer called the Avid editing system. The "nonlinear" part is that no tape is involved while you're editing. There's no rewinding or fast-forwarding; you jump instantly to any piece of footage as you piece your movie together.

Your interest in video may be inspired by any number of ambitions. Maybe you want to create great-looking shows for your local cable station's public-access channel. Maybe you want to create the next *Blair Witch Project,* which was also created by nonprofessionals using a camcorder and nonlinear editing software. Or maybe you just want to make better home movies—much, *much* better home movies. iMovie can accommodate you.

The world of video is exploding. People are giving each other videotapes instead of greeting cards. People are watching each other via video on their Web sites. People are quitting their daily-grind jobs to become videographers for hire, making money filming weddings and creating living video scrapbooks. Video, in other words, is fast becoming a new standard document format for the new century.

If you have iMovie and a camcorder, you'll be ready.

About this Book

Don't let the rumors fool you. iMovie may be simple, but it isn't simplistic. It offers a wide range of special effects and flexible features for creating transitions between scenes, superimposing text on your video, layering multiple soundtracks together, and more. Unfortunately, many of the best techniques aren't covered in the only "manual" you get with iMovie—its sparse electronic help screens.

This book was born to address two needs. First, it's designed to serve as the iMovie manual, as the book that should have been in the box. It explores each iMovie feature in depth, offers illustrated catalogs of the various title and transition effects, offers shortcuts and workarounds, and unearths features that the online help doesn't even mention.

Second, this book is designed to give you a grounding in professional filming and editing techniques. The camcorder and iMovie produce video of stunning visual and audio quality; they give you the *technical* tools to produce amazing videos. But most people don't have much experience with the *artistic* side of shooting—such as lighting, sound, and composition—or even how to use the dozens of buttons packed onto the modern camcorder. This book will tell you all you need to know.

About the Outline

iMovie: The Missing Manual is divided into four parts, each containing several chapters:

- Part 1, **Capturing DV Footage,** covers what happens *before* you get to iMovie. It explains the DV format, helps you buy and learn to use a camcorder, and offers a crash course in professional film technique.

- Part 2, **Editing in iMovie,** is the heart of the book. It leads you through the act of transferring your footage into iMovie, editing your clips, placing them into a timeline, adding crossfades and titles, working with your soundtracks, and more.

- Part 3, **Finding Your Audience,** helps you take the cinematic masterpiece on your screen to the world. iMovie excels at exporting your work in two different ways: either back to your camcorder (from which you can play it on TV, transfer it to your VCR, and so on), or to a QuickTime movie file (which you can burn onto a CD, post on a Web page, or send to friends by email). This part of the book offers step-by-step instructions for each of these methods.

- Part 4, **Beyond iMovie,** shows you how you can use QuickTime Player Pro to supplement the editing tools in iMovie. It also gives you a peek at such more advanced video-editing software as Final Cut Pro, Adobe Premiere, and EditDV.

At the end of the book, two appendixes provide a menu-by-menu explanation of the iMovie menu commands and a comprehensive troubleshooting handbook.

Note: Scattered through this book, you'll find special sidebar boxes labeled "On Location." These are real stories of real people whose lives have been changed by iMovie. Here's hoping that you find them entertaining or even inspiring.

About→These→Arrows

Throughout this book, and throughout the Missing Manual series, you'll find sentences like this one: "Open the iMovie→Resources→Plugins folder." That's shorthand for a much longer instruction that directs you to open three nested folders in sequence, like this: "On your hard drive, you'll find a folder called iMovie. Open that. Inside the iMovie window is a folder called Resources; double-click it to open it. Inside *that* folder is yet another one called Plugins. Double-click to open it, too."

Similarly, this kind of arrow shorthand helps to simplify the business of choosing commands in menus, as shown in Figure I-1.

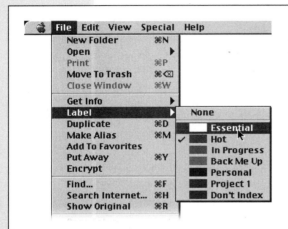

Figure I-1:
In this book, arrow notations help to simplify folder and menu instructions. For example, "Choose File→Label→ Essential" is a more compact way of saying, "From the File menu, choose Label; from the submenu that then appears, choose Essential," as shown here.

Technical Notes for PAL People

If you live in the Americas, Canada, Japan, or any of 30 other countries, your camcorder, VCR, and TV record and play back a video signal in a format that's known as *NTSC*. Even if you've never heard the term, every camcorder, VCR, TV, and TV station in your country uses this same signal.

What it *stands* for is National Television Standards Committee, the gang who designed this format. What it *means* is incompatibility with the second most popular format, which is called PAL (for *Phase Alternating Line,* if you care). In Europe, Africa, the Middle East, Australia, and China (among other places), everyone's equipment uses the PAL format. You can't play an American tape on a standard VCR in Sweden; in other words, you'll get nothing but static.

Tip: France, the former Soviet Union countries, and a few others use a third format, known as SECAM. iMovie doesn't work with SECAM gear. To find out what kind of gear your country uses—if you don't already know—visit a Web site like *www.vxc.com/wwtvs.html.*

Fortunately, iMovie converses fluently with both NTSC and PAL camcorders. When you launch the program, it automatically studies the camcorder you've attached and determines its format.

However, most of the discussions in this book use NTSC terminology. If you're a friend of PAL, use the following information to translate this book's discussions.

The Tech Specs of NTSC

Whether you're aware of it or not, using the NTSC format means that the picture you see is characterized like this:

- **30 frames per second.** A *frame* is one individual picture. Flashed before your eyes at this speed, the still images blend into what you perceive as smooth motion.

- **575 scan lines.** The electron gun in a TV tube paints the screen with this number of fine horizontal lines.

- **The DV picture measures 720 x 480 pixels.** This figure refers to the number of screen dots, or *pixels,* that compose one frame of image in the *DV* (digital video) version of the NTSC format. (These pixels translate to dimensions of *640* x 480 pixels on your Mac. That's because DV pixels aren't square, they're rectangular. Details on this anomaly on page 233.)

The Tech Specs of PAL

Fortunately, iMovie automatically notices when it's connected to a PAL camcorder. It makes the necessary adjustments automatically, including:

- **25 frames per second.** Video fans claim that the lower frame rate creates more flicker than the NTSC standard. On the other hand, this frame rate is very close to the frame rate of Hollywood films (24 frames per second). As a result, many independent filmmakers find PAL a better choice when shooting movies they intend to convert to film.

- **625 scan lines.** That's 20 percent sharper and more detailed than NTSC. The difference is especially visible on large-screen TVs.

- **The DV picture measures 720 x 576 pixels.** This information may affect you as you read Chapter 9 and prepare still images for use with iMovie.

About MissingManual.com

If you have an Internet account, visit the *MissingManual.com* Web site. Click the *iMovie: The Missing Manual* button to reveal a neat, organized, chapter-by-chapter list of every piece of shareware and freeware mentioned in this book. (As noted on the inside back cover, having the software online instead of on a CD-ROM saved you 25 percent on the cost of the book.)

But the Web site also offers articles, tips, and updates to the book. In fact, you're invited and encouraged to submit such corrections and updates yourself. In an effort to keep the book as up-to-date and accurate as possible, each time we print more copies of this book, we'll make any confirmed corrections you've suggested. We'll also note such changes on the Web site, so that you can mark important corrections into your own copy of the book, if you like.

In the meantime, we'd love to hear your own suggestions for new books in the Missing Manual line. There's a place for that on the Web site, too, as well as a place to sign up for free email notification of new titles in the series.

What's New in iMovie 2

In July 2000, Steve Jobs announced iMovie 2.0 at the Macworld Expo in New York City. The 2.0 version solves almost every limitation of the original iMovie, and makes the program much more flexible without making it much harder to use.

If you've used the original iMovie, here's a quick guide to the changes. The rest of this book covers each of these features in the appropriate chapters.

A New Look

The first thing you'll notice when you launch iMovie 2 is that it's had a dramatic visual overhaul. The accursed Shelf, with its 9- or 12-clip limit, has now become a scrolling palette that holds as many clips as your hard drive can take.

You'll notice a few other changes, too, both cosmetic and functional:

- The **Camera Mode/Edit Mode** switch is now a blue switch, featuring a "DV"-icon camera (for Camera Mode) and filmstrip icon (for Edit Mode).

- The **Pause and Stop buttons** are gone. To stop playback, click the Play button again.

- There's a new **Rewind to Start** button, for the benefit of people who never figured out that the Home key performs that function.

- The bizarrely placed **Full-Screen Playback** button has come home to roost, nestled just to the right of the big Play button. Better yet, when you click this button, iMovie no longer insists upon playing your entire movie from the beginning. It plays from the location of the Playhead, just as you'd expect.

- The **Effects and Sound** palette is no longer a separate entity. Now when you click the Transitions, Titles, Audio, or new Effects button, the Shelf disappears, replaced entirely by the palette you summoned—a much more efficient use of screen space.

Note, too, that you can now double-click a clip to open a special informational dialog box. (The File→Get Clip Info command does the same thing.) It tells you both the clip's name (which you can edit) *and* the name of its corresponding media file on your hard drive (called Clip 23, or whatever). You still can't rename that media file, and shouldn't mess with it on the hard drive; but it's sometimes nice to know which clip corresponds to which gigantic file on your hard drive.

Editing Changes

The changes in iMovie 2 have the biggest impact when it comes to actually editing your flick. The landscape is very different now—not as simple, but not as limiting either.

The Timeline Viewer

The Timeline Viewer (which appears when you click the little clock icon) has had a radical overhaul. Now iMovie offers a scrolling linear map of your movie, just like its $1,000 big brother Final Cut Pro.

Thanks to the newly incarnated Timeline, all kinds of new editing possibilities become available. For example:

- **Insta-black.** If you drag a video clip to the right, creating blank space to its left, you introduce a pure black moment of video. You're spared the hassle of importing a black square whenever you want a moment of visual silence.
- **Slo-mo and fast-mo.** When you highlight a video clip, the Faster/Slower slider at the bottom edge of the Timeline becomes available. Drag this slider to apply instant, gorgeous, smooth slow-motion and fast-motion effects to the clip you've highlighted. (You'll see a double-triangle arrow appear on the clip's bar to show that you've messed with its temporal head.)

New Commands

You can take advantage of a few cool new menu commands, too, during editing:

- **Edit→Create Still Clip** creates, on the Shelf, a "digital photo" of the frame you're looking at. You can now specify the default duration of such a still image (and all still images) by choosing Edit→Preferences.

  iMovie 1 could create still images from footage, too, but it took several steps (exporting a graphics file to your hard drive, then reimporting it).

- **Advanced→Reverse Clip Direction** makes a highlighted video clip play backward. Works great on splashes, things breaking, and people jumping off of walls. (Works not so great the 15th time your audience has to watch this effect.)
- **Advanced→Restore Clip Media.** iMovie automatically restores the highlighted clip to its full length, the way it was when you first imported it from the camera. That's a great safety net when you discover that you've cropped out too much, or that you really should use a different portion of the clip.

New Preferences

You'll discover that the new Edit→Preferences dialog box offers a long list of options that were never before available.

On the **Views** tab, for example, you're offered an option called "Show More Details." When you turn on this checkbox, the Timeline block representing each video clip doesn't simply show an icon representing the first frame; it also shows the clip's length ("6:20") and the name of its corresponding media file on your hard drive ("Clip 18"). (You see this extra info only if your Timeline Viewer is zoomed in enough for the clip to show it.) As for that icon—it's very helpful, but it also slows down scrolling and zooming. To hide it so that only empty colored bars represent your video clips, turn off "Show Thumbnails."

By turning off "Use Short Time Codes," you make all clip and effect durations show up in "minutes:seconds:frames" format wherever clip durations are displayed (instead of just "seconds:frames"). (The final option here, "Show Locked Audio Only When Selected," refers to the pushpins described on page 214. It means you won't see them until you actually click the audio clip in question.)

The new **Advanced** tab offers some juicy options, too. You can read about "Extract Audio in Paste Over" on page 220. "Filter Audio from Camera" is directly connected to the awful clicking and popping sounds that you sometimes find on your audio track after importing from your camcorder. Whether the "Filter" option *creates* those dropouts or *eliminates* them depends on whom you're asking, but at least you can experiment. Finally, "Video Play Through to Camera" lets you do all your editing without the jittery/blurry tradeoff described on page 102: Instead, you can watch all your footage at high resolution on your camcorder's LCD display panel (and on a TV too, if one is connected to the camcorder).

Titles and Text

Apple made some extremely welcome changes to the titles, text, and credits feature. In addition to a much less cramped display, just look at all you get:

- **Bigger type.** In iMovie 2, you no longer have to contend with two sets of text effects, such as "Centered Title" and "Centered Title Large." There's only one kind of each effect—and a text-size slider. The odds of creating type that shrinks to illegibility when converted to QuickTime movies are greatly lessened.

- **More colors.** The Color pop-up menu offers a few, slightly less timid color choices for your text.

- **TV awareness.** As a film editor, the *TV-safe area* is suddenly your concern (see page 174). The *overscanning* effect means that when you show your iMovie productions on a TV, you'll lose anything that's very close to the edges of the frame.

  iMovie 2 avoids that problem automatically; on effects that put text close to the edge of the frame, such as Music Video, your credits are now scooted inward to avoid getting chopped off. But what if you want to export your movie to a QuickTime file, where there *is* no overscanning problem? In that case, turn on the **QT Margins** checkbox. The program will put your text very close to the edge of the frame, as it always has.

- **Separate Speed/Pause sliders.** Most of the titling effects are animated: First, your words fly onto the screen; then they stop moving long enough for you to read them. In iMovie 2, you can control the timing of these events independently.

Special Effects

When you click the new Effects button in iMovie 2, you're offered some video effects, such as Brightness/Contrast and Sharpen, which can help to repair (or creatively distort) your original camcorder footage. See Chapter 6 for a complete discussion.

Audio Enhancements

The audio features in iMovie 2 are the crown jewel of the new software. They're juicy indeed. You no longer need all the workarounds, ingenious though they are, described in the original edition of this book.

The key change in iMovie 2 is that you can split the audio apart from its video and move it around independently. That's a gigantic development, which offers an almost overwhelming number of permutations and possibilities:

Overlaying video

One of the most popular editing techniques—both with editors and audiences—is the *video overlay.* That's where the video cuts away to a new picture, but you continue to hear the audio from the original clip.

In iMovie 2, overlaying video is easy, as described on page 219.

Splitting audio apart from video—and locking it

When you separate audio from its original video, a tiny pushpin thumbtack appears on both the audio and video clips (see page 214). That's iMovie's shorthand for this comment: "OK, you know and I know that this audio wasn't recorded with this video. I'll assume that for now, you want them to stick together: Whenever the video slides in the Timeline—because you drag it, or because you paste something or cut something in front of it—I'll keep this particular audio clip in sync with the video." More on locking audio on page 214.

Controlling fade in/fade out timing

In iMovie 1, you could make an audio clip fade in or fade out by clicking a checkbox. In iMovie 2, you get something much better: Control over how *fast* the fade-in or fade-out proceeds (see page 211).

Splitting audio clips

In iMovie 2, you can split an audio clip in half. Just highlight the audio clip, position the playhead at the right spot, and then choose Edit→Split Selected Audio Clip at Playhead.

The result: You get two audio clips side-by-side, exactly where they were. So far, you haven't accomplished much; your movie looks and sounds exactly as it did before. That's because splitting an audio clip is useful only when you *follow* it with another editing maneuver, such as deleting one of them (a great way to "bleep out" an obscenity) or adjust their volume settings independently, which lets you come very close to creating freeform volume fluctuations.

Extracting audio

When you click a video clip in the Timeline and then choose Advanced→Extract Audio, iMovie duplicates the audio track and pastes it into the Timeline's Audio 1 track. (It doesn't *delete* the video clip's audio—just turns its volume to zero and places a full-volume *copy* into the Audio track.) Now that the clip's audio is independent, you can move, edit, or otherwise manipulate it as described in Chapter 8.

The big picture

You've just read about the big-ticket items in iMovie 2, but dozens of smaller touches await. There are dozens of things you *won't* find in iMovie 2, too—bugs that have been fixed. For example, you no longer need a LANC cable to make iMovie 2 work with a Sony Media Converter box (you know who you are); you no longer get a hideous buzzing when you export your audio track to another program; and iMovie 2 can now export to both MP and ME cassettes in Sony Digital8 camcorders.

Overall, the big and small improvements bring every corner of the program up to a standard of simplicity and power you'll rarely find in the software world.

Part One:
Capturing DV Footage

1

The DV Camcorder

This book is called *iMovie 2: The Missing Manual*, but it's not just about iMovie. To edit video using iMovie, you must first *shoot* some video; that's why the first three chapters of this book have nothing to do with your iMovie software. Instead, this book begins with advice on buying and using a digital camcorder, getting to know the equipment, and adopting professional filming techniques. After all, teaching you to edit video without making sure you know how to shoot it is like giving a map to a 16-year-old without first teaching him how to drive.

Meet Digital Video

If you read the paragraph above carefully, you may have noticed the phrase "digital camcorder." To use edit footage in iMovie, you need a *digital* camcorder. This is a relatively new camcorder format, one that's utterly incompatible with the tapes you may have filled using these earlier camcorder types (see Figure 1-1):

- **VHS.** These gigantic machines were the original camcorders, circa 1980. Nearly a foot and a half long, you have to rest the butt of these cameras on your shoulder because of the weight. VHS camcorders accept full-size VHS cassettes that, after filming, you can insert directly into your VCR for playback.

  That convenience is nothing to sneeze at. Still, the size, weight, and bulk of these camcorders were too much for the general public to swallow. Only a handful of full-size VHS camcorders are still on the market. Nowadays, they offer a pop-out LCD viewscreen, just like the more compact camcorders listed next; but their reservations on the Obsolescence Train are almost certainly confirmed.

• **S-VHS.** This format, also known as Super VHS, accepts special, more expensive S-VHS tapes; requires a special, more expensive camcorder; and requires special, more expensive jacks on your TV or VCR. The advantage: sharper video quality.

The existence of the S-VHS format should be your first hint at a phenomenon you'll be reading, and hearing, a lot more about: For many home-video fans, the *quality* of the picture and sound is incredibly important. It's worth paying more for, buying add-on gear for, and re-shooting scenes for. (Fortunately, you, a soon-to-be experienced *digital*-video [DV] producer, are ready to create videos that easily surpass the work of all of those long-suffering, pre-DV camcorder owners, no matter how much they spent on equipment.)

• **VHS-C.** Here was Panasonic's attempt to solve the problems of the VHS camcorder's weight. This kind of camcorder is much smaller than full-size VHS units because it takes much smaller cassettes. After filming, you can pop one of these VHS-C (for "compact") cassettes into a VHS-sized *adapter* cassette, which you then insert into a standard VCR.

Clever, really, but still a nuisance. Now, when you want to play the video of the kids' birthday party, you have to find *both* the party cassette *and* the adapter cassette. Moreover, you can't send the tapes you make to friends or family without buying an adapter cassette for them, too.

• **8 mm.** The eight-millimeter cassette is smaller even than VHS-C, which makes 8 mm camcorders smaller still, now not much bigger than a 6-inch sub sandwich. Makers of these camcorders make no apology for their tapes' inability to fit into a standard VCR. If you want to play back your footage, you run a cable from the camcorder to your TV or VCR, so that the camcorder itself becomes the VCR.

Figure 1-1:
The evolution—and the shrinking—of the modern camcorder. From top left: the full-size VHS camcorder; the 8 mm/Hi-8 camcorder; and the modern DV camcorder—the one you need to work with iMovie.

8 mm camcorders are extremely inexpensive these days—around $300, at this writing. Among people who don't have computers, 8 mm is the most popular format.

- **Hi-8.** For about $150 more, you can get a camcorder that has higher-quality cir-cuitry and accepts a higher-quality 8 mm cassette—called Hi-8. (Most of these cameras accept *either* Hi-8 or regular 8 mm cassettes—which, apart from the label, look identical—and automatically detect which you've inserted.)

Hi-8 is the compact-camcorder equivalent of the S-VHS format described above. For several years, S-VHS and Hi-8 were popular *prosumer* camcorders—a cute way of saying that they bridged the gap between inexpensive *consumer* equip-ment and very expensive *professional* equipment. Because S-VHS and Hi-8 foot-age doesn't deteriorate as much from copy to copy as regular VHS and 8 mm tape, it was a popular format for recording wedding videos, legal depositions, and even low-budget cable TV commercials. (Today, of course, DV camcorders dominate these functions.)

Swallow hard and read it again: you can't use iMovie without *buying a new cam-corder.*

By no means does this imply that you can't use all your older *footage;* Chapter 4 offers several ways to transfer your older tapes into iMovie. But from this day for-ward, consider shooting all of your new footage with a DV camcorder. At this writ-ing, such camcorders cost about $600 for a basic model, and prices continue to sink, month by month. (See the end of this chapter for a DV buying guide.)

Tip: Selling your old camcorder for, say, $250 eases much of the pain of buying a DV camcorder. Remem-ber to transfer your old footage into DV format before you do so, however.

Why a DV Camcorder Is Worth It

A DV camcorder offers several enormous advantages over previous formats:

They're smaller

The size of the camcorder is primarily determined by the size of the tapes inside it. A *mini-DV cassette* (tape cartridge) is the smallest cassette yet designed, as shown in Figure 1-2, so the camcorders are also the smallest yet designed. The largest DV camcorder is about the size of the *smallest* 8 mm camcorder, and the smallest DV camcorder is the size of a Sony Walkman.

The small size has lots of advantages. You can film surreptitiously when necessary. DV camcorders don't make kids or interview subjects as nervous as bulkier equip-ment. The batteries last a long time, because they've got less equipment to power. And, of course, smaller means it's easier to bring with you.

DV cassettes aren't perfect. Most hold only an hour of footage, and they're expen-sive. As you'll soon see, however, both of these limitations quickly become irrelevant in the world of iMovie. The whole idea is that iMovie lets you edit your footage and then, if you like, dump it back out to the camcorder. In other words, it's common iMovie practice to delete the boring footage from DV tape #1, preserve only the good stuff by dumping it onto DV tape #2, and then reuse DV cassette #1 for the next shooting session.

Figure 1-2:
The various sizes of tapes today's camcorders can accept differ in size, picture quality, and cost. For both home and "prosumer" filming, the standard-size VHS cassette (back) is nearly extinct. 8 mm and Hi-8 cassettes (right) are extremely popular among people who don't *have a computer to edit footage, and are very inexpensive. Mini-DV tapes (left), like the ones required by most DV camcorders, are more expensive—but the enormous quality improvement makes them worth every penny.*

The quality is astounding

Video quality is measured in *lines of resolution:* the number of tiny horizontal stripes of color the playback uses to fill your TV screen. As you can see by this table, DV quality blows every previous tape format out of the water. (All camcorders, TVs, and VCRs have the same vertical resolution; this table measures *horizontal* resolution.)

Tape Format	Maximum Lines of Resolution
VHS, VHS-C	240
8 mm	280
Live TV broadcast	300
S-VHS, Hi-8	400
Digital satellite broadcast	400
Mini-DV	500

DV's 16-bit sound quality is dramatically better than previous formats, too. In fact, it's better than CD-quality, since DV camcorders record sound at 48 kHz instead of 44.1 kHz. (Higher means better.)

Tip: Most DV camcorders offer you a choice of sound quality modes: 12-bit or 16-bit. The lower quality setting is designed to leave "room" on the tape for adding music after you've recorded your video. But iMovie itself offers far more comprehensive soundtrack management features. You're unnecessarily sacrificing quality if you use the 12-bit setting on your camcorder.

You can make copies of copies

This is a big one. You probably know already that every time you make a copy of VHS footage (or other non-DV material), you lose quality. The copy loses sharpness, color fidelity, and smoothness of color tone. Once you've made a copy *of* a copy, the quality is terrible. Skin appears to have a combination of bad acne and radiation burns; the edges of the picture wobble as though leaking off the glass; and *video noise* (jiggling static dots) fills the screen. If you've ever seen, on the news or *America's Funniest Home Videos*, a tape submitted by an amateur camcorder fan, you've seen this problem in action. If the original was recorded in LP (long-play) or ELP (extended long-play) mode, which gains you more recording time per cassette at the expense of picture quality, these problems are compounded.

Digital video is stored on the tape as computer codes, not as pulses of magnetic energy. You can copy this video from DV camcorder to DV camcorder, or from DV camcorder to Mac, dozens of times, making copies of copies of copies. The last generation of digital video will be utterly indistinguishable from the original footage—which is to say, both will look fantastic.

Note: Technically speaking, you can't keep making copies of copies of a DV tape *infinitely.* After, say, 20 or 30 generations, you may start to see a few video *dropouts* (digital-looking specks), depending on the quality of your tapes and duplicating equipment. Still, few people have any reason to make that many copies of copies. (Furthermore, making infinite copies of a *single* original poses no such problem.)

A DV recording is forever

Depending on how much you read newspapers, you may have remembered the depressing story the New York Times broke in the late eighties: Because home video was such a recent phenomenon at the time, nobody had ever bothered to check out how long videotapes last.

The answer, as it turns out, was: not very long. Depending on storage conditions, the signal on traditional videotapes may begin to fade in as little as ten years! The precious footage of that birth, wedding, or tornado, which you hoped to preserve forever, could in fact be more fleeting than the memory itself.

Your first instinct might be to rescue a fading video by copying it onto a fresh tape, but making a copy only further damages the footage. The bottom line, said the scientists: There is *no way* to preserve original video footage forever!

Fortunately, there is now. DV tapes may deteriorate over a decade or two, just as traditional tapes do. But you won't care. Long before the tape has crumbled, you'll have transferred the most important material to a new hard drive or a new DV tape. Because quality never degrades when you do so, you'll glow with the knowledge that your grandchildren and *their* grandchildren will be able to see your movies with every speck of clarity you see today—even if they have to dig up one of those antique "Macintosh" computers or gigantic, soap-sized "DV camcorders" in order to play it.

No fuzzy snow when re-recording

As on any camcorder, a DV unit lets you re-record a scene on top of existing footage. But with DV, at the spot where the new footage begins or ends, you don't get five seconds of glitchy static, as you do with non-digital camcorders. Instead, you get a clean edit.

You can edit it

The fifth and best advantage of the DV format is, of course, iMovie itself. Once you've connected your DV camcorder up to your Mac (as described in Chapter 4), you can pour the footage from camcorder to computer—and then chop it up, rearrange scenes, add special effects, cut out bad shots, and so on. For the first time in history, it's simple for anyone, even non-rich people, to edit home movies with professional results. (Doing so in 1990 required a $200,000 Avid editing suite; doing so in 1995 required a $4,000 computer with $4,000 worth of digitizing cards and editing software—and the quality wasn't great because it wasn't DV.)

Furthermore, for the first time in history, you won't have to press the Fast-Forward button when showing your footage to family, friends, co-workers, and clients. There won't *be* any dull footage worth skipping, because you'll have deleted it on the Mac.

Tip: Before you get nervous about the hours you'll have to spend editing your stuff in iMovie, remember that there's no particular law that every video must have crossfades, scrolling credits, and a throbbing music soundtrack. Yes, of course, you *can* make movies on iMovie that are as slickly produced as commercial films; much of this book is dedicated to helping you achieve that standard. But many people dump an entire DV cassette's worth of footage onto the Mac, chop out the boring bits, and dump it right back onto the camcorder—after the transfer to the Mac, only about 20 minutes' worth of work.

What's It Good For?

If you're reading this book, you probably already have some ideas about what you could do if you could make professional-looking video. Here are a few possibilities that may not have occurred to you. All are natural projects for iMovie:

- **Home movies.** Plain old home movies—casual documentaries of your life, your kids' lives, your school life, your trips—are the single most popular creation of camcorder owners. Using the suggestions in the following chapters, you can improve the quality of your footage. Using a DV camcorder, you'll improve the quality of the picture and sound. And using iMovie, you can delete all but the best scenes (and edit out those humiliating parts where you walked for 20 minutes with the camcorder accidentally filming the ground bouncing beneath it).

- **Actual films.** Don't scoff: iMovie is perfectly capable of creating professional video segments, or even plotted movies. If the three kids who made *The Blair Witch Project* could do it with *their* camcorder, you can certainly do it with yours. *They* didn't even have iMovie; they had to get $60,000 in loans to do the editing and processing that you can do right on your Mac. (See *www.loop.com/~pirro* for the story of a guy who made a full-length feature film with his DV camcorder for under $500.)

Moreover, new film festivals, Web sites, and magazines are springing up everywhere, all dedicated to independent makers of *short* movies; more on this topic in Chapter 13 .

- **Business videos.** It's very easy to post video on the Internet or burn it onto a cheap, recordable CD-ROM, as described in Part 3. As a result, you should consider video a useful tool in whatever you do. If you're a realtor, blow away your rivals (and save your clients time) by showing movies, not still photos, of the properties you represent. If you're an executive, quit boring your comrades with stultifying PowerPoint slides and make your point with video instead.

- **Once-in-a-lifetime events.** Your kid's school play, your speech, someone's wedding, someone's birthday or anniversary party are all worth capturing, especially because now you know that your video can last forever.

- **Video photo albums.** A video photo album can be much more exciting, accessible, and engaging than a paper one. Start by filming or scanning your photos (you can read tips for doing this in Chapter 3). Assemble them into a sequence, add some crossfades, titles, and music; the result is a much more interesting display than a book of motionless images. This emerging video form is becoming very popular—videographers are charging a lot of money to create such "living photo albums" for their clients.

- **Just-for-fun projects.** Never again can anyone over the age of eight complain that there's "nothing to do." Set them loose with a camcorder and the instruction to make a fake rock video, a fake commercial, or a fake documentary.

- **Training films.** If there's a better use for video than providing how-to instruction, you'd be hard pressed to name it. Make a video for new employees, to show them the ropes. Make a video that accompanies your product, to give a humanizing touch to your company and help the customer make the most of her purchase. Make a tape that teaches newcomers how to play the banjo, grow a garden, kick a football, use a computer program—and market it.

FREQUENTLY ASKED QUESTION

What's Digital About DV

I was a little surprised to find, when I bought my DV camcorder, that it requires tapes, just like my old nondigital one. If it still needs tapes, how can they call it digital?

Your confusion is understandable. After all, digital cameras don't require film, and digital TV recorders (such as the tapeless TiVo and ReplayTV "VCRs") don't use videotape.

Today's DV camcorders are really only half digital. They store their *signal* in digital form as a bunch of computer codes, but still record it on videotape just like the old camcorders. You still have

to rewind and fast-forward to find a particular spot in the footage. (Until you transfer the footage to iMovie, that is.)

Put another way, today's DV camcorders are a temporary technology, a halfway step toward fully digital, hard-drive-, CD-, or memory-based camcorders that will surely become commonplace one day. Even today, for huge amounts of money, you can buy a camcorder that records onto a hard drive or CD. Such devices let you jump instantly anywhere in the footage without having to wait for a tape to roll.

- **Interviews.** You're lucky enough to live in an age where you can manipulate video just as easily as you do words in a word processor. Capitalize on this fact. Create family histories. Film relatives who still remember the War, the Birth, the Immigration. Or create a time-capsule, time-lapse film: Ask your kid or your parent the same four questions every year on his birthday (such as, "What's your greatest worry right now?" or "If you had one wish…?" or "Where do you want to be in five years?"). Then, after five or ten or twenty years, splice together the answers for an enlightening fast-forward through a human life.

- **Broadcast segments.** Want a taste of the real world? Call your cable TV company about its public-access channels. (As required by law, every cable company offers a channel or two for ordinary citizens to use for their own programming.) Find out the time and format restraints, and then make a documentary, short film, or other piece for actual broadcast. Advertise the airing to everyone you know. It's a small-time start, but it's real broadcasting.

- **Analyze performances.** There's no better way to improve your golf swing, tennis form, musical performance, or public-speaking style than to study footage of yourself. If you're a teacher, camp counselor, or coach, film your students, campers, or players so that they can benefit from self-analysis, too.

Buying a DV Camcorder

If you already own a DV camcorder, you can safely skip to the next chapter—unless you've always wondered what this or that button on your camcorder does. In that case, surveying the following pages may enlighten you.

DV Camcorder Features: Which Are Worthwhile?

Like any hot new technology, DV camcorders started out expensive ($2,500 in 1996) and continue to plummet in price. At this writing, basic models start at $600; prosumer models hover around $2,000; many TV crews are adopting $3,500 models like the Canon XL1; and the fanciest, professional, commercial-filmmaking models go for $10,000. All of them are *teeming* with features; each brochure is pages and pages long.

So how do you know which to buy? Here's a rundown of the most frequently advertised DV camcorder features, along with a frank assessment of their value. In general, the features of greatest importance to an iMovie owner who wants the highest quality are described first. The last few items described in this section aren't worth paying *anything* for.

FireWire connector

FireWire is Apple's term for the tiny, compact connector on the side of most DV camcorders. When you attach a FireWire cable, this jack connects the camera to your FireWire-equipped Mac. Other companies have different names for this connector—you may see it called IEEE-1394, i.Link, DV In/Out, or DV Terminal.

If the camera you're considering doesn't have this feature, don't buy it; you can't use that camera with iMovie or any other DV software.

Analog inputs

This single feature may be important enough to determine your camcorder choice by itself. *Analog inputs* are connectors on the camcorder itself (see Figure 1-3). Into these jacks you can connect older, pre-DV equipment, such as your VCR, your old 8 mm camcorder, and so on. There's no easier, less expensive method of transferring older footage into your DV camcorder—or directly into iMovie.

This technique is described in more detail in Chapter 4. For now, note only that the alternative method of getting pre-DV footage into DV format is to buy a $350 converter box—an unnecessary purchase if your DV camcorder has analog inputs.

Tip: Using analog inputs, you can fill a couple of DV cassettes with, say, a movie you've rented. Then flip out the camcorder's LCD screen, plug in your headphones, and enjoy the movie on your cross-country flight—in economy class. Smile: the people up front in first class paid $1,000 more for the same privilege.

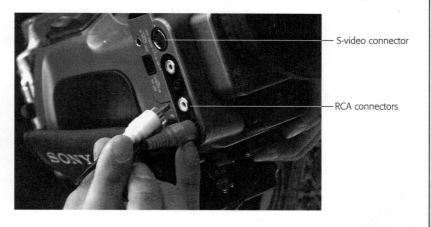

Figure 1-3:
Many camcorders offer inputs known as RCA connectors. Better models offer an S-video connector instead, for much higher quality. (Some Sony models require a special cable with RCA connectors on one end and a miniplug on the camcorder end. Don't lose this cable! You also need it to play your camcorder footage on TV.)

S-video connector

RCA connectors

Digital8 format

Here's another plan for getting your older footage into iMovie: Buy what Sony calls a *Digital8* camcorder. This fascinating hybrid doesn't use the mini-DV videotapes used by all other DV camcorders. Instead, it accepts the much less expensive 8 mm or, as Sony recommends, Hi-8 tapes.

Onto these cassettes, Digital8 camcorders record the identical DV signal found on mini-DV camcorders. But they can play back *either* digital video *or* traditional, analog video. (When recording digital video, however, the camera runs twice as fast—you still get only one hour of recording per tape, just as on mini-DV tapes.)

This kind of camcorder, in other words, is a good solution if you have a library of old 8 mm tapes that you'd like to edit in iMovie. Your Mac can't tell which kind of tape the Digital8 camcorder is playing.

Three chips (three CCDs)

Professional camcorders offer three individual image sensors, one for each color component of a video picture: red, green, and blue. These camcorders are advertised as having three chips or *CCDs* (*charge-coupled devices*—electronic plates, covered with thousands of individual light sensors, that convert light rays into a digital signal). The result is even more spectacular picture quality, resolution, and color rendition than the less-expensive, one-CCD cameras.

Unfortunately, you'll pay dearly for this breathtaking video quality. At this writing, these camcorders cost $1,700 or more, and are much larger than the very compact, less expensive models. However, if broadcast- or commercial-quality footage is your goal, these camcorders can get it for you. (The prices for these models are falling quickly.)

LCD viewfinder

In the olden days, you'd set up your shots and monitor your filming by looking through a tiny glass eyepiece, exactly like those on today's 35 mm still cameras. Today, most standard camcorders, and *all* inexpensive DV camcorders, offer an alternative to the eyepiece: a small TV screen known as an *LCD.* (LCD stands for *liquid crystal display,* the technology used to produce the image. As you may have noticed, it's the same technology used in laptop screens.) In most cases, this LCD panel swings out from the side of the camera (see Figure 1-4), though occasionally it's built into the body of the camcorder.

Either way, the idea is the same: When shooting, you can see what the camcorder sees without having to mash your face against the eyepiece. Better yet, after shoot-

Figure 1-4:
A well-designed LCD screen can be rotated 180 degrees to face front; that's useful when you want to film yourself. Without an LCD screen, you'd have no idea whether or not you were centered in the frame. (To ensure the longest possible videography career, don't actually film yourself while driving.)

ing, you can play back your footage. And thanks to the small, built-in speaker found on every sub-$1,500 camcorder, you can watch your work played back on the LCD screen while still "on location."

It's worth noting, by the way, that what you see isn't *exactly* what you get. For one thing, the LCD panel usually has its own brightness control, which, if not adjusted perfectly, may trick you into thinking a scene is better (or worse) lit than it actually is. The color and exposure revealed by the LCD screen may not exactly match what's going onto the tape, either.

Use your camcorder's eyepiece viewfinder instead of the LCD panel, therefore, when picture perfection counts. You may also want to use the eyepiece when it's very bright and sunny out (the LCD display tends to wash out in bright light), when you don't want people around you to see what you're filming, and when you're trying to save battery juice. The LCD display depletes your battery about 50 percent faster than when the LCD is turned off.

Tip: The size of the LCD viewfinder is relative to two things: the size of the camcorder and its price. A camcorder with a 2.5-inch screen may cost hundreds of dollars less than one with a 4-inch screen.

Electronic image stabilizer (E.I.S.)

As you'll read in Chapter 2, certain film techniques scream, "Amateur!" to audiences. One of them is the instability of handheld filming. In a nutshell, professional video is shot using a camera on a tripod (Woody Allen's "handheld" period notwithstanding). Most home camcorder footage, in contrast, is shot from the palm of your hand.

A *digital* or *electronic* stabilizing feature (which may have a marketing name, such as Sony's SteadyShot) takes a half step toward solving that problem. As shown in Figure 1-5, this feature neatly eliminates the tiny, jittery moves present in handheld video. (It can't do anything about the bigger jerks and bumps, which are especially difficult to avoid when you're zoomed in.) It also uses up your battery faster.

Optical image stabilizer

On Canon DV camcorders, higher-priced Sony models, and a few others, you get an *optical* image stabilizer. This mechanism involves two transparent plates separated by a special optical fluid. As the camera shakes, these plates create a prism effect that keeps handheld shots clearer and steadier than many electronic (digital) stabilizers. The images are clearer because optical stabilizers don't have to crop out part of the picture as a buffer, unlike the stabilizers illustrated in Figure 1-5.

Optical zoom

When you read the specs for a DV camcorder—or read the logos painted on its body—you frequently encounter numbers like, "12X/300X ZOOM!" The number before the slash tells you how many times the camera can magnify a distant image, much like a telescope. That number measures the *optical* zoom, which is the actual amount that the lenses themselves can zoom in. Such zooming, of course, is useful when you want to film something that's far away. (As for the number *after* the slash, see "Digital zoom," below.)

You should know, however, that the more you've zoomed in, the shakier your footage is likely to be, since every microscopic wobble is magnified by, say, 12 times. You also have to be much more careful about focusing. When you're zoomed out all the way, everything is in focus—things near you and things far away. But when you're zoomed in, very close and very far objects go out of focus. Put into photographic terms, the more you zoom in, the shorter the *depth of field* (the range of distance from the camera that can be kept in focus simultaneously).

Finally, remember that magnifying the picture doesn't magnify the sound. If you're relying on the built-in microphone of your camcorder, always get as close as you can to the subject, both for the sound and for the wobble.

Tip: As you'll discover in the next chapter, professional video and film work includes very little zooming, unlike most amateur video work. The best zooming is subtle zooming, such as when you very slowly "move toward" the face of somebody you're interviewing.

For this reason, when shopping for camcorders, *try out* the zooming if at all possible. Find out if the camcorder has *variable-speed* zooming, where the zooming speed increases as you press the Zoom button harder. Unfortunately, most camcorders offer only two different speeds—fast and faster—but that's still better than having no control at all. (Variable-speed zooming isn't something mentioned in the standard camcorder literature; you generally have to try the camcorder in the store to find out how it does.)

Figure 1-5:
Digital stabilization features work by "taking in" more image than you actually see in the viewfinder. Because the camcorder has some buffer, its computer can compensate for small bumps and jitters by keeping an "eye" on prominent features of the image. On less expensive camcorders, unfortunately, this buffer zone means that your camcorder is absorbing less video information, to the detriment of picture quality.

Digital zoom

Much as computer owners mistakenly jockey for superiority by comparing the megahertz rating of their computers (higher megahertz ratings don't necessarily make faster computers), camcorder makers seem to think that what consumers want most in a camcorder is a powerful digital zoom. Your camcorder's packaging may "boast" zoom ratings of "50X!", "100X!", or "500X!"

When a camcorder uses its *digital* zoom—the number after the slash on the camcorder box—it simply enlarges the individual dots that compose its image. Yes, the image gets bigger, but it doesn't get any *sharper*. As the dots get larger, the image gets chunkier, coarser, and less recognizable, until it ends up looking like the blocky areas you see superimposed over criminals' faces to conceal their identity on *Cops*. After your digital zoom feature has blown up the picture by 3X, the image falls to pieces. Greater digital zoom is not something worth paying extra for.

Manual override

Better DV camcorders let you turn off the automatic focus, automatic exposure control, automatic white balance, and even automatic sound level. This feature can be useful in certain situations, as you'll find out in the next chapter. If you've decided to pay extra for this feature, look for a model that lets you focus manually by turning a ring around the lens, which is much easier than using sliders.

Digital time-remaining battery readout

Fortunately, the problems exhibited by camcorder batteries of old—such as the "memory effect"—are a thing of the past. (When you halfway depleted a pre-DV camcorder battery's charge several times in a row, the battery would adopt that halfway-empty point as its new *completely* empty point, effectively halving its capacity.) Today's lithium-ion battery technology (used by DV camcorders) eliminates that problem.

Some batteries, such as Sony's InfoLithium series, even contain circuitry that tells the camera how much juice it has remaining. A glance at the viewfinder or a small side-panel readout tells you how many minutes of recording or playback you've got left—a worthy feature.

Tip: The number of minutes' recording time advertised for camcorder batteries is *continuous* recording time—that is, the time you'll get if you turn the camcorder on, press Record, and go out to lunch. If you stop and start the camera to capture shorter scenes, as almost everyone does, you'll get about half the advertised amount of time out of each battery charge.

Built-in light

As you can read in the next chapter, insufficient lighting is one of the leading causes of amateur-itis, a telltale form of poor video quality that lets viewers know that the footage is homemade. In the best—and most expensive—of all possible worlds, you'd get your scene correctly lit before filming, or you'd attach a light to the "shoe" (light connector) on top of the camera. Those few cameras that have such a shoe, or even have a built-in light, give you a distinct advantage in filming accurate colors.

Pre-programmed exposure options

Most DV camcorders come with a number of canned focus/shutter speed/aperture settings for different indoor and outdoor environments: Sports Lesson, Beach and Snow, Twilight, and so on. They're a useful compromise between the all-automatic operation of less expensive models and the all-manual operation of professional cameras.

Remote control

Some DV camcorders come with a pocket-sized remote control. It serves two purposes: First, its Record and Stop buttons give you a means of recording *yourself,* with or without other people in the shot. Second, when you're playing back footage with the camcorder connected to your TV or VCR, the remote lets you control the playback without having to have the camcorder on your lap. You may be surprised at the remote's usefulness.

Backlight mode

As you can read in the next chapter, modern camcorders take much of the guesswork out of shooting video. For example, they can focus automatically.

Although few consumers appreciate it, today's camcorders also set their *aperture* automatically. The aperture is the hole inside the barrel of your camcorder's snout that gets bigger or smaller to admit more or less light, preventing you from under- or overexposing your footage. (Inside the camera is an *iris*—a circle of interlocking, sliding panels that move together to reduce or enlarge the opening, much like the one in a still camera.)

The automatic aperture circuitry works by analyzing the image. If it contains a lot of light—such as when you're filming against a snowy backdrop or aiming the camera toward the sun—the iris closes automatically, reducing the opening in the lens and thus reducing the amount of light admitted. The result: you avoid flooding the image with blinding white light.

Unfortunately, there may be times when you have no choice but to film somebody, or something, against a bright backdrop. In those cases, as you may have discovered through painful experience, the person you're trying to film shows up extremely dark, almost in silhouette (see Figure 1-6). Now the background is correctly exposed, but the *subject* winds up *under*exposed.

Figure 1-6:
Without the backlight mode, your camcorder is likely to turn your subject into a silhouette (left). The Backlight button compensates by brightening every-thing up (right).

A Backlight button, then, is a valuable asset on a camcorder. Its purpose is to tell the camera: "OK, look, it's a bright scene; I can appreciate that. But I'm more interested in the subject that's, at the moment, coming out too dark. So do me a favor and open that aperture a couple of notches, will you?"

The camera obliges. Your subject no longer winds up too dark—in fact, modern camcorders do a great job at making sure the subject turns out just right. But over-riding the automatic aperture control undoes the good the automatic iris originally did you—and everything *around* your subject is now several shades too bright. Alas, there's no in between; *either* your subject or the background, but not both, can be correctly exposed in very bright settings.

Tip: If your camcorder has a manual-exposure knob, you can similarly compensate for backlit scenes—with much more control. Professionals and semi-pros, in fact, turn the auto-exposure feature off *completely.* True, they must now adjust the exposure knob for every single new shot, but their footage is then free from the bizarre and violent darkening or brightening that auto-exposure electronics can create as you pan across a scene.

FlexiZone or Push Focus

All camcorders offer automatic focus. Most work by focusing on the image in the center of your frame as you line up the shot.

That's fine if the subject of your shot *is* in the center of the frame. But if it's off-center, you have no choice but to turn off the auto-focus feature and use the manual-focus ring. (Using the camcorder isn't like using a still camera, where you can point the camera directly at the subject for focusing purposes, and then—before taking the shot—shift the angle so that the subject is no longer in the center. Camcorders continually refocus, so pointing the camera slightly away from your subject makes you lose the off-center focus you have established.)

Some Canon, Sony, and Sharp camcorders let you point to a specific spot in the frame that you want to serve as the focus point, even if it's not the center of the picture. (This feature is called FlexiZone on the Canon models, or Push Focus on high-end Sony models like the VX-1000.) If the model you're eyeing has this feature, it's worth having.

Night-vision mode

Some Sony camcorders offer a night-vision mode (called NightShot) that works like night-vision goggles. In this mode, you can actually film (and see, as you watch the LCD screen) in total darkness. The infrared transmitter on the front of the camcorder measures the heat given off by various objects in its path, letting you capture an eerie, greenish night scene. (Rent *The Silence of the Lambs* for an idea of how creepy night-vision filming can be.)

You'll soon discover that the infrared transmitter picks up only objects within 10 feet of the camcorder. Moreover, most camcorder owners go for years without ever running across a desired scene that's in total blackness. Whether or not this feature is valuable is a personal call.

Tip: Many Sony camcorders offer LaserLink, a method of watching your footage on your TV without having to connect a wire to the camcorder. It works by infrared—the camcorder sends its video signal through the air and into an optional receiver connected to your TV.

Unbeknownst to most camcorder owners, however, this infrared signal is the *same* signal used by NightShot. In other words, if you're a spy hiding in total blackness outside your subject's bedroom to film him sleeping, the joke may be on you. If he has a LaserLink receiver, he may be actually watching what you're filming on his TV!

Still-camera mode

All DV camcorders offer a snapshot, or still-photo, mode, in which you can "snap" a "still" picture. Behind the scenes, the camcorder freezes one frame of what it's seeing, and lays it down on, for example, seven seconds of videotape. You may also get an equivalent seven seconds of sound.

If the camcorder you're considering offers this feature, fine—but it's redundant for the iMovie owner. iMovie can perform the same feat far more efficiently, and with *any* frame of your captured video, as described in Chapter 9.

Note: Regardless of the camcorder you buy, the still-photo feature always captures a photo at 72 dots per inch (dpi). Such photos look fine on the screen or on a Web page, but are extremely low-resolution on the greater scale of graphics files. Put another way: No matter how you capture still photos from your camcorder, whether using iMovie or using the camcorder's own "digital camera" feature, you won't wind up with something that looks good when printed out. The result will be decidedly "dotty."

Progressive-scan CCD

This special kind of image sensor is primarily useful for capturing still images. It ensures that the *entire* image is grabbed, not just one set of alternating, interlaced scan lines (the usual video signal). If you plan to catch still frames from your camcorder, a progressive-scan CCD will spare you some of the jagged lines shown in, for example, Figure 9-7. However, if your primary goal is to make movies, this expensive feature is not worth paying for, especially since you can buy a digital *still* camera, with much greater resolution, for about the same added cost.

Title generator

Some camcorders let you superimpose *titles* (that is, lettering) on your video as you film. In your case, dear iMovie owner, a title-generating feature is useless. Your Mac can add gorgeous, smooth-edged type, with a selection of sizes, fonts, colors, and even scrolling animations to your finished movies, with far more precision and power than the blocky text available to your camcorder. (Chapter 7 shows you how.)

Tip: A title generator on the camcorder is *worse* than useless, because it permanently stamps your original footage with something you may wish you could amend later.

In fact, as a general rule, you should avoid using (or paying for) *any* of the in-camera editing features described in this chapter—title generator, fader, special effects—because you can do this kind of editing much more effectively in iMovie. Not only are they redundant, but they commit you to an editing choice in advance, thus limiting how you can use your footage.

Fader

Most DV camcorders offer a Fade or Fader button. If you press it once before pressing the Record button, you record a smooth, professional-looking fade in from blackness. If you press it *as* you're recording, and then press the Record button again to stop recording, you get a smooth dimming of the picture (and, usually, a fading of the sound), all the way to black (and silence).

Even if your camcorder has a Fader button, don't use it, for several reasons:

- Pressing the Fade button in order to trigger a fade out is very difficult to do. You're forced to look away from your subject to hunt for the button, and it's almost impossible to keep the camera steady in the process.

- iMovie offers much more graceful and controlled fade ins and fade outs. For example, you can specify exactly how many seconds long the fade should last, and you can even fade into a color other than black.

- When you use your camcorder's Fade button, you risk chopping off one last great wisecrack from your kid as she rides into the sunset, or one last backflip by the seal at Sea World. In other words, once you've started the fade, you can't stop it.

- If you need any more convincing, ask any camcorder owner about the embarrassment factor that comes from fading out on what he assumed would be the absolute perfect final shot, and then coming across another event that *had* to be included in the footage. When played back, the feeling of gentle, sighing finality created by the fade out is jarringly shattered by the sudden appearance of that tacked-on scene.

Audio dubbing

In a few fancy camcorders, a special button lets you re-record only the soundtrack on a piece of tape you've already shot. If you didn't have a Mac, you could conceivably use this feature to add, for example, an accompanying rock song to a montage of party scenes.

But iMovie offers far more flexibility in this department. For example, iMovie lets you add a piece of music to a scene *without* deleting the original voices, as your camcorder's audio-dub feature would. The bottom line: Don't pay extra for audio dubbing on a camcorder.

Special effects

Most DV camcorders offer a selection of six or seven cheesy-looking special effects. They can make your footage look solarized, or digitized, or otherwise processed (see Figure 1-7).

Unlike more expensive video editing software, iMovie offers no such special effects. Many other Mac movie-related programs do, however, including the $30 QuickTime Pro, which works well with iMovie (see Chapter 14). In other words, unless you're shooting a documentary about nuclear explosions or bad drug episodes, consider avoiding these built-in camcorder effects.

 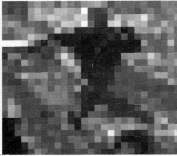

Figure 1-7:
Using the stock collection of special effects built into your camcorder, you can create special, hallucinogenic visuals. The question is: why? (These examples come from a Sony TRV10.)

Date/time stamp

Every camcorder offers the ability to stamp the date and time directly onto the footage. As you've no doubt seen (on *America's Funniest Home Videos* or *America's Scariest Cop Chases),* the result is a blocky, typographically hideous stamp that permanently mars the footage. Few things take the romance out of a wedding video, or are more distracting in spectacular weather footage, than a huge 7 **DEC 99 12:34 PM** stamped in the corner.

Nor do you have to worry that you'll one day forget when you filmed some event. As it turns out, DV camcorders automatically and invisibly date- and time-stamp *all* footage. You'll be able to see this information when you connect the camcorder to your Mac (see page 101); *then* you can choose whether or not to add it to the finished footage (and with much more control over the timing, location, and typography of the stamp).

Control-L or LANC

You'll find this feature on some Canon and all Sony camcorders. It's a connector that hooks up to special editing consoles.

You, however, have the world's best editing console—iMovie—and a far superior connection method—FireWire. Control-L and LANC are worthless to you.

Which Brand to Buy

Virtually every camcorder manufacturer has adopted the DV format, including Sony, Panasonic, JVC, Sharp, RCA, Hitachi, and Canon. Each company releases a new line of models once or twice a year; the feature list always gets longer, the price always gets lower, and the model numbers always change.

In magazine reviews and Internet discussion groups, Sony and Canon get the best marks for high quality and reliable FireWire connections. Some brands, notably JVC, have caused headaches for iMovie fans, thanks to a nonstandard version of the FireWire messages required to communicate with the Mac.

Still, each manufacturer offers different exclusive goodies, and each camcorder generation improves on the previous one. As a starting point, visit Apple's "Supported Camcorders" list at *www.apple.com/imovie/gear.* It's a list of models that Apple has tested to confirm that they work beautifully with iMovie; they are most certainly not, however, the *only* models that do. (They're the ones whose manufacturers have given units to Apple for testing and endorsement.)

Here's a guide to the most popular camcorder families as of mid-2000, along with the Web sites that feature photos and more detail.

Tip: Camcorders are famous for having hopelessly unrealistic list prices. The professional-level Canon XL1, for example, has an official price tag of $4,500, but you can find it for under $3,400 online. (All the prices in this book here are "street prices"—the prices you'll actually pay. And even these price numbers are falling rapidly. Still, they should provide a good indication of the relative quality of these cameras.)

Sony

Sony makes three lines of DV camcorders: Digital8 and Mini-DV, named for the kinds of tapes they accept, and a professional line.

- **Digital8.** As noted earlier, Digital8 camcorders accept traditional, inexpensive 8 mm tapes, but record them with digital information, exactly as though you're using mini-DV tapes. As a bonus, these camcorders can also play back your old 8 mm and Hi-8 cassettes, making these cameras great transitional models. Every Digital8 model includes analog inputs, too, for converting other kinds of footage into digital format (from your VCR, for example). (The larger cassette size makes these camcorders larger than mini-DV models, however. That means you'll get better optical zooming than you will with the ultra-compact models.)

  At this writing, Sony's Digital8 models are among those containing **TRV** in their names. The least expensive is about $600 for a model with a smallish LCD screen and a black-and-white eyepiece viewfinder. $100 more buys you a larger 3.5-inch LCD screen, and yet another $100 gets you an enormous 4-inch LCD screen *and* a color viewfinder. All include a number of features you probably won't use, including special effects and fade options.

- **Mini-DV camcorders.** The rest of Sony's consumer DV camcorder line accepts traditional mini-DV videocassettes. All of them feature a long-play mode that gets 90 minutes out of each cassette, an improved version of Sony's digital image stabilization, infrared-nighttime recording mode, a remote control, pre-programmed auto-exposure settings, and batteries that tell the camera how many minutes you have left. (These models also include a surprisingly intelligent feature for people who sometimes lose track of whether the camcorder is on or off: a mode that forces you to press the Record button continuously as long as you want the camera to shoot.)

You can buy two different kinds of Sony compact DV models. The ones whose names contain the letters **PC** are extremely small—about the size of a Walkman, as shown at top left in Figure 1-8. You hold them vertically while filming. All of the PC models offer the superior *optical* (instead of electronic) image stabilization. The relatively high price ($1,200 to $1,900) includes a fancy Carl Zeiss lens, but the small size means that the optical zoom is limited to "only" 10X, and the LCD is 2.5 inches.

The other Sony mini-DV series is the **TRV** line of compact horizontal-format camcorders (see Figure 1-8), which accommodates an extra-large 3.5-inch LCD screen. Some of the goodies include manual exposure and focus override (using a lens ring), Carl Zeiss lenses, and the LaserLink transmitter described earlier.

These models use electronic image stabilization. Although electronic is usually inferior to optical stabilization, Sony's implementation produces no visible deterioration of the image. Of particular note is the highly reviewed TRV900. The $1,700 price buys you the broadcast quality of a *three-CCD* camera—in fact, it's among the least expensive three-CCD models you can buy—along with a large LCD screen, analog inputs, and a long list of other features.

Figure 1-8:
The model lineup changes constantly, but the various families of Sony DV models generally include the PC series (top left), with a removable Memory Stick for transferring still photos; the three-CCD, semi-pro VX2000 (top right; the TRV family of medium-size mini-DV models (lower left); and a Digital8 model that accepts Hi-8 cassettes instead of DV cassettes (lower right).

- **VX1000.** If you work in film or TV, this $3,300, three-chip, professional camcorder may appeal to you. It offers quality that's as good as, or better than, TV-station equipment. Like its rival, the Canon XL1, it has no flip-out LCD screen; but the picture and sound are breathtaking. You'll note that this model's shotgun-type microphone is mounted well away from the camera body. That design lessens (but doesn't eliminate) a common problem of camcorder microphones: During low-volume scenes, they pick up the noise of the camcorder itself.

Details on Sony's camcorder lines are at *www.sel.sony.com/SEL/consumer/handycam/home.html.*

Tip: Another reason for the popularity and high regard of Sony's camcorders is that you can buy various longer-life batteries for a little extra money. The thickest and most expensive one can power the device for up to eight hours before needing a charge.

Canon

Canon offers an impressive array of camcorder models that trade heavily on the company's expertise as a still-camera manufacturer. They're distinguished by *optical* stabilizers that reduce camera shake better than most digital stabilization systems; an LP mode that lets you squeeze 90 minutes of recording time out of the standard mini-DV cassette; and the FlexiZone off-center auto-focus feature.

- **Consumer line.** The ZR-10 ($700), Ultura ($760), Vistura ($850), Optura Pi ($1500), and Elura 2 ($1150) are Canon's consumer models (see Figure 1-9). They're compact, handheld camcorders, with optical zooms between 10 and 16X. All have the standard features you need—a flip-out LCD screen, color eyepiece viewfinder, FireWire jacks, manual override for the focus controls, and so on. They also include several features you don't need—digital still-photo mode, special effects, and so on. Most, including the delightfully tiny ZR-10, offer analog inputs that accommodate footage from your VCR and from older camcorders.

FREQUENTLY ASKED QUESTION

The MiniDisc Camcorder

What about the new Sony camcorder that records onto a CD instead of tape?

Sounds cool, doesn't it? The DCM-M1 is certainly one of a kind. It doesn't accept mini-DV tapes. Instead, you insert a special, recordable CD—a Sony MiniDisc.

This camcorder offers two profound drawbacks: You can record only 10 minutes of footage on each disk, and the quality isn't as good as it is on a mini-DV tape (because the camcorder must compress it to fit on the CD).

So why would anyone buy one of these? Because it offers *in-camera editing.* You can direct the camera to jump automatically from one shot to another, anywhere on the CD, without having to transfer the footage to another machine, re-record, or go through any other rigamarole.

Of course, as an iMovie owner, you don't benefit much from this feature, since you can perform that editing and much more, much more easily, on your computer. The $2,300 you save could be your own.

• **Professional line.** For semi-pros, Canon offers the GL1 ($2,100, as shown in Figure 1-9)—a much more expensive, larger, pro-oriented camera with superior optics and three CCDs, plus a flip-out LCD screen.

Canon's top-of-the-line model, however, is the XL1 ($3,400). Shaped like a slim TV cameras, its big-ticket feature is that it accepts interchangeable lenses. Like the Sony professional model, its microphone is situated where it's less likely to pick up the sounds of the camera motor itself, and the sound quality is outstanding. Professionals adore the results they get from this camera, but complain only that its six pounds rest largely in your hand, instead of on your shoulder, when shooting. (Note, too, that this camera has no LCD screen at all. Like a TV camera operator, you have to keep this camera up to your eye while shooting.)

Acres of information await at *www.canondv.com*.

Figure 1-9:
Canon's "-ura" camcorders come in both horizontal and vertical orientations. Clockwise from top left: the Elura; the GL1; the original Optura, which looks something like a 35 mm camera; and the Ultura. Some people consider vertical-oriented camcorders (top left) more difficult to hold than horizontal models (bottom left).

Panasonic

Panasonic makes several basic, inexpensive DV camcorders, each gracefully designed. Each includes a remote control, a rotating LCD screen, two tape speeds, 18X optical zoom, and digital (not optical) stabilization.

At the high end, Panasonic offers the **DV950,** a three-CCD camcorder. Panasonic says that, at under 1.5 pounds, this is the smallest and lightest three-CCD camcorder you can buy. (At $1,700, it's also among the least expensive.) It comes with a 2.5-inch color LCD screen, color viewfinder, manual override for every automatic function, and other pro features. Details: *www.panasonic.com/consumer_electronics/video/index.htm*

Sharp

Sharp's camcorders, called ViewCams, aren't state of the art, but they're fine (and under $700). There are two models, both compact and silver. One looks like other horizontal-oriented models. The other has the unusual design of the original Sharp ViewCam lines. In the latter, the entire back of the body is the LCD screen. The lens apparatus is on a separate, rotating segment of the camera.

Unfortunately, most reviewers give the Sharp models poor marks on image quality and FireWire compatibility. Online info: Drill down, starting at *www.sharp-usa.com.*

JVC

Standard features on the JVC line include pivoting LCD screens and extremely compact sizes. Unfortunately, at this writing, JVC hasn't worked the kinks out of its FireWire implementation. You'll have the fewest headaches if you stick with one of the other brands. More info: *www.jvc.com.*

Where to Buy

You can find DV camcorders at electronics and appliance superstores (The Wiz, Circuit City, and so on), mail-order catalogs, and even photo stores.

If you're interested in saving money, however, look online. Such comparison Web sites as *shopper.com, dealtime.com,* and *etown.com* specialize in collecting the prices from mail-order companies all over the world. When you specify the camcorder model you're looking for, you're shown a list of online stores that carry it, complete with prices. (All of the prices in this chapter came from listings on those Web sites.)

As you'll quickly discover, prices for the same camcorder cover an *extremely* large range—one Sony model, for example, ranged from $710 to $980 in one search. Use the price-comparison Web sites if saving money is your priority.

Note: Even though some of the cameras described in this chapter may strike you as expensive, they're not the most expensive camcorders available. If you're a professional broadcaster or filmmaker, $5,000 or $10,000 buys you a much more rugged, shoulder-mounted, interchangeable-lens pro model, whose lenses can cost $10,000 alone. These cameras have batteries that seem to last forever, broadcast-oriented color balance controls, and higher *color-sampling* rates (for even more accurate color representation).

BUYERS' GUIDE

Smaller Isn't Always Better

Much camcorder marketing is based on the idea that smaller is better—but it isn't always.

For example, it's difficult to hold the tiny, box-like camcorders steady, especially as you're trying to use the eyepiece viewfinder. Smaller camcorders come with smaller LCD pan-els, too. And it's *very* difficult to push the tiny buttons on one of the micro-camcorders while you're trying to film.

By all means, go for tiny if traveling light is a priority, or if you do a lot of undercover filming. But buy armed with the realization that tininess requires tradeoffs.

IMOVIE 2: THE MISSING MANUAL

Turning Home Video into Pro Video

W hen you turn on the TV, how long does it take you to distinguish between an actual broadcast and somebody's home video? Probably about ten seconds.

The real question is: *How* can you tell? What are the visual differences between professionally produced shows and your own? Apple's advertising claims that a DV camcorder and iMovie let you create professional-quality video work. So why do even iMovie productions often have a homemade look to them?

Maybe Homemade is What You Want

If you want to learn how to upgrade your filming techniques to make your finished videos look more professional, then this chapter is your ticket.

That's not to say, however, that "professional" *always* means "better." Not every video has to be, or should be, a finished-looking production. There are plenty of circumstances in which homemade-looking video is just fine. In fact, it's exactly what an audience of family members is probably expecting. When watching your footage of a one-of-a-kind scene for which preparation was obviously impossible, such as a baby's first steps or the eruption of a local volcano, rest assured that nobody will be critiquing your camera work.

Furthermore, sometimes amateur-looking video *is* the look your professional project calls for. In some movies, filmmakers go to enormous lengths to simulate the effect of amateur camcorder footage. (The color segment of *Raging Bull,* for example, is designed to look as though it's composed footage shot by a home movie camera.)

In other words, polished-looking video isn't necessarily superior video in every situation. Nonetheless, you should know how to get professional results when you want them; even Picasso mastered traditional, representational drawing before going abstract.

As it turns out, there are a number of discernible ways that home movies differ from professional ones. This chapter is dedicated to helping you accept the camcorder deficiencies you cannot change, overcome the limitations you can, and have the wisdom to know the difference.

Film vs. Videotape

There's only one crucial aspect of Hollywood movies that you can't duplicate with your DV camcorder and iMovie: Real movies are shot on *film,* not video. Film, of course, is a long strip of celluloid with sprocket holes on the edges. It comes on an enormous reel, loaded onto an enormous camera. After you've shot it, a lab must develop it before you can see what you've got.

Videotape is a different ballgame. As you know, it comes on a cartridge, pops into a compact camera, and doesn't have to be developed. Many TV shows, including sitcoms and all news shows, are shot on video.

Visually, the differences are dramatic. Film and videotape just look different, for several reasons:

- Film goes through many transfer processes (from original, to positive master, to negative master, to individual "prints," to movie screen), so it has a softer, warmer appearance. It also has microscopic specks, flecks, and scratches that tell you you're watching something filmed on film.

- Film has much greater resolution than video—*billions* of silver halide crystals coat each frame of the film. As a result, you see much more detail than video can offer. It has a subtle grain—a texture—that you can spot immediately. Furthermore, these specks of color are irregularly shaped, and different on every frame; a camcorder's sensors (CCDs), on the other hand, are all the same size and perfectly aligned, which also affects the look of the resulting image.

- Film is also far more sensitive to color, light, and contrast than the sensors in camcorders. And different kinds of film stock offer different characteristics. Hollywood directors choose film stock according to the ambiance they want: One type of film might yield warmer colors, another type might be more contrasty, and so on.

- Film is composed of 24 individual frames (images) per second, but NTSC video (see page 5) contains more flashes of picture per second (30 complete frames, shown as 60 alternating sets of interlocking horizontal lines per second). All of that extra visual information contributes to video's hard, sharp look, and lends visual differences in the way motion is recorded. This discrepancy becomes particularly apparent to experts when film is *transferred* to video for broadcast on TV, for example. Doing so requires the transfer equipment to *duplicate* a frame of the original film here and there.

Of course, the *content* of the film or video is also a telltale sign of what you're watching. If it has a laugh track and a brightly lit set, it's usually videotape; if it's more carefully and dramatically lit, with carefully synchronized background music, it's usually film.

Film-Technique Crash Course

The bottom line is that two different issues separate film from video: the *technology* and the *technique*. What you can't change is the look of the basic medium: You're going to be recording onto tape, not film.

Tip: If the grain and softness associated with film are crucial to your project, you're not utterly out of luck. With the addition of a $1,500 video-processing program called Adobe After Effects and a $6,000 software add-on called CineLook (from DigiEffects), you can get very close to making video look like film. CineLook adds the grain, flecks, and scratches to taped footage, and plays with the color palette to look more like that of film. Another popular add-on called CineMotion (from the same company) adds subtle blur processing to make the *motion* of video look more like film, simulating 24-frames-per-second playback. (Needless to say, few iMovie fans go to that expensive extreme.)

What you can change with iMovie alone, however, is almost every remaining element of the picture. Some of the advice in this chapter requires additional equipment; some simply requires new awareness. Overall, however, the tips in this chapter should take you a long way into the world of professional cinematography.

The Very Basics

If you're using a camcorder for the first time, it's important to understand the difference between its two functions: as a camera and as a VCR.

The most obvious knob or switch on every camcorder lets you switch between these two modes (plus a third one known as Off). These two operating-switch positions may be labeled *Camera* and *VTR* (for Video Tape Recorder), *Camera* and *VCR*, or *Record* and *Play.*

But the point is always the same: When you're in Camera mode, you can record the world; the lens and the microphone are activated. When you're in VTR mode, the lens and the mike are shut down; now your camcorder is a VCR, complete with Play, Rewind, and Fast-Forward buttons (which often light up in VTR mode). When you want to *film* a movie, use Camera mode; to *watch* the movie you've recorded, put the camcorder into VTR mode. (You'll also have to put the camera in VTR mode when it comes time to record your finished iMovie creation, or when you want to copy video to or from another camcorder or VCR.)

Here, then, is the usual sequence for filming:

1. **Prepare the microphone, lighting, angle, and camera settings as described in this chapter.**

   This is the moment, in other words, to play director and cinematographer—to set up the shot. You can read about all these important techniques in the rest of this chapter. They're extremely important techniques, at that—if the raw footage has bad sound, bad lighting, or the wrong camera settings, no amount of iMovie manipulation can make it better.

2. **Turn the main knob or switch to Camera (or Record) mode.**

   You've just turned the power on. The camera's now in standby mode—on, but not playing or recording anything. (See Figure 2-1.)

Figure 2-1:
The main button on every camcorder lets you turn the camera on by switching it into Camera or VTR mode (left). The red Record button is the trigger that makes the tape roll (right).

3. **Take off the lens cap.**

   The lens cap usually dangles from a short black string that you've looped around a corresponding hole on the front of the camera (or hooks onto the handstrap), unless you're lucky enough to have a camcorder blessed with a built-in, auto-opening lens cap.

4. **Frame your shot (aim the camera).**

   Do so either by looking at the LCD screen or by looking through the eyepiece. Adjust the zoom controls until the subject nicely fills the frame. Get your performers ready (if they're even aware that they're being filmed, that is).

5. **Press the Record button.**

   It's usually bright red and located next to your right thumb. (The left-handers' lobby has gotten absolutely nowhere with camcorder manufacturers.)

   Some camcorders have an additional Record button on the top or side, plus another one on the remote control, for use when you're filming yourself or holding the camcorder down at belly level.

   In any case, now you're rolling.

6. Film the action as described in this chapter. When you've filmed enough of the scene—when you've *got the shot*—press the Record button a second time to stop rolling.

At this point, the camcorder is back in standby mode. It's using up its battery faster than when it's turned off. Therefore, if you don't expect to be filming anything more within the next few minutes, push the primary switch back to its Off position. (If you forget, no big deal; most camcorders turn off automatically after five minutes or so since your last activity.)

Now you, like thousands before you, know the basics. The rest of this chapter is designed to elevate your art from that of camera operator to cinematographer/director.

Get the Shot

Rule No. 1: Get the shot.

If you and the camcorder aren't ready when something great happens—whether you're trying to create a Hollywood-style movie with scripted actors or just trying to catch the dog's standoff with a squirrel—then everything else in this book, and in your new hobby, are for naught.

FREQUENTLY ASKED QUESTION

The Slate: Lights, Lens Cap, Action!

I'm getting so tired of seeing that stupid black and white "clapper" board—it's the iM-ovie icon, it's the picture that shows up when you choose ⬛—About iMovie, *it's the icon of every iMovie document. In fact, it's the world's most over-used symbol—everybody uses it to symbolize filmmaking. What the heck is that thing?*

It's called the *slate* or *clapstick,* and they really do use it when they make commercial movies. Using chalk, an assistant writes the movie's name, scene number, and date onto this black-board. As soon as the camera is rolling, the slate is held in front of the lens and the clapstick on top is slammed shut. Only then does the director shout, "And, *action!"*

The purpose of this exercise is to make editing easier later. The director can say, "I thought that the second take was the best one," and the editors will quickly be able to find that particular spot in the raw footage.

Oh, and the clapstick business : Although your camcorder records sound and video simultaneously, the soundtrack for *film* is actually recorded on a different machine. When editing, technicians must manually fiddle with the picture and sound tracks so that they line up. The action of the opened clapstick closing is designed to help film editors synchronize the audio with the video—the loud, crisp sound is easy to align with the visual moment when the clapstick closes.

Both human and mechanical obstacles may conspire to prevent you from capturing the perfect footage. Here are some examples:

Is the Camera Ready?

Your camcorder is only ready when its battery is charged and it's got fresh tape inside. If you have a Digital8 camera, whose Hi-8 cassettes are $4.50 apiece, you have no excuse not to have a stack of blanks, at least a couple of which should live in your camcorder carrying case for emergency purposes. Mini-DV tapes cost $8 to $10 each (from, for example, *www.bhphotovideo.com*), but if you bite the bullet and buy a box of ten, you'll save even more money, you won't have to buy any more for quite a while, and you'll be able to keep a couple of spares with the camera.

Tip: Professional broadcast journalists never go anywhere without fully charged batteries and blank tape in the camera. Even if you're not a pro, having enough tape and power at all times can pay off, since you can make good money selling your video to news shows because you caught something good on tape.

The same goes for battery power. The battery that comes with the camcorder is adequate as a starter battery, but buying a second one—especially if it's one of the fat, heavy, longer-capacity batteries—is further insurance that some precious shooting opportunity won't be shut down by equipment failure.

Remember, too, that today's lithium-ion batteries are extraordinarily sophisticated. But even though they're rechargeable, they're not immortal; most can be recharged only a few hundred times before you start to notice a decrease in capacity. In other words, use the power cord whenever it's practical.

Tip: Camcorder batteries are far more fragile then they appear. Keep them dry at all costs. If one gets damp or wet, you may as well throw it away.

Are You Ready?

There's a human element to being ready, too. For example, remember that from the moment you switch on the power, your camcorder takes about eight seconds to warm up, load a little bit of tape, and prepare for filming. It's a good idea to flip the power on, therefore, even as you're running to the scene of the accident, earthquake, or amazing child behavior.

Is the Camera Actually Recording?

Every day, somewhere in the world, a family sits down in front of the TV, expecting to watch some exciting home movies—and instead watches 20 minutes of the ground bumping along beneath the camcorder owner's hand.

As you begin to shoot, *always* glance at the viewfinder to confirm that the Record indicator—usually a red dot, or the word REC or RECORD—has appeared. Make it a rigid and automatic habit. That's the only way you'll avoid the sickening realization later that you punched the Record button one too many times, thus turning the camera *on* when you thought it was *off,* and vice versa.

If your subject is a family member or friend, they may be able to confirm that you're getting the shot by checking the *tally light*—the small light on the lens end of the camcorder that lights up, or blinks, while you're recording. Most videographers, however, turn off the tally light (using the camcorder's built-in menu system) or put a piece of black tape over it. If you're trying to be surreptitious or to put your subject at ease, the light can be extremely distracting, especially when it starts *blinking* to indicate that you're running out of tape or power.

Similarly, make sure the indicator disappears when you punch the Record button a second time—sometimes this button sticks and doesn't actually make the camera stop filming.

Tip: If the recording-the-ground syndrome has struck you even once, check your camcorder's feature list. Some models, including most Sony camcorders, offer a special feature that's designed to eliminate this syndrome. When you slide a switch into a mode Sony calls Anti-Ground Shooting, the camcorder records only *while* you're pressing the Record button. As soon as you remove your thumb, the camera stops recording. This scheme isn't ideal for long shots, of course, and it ties up your hands during shots when you might need to adjust the zoom or focus while filming. But it's extremely good insurance against missing important moments.

How Much to Shoot

For years, books and articles about camcorders have stressed the importance of keeping your shots *short.* In the pre-iMovie era, this was excellent advice. When you show your footage to other people, there's absolutely nothing worse than endless, monotonous, unedited scenes of babies/speeches/scenery. If you don't want your guests and family members to feel that they're being held hostage during your screenings (goes the usual advice), strive for short shots and very selective shooting.

But the iMovie revolution turns that advice on its head. Yes, it's still agonizing and tedious to watch hours of somebody's unedited video, but thanks to iMovie, you won't be *showing* unedited video. By the time an audience sees it, your stuff won't be endless and boring. In fact, it will be far better than a bunch of short, selective shots on the average person's camcorder, because you'll have had a much greater selection of footage from which to choose the most interesting scenes.

In other words, it's safe to relax about how much you're shooting. It's much better, in the iMovie Age, to shoot too much footage than too little; if your camcorder stops rolling too soon, you might miss a terrific moment. (Almost everyone who's used a camcorder has experienced such unfortunate timing.)

In Hollywood and professional TV production, in fact, shooting miles of footage is standard practice. When filming movies, Hollywood directors shoot every scene numerous times, even if nothing goes wrong in most of them, just so that they'll have a selection to choose from when it comes time to assemble the final film. (As an extreme example, legend has it that during the making of Stanley Kubrick's *Eyes Wide Shut,* the director asked the actors to repeat a scene 140 times, on the premise that eventually they'd no longer be acting—it would be *real.*) The more takes you get "in the can," especially if they're shot different ways (different angles, zoom levels, and so on), the more flexibility and choice you'll have when editing, and the better the finished product will be.

Don't go overboard, of course; there *is* still such a thing as shooting too much footage. You should still think in terms of capturing *shots* that you've thought about and framed in the viewfinder; don't just roll continuously, pointing the lens this way and that. And you should still remember all the extra time you'll have to spend transferring the footage into iMovie, reviewing it, and editing it. The more you shoot, the greater the editing time.

There's a hard drive limitation, too. A fruit-colored iMac DV or base-model Power Mac G4 can hold only about 45 minutes of raw footage at a time (if there's not much else on the hard drive); a high-end PowerBook can hold about an hour and 20 minutes. (You can certainly create longer shows, but you'll have to piece them together one section at a time. Those 45 or 80 minutes represent the raw footage you can *edit* at a time—unless you buy a bigger hard drive, as described in Chapter 4.)

But it's certainly safe to say that in the age of iMovie, you'll improve your odds of catching memorable moments on tape if you keep the camera rolling as long as the kid/animal/tornado is performing.

Replace the Microphone

The built-in microphone on your camcorder can't be beat for convenience. It's always there, it's always on, and it's always pointing at what you're filming.

Unfortunately, camcorder microphones have several profound disadvantages. For example:

- They're usually mounted right on the camera body. In quiet scenes, they can pick up the sound of the camcorder itself—a quiet grinding of the electronic motor, or the sound of the lens zooming and focusing.

- They're on the camera, not where the subject is. If your subject is farther than a few feet away, the sound is much too faint. The powerful zoom lens on modern camcorders exaggerates this problem. If your subject is 50 yards away, the zoom may make it look as though you're right up close, but the sound still has to come from 50 yards away.

"Camcorder sound," that hollow, faraway sonic quality present on most home videos (including the ones shown on your cable station's public-access channel late at night), is one of the most obvious differences between amateur video and professional work. Even if viewers can't quite put their finger on *how* they know that something was shot with a camcorder, they'll know that it *was* shot with a camcorder just by listening.

Clip-on (Lavalier) Microphones

Few camcorder accessories, therefore, are more useful than an external microphone. And it doesn't have to cost a lot. For $20, Radio Shack will sell you a high-quality tie-clip microphone that resembles the one worn on the lapels of newscasters (see Figure 2-2).

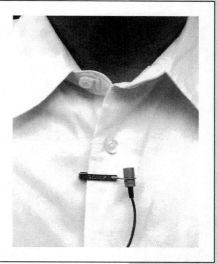

Figure 2-2:
A tie-clip microphone, known in the business as a Lavalier *mike ("lava-LEER"), is a very inexpensive way to dramatically improve the audio on your footage, especially when accompanied by an extension cable or two. You plug it into the Mic In jack on the side of almost every DV camcorder. (This jack may be concealed by a protective plastic cap.)*

Of course, if the problem of camcorder audio is that it gets worse when the subject is far away, an external microphone with a six-foot cord isn't of much use. Therefore, consider buying a couple of extension cords for your microphone; they come in lengths of 20 feet or more, and cost about $10. You can plug one into the next, using standard miniplug connectors (like the ones on the end of Walkman headphones).

Tip: In certain situations, plugging one cable into the next, as you do when connecting an external microphone to an extension cable, can introduce a hum on your soundtrack. To avoid ruining otherwise great footage, carry with you a pair of cheap Walkman headphones. Whenever you're using an external microphone, plug these headphones into the headphone jack on your camcorder and listen as you film. (In fact, you're wise to use headphones *any* time you're filming.)

If a humming or buzzing does arise, try exchanging cables, eliminating extension cords, and running the camcorder on battery instead of AC power, until you've isolated the source of the problem.

Wireless Mikes

One of those inexpensive tie-clip microphones is ideal when you're filming interviews, speeches, or scripted dialog with actors. But in other situations, a cabled microphone like this is impractical, such as when you're shooting a jogger, somebody in a car, or an undercover agent.

For those circumstances, consider buying or renting a *wireless* microphone. These microphones come in two parts: the microphone held or worn by the actor or speaker, and a receiver that clips onto your camcorder and plugs into the Mic In jack. The receiver picks up the sound signal that's transmitted by radio waves. (Here again, be aware of interference. As you film, wear Walkman headphones to monitor the incoming sound. There's nothing worse than tender words of love being drowned out by a nearby trucker cursing on his overamplified CB radio that's picked up by your receiver.)

Other Microphones

If you're shooting documentary-style, it's impractical to attach *any* kind of microphone to the people you're filming. Depending on how serious you are about your filming, you have alternatives. A *shotgun mike* is elongated and thin; it's designed to pick up a distant sound source with pinpoint accuracy. (In Hollywood thrillers, shotgun mikes appear on-screen in the hands of the characters almost as often as they

---

BUYERS' GUIDE

How to Buy a Microphone

When you shop for an add-on mike for your camcorder, you'll have to choose between models based on three important microphone characteristics: its *technology* (dynamic vs. condenser), its *pickup pattern,* and its *connector.*

Dynamic microphones sense changes in air pressure caused by sound waves. They use relatively simple technology that's usually rugged, but not very sensitive to quiet sounds. These are the least expensive microphones.

A *condenser* mike (also called *electret condenser*), on the other hand, has a built-in amplifier, making it much more sensitive to both sound levels and frequency. These microphones require extra power; some use batteries; some can get their power from the cable that plugs into your camcorder using what's called "phantom power." The important thing to remember when using a condenser mike is to carry spare batteries, because the microphone may go dead at any time during shooting. These mikes are also more expensive and less rugged than dynamic models.

The *pickup pattern* refers to the area in space from which a particular microphone picks up sounds. For example, *omnidirectional* mikes pick up sound from every side—in front, to the side, from behind. They're great if you need to record groups of people or general environmental sounds, but they pick up too much ambient noise when you're trying to record dialog in a noisy environment.

Cardioid microphones block sound from behind, and dampen sound coming from the sides. In other words, they mostly capture sounds they're pointed at, but still pick up some general surrounding sound. This is the most common type used in Hollywood productions.

Supercardioid microphones, such as shotgun mikes, are extremely directional. They must point *straight* at the subject, or they may not pick up its sound at all. These specialized mikes are great in noisy environments, but they're expensive. They usually require an operator, someone who does nothing but point the mike at the sound's source.

Finally, consider the *connector* at the end of the microphone cable. *XLR* is the professional connection: a big, round, three-pin jack that doesn't fit any camcorder under $4,000. Instead, your camcorder probably accepts *eighth-inch, mini-phono* plugs, which look like the end of a pair of Walkman headphones.

Several companies manufacture XLR to eighth-inch adapters, which let you use professional mikes on less expensive camcorders. These converters also have one or two *extra* jacks, so that you can plug in a second microphone, when necessary—a great feature for interviews. Such converters usually include signal-level control knobs, too, that let you manually adjust the sound volume as you're recording.

---

do behind the scenes.) DV camcorders in the $3,000 range, such as the Canon XL1 and the Sony VX1000, have a shotgun mike built right in; clip-on shotgun mikes are available for less expensive Canon and Sony camcorders, too.

There's also the *boom mike,* which requires a helper to hold over the head of the actor on a long pole—another staple of professional film production. Unfortunately, this kind of mike, too, is likely to dampen your spontaneity.

Where to Buy Them

You won't find these fancier microphone types, which cost $100 or more, in the local Radio Shack. Online, however, they're everywhere. Video-supply companies like *www.rentgear.com, www.markertek.com,* and *www.bhphotovideo.com* are good starting points for your shopping quest. For good information about microphones in general, visit *www.audiotechnica.com/using/mphones/guide.*

FREQUENTLY ASKED QUESTION

Automatic Gain Control

Where's the recording-volume knob on my camcorder?

There isn't one. Modern consumer camcorders use something called *automatic gain control* (AGC). They set the volume level automatically as you record.

That may sound like a neat feature, but it drives professionals nutty. AGC, in essence, strives to record all sound at exactly the same level. When something is very loud, the AGC circuit quiets it down to middle volume; when something is very soft, the AGC circuit boosts it to middle volume.

Over the years, automatic-gain circuitry has dramatically improved. The electronic boosting or quieting is smoother and less noticeable than it once was. Even some modern camcorders, however, sometimes exhibit the unpleasant side effects of AGC circuitry: Try filming something that's very quiet, and then suddenly clap right next to the micro-

phone. On lesser camcorders, when you play the footage back, you'll hear how the sudden, loud sound made the AGC back off, cutting the volume way down in anticipation of further loud noises. It takes the camcorder several seconds to realize that the surrounding sound is still quiet (and to boost the volume level back up where it had been).

Fortunately, that sudden-adjustment syndrome is a rare and usually harmless occurrence. For most purposes, camcorders do an excellent job of setting their own volume level (although it certainly evens out the dynamic highs and lows of, say, a symphony performance).

Besides, you don't have much of an alternative. Only a few, more expensive camcorders permit you to override the AGC circuit (and adjust the sound level manually). Even if you plug in an external microphone, most camcorders take it upon themselves to adjust the sound level automatically.

Limit Panning and Zooming

In a way, camcorder manufacturers are asking for it. They put the zoom-in/zoom-out buttons right on top of the camcorder, where your fingers naturally rest. That tempting placement has led millions of camcorder owners to zoom in or out in almost every shot—and sometimes even several times *within* a shot. For the camcorder operator, zooming imparts a sense of control, power, and visual excitement. But for the viewer, zooming imparts a sense of nausea.

In other words, most home-movie makers zoom too much. In professional film and video, you almost never see zooming, unless it's to achieve a particular special effect. (Someday, rent a movie and note how many times the director zooms in or zooms out. Answer: almost never.)

Tips for Keeping Zooming Under Control

To separate yourself from the amateur-video pack, adopt these guidelines for using the zoom buttons:

- The zoom button is ideal for adjusting the magnification level *between* shots, when the camcorder is paused—to *set up* a new shot. Be conscious of how many times you're using the zoom while the tape is rolling.

- Sometimes you may be tempted to zoom in order to create an *establishing shot*—to show the entire landscape, the big picture—before closing in on your main subject.

  That's a worthy instinct, but zooming isn't the best way to go from an establishing shot to a close-up. Instead, consider an effect like the extremely effective,

Zooming   Cutting

Figure 2-3:
Zooming, as represented here by several sequential frames (left), is a dead giveaway that the movie is homemade. Try a more professional sequence to set up your shot: Hold on a wider, scene-establishing shot, cut to a medium shot, and then cut to a close-up (right).

more interesting one that opens *Citizen Kane:* a series of successive shots that dissolve, one into the next, each closer to the subject than the previous. (See Figure 2-3.) Open with a wide shot that shows the entire airport; fade into a medium shot that shows the exiting masses of people; finally, dissolve to the worried face of the passenger whose luggage has vanished. Naturally, you can't create the fades and dissolves while you're shooting, but it's a piece of cake to add them in iMovie. Your job while filming is simply to capture the two or three different shots, each at a different zoom level.

- You don't have to avoid zooming altogether. As noted above, professional moviemakers rarely zoom. One of the exceptions, however, is when the director wants to pick one face out of a crowd, often just as some horrific realization is dawning. Furthermore, when you're filming somebody who's doing a lot of talking, a very slow, almost imperceptible zoom is an extremely effective technique, especially if you do it when the speech is getting more personal, emotional, ominous, or important.

The point is to use zooming *meaningfully,* when there's a reason to do it.

- For the lowest motion-sickness quotient, use the *hold-zoom-hold* technique. In other words, begin your shot by filming without zooming for a moment; zoom slowly and smoothly; and end the shot by holding on the resulting close-up or wide shot. Don't begin or end the shot in mid-zoom.

Tip: Documentary makers frequently film with this pattern: Hold for five seconds; zoom in, and then hold for five seconds; zoom out again, and hold for five, then stop the shot. This technique gives the filmmaker a variety of shots, providing choice when editing the final movie.

All of this sheds light on another reason to hold at the end of a zoom, and another reason to avoid zooming in general: When editing, it's very difficult to make a smooth cut during a zoom. Cutting from one nonzooming shot to another is smoother and less noticeable than cutting in mid-zoom.

- Consider how much to zoom. There's no law that says that every zoom must utilize the entire 500X magnification range of your camcorder. Start or stop zooming at the point where it's most artistically satisfying.

- Did you ever see *Wayne's World*—either the movie or the *Saturday Night Live* skit on which it was based? *Wayne's World,* of course, was a spoof of a hilariously amateurish public-access cable TV show that was supposedly shot with a camcorder in somebody's basement. The show's trademark camerawork: multiple zooms in a single shot. (Such annoying shots are always accompanied by Wayne and Garth shouting, "Unnecessary zoom!")

As rare as zooming is in professional TV and film, *multiple* zooms in a single shot is virtually unheard of. To avoid creating a *Wayne's World* of your own, consider zooming only once, in only one direction, and then *stop* to focus on the target. Don't zoom in, linger, and then continue zooming; and don't zoom in, linger, and then zoom back out (unless you intend to discard half of that shot during editing). Furthermore, on camcorders equipped with a variable-speed zoom, keep the zoom speed consistent. (The slowest zoom is usually the most effective.)

Note: There's an exception to the avoid-zooming-in-and-out-while-shooting rule. That's when you're filming a one-of-a-kind event and you're desperate to keep the camera rolling for fear of missing even a second of priceless footage. In that case, zoom all you want to get the shots you want. But do so with the understanding that the good stuff won't be the zooming footage—it will be the scenes *between* zooms.

Later, you can eliminate the unnecessary zooms during iMovie editing.

Panning and Tilting

Panning is rotating the camera while recording—either horizontally, to take in a scene that's too wide to fit in one lens-full, or vertically (called *tilting)*, to take in a scene that's too tall.

In general, panning is justifiable more often than zooming is. Sometimes, as when you're filming a landscape, a skyscraper, or a moving object, you have no alternative. Standard camcorder lenses simply aren't wide-angle enough to capture grand panoramas in one shot, much to the frustration of anyone who's tried to film New Zealand landscapes, New York skyscrapers, or the Grand Canyon.

Even so, some of the guidelines listed above for zooming also apply to panning:

• Pan only when you have good reason to do so. One of the most common reasons to pan is to *track* a moving target as it moves through space. (Interestingly, pro-

---

POWER USERS' CLINIC

Recording Entrances and Exits

When it's possible, record the "entrances and exits" of moving subjects into, and out of, your camcorder's field of vision. For example, if you're filming two people walking, film the space where they're *about* to appear for a moment—and then, when they enter the frame, pan the camcorder to follow their movement. Finally, stop panning and let your subjects walk clear out of the frame.

Entrances and exits like this make more interesting footage than simple follow-them-all-the-way shots. By letting the motion occur within the frame, for example, you emphasize the motion. If a car zooms *across* the screen, and then exits the frame, your viewers can *see* how fast it was going. But if you track the car by panning all the way, you diminish the sense of motion; it's hard to tell how fast a car is moving if it's always centered in a panning shot.

More important, frame entrances and exits can help make your editing job easier, thanks to their ability to disguise discontinuous action. Suppose, for example, that you've got a medium shot of a schoolgirl starting to raise her hand. But the shot ends when her hand is only as high as her stomach. Now suppose that the next shot, a close-up of her face, begins with her hand *entering the frame* from below, whereupon it heads for, and finally scratches, her nose. You can safely cut from the stomach shot to the nose shot; because of the hand's entrance into the frame, your cut looks natural and motivated. The "entrance" disguises the fact that the hand was at stomach level in one frame and at face level in the next.

Without that entrance, you'd wind up with a *jump cut*—an irritating discontinuity in time from one shot to the next.

---

fessionals pan most of the time from left to right, the way people read, except when a shot is meant to be deliberately disturbing.)

In fact, almost *any* pan looks better if there's something that "motivates" the camera movement. A car, train, bird flying, person walking, or anything else that draws the eye justifies the pan and gives a sense of scale to the image.

• Begin and end the pan by holding, motionless, on carefully chosen beginning and ending images.

• Make an effort to pan smoothly and *slowly*. This time, you can't rely on the camcorder's electronics to ensure smoothness of motion, as you can when zooming. Bracing your elbows against your sides helps. (If you pan too fast, you may create what's known as a *swish pan*—a blurry shot that's *intended* to be disorienting, as when the main character, being chased through a crowd, is desperately turning his head this way and that in an effort to spot his pursuers.)

• Avoid panning more than once in a shot. Make an effort not to perform such classic amateur maneuvers as the Pan/Linger/Pan or the Pan-to-the-Right, Get-Distracted, Pan-Back-to-the-Left.

• If you're especially gifted with your camcorder, remember that you can also pan and zoom simultaneously. This, too, should be considered a special effect used rarely. But when you are, in fact, filming a close-up of somebody saying, "Look! The top of the building is exploding!", nothing is more effective than a smooth zoom out/pan up to the top of the building.

• *Practice* the pan, tilt, or zoom a couple of times before rolling tape. Each time, the result will be smoother and less noticeable.

• Be careful about panning when your camcorder's electronic image stabilizer is turned on. If you're doing a slow pan when the camcorder is on a tripod (as it should be), the shot gets jittery and jumpy as the camera tries to hold onto (or "stabilize") one scene as you rotate a new one into view. If your camcorder is on a tripod, you're safe to turn off the electronic stabilization anyway. (*Optical* stabilization doesn't exhibit this problem.)

Tip: If you plan to save your finished iMovie work as a QuickTime movie—a file that plays on your computer screen, rather than a tape that will play on your TV (see Part 3)—panning and zooming slowly and smoothly is especially important. iMovie's compression software works by analyzing the subtle picture differences from one frame to another; if you zoom or pan too quickly, the QuickTime compressors won't understand the relationship between one frame and the next. Blotchiness or skipped frames (which cause jerky motion) may result in the finished QuickTime movie.

Keep the Camera Steady

Here's another difference between amateur and pro footage: Most camcorder movies are shot with a camera held in somebody's hand, which is extremely obvious to

---

people who have to watch it later. Real TV shows, movies, and corporate videos are shot with a camera on a *tripod*. (There are a few exceptions, such as a few annoying-to-watch Woody Allen movies. However, they were shot with handheld cameras for an artistic reason, not just because it was too much trouble to line up a tripod.)

It's impossible to overstate the positive effect a tripod can have on your footage. Nor is it a hassle to use such a tripod; if you get one that's equipped with a quick-release plate, the camcorder snaps instantly onto the corresponding tripod socket. Tripods are cheap, too. You can buy one for as little as $20, although more expensive tripods have more features, last longer, and are less likely to nip your skin when you're collapsing them for transport.

Tip: If the camcorder on the tripod isn't perfectly level, the picture will start to tilt diagonally as you pan (the car will appear to be driving up or down a hill instead of across a flat plain). To prevent this phenomenon, make sure that the camera legs are carefully adjusted—slow and tedious work on most tripods. But on tripods with *ball-leveling heads* (an expensive feature, alas), achieving levelness takes just a few seconds: Just loosen a screw, adjust the head until it is level, and tighten the screw down again.

Of course, tripods aren't always practical. When you're trying to film without being noticed, when you don't have the luggage space, or when you must start filming *immediately*, you may have to do without. In those instances, consider one of these alternatives:

- **Turn on the image stabilization feature.** As noted in Chapter 1, every modern DV camcorder includes an *image stabilization* feature, which magically irons out

---

BUYERS' GUIDE

How to Buy a Tripod

A tripod has two parts: the legs and the *pan head.* The camera attaches to the pan head, and the legs support the head.

You can buy a tripod with any of three pan head types. *Friction heads* are the simplest, least expensive, and most popular with still photographers; unfortunately, they provide the bumpiest pans and tilts when used for videotaping. *Fluid heads* are the most desirable kind; they smooth out panning and tilting. They're more expensive than friction heads, but are well worth the money if you're after a professional look to your footage. Finally, *geared heads* are big, heavy, expensive, and difficult to use; these are what Hollywood productions use, because they can handle heavy film cameras.

The tripod's legs may be made of metal, wood, or composite. Metal is light and less expensive but easier to damage by accident (thin metal is easily bent). Wood and composite legs are much more expensive; they're designed for heavier professional broadcast and film equipment. The bottoms of the legs have rubber feet, which is great for use indoors and on solid floors. Better tripods also have spikes, which work well outdoors on grass and dirt.

Good tripods also have *spreaders* that prevent the legs from spreading apart and causing the entire apparatus to crash to the ground. If your tripod doesn't have spreaders, you can put the tripod on a piece of carpet, which prevents the legs from slipping apart.

In general, you adjust a tripod's height by extending the legs' telescoping sections. Some tripods have a riser column, too, that lets you crank the pan head higher off the legs. Remember that the higher the camera is lifted up, the more unsteady it becomes, so sturdiness is an important characteristic.

the minor jiggles and shakes associated with handheld filming. Using electronic/ digital (as opposed to optical) image stabilization drains your battery faster, so feel free to turn it off when you *are* using a tripod. But at all other times, the improvement in footage is well worth the power sacrifice.

- **Make the camera as steady as possible.** If you can steady it on top of a wall, on top of your car, or even your own knee, you'll get better results. If there's absolutely nothing solid on which to perch the camcorder, keep your camcorder-hand elbow pressed tightly against your side, use two hands, and breathe slowly and with control. When you pan, turn from the waist, keeping your upper body straight. Bend your legs slightly to serve as shock absorbers.

Tip: Regardless of your camcorder model, you'll get the best and steadiest results if you use your free hand to brace the *bottom* of the camera. Holding both *sides* of the camcorder isn't nearly as steady.

- **Zoom out.** When you're zoomed in to film something distant, magnifying the image by, say, 10 times, remember that a one-millimeter jiggle gets magnified many times. When you're zoomed in a lot, it's easy to produce extremely unsteady footage. Keep this in mind when deciding how much you want to zoom; the most stable picture results when you're zoomed out all the way. (Zooming also makes focus more critical, as described later in this chapter.)

- **Consider a monopod.** Despite the enormous boost in stability that a tripod gives your footage, you don't always have the time to unlatch, extend, and relatch each of the three legs. If the kind of shooting you do frequently requires such fast setup and takedown, consider a *monopod*. As much as it sounds like a creature from a sci-fi movie, a monopod is actually a closer relative to a walking stick: It's a collapsible metal post for your camcorder. When using a monopod, you still have to steady the camcorder with your hands (jiggles are still possible), but the monopod eliminates motion from one of the three dimensions (up and down), which is much better than nothing. And the monopod, of course, takes very little time to set up and take down.

- **Get a clamp.** You can also buy vise-like clamps equipped with camera plates. You can clamp them to car windows, chair backs, tops of ladders, skateboards, and so on, for even more stable-shooting options. (Put a piece of cloth between the clamp and the surface to prevent scratching.)

Video Lighting: A Crash Course

Today's camera optics are good, but they're not human eyeballs. Every camera, from your camcorder to professional TV and film models, captures truer color, depth, and contrast if lighting conditions are good. The need for bright light grows more desperate if:

- **You record onto videotape instead of film.** Video picks up an even smaller range of light and shadow than film, so having enough light is especially important

---

when using your camcorder. Figure 2-4 illustrates how a movie whose acting, sound, and dialog are exceptional can be ruined by poor lighting.

- **You plan to turn your finished production into a QuickTime movie.** If the final product of your video project is to be a QuickTime movie, as described in Part 3 (as opposed to something you'll view on TV), you need even *more* light.

The compression software *(codecs)* that turn your video into QuickTime files do excellent work—*if* the original footage was well lit. When you turn a finished *dim* iMovie production into a QuickTime movie, you'll notice severe drops in color fidelity and picture quality—and a severe increase in blotchiness. Take a look at some of the iMovie films that Apple has posted online at *www.apple.com/imovie;* you'll see that fully half of them suffer dramatically from this dim, QuickTime-darkening problem.

This desperate need for light explains why some camcorders have a small built-in light on the front. Unfortunately, such lights are effective only when shooting subjects only a few feet away. Better still are clip-on video lights designed precisely for use with camcorders. Not every camcorder has a *shoe*—a flat connector on the top that secures, and provides power to, a video light. But if yours does, consider buying a light to fit it. The scenes you shoot indoors, or at close range outdoors, will benefit from much better picture quality.

If your camcorder doesn't have a light attachment, or if you want to get more serious yet, consider deliberately lighting the scene, just like TV and film cinematographers the world over.

Figure 2-4:
At the end of 1999, Apple invited several celebrities to spend two days making movies with iMovie. The results were posted on Apple's Web page, as shown here. But Apple should have instructed these stars in basic film technique, not just iMovie technique. As shown here, several of the finished movies are marred by bad lighting. First rule: The primary light source should never be behind your subject, as it is in each of these "what-not-to-do" examples.

Going to this extreme isn't always necessary, of course. If it's just you filming the New Year's Eve party, you're better off not asking the revelers to sit down and be quiet while you set up the lights. But when you're conducting interviews, shooting a dramatic film, making a video for broadcast, or making a QuickTime movie for distribution on a CD-ROM, lights will make your footage look much better.

The following discussion is dedicated to illuminating those more important filming situations. When you want the very best footage, lit the way the pros would light it, the following guidelines, theory, and equipment suggestions will serve you well indeed.

(If you're just shooting kids, relatives, or animals indoors, at least turn on every light in the room.)

Lighting Basics

Cinematographers spend entire careers studying lighting; it's a fantastically complex science. Here's what they worry about.

Exposure

Exposure refers to light—the amount of illumination the camera picks up. When the scene is too dark, you lose a lot of detail in dark shadows. Worse, your camcorder's AGC (Automatic Gain Circuit, the video equivalent of the audio-leveling circuitry described in the previous section) tries to amplify the available light. The result, which you can see for yourself by filming in dim light, is in "video noise" (colored speckles) and unrealistic colors (black becomes a noisy, milky dark grey).

If the scene is too bright, on the other hand, details can wash out, disappearing in white areas.

Contrast

The *contrast ratio* is the ratio of the brightest highlights in a scene to the darkest shadows. Professional filmmakers often set up huge arrays of extra lights to *reduce* the contrast ratio, thus evening out the illumination so that the camera can record more detail accurately. (When watching a movie being filmed, you sometimes see huge lights set up, even in daylight: they're there to fill in the shadow areas, so that the camera can "see," for example, the actors' eyes.)

Film cameras can photograph details in a scene that has a 10:1 contrast ratio (highlights are ten times brighter than the dark shadow areas). Video, on the other hand, can't capture details outside a contrast ratio of about 3:1 or 4:1. That's another reason lighting is much more important when using a camcorder, as noted above.

Hard light vs. soft light

Hard light comes from a small light source falling directly on an object. It creates hard edges between the highlight and shadow areas. For example, when someone's standing in direct sunlight, the shadows on his face are harsh and dark. This high contrast emphasizes wrinkles, skin blemishes, baggy eyes, and other facial features—in other words, hard light is unflattering light.

Soft light, on the other hand, is less direct; it offers softer, much smoother gradations of light from brightest to darkest areas. You get soft light from a large light source, usually reflected or diffused (like the outdoors light on an overcast day, or like the light reflected from the umbrellas used by photographers). The result: soft shadows or no shadows; everything is lit fairly evenly.

Soft light is much more flattering to human subjects, because it de-emphasizes wrinkles and other facial contours. Unfortunately, soft light can also make your subjects appear flat and lifeless. Harder light can reveal contours, shapes, and textures, making objects more interesting and three-dimensional.

The best video lighting, therefore, comes from direct light sources that are mechanically softened. That's why many video lights have milky translucent covers.

Key, fill, and backlights

In professional film and TV work, the most common lighting arrangement is called the *three-point lighting setup.* It requires that you set up at least three light sources, as shown in Figure 2-5:

- The *key* light is the primary source of illumination in a scene. This can be the light on the camera, the sun, the overhead light above a table, or the light from a window, for example.

- The *fill* light comes from a second light source. It's designed to fill in the shadows caused by the key light. By doing so, fill light reduces the *contrast ratio,* allowing the camcorder to pick up more details. If your camcorder has a built-in light, that's usually a fill light, too. It softens the shadows cast by the key light (such as the room lights).

- The *backlight* comes from behind the subject. It helps to separate the subject from the background. Backlight is especially helpful in distinguishing a dark sub-

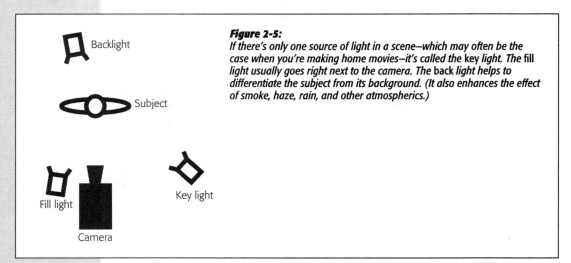

Figure 2-5:
If there's only one source of light in a scene—which may often be the case when you're making home movies—it's called the key light. The fill light usually goes right next to the camera. The back light helps to differentiate the subject from its background. (It also enhances the effect of smoke, haze, rain, and other atmospherics.)

ject (such as a person's hair) and a dark background, because it casts a glow around the rim of the subject's outline.

Be careful, of course: When the light behind the subject is *too* bright, camcorders respond by dimming the entire picture, as described on page 26.

- In professional film and video, technicians sometimes set up a fourth light: the *background* light, which is pointed at the background to make it easier to see (especially in very dark scenes).

Color temperature

Believe it or not, even ordinary daylight or room light also has a *color*. In general, daylight has a bluish cast, fluorescent light is greenish, and household bulbs give off a yellowish light.

Filmmakers call these color casts the *color temperature* of the light. We don't usually notice the color casts of these common light sources because our eyes and minds have adjusted to it. DV camcorders usually do an excellent job of compensating to avoid noticeable color casts, thanks to the *automatic white balance* in the circuitry of every modern model.

If, even so, you notice that certain shots are coming out too blue, green, or yellow, you can help the camcorder along by switching on one of its Programs (as several manufacturers call them)—presets for Daylight, Indoor Light, Snow and Ski, and so on. Each is represented in your viewfinder by an icon (such as a sun or a light bulb). When you use these presets, the camcorder shifts its color perception accordingly.

And if even those adjustments don't fix a particular color-cast problem, your camcorder may offer a *manual* white-balance feature. White balancing means identifying to the camera some object that's supposed to look pure white (or colorless), so that it can adjust its circuitry accordingly. To use the manual white-balance feature, focus on something white that's illuminated by the key light—for example, a clean T-shirt or piece of paper. Zoom in until the white area fills the screen, then press the White Balance button. The camcorder responds by compensating for the dominant color in the light.

The 45/45 Rule

This lighting guideline suggests that the key light be at a 45-degree angle to the camera-subject line and at a 45-degree angle above the ground (see Figure 2-6).

General Guidelines for Lighting

The preceding discussion gives you the theory of lighting design. Here's the executive summary—a distillation of that information down into just a few points to remember for the most professional-looking lighting.

- The subject should be brighter than the background. As noted in Figure 2-4, don't shoot people with a bright window or doorway behind them, unless you want them to disappear into silhouette.

- If the background is bright, shine additional lights on the subject. If you can't do that, use your camcorder's Backlight button or its manual-exposure knob, as described on page 26, so that the subject is correctly exposed (even if that makes the background too bright).

- Stand so that the key light—the sun, for example—is behind you. Don't shoot a subject with the sun behind her (unless you want silhouettes).

- Avoid a key light that's *directly above* your subject. That arrangement causes ugly, heavy shadows under the eyes, nose, and chin. (The cinematographers for the *Godfather* movies set up lights this way on purpose, so that the mobsters' eyes would be hidden in shadows. That's not the effect you want when filming the mother-in-law at the wedding ceremony. Usually.)

- If you decide to add lights to your setup, you don't need expensive movie lights. At the hardware store, buy some inexpensive photoreflector lights (those cheap, silver, bowl-shaped fixtures) and equip them with photoflood or tungsten work-light bulbs.

- If you're aiming for professional quality, create soft fill lights by bouncing light off of a big square of white foam-core board (which you can get at K-Mart, Home Depot, and so on), or a big piece of cardboard covered by foil or newspaper. This arrangement creates a beautiful soft light—great for close-ups.

  Bouncing lights off a white ceiling makes for a pleasantly soft key light, too.

- Tracing paper, tissue paper, and translucent plastic (such as shower-door material) make great diffusers for soft light, too. (Just don't put the paper in *contact* with the bulb; this kind of paper, especially tissue paper, ignites easily if it gets too hot.)

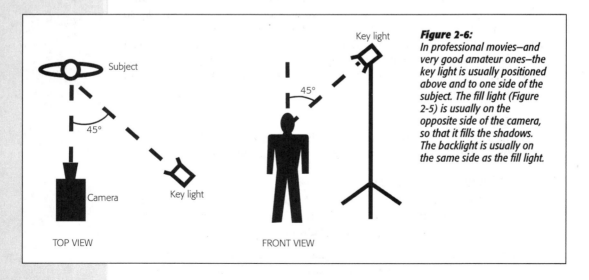

Figure 2-6:
In professional movies—and very good amateur ones—the key light is usually positioned above and to one side of the subject. The fill light (Figure 2-5) is usually on the opposite side of the camera, so that it fills the shadows. The backlight is usually on the same side as the fill light.

- Be alert to the presence of shiny surfaces like windows, glass, chrome, and highly polished wood in your shots. They can reflect your lights into the camera, making it look as though someone is shining a light directly into the lens.

- If the backlight spills into the lens, you get *flares*—those oddly shaped patches of light that move across the frame as the camera pans. The sun behind the subject, or car headlights, often cause flares. If you can avoid this effect, do so.

Keep It in Focus

A camcorder is a camera, just like any other. If its lenses aren't focused on the subject, you wind up with a blurry picture.

In theory, the auto-focus feature of every DV camcorder takes care of this delicate task for you. You point the camera; it analyzes the image and adjusts its own lens mechanisms; and the picture comes out in sharp focus.

In practice, the auto-focus mechanism isn't foolproof. Camcorders assume that the subject of your filming is the *closest* object; most of the time, that's true. But now and then, your camcorder may focus on something in the foreground that *isn't* the intended subject; as a result, what you actually wanted to capture goes out of focus. Figure 2-7 makes this point clear.

Another auto-focus hazard is a solid or low-contrast background (such as a polar bear against a snowy background). The auto-focus method relies on contrasting

Figure 2-7:
When you're filming the school play, somebody's head or hat may confuse the auto-focus. When you're filming scenery, a nearby branch may similarly fool it (top). The front bars of zoo cages are also notorious for ruining otherwise great shots of the animals inside them. The only solution is to use manual focus (bottom).

colors in the image. If you're aiming the camcorder at, say, a white wall, you may witness the alarming phenomenon known as auto-focus *hunting,* in which the camcorder rapidly goes nearsighted, farsighted, and back again in a futile effort to find a focus level that works.

Other situations that freak out the auto-focus include shooting when it's dark, shooting through glass, filming a subject that's not centered in the frame, and high-contrast backgrounds (such as prison or cage bars, French-window frames, and so on), which compete for the auto-focus's attention.

Manual Focus

Fortunately, most DV camcorders offer a *manual-focus* option: a switch that turns off the auto-focus. Now you can (and must) set the focus by hand, turning a ring around the lens (or pushing + and – buttons) until the picture is sharp.

If neither you nor your subject has any intention of moving during the shot, that's all there is to manual focus. Moving shots are trickier, because as the distance between you and your subject changes, you don't have time to fiddle with the focus ring. The best approach is to keep the camera zoomed out all the way as you pan to track the action.

Another potential problem: zooming. When you zoom, your focus changes, too. Fortunately, there's an ancient and very clever trick that circumvents this problem: the zoom-out-and-focus trick. It goes like this:

Figure 2-8:
For freedom of zooming without worrying about going out of focus, begin by zooming in all the way (top). Then use the focus ring to focus (middle). Now you can zoom in or out to any level, before or during the shot (bottom), and your focus remains sharp all the way.

Be careful, though: Don't zoom in so far that you make the camcorder's digital zoom kick in, as described in Chapter 1. Most camcorders zoom in optically (true zoom) for several seconds, and then, as you continue to press the Zoom button, begin the artificial digital zoom that makes the image break up. You can detect the end of the optical zooming in two ways: First, a bar graph in the viewfinder usually identifies the ending point of the true zoom's range. Second, your camcorder may introduce a very short pause in the zooming as it switches gears into digital mode.

Either way, when using the manual-focus trick described here, you want to zoom in all the way using your true, optical zoom only.

1. **Zoom all the way in to your subject.**

   You haven't yet begun to record. You're just setting up the shot.

2. **Focus the camcorder manually.**

3. **Zoom back out again.**

   As you zoom out, notice what happens: The camcorder remains in perfect focus all the way. (Figure 2-8 shows this sequence.) Now you can begin to film, confident that even when you zoom in, the picture will remain in sharp focus.

In other words, once you've focused at the maximum zoom level, you're free to set the zoom to any intermediate level without having to refocus (*if* you're zooming sparingly and with a purpose, of course).

Video Composition: A Crash Course

The tips in this chapter so far have been designed to turn you from an amateur into a more accomplished technician. Now it's time to train the artist in you.

Even when shooting casual home-movie footage, consider the *composition* of the shot—the way the subject fills the frame, the way the parts of the picture relate to each other, and so on. Will the shot be clearer, better, or more interesting if you move closer? What about walking around to the other side of the action, or zooming in slightly, or letting tall grass fill the foreground? Would the shot be more interesting if it were framed by horizontal, vertical, or diagonal structures (such as branches, pillars, or a road stretching away)? All of this floats through a veteran director's head before the camera starts to roll.

As an iMovie-maker, you, unlike millions of other camcorder owners, no longer need to be concerned with the sequence or length of the shots you capture; you can rearrange or trim your footage all you want in iMovie. Your main concern when filming is to get the raw footage you'll need. You can't touch the composition of a shot once you're in iMovie.

Kinds of Shots

You'll hear film professionals talk about three kinds of camera shots: *wide, medium,* and *close* (see Figure 2-9):

- When you're zoomed out all the way, so that the camera captures as wide a picture as possible, you're using a *wide shot*. Wide shots establish context. They show the audience where we are and what's going on. Wide shots make great *establishing* shots, but they can also reveal a lot about the scale and scope of the action even after the scene has begun. (There's a famous crane shot in *Gone With the Wind* that starts on a medium shot of Scarlett O'Hara and then moves up and wide as she walks through a compound filled with hundreds of dying confederate soldiers to reveal a tattered Confederate flag. Thanks to the wide shot, you can see the people she's passing completely, from head to foot.

- *Medium shots* are useful because they eliminate many distractions from the background. By zooming in part way, you let your viewers concentrate more on individuals, and you establish a relationship between objects in the frame. People in medium shots are usually visible only from the waist up. Medium shots are by far the most common ones on TV.

- When you're zoomed in a lot, so that your subject fills the screen, you're using a *close shot, tight shot,* or *close-up.* These shots reveal detail, such as a character's reactions, which have a huge impact on how the *audience* reacts. Close shots are the best kind of shot if you plan to show your movie on a small screen, such as in a QuickTime movie or on a small TV.

Note: You'll hear professionals talk about lots of other kinds of shots, too: the extreme close-up, the extreme long shot, the medium close-up, and so on—but they're all variations on the Big Three.

Choosing your shots

After you're finished editing your film in iMovie, will it mostly be viewed on a computer screen or a TV screen? This important question may affect your choice of zoom level for each shot.

Figure 2-9:
A wide shot captures the camcorder's biggest possible picture (top). It gives viewers a sense of place and direction. A medium shot (middle) begins to direct the audience's attention, but still captures some of the surroundings. And a close-up (bottom) is delightful for all concerned, especially if you plan to export your finished iMovie production as a QuickTime movie.

If you plan to make QuickTime movies (for playback on computer screens), use a lot of close-ups. Remember that most QuickTime movies play in a small window on the computer screen. Beware the wide shot that looks great on the TV or in the viewfinder, but when shrunk to QuickTime-movie size, reduces faces to white specks on the screen.

Tip: If you're concerned about the *file size* of the finished QuickTime movies—if you intend to email them or post them on a Web site, for example—simpler and steadier shots work best. When iMovie creates the QuickTime movie, it reduces the file size by *discarding* information about parts of the frame that don't change from one frame to the next. Frames filled with clutter, and moving shots, therefore, result in larger QuickTime movie files that take longer to email and download from the Web.

If your iMovie productions are instead destined to be sent back to your camcorder for viewing on a TV, you don't need to be quite so worried about using mostly close-ups (although they're still extremely effective on TV). Medium shots are fine, and so is *variety* in your shots, as described in the next section.

Combining shots

When editing footage, professional editors often use a wide shot to show where something is happening, then cut between medium and close shots. Example:

1. **A wide shot reveals the hustle and bustle of a city market.**

   No individual details stand out.

2. **Cut to a medium shot of two people standing next to each other, back to back.**

   Their hands are by their sides.

3. **Cut to a close-up showing the hand of one person passing a small envelope to the other.**

4. **Cut back to a medium shot.**

   The exchange was barely noticeable.

5. **Cut away to someone reading a newspaper.**

6. **Cut in to a close-up of the newspaper guy, showing that he's not actually reading, but is looking over the top of the paper.**

7. **Cut to a wide shot of the two people who made the hand-off, now starting to walk away from each other.**

8. **Cut to a medium shot of the person with the newspaper. As he stands up, someone sitting at the table behind him also gets up.**

   The audience didn't even notice the second person before, because the first shot of the newspaper guy was a close-up.

Of course, you'll do all of this fancy footwork in iMovie, during the editing phase. But you can't create such a dramatic sequence unless you capture the various close, medium, and wide shots to begin with—as you're filming.

As noted earlier, footage that you'll eventually save as a QuickTime movie file should consist mostly of close-ups. But regardless of the final format, the best movies feature a variety of shots—a fact that doesn't occur to every camcorder operator.

Tip: It's an excellent idea to set a new scene with an establishing shot, but *when* you film that shot is unimportant. Ever watch a TV sitcom? Almost every segment that takes place in, for example, the Cosby family's apartment begins with an exterior establishing shot of the brownstone building's exterior. Needless to say, those interior and exterior apartment shots were filmed on different days, in different cities, by different film crews. The magic of video editing made it seem like the same time and place.

The Rule of Thirds

Most people assume that the center of the frame should contain the most important element of your shot. As a result, 98 percent of all video footage features the subject of the shot in dead center. For the most visually *interesting* shots, however, dead center is actually the *least* compelling location for the subject. Artists and psychologists have found, instead, that the so-called Rule of Thirds makes better footage.

Imagine that the video frame is divided into thirds, both horizontally and vertically, as shown in Figure 2-10. The Rule of Thirds says that the intersections of these lines are the strongest parts of the frame. Putting the most interesting parts of the image at these four points, in other words, makes better composition.

Save the center square of the frame for tight close-ups and "talking heads" (shots of people standing alone and talking to the camera, as in a newscast). Even then, try to position their eyes on the upper-third line.

Figure 2-10:
The Rule of Thirds: Don't put the good stuff in the middle. When shooting someone's face, frame the shot so that the eyes fall on the upper imaginary line, a third of the way down the frame. When two people are in the frame, zoom in so that they're roughly superimposed on the two vertical "rule of thirds" lines. When shooting a panorama, put the horizon line at the bottom-third line to emphasize the sky or tall objects like mountains, trees, and buildings; put the horizon on the upper-third line to emphasize what's on the ground, such as the people in the shot.

Mind the Background

Most home videographers don't pay much attention to the background of the shot, and worry only about the subject. The result can be unfortunate juxtapositions of the background *with* the foreground image—tree branches growing out your boss's head, for example, or you and your camcorder accidentally reflected in a mirror or glass, or a couple of dogs in furious amorous passion 20 feet behind your uncle.

When possible, set up the shot so that the background is OK, and then place your subjects in front of it. If you have no such control—if you're shooting, home-movie, reality-TV, or documentary style—move *yourself.* Find a spot where the subject looks better relative to the background, whether it's 6 inches away or 20 feet away.

Professional camera operators, in fact, train themselves to watch the *edges of the frame* while filming, rather than the actors' faces. Doing so ensures that they take in the background, spot such accidental intrusions as reflections of people standing behind the camera, and stand ready to pan or tilt if the subject should move into or out of the frame. If you pay some attention to the shapes rather then people in the frame, composing the shot well becomes much easier. (You can always watch the subject later when you play back your footage.)

> **Note:** Even despite years of training, Hollywood film crews nonetheless occasionally catch unwanted reflections, equipment, and technicians on film. The Internet Movie Database (*www.imdb.com),* for example, maintains message boards where observant moviegoers can report gaffes, such as the scene in *Titanic* where both crew members and equipment are visible as a reflection in Rose's TV.

Framing the Shot

Another way to make a shot more interesting is to let something in the environment *frame* it, subtly altering the shape of the square image of the frame. You might, for example, shoot through a door or window, shoot down a hallway, and so on. Even a tree branch stretching across the top of the frame, emphasizing the horizontal component of the image, makes an interesting shot.

Camera Angle

The camera angle—that is, where you place the camcorder relative to your subject—is your greatest compositional tool. What position in the room or setting gives you the best framing, the best lighting, the least background distraction? Which position gives the shot the best composition?

You know the old stereotype of the movie director who walks slowly in a circle, squinting, peering through a square he frames with his thumbs and index fingers? It's a cliché, for sure, but old-time directors did it for a good reason: They were trying out different camera angles before committing the shot to film.

If you want to capture the best possible footage, do exactly the same thing (although you can just check the camcorder's LCD screen as you walk around instead of looking through your fingers like a weirdo). Before recording *any* shot, whether it's for a casual home movie or an independent film you plan to submit to the Sundance Film Festival, spend at least a moment cataloging your camera-placement options.

Tip: When framing any shot, take a step to the left, then a step to the right, just to check things out. You may discover that even that slight a movement improves the shot substantially.

The *vertical* angle of the camera counts, too. Will you be shooting down on your subject, up at it, or straight on? In commercial movies, camera angle is a big deal. Shooting up at somebody makes her look large, important, or threatening; shooting down from above makes her look less imposing.

In home movies, you don't have as much flexibility as you might when shooting a Hollywood film. About all you can do is hold the camcorder while lying down, squatting, sitting up, standing, or standing on a chair. Still, that's a lot more flexibility than most camcorder owners ever exploit.

Tip: Choosing the angle is especially important when filming babies, toddlers, or other cuddly animals. Too many people film them exclusively from a parent's-eye-view; you wind up with tapes filled with footage shot from five feet off the floor. As anyone who has ever watched a diaper commercial can tell you, baby footage is much more compelling when it's shot from baby height. Kneel or squat so that the camera puts the viewer in the baby's world, not the parent's.

Capturing Multiple Angles

When you make a movie, you're trying to represent a three-dimensional world on a two-dimensional screen. To give the audience the best possible feeling for the envi-

POWER USERS' CLINIC

The "180 Degree" Rule

When you're filming a scene from several different angles, don't cross "the Line." That's the invisible line that connects two people who are conversing, the two goalposts of the football field, and so on. Change camera angles and positions all you like, but stay on the same *side* of the action.

That's the "180-degree" rule they'll teach you about in film school. If you were to cross this 180-degree angle between the right and left objects in your shot, you'd confuse the audience. Imagine, for example, how difficult it would be to follow a football game if one shot showed the Browns rushing to the right side of the screen, and the next shot (of the same play) showed them running left. Similarly, the audience would become confused if an interviewer and interviewee shifted sides

of the frame from one shot to another. And if you're showing two people talking, you can imagine how disconcerting it would be if you cut from a close-up of one person to a close-up of the other, each facing the *same direction*.

As you watch TV and movies in the coming days and weeks, notice how rigidly directors and cinematographers obey the 180-degree rule. Once the right-to-left layout of the room, scene, or conversation has been established, it doesn't change for the duration of the scene.

The only exception: when the audience *sees* the camera cross the line, so that they get their new bearings as the camera moves. What you should avoid is *cutting* to a different shot on the other side of the 180-degree line.

ronment where the filming was done—and to create the most interesting possible videos—consider *varying* your shots.

When you're shooting longer scenes, such as performances, interviews, weddings, and scripted movies, consider changing the camera position during the same shooting session. Doing so gives you two benefits: First, it gives your audience a break; whenever the camera angle changes, your footage benefits from a small boost of energy and renewed interest.

In fact, whenever you're shooting something important, cover the same action from different angles and with different kinds of shots. Get wide shots, medium shots, *and* close-ups. If you're shooting a scripted movie, have the actors repeat their actions for the different shots, when possible.

When shooting two people in conversation, get more than the standard "two shot" (a composition containing two people, equally prominent, in the same frame). Shoot the two people talking in a wide shot that establishes where they are and how their positions relate. Get a close-up of one person by shooting over the shoulder of the other subject (whose back is therefore to you). If you can shoot the scene a second time, shoot the conversation again, this time from over the other person's shoulder. Keep rolling even when that person's just listening, so that you'll have some *reaction shots* to edit into your finished iMovie.

The second advantage of capturing the same scene from different angles is that it gives you the luxury of *choice* when it comes time to assemble your movie in iMovie. You'll be able to conceal a flubbed line or a bad camera shot by cutting to a continuation of the action in different piece of footage. Because the new footage will have been shot from a different angle or zoom level, the cut won't feel forced or artificial.

Capture Footage for Cutaways and Cut-Ins

Capturing a scene from more than one angle is a great precaution for another reason, too: You'll often find it extremely useful to be able to *cut away* to a shot of a secondary subject, such as an onlooker or the interviewer's face.

For example, when you're making a scripted movie, the first 30 seconds of dialog may have been terrific in the first take, but the next few lines may have been better in take #4. You'd want to avoid simply editing the second take onto the end of the first; doing so would introduce a *jump cut,* an obvious and awkward splice between two shots of exactly the same image. But if you conceal the snip by briefly cutting away to, for example, the reaction of an onlooker, your viewers will never suspect that the dialog came from two different takes.

Another example, one that's especially pertinent when you're making training or how-to videos: Capture some footage that you can use for *cut-ins.* Cut-ins are like cutaways, in that they're brief interpolated shots that inject some variety into the movie. But instead of splicing in a wider shot, or a shot of somebody who's observing the scene, you splice in a *closer* shot.

When you're filming somebody for a cooking show, you can cut in to a close-up of the whisk stirring the sauce in the bowl; if it's a technology show, you can cut in to the computer screen, and so on. When you're filming a dramatic scene, you can cut to a close-up of the actor's hands twitching, a trickle of sweat behind the ear, or a hand reaching slowly for a weapon.

You'll do all of this cutting in and cutting away during the editing process, not while you're actually filming. Nonetheless, the point, in all of these cases, is to make sure you've captured the necessary footage to begin with, so that you'll have the flexibility and choice to use such techniques when it comes time to edit. Shoot cutaway candidates near and around your subject—clouds in the sky, traffic, someone sitting at a café table sipping cappuccino, a bird in a tree, and so on—*something* so that you'll have some shot variety when you assemble your final footage. (You can always film your cutaway material after the main shooting is over; when, or even *where*, this supplementary footage is shot makes no difference. In iMovie, you'll make it seem as though it all happened at once.)

Tip: Imagine the difficulty of shooting and editing a movie like *My Dinner With André* (1981)—a conversation between two men seated at the same restaurant table for the *entire* two-hour movie. If this movie had been shot with a single camcorder on a tripod, its audiences would have gone quietly insane. Only the variety of shot types, angles, shot length, and so on make the single setting tolerable. (That and the conversation itself, of course.)

Dolly Shots

One of Hollywood's most popular shot types is one that never even occurs to most camcorder owners: the *dolly shot* or *tracking shot*. That's when the camera moves while shooting.

To create a dolly shot, filmmakers mount the camera on a platform car that glides along what looks like baby train tracks. The purpose of this elaborate setup is, of course, to move the camera along with a moving subject—to follow Kevin Costner running with wolves, for example, or to show the axe-murderer-eye's view of a teenager running away in terror, or to circle the passionately embracing Joseph Fiennes and Gwyneth Paltrow at the end of *Shakespeare in Love*. As a film technique, this one works like gangbusters—not only is it a very exciting shot to watch, but it also puts the viewer directly into the action.

Note: A dolly shot that moves forward isn't the same as simply zooming in. As a quick experiment will show you, the visual result is completely different.

When you zoom, the camera enlarges everything in the picture equally, both foreground and background. When you move forward through space, on the other hand, the distant background remains the same size; only the subject in the foreground gets bigger, which is a much more realistic result. Your viewers are more likely to feel as though they're part of the action and actually in the scene if you dolly forward instead of just zooming.

As a camcorder owner hoping to film, for example, your daughter's field hockey championship, you may find that this business of laying down train tracks on the field isn't always well received by the other parents.

But don't let the expense and dirty looks stop you. When it counts, you can improvise. You can lean out of a car window or sunroof, holding the camcorder as steady as you can, as a friendly relative drives slowly alongside the action. You can film while riding a bicycle. You can persuade a family member to drag you along in an actual Radio Flyer-style wagon in the name of getting more interesting, more professional footage.

The wheelchair solution

Or use a wheelchair. Wheelchairs are remarkably popular with low-budget filmmakers who want to create dolly shots inexpensively. Wheelchairs don't require tracks, are comfortable to sit in while shooting, and provide a stable moving platform.

GlideCam and Steadicam JR

You might also consider buying or renting a special camera mount called GlideCam, a padded brace that keeps the camera steady against your body (about $300, shown in Figure 2-11), or even a Steadicam JR (about $450), a scaled-down version of the popular Hollywood tracking camera device. Both of these devices incorporate variations of a *gimbal* (a universal ball joint) that intercepts jerks and twists before they can reach the camera; it also distributes the camcorder's center of gravity to keep it even steadier. As a result, a Steadicam or GlideCam lets keeps the camera level and stable even while you're running in a crowd, up and down stairs, following your actors into an elevator and then out again when they reach their floor, and so on.

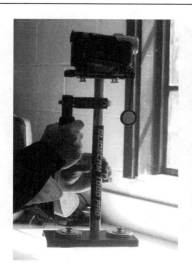 

Figure 2-11:
Both the GlideCam, shown here, and the Steadicam JR require lots of practice and a strong arm, but can create spectacular moving shots. Both Bonfire of the Vanities *and* Goodfellas *include very long shots where we follow the main character as he crosses the street, enters a building, goes downstairs, through a hallway, and so on—all in one continuous, very steady shot, thanks to the Steadicam.*

These ideas may sound extreme, but you'd be surprised at how effective they are. Suddenly you have access to one of Hollywood filmmakers' favorite tricks. Sure you'll feel silly riding through the neighborhood in your kid's Radio Flyer wagon—but how do you think professional camera operators feel riding along on their little choo-choos?

ON LOCATION

iMovie 1, Compaq 0

A quick iMovie story.

I was doing a demo of iMovie at CompUSA on behalf of Apple. A man had just selected a Compaq computer with all the trimmings. Everything was in his shopping cart. He was headed up to the cashier.

My iMovie was playing on the iMac. He stopped to watch and listen.

"Can my computer do that?" he said.

"No," I told him.

"OK then," he said. "I want that computer instead."

*—Amy Carson
Baltimore, MD*

Special-Event Filming

If all you intend to do with your camcorder is to capture random events of childhood charmingness around the house, you can skip this chapter. Just keep your camcorder lying handy , its battery charged and its tape compartment occupied, and you'll be all set.

Chances are, however, that once you've got the iMovie bug, you may become more inspired. It may occur to you to take your camcorder out of the house—to shoot the school play, your kid's sports game, your cousin's wedding, and so on. Maybe you'll decide to use the camcorder for more serious work, such as transferring your old photos to DV to preserve them forever, creating a family history by interviewing relatives, shooting a documentary, or even making a scripted movie.

Each of these situations can benefit from a little forethought, plus a few tips, tricks, and professional techniques. This chapter is designed as a handbook to help you make the most of these common camcorder-catchable events.

Interviews

What's great about an interview is that you know it's coming. You've got time to set up your tripod, arrange the lighting, and connect an external microphone, as described in Chapter 2. (Do all of this before your subject arrives, by the way; nothing contributes to a nervous interview subject more than having had to sit around, growing apprehensive, before the interview begins.) Because you've got this extra time to plan ahead, there's no reason your interview footage can't look almost identical in quality to the interviews you see on TV.

Chapter 2 describes the basics of good camcorder footage; in an interview situation, the same tips apply. Lighting is important—avoid having the brightest light behind the subject's head. Sound is critical—fasten a tie-clip microphone to your subject's lapel or collar.

Above all, use a tripod. You'll be glad you did, not only because the picture will be stable, thus permitting the audience to get more "into" the subject's world, but also for your own sake. Even the lightest camcorder is a drag to hold absolutely motionless for more than five minutes.

But interviews offer some additional challenges. If you've ever studied interviews on TV, such as the *60 Minutes* interviews that have aired every Sunday night since 1968, you realize that the producers have always thought through these questions:

- **What's the purpose of the interview?** The answer affects how you shoot the scene. On *60 Minutes,* the purpose is often to demonstrate how guilty or shifty the subject is. Bright lights and a black background help to create this impression, as do the ultra-close-ups favored by the *60 Minutes* crew, in which the camera is zoomed in so tight that the pores on the subject's nose look like the craters on Mars.

  In interviews that aren't designed to be especially incriminating, however, the purpose of the interview is often to get to know the subject better. The setting you choose can go a long way toward telling more of the subject's story. Set the interview somewhere that has some meaning for, or tells something about, your subject. If it's a CEO, shoot it in her office across her handsome mahogany desk; your wide establishing shot will telegraph to your viewers just how magnificent this office is. If it's your grandfather, shoot it in his study or living room, where the accumulated mementos on the end tables suggest his lifetime of experiences. (When possible, get these cutaway and establishing shots before or after the actual interview, so as not to overwhelm your interviewee or waste his time.)

- **Who's going to ask the questions?** In professional interviews, of course, the camera person doesn't ask the questions. One person operates the camera, while another conducts the interview. If you can arrange to have a buddy help with your interview, it'll go a *lot* better. He (or you) can chat with the subject while the lights and microphones are being adjusted, for example.

  If you, the camcorder operator, absolutely must double as the interviewer, take your microphone situation into account. If your subject is wearing a tie-clip microphone, then your questions will be recorded very softly, as though coming from far away. If you're not using an external microphone, you'll have the opposite problem: You're standing right next to the camera, so the sound of your voice will be very loud on the finished tape, in unfortunate contrast to the much fainter sound of your subject's replies.

  You can usually find solutions to all of these problems. For example, you can use a single, *omnidirectional* mike (see page 46) that sits between you and your subject. Or you could connect *two* external mikes to your camcorder by way of a portable mixer, which accepts (and lets you adjust the volume of) several inputs simulta-neously. (Radio Shack and video-equipment Web sites sell these items.)

Tip: If you are both the camera operator and the interviewer, and you decide that you want to be on camera along with your interview subject, use the remote control that comes with most camcorder mod-els. Open the LCD screen and rotate it so that it's facing you as you sit in front of the camera—that's the only way for you to frame the shot when you're not actually standing behind the camcorder. Figure 3-1 shows the setup.

Figure 3-1:
The beauty of interview footage is that you can prepare for it. You can arrange the lights and the microphone. If you're going to be filming yourself as part of the interview, use the remote control (inset), a tripod, and the LCD screen rotated so that you can see yourself. You may have to dash over to the tripod a few times, tweaking the position of the camcorder until it captures both of you, but once that's done, you can roll with the interview. (The clip-on microphones are difficult to see in this photo, but they're there—and important.)

- **Is the interviewer part of the interview?** In other words, will the audience see the person asking the questions? If so, you've got a challenge on your hands. You've got two people to film, who usually sit across from each other, facing opposite directions, but only one camera.

If you ever saw the 1987 movie *Broadcast News,* you know how TV professionals solve this problem: before or after the interview, they capture some establishing-shot footage of the two people sitting there face-to-face. They also take some footage of the interviewer alone: nodding sagely in agreement, smiling in under-standing, frowning in concern, and so on. They film him asking the questions again, even after the interview subject has left the scene. Later, when editing the finished product, they splice these reaction shots into the interview footage, as you can do in iMovie. The audience never suspects that the entire interview was shot with one camera.

On the other hand, in many interviews, you don't see the interviewer at all. You hear her voice, but you don't see her on camera. (A disembodied voice like this is called a *voice-over.* Voice-overs are extremely common in TV ads, movies with narration, and episodes of *The Wonder Years.*)

Sometimes you don't see *or* hear the interviewer, such as when the producer just wants a comment (or a sound bite) from the interview subject. In those situations, invite your subject to phrase his answers as complete sentences; otherwise, after the questions have been edited out, you'll be left with an interview subject saying, "Yes... that's right... no, I don't think so," and other unhelpful utterances.

Tip: If you, the interviewer, will ultimately be edited out of the movie, you can greatly assist your own cause by framing your questions cleverly. Avoid yes-or-no questions. Don't ask, "Were you happy with your performance?" Instead, ask, "Tell us about how you felt," for example.

That's what professionals do. Now you know why, when asked "You just won the Olympics. Where are you going to go now?", nobody in the Disney World ads ever just says, "Disney World!"

- **How long will the interview be after editing?** If the finished product will be more than a couple of minutes long, think about keeping your viewers' interest up by introducing some variety into the camera work, as described in the previous chapter.

  Capture some wide shots, for example, for use as cutaways (see page 67); that way, when you edit the interview in iMovie, you'll be able to offer a refreshing change of shot now and then.

  Cutaways are also ideal for masking cuts in the interview footage. It's a convenient fact of life that you can't see somebody's lips moving when filming from behind them, or when the camera is far away. In other words, you can use a cutaway even while your interview subject is still talking. Your viewers won't be able to detect that the cutaway footage was actually shot at a different time. (TV news editors use this technique all the time—they briefly cut to a shot behind the subject's head in order to conceal an edit between two parts of the same interview.)

- **How conservative is the interview?** The answer to this question affects how you frame the subject in your lens. Some interviews are designed to be hip, such as the ones on MTV, the *Bunting's Window* computer show shown on airplanes, or fight sequences in the old *Batman* series. These might feature a hand-held camera, off-center framing, or even a camera mounted off-kilter on its tripod for that added wackiness.

  If wackiness isn't exactly what you're going for, however, the framing shown in Figure 3-2 is about right.

- **How is the shot set up?** In most interviews, the interview subject doesn't look directly into the camera—except when he's recording a Last Will and Testament. Usually he's looking just off-camera, at a spot a couple of feet to one side of the camcorder, or even directly across the camcorder's line of vision. That's where the interviewer should sit, so that the subject looks at the right spot naturally.

  The camcorder should be level with the subject's face, which is yet another argument for using a tripod.

Tip: If you're the interviewer, here's one tip that has nothing to do with the technicalities of your camcorder and tripod: *Listen* to the answers. Many inexperienced interviewers are so busy thinking about the next question that they miss great openings for further lines of questioning. Worse, the interview subject will detect that you're not really paying attention; therefore, the interview won't go nearly as well as it could.

Figure 3-2:
As in any footage, interviews should offer some variety of composition and zoom amount. But for maximum viewer comfort, most pro video interviews capture the speaker from shoulders up, with a little bit of space left above the head. (Here, you're seeing more of the subject's torso, just so you can see the tie-clip microphone.) If the subject is supposedly looking at something off-camera—the interviewer, for example—professionals leave some talk space in the shot—that is, a little extra room in front of the person's face, as shown here.

Music Videos

Few camcorder endeavors are as much fun as making a music video, whether it's a serious one or a fake one just for kicks.

Of course, your interest in this kind of video technique may depend on your age and taste. But music videos are worth studying, no matter who you are, because they frequently incorporate every conceivable camera trick, editing technique, and shooting style. The day you shoot a music video is the day you can try punching every button on your camcorder, unlocking those weird special effects you've never even tried, and using all the unnecessary zooms you want. Better yet, this is the day when you don't care a whit about microphones or sound. Eventually, you'll discard the camcorder's recorded sound anyway. As you splice your footage together in iMovie, you'll replace the camcorder's sound track with a high-quality original recording of the song.

Some music videos are lip-synced; that is, the performers pretend that they're singing the words on the soundtrack. Other videos are voice-over, narrative, or experimental videos. In these videos, you don't actually see anybody singing, but instead you watch a story unfolding (or a bunch of random-looking footage). If you decide to create a lip-synced video, take a boom box with you in the field. Make sure it's playing as you film the singers, so that they're lip-syncing with accurate timing.

When it comes time to edit the music video in iMovie, you'll be able to add the little lower-left-corner credits (the name of the song, the group name, and so on) with extremely convincing results. You'll also be able to add crossfades, transitions, graphics, and other common rock-video elements (see Figure 3-3).

Figure 3-3:
Because you have iMovie, you can pull off a fascinating visual stunt that's very common in rock videos: the jumping-flea musician effect, in which, every few seconds, everybody in the scene blips into a new position (or appears and disappears), sometimes in time to the music. (You're actually creating jump cuts, which you should avoid except when creating special effects like this.) Creating this effect is simple—if your camcorder has a tripod. Just shoot each segment, moving your musicians around when the camera isn't moving. In iMovie, the splices will be exactly as sharp and convincing as they are on MTV (or Bewitched).

Live Stage Performances

Filming a live stage performance, such as a play, musical, concert, or dance, is extremely challenging. It poses three enormous challenges: capturing the sound, capturing the picture, and getting permission in the first place.

Getting Permission

At most professional performances, the management doesn't permit camcorders. Union rules, copyright rules, house rules, or simple paranoia may be at play; but the bottom line is that using a camcorder (or any camera) is usually forbidden.

That leaves you two alternatives: Confine your footage to performances where camcorders are OK, such as the choir concert at the elementary school—or film surreptitiously. (As the size of DV camcorders shrinks year by year, the latter option is becoming ever more popular among people who don't mind flaunting the rules.)

Capturing the Sound

When you're filming a performance from the audience, your camcorder gets hopelessly confused. It's programmed to record the closest sounds, which, in this case, are the little coughs, chuckles, and seat-creaks of the audience members around you. The people onstage, meanwhile, come through only faintly, with the hollow echo that comes from recording people who are far away from the microphone. As any camcorder buff who's filmed her kid's school play can tell you, the resulting video is often very unsatisfying.

You have alternatives, but they require some effort. You can equip your camcorder with an external microphone—a *unidirectional*-style one. Mount it on a pole that puts the microphone over the audience's heads.

If the show has its own sound system—that is, if it's miked and amplified—you may be able to snake an external microphone up to the speaker system, so that your camcorder is benefiting from the microphones worn by every actor. Better yet, you can sometimes persuade the management to let you hook up your camcorder to the sound system itself. Connect the cable to the *audio* input of your camcorder, if you have one—unfortunately, connecting it to the *microphone* input may overload your sound circuitry and produce distortion.

Getting Power

Before worrying about the visual quality of your live-performance footage, worry about the power. Are the batteries charged? Do you have enough battery power to film the entire show? If so, have you thought about when you can swap batteries without missing something good?

If you're filming with permission, you may be able to plug your camcorder into a power outlet, which neatly solves this problem. Unfortunately, because of the extension-cord tripping hazard, this solution presents itself fairly rarely. (If you do get permission to lay down extension cords, tape them to the floor using duct tape, like generations of professional film crews before you.)

Capturing the Picture

Now you've got to worry about where you're going to sit or stand. Sometimes you don't have a choice—you'll just have to sit in your seat and do the best you can. (Keep your LCD screen closed when shooting; keeping it open both distracts the other audience members and gets you in trouble with management.)

Thanks to the powerful zoom feature on today's camcorders, standing at the back of the theater is frequently a more attractive alternative. There you may even be able to use a tripod, much to the benefit of your footage and the relief of your muscles. Doing so means that the camcorder will be able to shoot over the audience's heads—another great advantage over shooting from your seat.

Technically speaking, filming a live performance on a fairly distant, brightly lit stage requires three special considerations:

- **Use the manual-focus trick.** You'll find this secret described on page 61; nowhere is it more useful than when you're filming a live stage performance. Auto-focus generally fails you in these circumstances, because the camera tries to focus on the nearest object—the head of the lady in row 34. This auto-focus syndrome, which arbitrarily blurs the picture as you film, is the number-one destroyer of homemade performance videos.

  Use the manual focus to get the picture sharpened up in its fully zoomed-in state before you begin rolling tape. Then you'll be able to zoom in or out during the performance without ever having to worry about the focus.

- **Adjust the exposure.** Stage lights and spotlights throw camcorders for a loop. These lights pour very bright light onto the performers' faces, but throw normal light on the rest of the set. The result is a broad spectrum of brightness—too broad for a camcorder's sensors. The auto-exposure feature of your camcorder does its best to figure out its mission, but it usually makes a mess of things in medium or wide shots, turning every actor's face into a radioactive white blur with no features at all (see Figure 3-4).

Solving the problem requires you to *override* the auto-exposure feature. Consult the camcorder's manual for instructions. On Sony camcorders, for example, you press the Exposure button on the left side of the camera and then turn a thumb knob to adjust the exposure. Turn this knob downward to make the picture darker. After a moment, you'll see the features return to the actors' faces.

Be ready to turn that exposure knob the other way on short notice, however. You can expect the stage lights to be full up during the big, full-cast, song-and-dance numbers, but other scenes may be lit dimly for dramatic effect. Such scenes are equally troublesome for camcorders; turning up the exposure knob can help a lot, but may introduce graininess to the picture. There's not much you can do in this situation, since camcorders simply thrive on light.

Figure 3-4:
The solution to the bright-face syndrome in shows (left) is to turn down the exposure (right). Unfortunately, when the actors' faces look good, the set may wind up too dark.

Tip: Whenever you use your camcorder's manual exposure control, be very careful about trusting your LCD monitor for feedback. On most camcorders, this screen has its *own* brightness control, which, when set to a very bright or very dim setting, can lead you astray as you set your exposure knob. For best results, gauge the effect of your manual-exposure fiddling by looking only through the eyepiece viewfinder.

- **Know the show.** The best performance videos are made by somebody who's familiar with the performance. Only they know in advance when to use a wide shot, when to use a close-up, and so on.

When you're zoomed out all the way, you can't see any faces—a distinct drawback in a dramatic performance. For this reason, you'll be tempted to use the zoom a lot when you're filming a theatrical performance. Unfortunately, actors have a habit of *moving* during the scene—from the camcorder operator's standpoint, a distinctly annoying behavior. No sooner have you found your kid and zoomed into his face when he *moves*, leaving you to film seven seconds of empty set as you try to hunt for a human being. (Professionals learn to keep both eyes open when shooting. One eye is on the eyepiece when framing, and the other eye occasionally looks around to see what else is happening in the scene and to prepare for subjects that may be about to enter the frame.)

If it's possible to attend a dress rehearsal or a previous performance, therefore, your footage will be vastly improved. You'll know in advance when the big, full-stage moments come, and when to zoom in for close-ups.

Tip: If the show is really important, consider shooting it *twice;* at the second performance, position the camera in a different place and shoot different kinds of shots. Later, you can use iMovie to combine the footage from the two performances. By splicing in one camera's shot, then the other, changing camera angles and zoom amounts without missing a beat, you simulate having had two cameras at the same performance.

You also have a backup in case you missed a key entrance, joke, or pratfall during the first performance.

Speeches

What to worry about when filming talks, presentations, and speeches: the sound. Exactly as when filming live stage performances, your camcorder's built-in microphone does a lousy job of picking up a speaker more than 10 feet away. To remedy the problem, use a tie-clip microphone on extension cords, get a wireless mike, or run an external microphone to the loudspeakers (if the talk is amplified) or even directly to the sound system's mixing board.

Otherwise, the only other problem you'll encounter is the question-and-answer session, if there is one. In an auditorium situation, not only will you have a terrible time (because there isn't *enough* time) trying to train the camera on the person asking the question, but you won't pick up the sound at all. You can only pray that the guest speaker will be smart enough to repeat the question before providing the answer.

Tip: Capturing audience reaction shots for use as cutaways is a great idea when you're recording a talk. Splicing these shots into the finished iMovie film can make any speech footage more interesting, and gives you the freedom to *edit* the speech if necessary.

If your goal is to capture the entire talk, and you've got only a single camcorder, you'll have to get the reaction shots *before or after* the talk. Don't just pan around to the audience while the speaker is speaking.

Sports

Filming sporting events is, in general, a breeze. Most take place outdoors, neatly solving all lighting problems, and the only sound that's important at a sporting event is usually the crowd's reaction, which your camcorder captures exquisitely. Most of the time, you'll be zoomed out all the way, because there's too much motion to worry about close-ups. (And when you *do* want close-ups, you'll know exactly when to zoom out again, thanks to the structured nature of most sports. Every baseball play begins the same way, for example.)

If your aim is to film a player for training purposes, or to study a golf swing or tennis stroke as it's played back in slow motion or frame by frame, consider using your camcorder's *high-speed shutter* feature. When you use this special recording mode, the camcorder records the action in a strange, frame-flashing sort of way. When you play this footage back, you can use the slow-motion or freeze-frame controls on your camcorder with sensational, crisp, clear results.

Caution: The high-speed shutter is effective only in *very* bright, sunny, outdoor light. If you try to use it indoors, outdoors when it's overcast, or in shadow, all kinds of unpleasant side effects result. You may get flickering, stuttering motion; the auto-focus feature may stop working; colors may not look right; and the picture in general will seem too dim.

Photos and Old Movies

Most people associate video with *moving* images, but video "slide shows" can be extremely satisfying to watch, especially if you add commentary or music in iMovie, as described in Chapter 8. With a tripod, a music stand, and good lighting, your camcorder is all set to preserve your family photos forever.

Shooting Photos

Take each photo out of its frame; prop it on a music stand or tape it to the wall; slip a big black piece of cardboard behind it, just in case you pan beyond the borders of the photo. Set up the camcorder so that it's directly aimed at the photo (otherwise, the photo may look skewed or distorted when filmed). Use the manual focus on your camcorder, zoom in an appropriate amount, position the tripod and lights so that there's no glare, and begin shooting. If you're getting glare from the photo, use two lights, one on each side of the photo, each at a 45-degree angle to it.

What's great about filming photos is the flexibility the camcorder gives you. By no means should every shot be five motionless seconds of an entire photo. It's very easy, for example, to get several shots out of a single photo—just zoom into, and shoot, each of several faces in the photo individually. Along the same lines, you can add interest and even surprise to a photo shoot by slowly zooming or panning within the same photo.

Note: The panning trick is especially popular with documentary makers. "Little Harry graduated from junior high school in 1963"—slow pan to someone else in the school photo—"little suspecting that the woman who would one day become his tormentor was standing only a few feet away."

When you're zoomed in to film photos, every little jiggle and bump of the camcorder is magnified. Fortunately, most tripods are designed for smooth panning—that is, you can turn the entire camera apparatus slowly by pushing on a handle. But because you can pan in any of three possible dimensions, figuring out which tripod handles to tighten, and which to push, requires some experimentation before you begin.

Tip: Another trick for getting photos into your movie: Get them directly into the Mac using a scanner. As described in Chapter 9, you can then drop them into your iMovie storyboard electronically, without having to mess with lights, focusing, the tripod, and so on.

Unfortunately, using this trick deprives you of the flexibility of panning and zooming. But by using scanned photos as well as filmed ones, you save time and hassle *and* provide some variety.

Shooting Slides

You can transfer slides to your movie in either of two ways:

- Project the slides onto a slide screen or white wall—and film it with your camcorder. To make the slide's image sharper, put the projector as close as possible to the screen. Position the camera right next to the projector, so that it doesn't wind up filming the projected slide at an angle.

- Have a Kodak shop or a local service bureau scan your slides, transferring them to a CD-ROM. (If your scanner has a slide attachment, you may even be able to do this yourself, although doing so is sometimes a finicky procedure.) Then you can import the slides electronically into iMovie, as described in Chapter 9. This method ensures the highest possible quality and saves you a lot of setup hassle.

Transferring Old Movies to DV

Transferring old movies to the camcorder is another good idea. If these older movies are on videotape, such as VHS cassettes or 8 mm videotapes from an older camcorder, you're in good shape. Transferring them onto your DV camcorder is fairly easy, if you have the right equipment; see Chapter 4.

Transferring old *film* to your camcorder is a more difficult proposition. Photographic catalogs sell mirror-based gadgets just for this purpose. In essence, this apparatus lets you run the film projector, which projects the old movie onto a tiny movie screen. Your camcorder simply films the film. Unfortunately, the camcorder can pick up quite a bit of grain and picture deterioration in the process.

You can also send your old reels out to a commercial transfer shop; most local photo-developing outfits and camera shops handle this transaction for you.

Weddings

Ah, weddings! Everybody loves weddings—especially camcorder manufacturers. Talk about once-in-a-lifetime (all right, *very-few*-times-in-a-lifetime) occasions! What bigger event could there be to drive somebody to buy a camcorder?

Where to Stand

If you're just a friend or family member in the audience, you've got no choice about where to position the camcorder; you'll have to shoot from your seat or stand in the back.

But suppose that you're a wedding videographer—or becoming one. (That's an excellent idea, by the way, if you've been thinking about going into business for yourself. You, with your *digital* camcorder and iMovie, can advertise your superior equipment, lower costs, and greater editing flexibility when compared with all the poor slobs still lugging around older, analog equipment.)

From the videographer's standpoint, weddings are tricky. If you've only got one camcorder, where do you stand during the vows? From the spectators' side, where you can't capture the faces of the bride and groom? Or from the opposite side, where you get the bride and groom, but can't see the scene the way the spectators see it? Here are a few solutions:

- **Film the rehearsal.** The idea is that later, in iMovie, you can splice in some of this footage as though it was captured with a second camera on the day of the wedding. The rehearsal isn't usually "in costume," of course, so you won't fool anyone with your footage of the bride and groom in their sweatshirts and blue jeans. But the presiding official (minister, rabbi, justice of the peace) may well be in official garb at rehearsal time. At the very least, you can grab some footage of him at the rehearsal. With his lines and reaction shots already in the can, you can spend your time during the actual ceremony standing, and filming from, behind him.

- **Really use a second camera.** Videographers make about $1,000 per wedding—after one wedding, you'll have made enough money to buy a second camcorder. If you have an assistant who can operate it, great; now you've solved your "where should I stand?" dilemma.

  But if you don't have an assistant, you can set this second camcorder up in the back of the hall, in the balcony, or behind the presiding official, and just let it run unattended. Once again, iMovie will be your salvation; you'll be able to incorporate footage from the second camcorder whenever your editing instincts tell you that it's time for a refreshing new angle.

- **Shoot from behind the official.** If none of these ideas work for you, film some of the wedding from the audience's point of view. But during the vows, get yourself up onto the dais and shoot over the official's shoulder. In the end, what everybody wants from your wedding video is to see the faces of the bride and groom as they pledge their love forever—something they *didn't* get to see during the actual wedding.

Getting the Sound

This is the big one. If there were ever an event where recording the words was important, this is it. If you're just a friend shooting from the audience, the sound will probably be weak unless you use one of the tricks described on page 77.

If you're the hired videographer, however, your responsibility to get good sound is even greater. Maybe you bought one of the pro camcorders that has a shotgun mike (see Chapter 1). It will do splendidly if you film from behind the presiding official, only a few feet from the bride and groom.

Otherwise, equip the groom with a wireless mike, if he'll permit it. This usually entails slipping a little transmitter into his pocket and running a tiny wire up to his lapel.

If he objects, well, it's his wedding. But remind him that his one wireless mike will also pick up the words of the bride and the official, too, thanks to their close proximity during the vows.

And for goodness' sake, wear Walkman headphones to monitor the sound when you shoot the actual ceremony. Your videography career will come to a quick and miserable end if you play back the footage and discover that the wireless mike wasn't transmitting.

Tip: Many professional videographers these days invest in a Sony MiniDisc recorder, which looks like a Walkman but contains a half-size, recordable CD. It records extremely high-quality sound, and serves as a great backup sound-recording unit at weddings. When you return to your Mac, you can transfer the audio into the computer and then import it into iMovie (as described in Chapter 8). The sound won't perfectly match the video for more than a few minutes at a time, but your clips are probably short enough that such "sync drift" won't be a problem.

Being Unobtrusive

Anyone who hires a wedding videographer has already swallowed hard and accepted that there's going to be somebody running around the ceremony with a bunch of electronics. Fortunately, your equipment is much smaller than non-DV equipment—a great feature at weddings.

Still, you should use as much tact and foresight as possible. Scope out the hall before the ceremony, and speak to the presiding official to discuss your plans. Use video lights if you can, but accept that your clients may object to the clutter. And use only battery power; duct-taping extension cords to the carpeting doesn't always go over well in houses of worship.

Tip: If it's your responsibility to film a wedding or some other important event, take an extra fully charged battery and extra blank tapes. You may think that this is obvious advice, but there's absolutely nothing worse than forgetting it and missing half of the most important day of your client/friend/sister's life.

Actual Scripted Films

For a steadily growing subset of camcorder owners, this is the Big Kahuna, the *raison d'être,* the piece of resistance: making a real movie, complete with dialog, actors, and a plot. Ever since *The Blair Witch Project* made $140 million—a movie made by recent film-school grads with a camcorder, no funding, and no Hollywood connections—independent films have become a *very* big deal.

You can post your homemade movies on the Web sites listed in Chapter 13, where 200 million Internet citizens can watch them; the most popular ones get Hollywood-studio attention. There are even a growing number of film festivals dedicated to showing homemade (usually DV) films. In the sixties, Americans used to say that anyone could grow up to be president. Today, we say that anyone can make a Hollywood movie.

The world, and the library, is filled with books on making traditional movies. The process is much more difficult than making the kinds of movies described so far in this chapter; in addition to all of the technique and technical considerations you've read about so far, you now have to worry about plot, scripts, continuity, marketing, actors, character, costumes, props, sets, locations—and budget. You'll go through these phases of creation:

- **Writing the screenplay.** Most movies begin with a script—or at the very least, a *treatment* (a five- to thirty-page prose synopsis of the movie's story line that's usually designed to attract interest from backers).

  If you send your screenplay to Hollywood in hopes of getting it made into a movie, your competition is 250,000 other people every year who also send unsolicited scripts. Like them, you'll get yours back soon enough, too; to avoid being accused of stealing ideas, Hollywood studios don't even open unsolicited scripts. Even if you have a connection to someone who'll look at your screenplay, it won't be taken seriously unless it's prepared using extremely specific page formatting, which you can read about in any of dozens of screenwriting books.

  Fortunately, if you're going to make your own movie, it doesn't make one bit of difference how your screenplay is formatted. Format it however you like, just so your actors can read it.

- **Location.** You'll have to figure out where you're going to shoot each scene—and get permission to shoot there. Does the restaurant owner know, for example, that you'll be bringing in lights and sound equipment?

FROM THE FIELD

22 Shots for Your Wedding Video

Take it from a wedding-video veteran, Doug Graham of Panda Video Productions: There's a certain set of shots you've *got* to include in the video if you're the one who's been asked to film it. Here they are:

1. Bride and bridesmaids dressing. (Keep it G-rated!)

2. Exterior of the church.

3. Wedding party arriving at church.

4. Continuous roll of the ceremony, from prior to bride's entrance to the couple's walk down the aisle at the end. Use two cameras, if you can—place one in the back third of the church. Using the handheld, position yourself on the bridesmaids' side of the aisle at the altar steps. Shoot the procession. After the bride arrives, move to a tripod placed behind the officiant and on the groom's side. This gives the best shot of the bride during the vows. (Coordinate and clear this with the officiant beforehand.)

If you can, take a moment later to film a reenactment of the ring ceremony, so that you can get a good close-up of rings being slipped onto fingers, which you can splice into iMovie later.

5. Any special touches in the ceremony, like a solo song, unity-candle lighting, etc.

6. Reaction shots of bride and groom's families.

7. The photographer's formal posed shots.

8. Wedding party leaving church.

9. Wedding party arriving at reception. (This'll take some good planning and fast driving on your part!)

10. Bride and groom entering reception.

11. First dance.

12. Mom's dance with the groom.

13. Dad's dance with the bride.

14. Best man's toast.

15. Cake cutting.

16. Garter toss.

17. Guestbook signings.

18. Special dances and ceremonies at the reception.

19. Interviews with guests.

20. Interview with the bride and groom.

21. Footage for use as cutaways: cake, presents, decorations, flower arrangements, the DJ or band. Get a copy of the wedding announcement, and souvenirs (such as specially printed napkins), so that you can film them for close-ups later.

22. Guests saying goodbye.

Don't shoot: People eating. Backs of heads. People backlit by windows. Drunks.

Interviews at a wedding are a real art. I just have the guests pass around the mike and ask them to "say a few words to the happy couple." Some good leading questions might be:

- What can you tell me about how Bill and Sue met?

- What did you feel when you learned they were engaged?

- What do you think Bill should do to keep Sue happy?

- Where do think Bill and Sue will be ten years from now?

- What do you think Sue loves most about Bill?

When interviewing the bride and groom, I do it individually, rather than together. I ask each of them the same questions: How did you meet? Tell me how the relationship deepened and grew. When did you first know Tim was the "one"? Tell me about how he proposed? What are your plans for the future?

Then I cut the responses together when editing. The juxtaposition of the two viewpoints can be funny, touching, or poignant.

I always remind my on-camera folks to answer questions in a complete sentence. For example, if I ask "What's your name?", I don't want, "Joe." I want, "My name is Joe." That way, I can edit out my questions later, and the response will be complete in itself.

Tip: Instead of traveling to a special location for shooting, you can often save money and hassle by turning your own backyard or living room into a set. Just a few key props and set dressings may be enough to suggest, for example, an office, jungle, or police station—especially if it's preceded, in your movie, by an establishing shot showing your characters going *into* such a building.

- **Preproduction.** Before shooting, make "shopping lists." Go through the script and make lists of which actors are in which scenes, what clothes and props they'll need for those scenes, and so on. *Preproduction,* the planning phase, is where a production is set up to succeed or to fail.

  You should also make a list of the shots that you'll want to get, so that when everyone arrives on the set and all hell breaks loose, you won't forget to get one critical shot or another. Lists prevent memory blocks.

- **Actors.** Who's going to star in your movie? You can get friends to do it, of course. You can recruit people from acting classes, colleges, or theaters in your area. They'll probably be delighted to participate, in exchange for nothing but the experience, good treatment, and *good food.* (You'd be surprised how important the food is.)

  Or you can get professional actors, with the help of a talent agency. You choose them by holding an audition, and you pay for their participation.

- **Editing.** After you've shot the various scenes of your movie—which, of course, you don't have to do in sequence—you'll assemble the film in iMovie. This is where you decide how long each shot should take, which camera angle to use, which *take* to use (which of several versions of the scene you've shot), and so on.

  In the real film world, this editing phase, called *postproduction,* often takes longer than the actual filming. Incredible magic takes place in the cutting room; the film editor alone can make or break the feeling, mood, and impact of the movie. You can read more about editing tricks in Chapter 10.

If you've never made an actual movie before, start small. Make a *short* (a brief movie), which, in the age of independent films, is becoming an increasingly popular format. (In March 2000, Woody Allen made a *six-minute* movie to protest the construction of a skyscraper in a beloved area of Manhattan.) Starting with a short film is a great idea not just because it prevents you from biting off more than you can chew, but also because the average Mac's hard drive can't hold more than about 60 minutes of raw footage at a time.

Making a short is also excellent practice for reducing a movie down to its absolutely essential elements, trimming out the superfluous shots and scenes—a highly prized talent that will pay off when you graduate to full-length movies. As they say in the biz: "If it doesn't move the story forward, it holds it back." (More editing advice in Chapter 10.)

Part Two:
Editing in iMovie

2

Camcorder Meets Mac

P hase 1 is over. You've captured the raw footage on your camcorder, you've now assembled the ingredients you need, and you're ready to enter the kitchen. Now it's time for Phase 2, the heart of this book: editing your footage on the Mac using iMovie.

This chapter introduces you to both iMovie and *FireWire* (the high-speed cable system that transfers footage from the camcorder to the Mac), gives you a tour of the iMovie interface, and walks you through your first transfer.

iMovie 2: The Application

So far in this book, you've read about nothing but *hardware*—the equipment. In the end, however, the iMovie story is about *software*—both the footage as it exists on your Mac and the iMovie program itself.

Getting iMovie on a New Mac

Starting in late 2000, Apple began including iMovie 2 on the hard drive of every new FireWire-equipped Mac. If you're lucky enough to have a Mac that falls in this category, iMovie is easy to find. Open the Macintosh HD icon→Applications folder→iMovie folder. Inside is the icon for iMovie itself.

For all its power, this is a fairly compact piece of software, as it consumes only 1.8 MB of disk space. It requires quite a bit of memory to run, however: 29 MB or more to run smoothly. That requirement and iMovie's dependence on a fast processor and FireWire jack explain why iMovie is happiest when it's running on the current crop of Mac models.

If you plan to use iMovie a lot, consider making an alias of it on your desktop. Do that by holding down the ⌘ and Option keys; while they're down, drag the iMovie application icon (not the iMovie *folder*) directly onto your colored backdrop.

Tip: If somehow you've managed to throw away or misplace iMovie or one of its components, run the installer on the iMovie CD-ROM. It will put a new iMovie folder on your hard drive—just in the hard drive window, *not* in your Applications folder, where the original copy was—complete with all its necessary accompanying files.

If you like, you can drag this iMovie folder into the Applications folder if you want to keep iMovie where it once was. You'll be asked if you're sure you want to replace the *existing* iMovie folder. If you're sure there's nothing important (like one of your movies) inside that iMovie folder, click OK.

Buying iMovie 2

If your Mac didn't come with iMovie 2, but it's still powerful enough to run the program you can download iMovie 2 from the Apple Web site *(http://store.apple.com)* for $50. Getting the software this way means that you don't get the tutorial files described on page 96. (Don't spend much time mourning your loss; what you can do with this book puts that simple tutorial to shame anyway, and meanwhile you save a few hundred megabytes of hard drive space.)

Apple says that iMovie 2 requires a machine with at least 64 MB of memory and a monitor that can zoom out to at least 800 x 600 pixels. That much is true.

But Apple also says that iMovie requires a FireWire-equipped Mac running Mac OS 9.0.4 or later. That part isn't true. The program *runs* just fine on Mac OS 8.6—but the *installer* doesn't like Mac OS 8.6 (it gives you only the Read Me files). The solution is to copy the program from a Mac where iMovie 2 has already been successfully installed.

Tip: On the other hand, having the latest Mac OS version ensures that you also have the latest version of QuickTime, the set of QuickTime files in your System Folder→Extensions folder that let your Mac "speak" the language of video. Each successive QuickTime version makes a huge quality improvement to video-editing work.

And although iMovie certainly thrives on FireWire machines, it doesn't require them. The program runs on almost any relatively young Mac.

Of course, "runs" has different meanings to different people:

- If you want to transfer footage from your DV camcorder, you must run iMovie on a Mac that has FireWire jacks. Most add-on FireWire cards (for Power Macs and PowerBooks) qualify for this requirement.

- If you simply want to *edit* your movies on your Mac, without involving the camcorder, then almost any fast Mac will do. It doesn't have to have FireWire circuitry. You can use a 1999-era PowerBook or iMac, for example.

This presumes, of course, that you've got some footage to work on. You can edit still pictures or QuickTime movies (Chapter 9) without even involving a camcorder or FireWire. Or you can work with DV clips that you've copied from a Mac that *does* have FireWire. Transferring this footage from the FireWire Mac to your non-FireWire Mac is fairly easy once you understand how iMovie organizes its files, as described on page 108.

Note: Using iMovie on anything besides a FireWire-equipped Mac is, as far as Apple is concerned, an extracurricular activity. If you call Apple's help line, you'll be told, in effect: "You're on your own, pal."

Once you've downloaded iMovie 2, you wind up with a *disk image* file (.smi) on your desktop. Double-click it to open a pseudo-floppy disk on your desktop, which contains the iMovie 2 installer. When the installer is finished, you'll find a folder called iMovie (not iMovie 2) in your main hard drive window (although you can use the pop-up menu at the bottom of the installer's main window to install iMovie anywhere you like).

Tip: If you've got iMovie 1 already on your Mac, don't install iMovie 2 until you've moved the earlier version to a folder with a different name—or thrown it away.

If you decide to trash it, however, open its folder and rescue any movies you've stored there by dragging them out of the iMovie folder. iMovie 2 can open and edit them just fine, but not if you've thrown them away by accident.

Updating Your Copy of iMovie

Like any software company, Apple occasionally releases new versions of iMovie. Version 2.0.1 was an important bug-fix update that appeared almost immediately after the original 2.0 version; the 2.0.3 version added compatibility with iDVD (see page 299) and even more bug fixes.

These updates are well worth installing; in fact, the rest of this book assumes that you've got 2.0.1 or later. Fortunately, the updates are free. You download them from *www.apple.com/imovie*. In general, they arrive on your desktop as an .smi file (a disk-image file), which you double-click to create a simulated floppy-disk icon on your desktop. Inside is the updater program.

Tip: If the updater gives you the message, "An error occurred that prevented the installation from completing. File not found: Find iMovie," it's because your copy of iMovie is *already* the latest version. The updater is wondering what's the matter with you.

When the updater is finished with its installation, your original copy of iMovie, wherever you've been keeping it, has now morphed into the newer version of the program. It's in the same place it was before, but now it has the new features and enhancements of the updated version. (One way to find out what version of iMovie you have is to launch program and then choose ⌘→About iMovie. After the cute movie plays, you'll see the version number appear.)

You might want to keep the updater around; if you ever have to reinstall your original version of iMovie, you'll have to update it again.

Tip: The iMovie home page offers more than updaters—more transitions, special effects, music tracks, backgrounds, and sound effects are also available for free download. Because iMovie 2 comes with a paltry collection of titles and transitions, downloading these free add-ons is especially important.

Connecting to FireWire

The FireWire jack on the side or back of your computer is marked by a radioactive-looking Y symbol.

If you got iMovie with your Mac, you also received an attractive, silvery FireWire *cable*, something like the one shown in Figure 4-1. One end is a plug that perfectly fits a FireWire jack on your computer. (Apple calls it the six-pin connector.)

On the other end is a much smaller, squarish plug (the four-pin connector). Plug this tiny end into the FireWire connector on your camcorder, which—depending on the brand—may be labeled "FireWire," "i.Link," or "IEEE 1394." This tiny end may look almost square, but it connects to the camcorder in only one particular way, thanks to a little indentation on one side. If it doesn't seem to want to connect, rotate the plug and try again—gently, because this end is fragile.

That's all the setup your Mac needs. This single FireWire cable communicates both sound and video, in both directions, between the Mac and the camcorder.

Tip: Like anything attached to the Mac, your FireWire jacks require software *drivers.* And like any drivers, those Apple makes for FireWire are constantly being updated, debugged, and improved. (iMovie requires FireWire 2.4 or later.) Since iMovie's debut, the Apple FireWire drivers have been released in several new versions, each set of which is compatible with more camcorders and solves more problems. To check for updates, visit *http://asu.info.apple.com,* where a search for *FireWire* will produce a list of the latest driver versions.

Figure 4-1:
Plug the larger end of the FireWire cable into the corresponding jack on the Mac. The tiny end goes into your camcorder. The FireWire connectors are convenient, but not necessary made of concrete; the small end is especially fragile. Take care to insert and remove these connectors straight into or out of the jacks.

Now, if you plan to transfer video to your Mac from a *tape* in the camcorder, turn the camcorder to its *VCR* or *VTR mode*. This is what most people do most of the time.

But if, instead, you want to capture *live* video into iMovie—to pass whatever your camcorder lens is seeing directly to the Mac, without ever recording it on tape—put the camcorder into *Camera* mode instead.

For best results, plug your camcorder's adapter into the wall instead of running it from battery power. At last you're ready to begin editing video!

Getting into iMovie 2

After you've connected and turned on your camcorder, launch iMovie 2. But before you're treated to the actual iMovie screen shown in Figure 4-4, iMovie may ask you to take care of a few housekeeping details.

Changing the Monitor Resolution

All modern Mac monitors let you adjust the *resolution*, which is a measurement of how much it can show, as measured in *pixels* (the tiny dots that make up the screen picture). If you choose →Control Panels→Monitors, you'll see the choices awaiting you. On an iMac, for example, you can choose from among three resolution settings:

- **640 x 480.** At this resolution, the pixels are very big, which magnifies the screen image. As a result, less image fits on the glass; when word processing, a single page might fill the entire screen. Poor iMovie can't even run at this setting.

- **800 x 600.** At this medium setting, you can see much more at a time—a page and a half side-by-side, for example. But everything is smaller now. At this resolution, iMovie has enough room to offer nine cubbyholes for footage in the *Shelf* (the storage area shown in Figure 4-4), and about eight cubbyholes on the Clip Viewer.

- **1024 x 768.** This maximum resolution of the iMac makes the individual pixels extremely small. (At this setting, you may have trouble reading 12-point text.) On the other hand, your monitor shows a very large overall area, enough to fit two side-by-side word processing pages—and, in iMovie, enough to fit fifteen clips on the Shelf, or ten on the Clip Viewer, without scrolling.

Note: If you have Apple's top-of-the-line, gargantuan Apple Cinema Display, your screen's added resolution doesn't help much with the Shelf situation. Instead of expanding the Shelf to fit your generously endowed monitor, iMovie 2 locks it at fifteen clips (without scrolling).

In return, you get an even more valuable gift: a much larger Clip Viewer and Monitor window, which make your iMovie setup feel much more like a professional studio setup.

Why is it important to understand monitor resolution when you're about to edit video? Because iMovie likes a very big screen—such as you can get only from a *high-*

resolution monitor. If your monitor is set to one of the lower resolution settings when you launch iMovie, you'll get an error message like those shown in Figure 4-2.

If you get the error message shown at top in Figure 4-2, click OK to quit iMovie. Then change the resolution to a higher setting, either by choosing →Control Panels→Monitors or by using the Control Strip, the gray tab that usually peeks out from the left edge of your screen. Click the tab to expand it; click the monitor resolution tile (which looks like a checkerboard); and choose a higher resolution from the pop-up menu. (For more on the Control Strip, see *Mac OS 9: The Missing Manual*.)

If you get the error message shown at bottom in Figure 4-2, on the other hand, you can click either Don't Change (to open iMovie at the current monitor resolution) or Change Resolution (which switches your monitor automatically to 1024 x 768). There's absolutely nothing wrong with using iMovie at 800 x 600. Indeed, you may find that the enlargement of the controls and icon labels makes them much easier to read. You should understand, however, that at this lower resolution, you'll have to scroll more to work with the Clip Viewer (also shown in Figure 4-4).

The bottom line: Experiment to see which monitor setting makes your editing work more comfortable.

Caution: iMovie can't run at monitor resolutions lower than 800 x 600. If you switch your resolution to 640 x 480 *while* iMovie is running, therefore, the program has no choice but to quit abruptly. (At least it does you the courtesy of offering to save the changes to the project file you've been working on.)

The program is more graceful when you switch between two *higher* resolutions; it instantly adjusts its various windows and controls to fit the resized screen. In other words, whenever you switch resolutions while the program is open, be extra careful not to choose 640 x 480 by mistake.

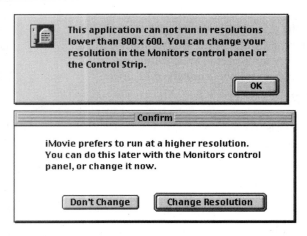

Figure 4-2:
If your monitor is set to 640 x 480, iMovie won't run. You get the error message shown at top. If it's set to 800 x 600, you'll get the message shown below. The program will still run if you click Don't Change, but you won't be able to see as many clips on the Shelf without scrolling, as shown in Figure 4-4.

The New/Open Dialog Box

If everything has gone well, and iMovie approves of your monitor setting, your next stop is the New Project/Open Project dialog box (Figure 4-3).

Figure 4-3:
The first time you open iMovie by double-clicking its icon, you're offered this dialog box—plus dancing children and this clapstick. Click New Project to begin working on a new movie, Open Project to open an existing movie, or Quit to back out of the whole thing. Of course, if you're going to work on an existing movie, it would have been much more efficient to just double-click its icon when you were at the desktop.

Substituting Your Own "Splash Screen" Movie

Two gloriously filmed demo movies come built right into the software. The first one, a small one, appears the very first time the New File/Open File dialog box appears (see Figure 4-3). It features photogenic dancing kids and a sweet guitar jingle. As noted above, most people never see this clip again once they start working in iMovie.

The other demo movie appears when you choose ⌘→About iMovie. It's a much larger, almost full-screen version of the same dancing-kids movie.

Why devote perfectly good paper and ink to documenting these five-second iMovie promotional videos? Because of what lurks in the iMovie→Resources folder on your hard drive. Inside, as shown here, are two standard QuickTime movie files: *Splash.mov* and *SplashSmall.mov*. These are, sure enough, precisely the movies you see in iMovie—that danc-

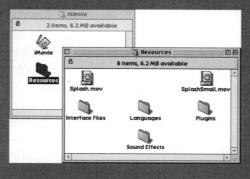

ing-kids movie, in large-screen and small-screen formats.

This knowledge is power. You can double-click these files to view the iMovie jingle movies any time you like. But the real fun comes from substituting your *own* finished iMovie movies.

Following the instructions in Chapter 12, make QuickTime movies of your kids saying, "Pick a movie to open, silly!" (for the small-format movie) and, "I wrote this software!" (for the larger one). Put these movie files in the iMovie→Resources, and give them exactly the same names as the movies already there (*Splash.mov* and *SplashSmall.mov*), replacing the original ones. Now, whenever you choose ⌘→About iMovie or face the New File/Open File dialog box, your own movies fill the screen.

The very first time you use iMovie 2, you get to hear the iMovie jingle: a catchy little
guitar lick accompanied by looping footage of children dancing in exquisite lighting
conditions. As noted in Figure 4-3, you've reached a decision point: You must now
tell the program whether you want to begin a new movie—called a *project* in iMovie
lingo; open the Tutorial project, if you have it; open one you've already started; or
quit the program.

Tip: You can get a fix of that catchy little jingle and those catchy little kids whenever you like by choosing
 →About iMovie.

The first time you run iMovie is probably the only time you'll ever see the dialog box
shown in Figure 4-3. After that, each time you launch iMovie, it automatically opens
up the movie you were most recently working on.

You'll run into the New Project/Open Project dialog box only if you do one of the
following:

- Discard the last movie you were working on (by trashing it from your hard drive).
- Throw away the iMovie Preferences file (inside your System Folder→Preferences
  folder).

The iMovie Tutorial

iMovie doesn't come with any printed instructions. The comes-with-your-Mac version does, however, include a tutorial—special help screens that are accompanied
by some raw footage that you're free to manipulate. If you're interested in taking this
miniature lesson, click the Open Tutorial Project that appears on the Open Project/
New Project screen. (The Open Tutorial button appears only if you do, in fact, *have*
the tutorial files. If you downloaded iMovie 2 from the Web, you didn't get the tutorial files.)

Six video clips now appear in the Shelf, as shown in Figure 4-4. iMovie comes with
about 45 seconds of ready-to-use footage, constituting a useful starter kit if you
want to try out iMovie but don't yet have a camcorder.

For instructions, choose Help→iMovie Tutorial. After a moment, the iMovie Help
window appears at the left side of your screen. These instructions guide you through
the creation of a short, happy, kids-washing-the-dog flick. (You may find it exceed-
ingly awkward to have to switch back and forth between the help screen and the
iMovie program behind it. Many iMovie fans, giving up in frustration, wind up
printing out the entire tutorial, no matter how many ink cartridges are sacrificed in
the process.)

iMovie Controls

Whether or not you decide to follow the tutorial instructions, opening the tutorial
project document is a quick and convenient way to get to know the various windows and controls of the iMovie *interface*. Figure 4-4 shows the basics.

Here's the cheat sheet for what these various screen elements do—a crash course in iMovie. Spend no time now memorizing their functions; the rest of this book covers each of these tools in context and in depth.

Tip: You can choose Help→Show Balloons to remind yourself of these control names. As you move the pointer to each part of the iMovie 2 window, a pop-up balloon identifies its function.

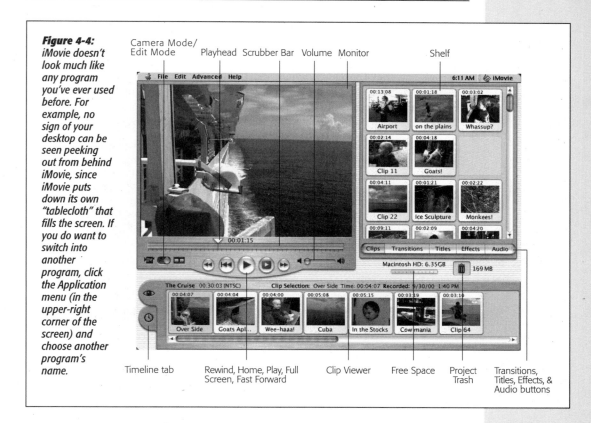

Figure 4-4:
iMovie doesn't look much like any program you've ever used before. For example, no sign of your desktop can be seen peeking out from behind iMovie, since iMovie puts down its own "tablecloth" that fills the screen. If you do want to switch into another program, click the Application menu (in the upper-right corner of the screen) and choose another program's name.

Camera Mode/ Edit Mode   Playhead   Scrubber Bar   Volume   Monitor   Shelf

Timeline tab   Rewind, Home, Play, Full Screen, Fast Forward   Clip Viewer   Free Space   Project Trash   Transitions, Titles, Effects, & Audio buttons

- **Monitor.** You watch your footage in this window.

- **Shelf.** These little cubbyholes store the *clips*—pieces of footage, individual shots—that you'll rearrange into a masterpiece of modern storytelling.

- **Project Trash.** You can drag any clip onto this icon to get rid of it. When you trim your footage, meanwhile, the trimmed portions go into this "can," too.

- **Transitions, Titles, Effects, and Audio buttons.** These five buttons each replace the Shelf with special tools that let you add professional touches to your movie, such as controls for crossfade styles, credit sequences, footage effects (such as brightness and color shifting), sound effects, and music. (Chapters 6, 7, and 8 cover these video flourishes in detail.)

- **Clip Viewer/Timeline.** When you work in iMovie 2, you spend most of your time down here. If you're an iMovie 1 veteran, it's especially important to understand the difference between the Clip Viewer, which remains largely unchanged, and the Timeline, which is radically different. Each of these tools offers a master map that shows which scenes will play in which order, but there's a dramatic and crucial difference in the way they do it.

When you click the Clip Viewer tab (marked by the eyeball), you see your movie represented as *slides*. Each clip appears to be the same size, even if some are very long and some are very short. The Clip Viewer offers no clue as to what's going on with the audio, but it's a supremely efficient overview of your clips' sequence.

When you click the Timeline tab (marked by the clock), on the other hand, you can see the relative lengths of your clips, because each shows up as a colored band of the appropriate length. Parallel bands underneath indicate blocks of sound that play simultaneously.

- **Camera Mode/Edit Mode buttons.** In Camera Mode, the playback controls operate your camcorder, rather than the iMovie film you're editing. In Camera Mode, the monitor window shows you what's on the tape, not what's in iMovie, so that you can choose which shots you want to transfer to iMovie for editing.

In Edit Mode, however, iMovie ignores your camcorder. Now the playback controls govern your captured clips instead of the camcorder. Edit Mode is where you start piecing your movie together.

Tip: You can drag the blue dot between the Camera Mode and Edit Mode positions, if you like, but doing so requires sharp hand-eye coordination and an unnecessary mouse drag. It's much faster to click *on* one of the icons, ignoring the little switch entirely. Click directly on the little camera symbol for Camera Mode, for example, or on the filmstrip for Edit Mode.

- **Rewind/Review.** In Edit Mode, these transport controls manipulate the playback of your movie (or a highlighted clip). When you're in Camera Mode, described above, you can click these buttons on the screen to make your camcorder, sitting beside you on the desk and connected by the FireWire cable, respond as if by magic.

The Rewind/Review button, of course, lets you skip to an earlier part of the movie or tape; if you're in Play mode, you see the camcorder footage flying backwards. (If you're looking at footage you've already brought into iMovie, you see the footage flying by regardless of whether you're in Play mode or not.) Click once to start, again to stop.

Tip: All of the transport buttons work like the "soft logic" buttons on an expensive tape deck. That is, you can click the Play button while you're rewinding, or vice versa. You never have to stop one function before clicking the next button.

- **Home.** Means "rewind to the beginning." *Keyboard equivalent:* the Home key on your keyboard.

   In Camera Mode—that is, when you're operating the camcorder using these controls—this button turns into a Pause button, so that you can freeze the tape on a certain frame.

- **Play/Stop.** Plays the tape, movie, or clip. When the playback is going on, the button turns blue; that's your cue that clicking it again stops the playback.

- **Play Full Screen.** Clicking this button makes the movie you're editing fill the entire Mac screen as it plays back, instead of playing just in the small Monitor window. (It still doesn't look nearly as good as it will on your TV, however, for reasons detailed on page 102.)

   In Camera Mode, this button turns into a Stop button. It does exactly the same thing as clicking the Play button a second time.

Tip: In iMovie 2, the Play Full Screen button doesn't play your movie back from the beginning (a behavior that drove many iMovie 1 users quietly postal). Instead, it plays back from the location of the Playhead.

If you *do* want to play in full-screen mode from the beginning, press the Home key (or click the Home button just to the left of the Play button) before clicking the Play Full Screen button.

- **Fast Forward.** Speeds forward through either the movie you're editing or the playback of your camcorder.

- **Scrubber bar.** This special scroll bar lets you jump anywhere in one piece of footage, or the entire movie. (Drag the handle, or just click in the "track.")

- **Playhead.** The Playhead is like the little box handle, or *thumb,* of a normal scroll bar. It shows exactly where you are in the footage.

- **Volume slider.** To the delight of interface-design nerds everywhere, the awkward "thumbwheel" speaker-volume knob of iMovie 1 has been replaced by this easy-to-drag slider. Actually, you don't even need to drag it; you can simply click anywhere in the slider's "track" to make the knob jump there. (Or just press the up or down arrow keys to change the volume.)

- **Free Space.** This indicator lets you know how full your hard drive is. In the world of video editing, that's a very important statistic.

- **Project Trash.** Tells you how much material you've cut out of your footage; see page 120 for details.

Saving a New Project File
If you played with the iMovie tutorial, great; save your work if you like.

Now choose File→New Project. If you didn't play with the tutorial, and you're still looking at the dialog box shown in Figure 4-3, click New Project.

Either way, you're now asked to select a name and location for the movie you're about to make—or, as iMovie would say, the *project* you're about to make. (iMovie 2 coyly proposes "Robin's Movie" as the title of any newly saved project file [but using *your* name, of course]. And how does it know your name? It consults the "Owner Name" blank in the File Sharing control panel, which you can open by choosing →Control Panels→File Sharing.)

This is a critical moment. Starting a new iMovie project isn't anywhere near as casual an affair as starting a new word processing file. For one thing, iMovie requires that you save and name your file *before* you've actually done any work. For another, you can't transfer footage from your camcorder without *first* naming and saving a project file.

Above all, the *location* of your saved project file—your choice of hard drive to save it on—is extremely important. Digital video files are enormous. Your footage consumes about 3.6 MB of your hard drive *per second*. Therefore:

This much video	Needs about this much disk space
1 minute	228 MB
15 minutes	3.5 GB
30 minutes	7 GB
60 minutes	13 GB
2 hours	28 GB
4 hours	53 GB

When you save and name your project, you also tell iMovie *where* to put these enormous, disk-guzzling files. If, like most people, you have only one hard drive—the one built into your Mac—fine; make as much empty room as you can, and proceed with your video-editing career.

But many iMovie fans have more than one hard drive. They may have decided to invest in a larger hard drive, as described in the box on page 101, so that they can make longer movies. If you're among them, you must save your new project *onto* the larger hard drive if you want to take advantage of its extra space.

Note, by the way, that digital video requires a fast hard drive. Therefore, make no attempt to save your project file onto a floppy disk, Zip disk, Jaz disk, SuperDisk, iDisk, or another disk on the network. It simply won't be fast enough, and you'll get nothing but error messages.

Tip: If you need more free space on your hard drive for iMovie work, one of the fastest ways to find out what's eating up all the megabytes is Mac Disk Explorer, a shareware program written, coincidentally, by the lead programmer on iMovie and iMovie 2. It shows a tidy list of every folder on your drives, listed by size, so that you can immediately target the space hogs. It's available from *missingmanual.com* and *macdiskexplorer.com.*

FREQUENTLY ASKED QUESTION

Saving to External FireWire Drives

I need more hard drive space. What should I do? Can I save a project onto an external FireWire drive?

The answer is: You can if you can.

It's a natural question; most Macs have two FireWire jacks. What better way to capitalize on them by hooking up the camcorder and an external FireWire hard drive simultaneously?

Yet Apple's help files warn that you shouldn't try saving iMovie projects onto an external FireWire hard drive.

But in fact, such an arrangement works fine if you have both a fast Mac and a fast external hard drive. Inquire online in one of the discussion groups described on page 383; you'll find out which drives have succeeded with your fellow iMovie mavens. (Check *www.dealmac.com* for best prices.)

For example, a fast-enough-for-iMovie 45 GB FireWire hard drive costs, at this writing, about $400 (from *www.promax.com,* for example); a 75 GB drive is $700. (The 45 GB drive holds just under four hours of footage; the 75 holds six

hours.) But the prices are falling rapidly. And FireWire hard drives have several advantages over hard drives you may have known in the past: They're smaller and faster, can be plugged and unplugged from the Mac without turning anything off, and don't require power cords of their own.

Even if you buy an external hard drive that's too slow to handle incoming DV footage in real time, remember that it's still not a loss. You can always move whatever non-video files are now on your *internal* drive to the external one, thus freeing up the built-in drive's space for DV files.

If you're technically inclined, you can save a lot of money *and* avoid the "not fast enough" problem by adding a new *internal* drive to your Mac (or replacing the one it's got). For example, at this writing, you'd pay about $250 for a 60 GB hard drive—enough to hold *five hours* of footage. Of course, this option involves taking the computer completely apart, a job you may want to leave to a technician. (And if you *are* a technician, you can find step-by-step instructions online at *www.imac2day.com/installhd.shtml* and other sites.)

Importing Camcorder Footage

Suppose you've now opened iMovie, enjoyed the dancing-kids video, and clicked the New Project button. At this moment, then, you're looking at an empty version of the screen shown in Figure 4-4. Your camcorder is turned on and connected to the FireWire cable. This is where the fun begins.

Click the little movie-camera symbol on the iMovie screen to switch into Camera Mode, as shown in Figure 4-4.

Tip: If you turn on your camcorder after iMovie is already running, the program notices that you've done so, and switches into Camera Mode automatically as a convenience. (iMovie only does so the *first time* you power up the camcorder during a work session, however, to avoid annoying people who like to turn the camcorder on and off repeatedly during the editing process to save battery power.)

The monitor window becomes big and blue, filled with the words "Camera Connected." (If you don't see those words, check the troubleshooting steps in Appendix B.) This is only the first of many messages the Monitor window will be showing you. At other times, it may say, "Camera No Tape," "Camera Fast Forward," "Camera Rewinding," and so on.

Now you can click the Play, Rewind, Fast Forward, and other buttons on the screen to control the camcorder. You'll probably find that you have even more precision using the mouse to control it than you would by pressing the actual camcorder buttons.

Tip: The Rewind and Fast Forward buttons work exactly as they do on a VCR. That is, they speed through the tape much faster if you stop playback first. If you click Rewind or Fast Forward while the tape is playing, the tape moves at only twice its usual speed—still not bad—while playback continues.

What you're doing now, of course, is scanning your tape to find the sections that you'll want to include in your edited movie. Unfortunately, iMovie offers no keyboard shortcuts for the playback controls. The only keys that work are the up- and down-arrow keys, which adjust the Mac's speaker volume, and the Space bar, described in a moment.

The Monitor Window's Video Quality

Today's personal computers are incredibly powerful, but not all of them are powerful enough to blast 3.6 MB of video data to the screen per second. Power Mac G4 models with 350 MHz or faster processors can keep up, but on slower Macs, you may notice that the Monitor window's playback of motion is slightly jerky. The colors look great, and the picture quality is terrific, but the motion just isn't as smooth as it is on TV, which may come as a shock to anyone who's been eagerly awaiting the famously high video quality of DV camcorders.

It's important to realize that this compromised video quality is *temporary;* it's visible only on the Mac screen. The instant you send your finished movie back to the camcorder, or when you export it as a QuickTime movie, you get the pristine, stunning DV quality that was temporarily hidden on the Mac screen.

You'll spend much of your moviemaking time watching clips play back, so it's well worth investigating the different ways iMovie can improve the picture. Here are your alternatives, in order of preference.

Use the camcorder—or a TV

By choosing Edit→Preferences, clicking the Advanced tab, turning on Video Play Through to Camera, and clicking OK, you tell iMovie to show the smooth, crisp picture it's been hiding all along *through your camcorder.*

In other words, if you're willing to watch your camcorder's LCD screen as you work instead of the onscreen Monitor window, what you see is what you shot: all gorgeous, all the time. (iMovie 2 automatically cuts out the Mac's audio, too, so that you hear all the sound through the camcorder.)

Better yet: If you hook up a TV to your camcorder's analog outputs, you get to edit your footage not just at full quality, but also at full size. This, by the way, is exactly the way professionals edit digital video—on TV monitors on their desks. The only difference is that you paid about $98,000 less for your setup.

Use the "Smoother Motion" option

The Preferences command offers another solution to this problem. Choose Edit→Preferences; in the resulting dialog box (see Figure 4-5), click the Playback tab. Now click Smoother Motion, and then click OK.

Tip: If you're using a fast Mac—one with a 350 MHz or faster G4 chip—the Playback tab doesn't appear at all in your Preferences dialog box. That's because these machines are powerful enough to show you high-quality, smooth, *and* clear video in the Monitor window. No compromise, of the type described in this section, is necessary.

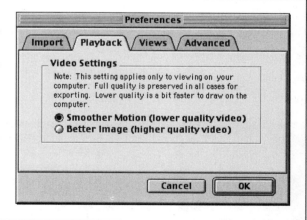

Figure 4-5:
You can watch smooth motion with a blurry picture, or jerky motion with a crisp picture, but not both (except on very fast Macs). The Preferences dialog box lets you choose which compromise you want to make.

Sure enough, the motion is now almost as smooth as television. But you pay for the smoothness with a slight degradation of picture quality—a slight blurriness or chunkiness. Still, this smooth-but-blurry look (the Smoother Motion option in Figure 4-5) is the best way to make frame-accurate cuts, splices, and trims of your footage, because only then are you seeing every single frame of the movie.

Capturing Footage

When you're in Camera Mode, an oval-shaped Import button appears just below the Monitor window. Every time you click this button—or press the Space bar—iMovie imports the footage you're watching. Technically speaking, the program records the incoming video as a series of special digital-video movie clips on the Mac's hard drive.

During this process, you'll notice a number of changes to your iMovie environment:

- The Import button lights up, as though illuminated by a blue spotlight. As shown in Figure 4-6, the Free Space indicator is active, too.

- As soon as you click Import, what looks like a slide appears in the first square of the Shelf, as shown in Figure 4-6. That's a *clip*—a single piece of footage—one of the building blocks of an iMovie movie. Its icon is a picture of the first frame.

- Superimposed on the clip, in its upper-left corner, is the length of the clip expressed as "seconds:frames" or (if it's a longer clip) "minutes:seconds:frames." You can see this little timer ticking upward as the clip grows longer. For example, if it says *1:23:10,* then the clip is 1 minute, 23 seconds, and 10 frames long.

Getting used to this kind of frame counter takes some practice for two reasons. First, computers start counting from 0, not from 1, so the very first frame of a clip is called 00:00. Second, remember that there are 30 frames per second (in NTSC digital video; 25 in PAL digital video). So the far-right number in the time code (the frame counter) counts up to *29* before flipping over to 00 again (not to 59 or 99, which might feel more familiar). In other words, iMovie counts like this: 00:28…00:29…1:00…1:01.

Tip: DV camcorders record life by capturing 30 frames per second. (All right, 29.97 frames per second; see page 286.)

That, for your trivia pleasure, is the standard frame rate for *television.* Real movies, on the other hand—that is, footage shot on film—rolls by at only 24 frames per second. The European PAL format runs at 25 frames per second.

A Wrinkle in Timecode

If a clip is shorter than one minute—as most clips are—iMovie 2 drops the "00:" minutes display from the beginning of the clip-length time code shown on every clip. You see a two-colon number (such as "1:22:03") if the clip is longer than a minute.

If you'd prefer to see the full three-segment time-code display ("minutes:seconds:frames") all the time, a new iMovie 2 preference can accommodate you. Choose Edit→

Preferences; click the Views tab; and turn off "Use Short Time Codes." When you click OK, you'll find that *all* time codes appear in the full form.

And if you'd rather do without the time code altogether, you can make it disappear from your clips' corners by editing the secret iMovie Preferences document, a procedure described on page 377.

- Your Mac devotes every atom of its energy to capturing the massive amounts of information that flows into its circuitry. While the importing is going on, the Mac won't let you switch into another program, use any menu command except Help or Quit, or do any editing. If you click any of the transport buttons (such as Rewind or Play/Stop), open one of the transition palettes (see Chapter 6), or click one of the clips on the Shelf, importing stops immediately.

Tip: iMovie is so single-minded by default. But if you edit the secret preferences file described on page 377, you can indeed enjoy background video capturing; while your Mac grabs footage from the camcorder, you can go off to read your email in another program.

If you click Import (or press the Space bar) a second time, the tape continues to roll, but iMovie stops gulping down footage to your hard drive. Your camcorder continues to play. You've just captured your first clip.

Figure 4-6:
While you're importing footage, the time code in the upper-left corner of the clip on the Shelf steadily ticks away to show you that the clip is getting longer (left). Meanwhile, the Free Space indicator updates itself, second by second, as your hard drive space is eaten up by the incoming footage (right).

FREQUENTLY ASKED QUESTION

Killing the Sound-Delay Echo

When I'm capturing footage, I get this annoying echo in the sound, as though a delay unit is processing the soundtrack. What's going on?

You're probably trying to watch the footage on your camcorder's LCD screen and on the Mac screen at the same time. As a result, you're hearing the soundtrack twice—once from the camcorder's built-in speaker, and then, a fraction of a second later, from the Mac's speaker. (It takes that

long for the sound to make its way through the Mac's sound circuitry and various layers of software.)

You can, of course, simply close the LCD screen, and presto!—no more echo. If you still want to be able to watch the superior picture on the LCD screen, then mute, or fully turn down, either the camcorder's speaker or the Mac's. Now you get two ways to watch the movie play, but only one sound source.

Using automatic scene detection

If you let the tape continue to roll, however, you'll notice something amazing. At the end of the current shot on the tape, at the point where the next scene begins, a new clip icon appears in the Shelf. What iMovie is actually doing is studying the *date and time stamp* that DV camcorders record into every frame of video. When iMovie detects a break in time, it assumes that you stopped recording, if only for a moment—and therefore that the next piece of footage should be considered a new shot. It turns each new shot into a new clip—a feature not found even in the $1,000 professional editing programs.

At first, iMovie's insistence upon ending every clip as each camera shot ends may annoy you. You may mutter to yourself, "Darn it, if I wanted to end the clip there, I would have done it myself by clicking the Import button again."

This is an optional behavior, however, and it can be useful. It lets you just roll the camera, unattended, as iMovie automatically downloads the footage, turning each scene into a clip in successive Shelf cubbyholes, while you sit there leafing through a magazine. Then, later, at your leisure, you can survey the footage you've caught and set about the business of cutting out the deadwood.

Tip: If you prefer, you can ask iMovie 2 to dump incoming clips into the Clip Viewer at the bottom of the screen instead of the Shelf.

In the days of iMovie 1, this feature was primarily useful because the Shelf, with its measly 12 cubbyholes, quickly ran out of space for new footage (whereas the Clip Viewer was limited only by your hard drive space). Fortunately, in iMovie 2, the Shelf scrolls as much as necessary to hold the imported clips.

Still, there's one circumstance where you still might like iMovie to put incoming clips directly into the Clip Viewer: if you filmed your shots roughly in sequence. That way, you'll have that much less Shelf-to-Clip Viewer dragging to do when it comes time to edit.

To bring this about, choose Edit→Preferences; click the Import tab; click Movie; and then click OK. Now when you begin importing clips, iMovie stacks them end-to-end in the *Movie Track* instead of on the Shelf. The Movie Track is endless; it won't run out of room until your hard drive does.

Turning off automatic scene detection

If you would prefer to have manual control over when each clip begins and ends, iMovie is happy to comply. Choose Edit→Preferences, and proceed as shown in Figure 4-7.

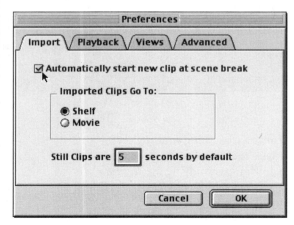

Figure 4-7:
The Import tab of the Edit→Preferences dialog box gives you control over the automatic clip-logging feature. You can turn this feature off entirely by clicking to turn off the checkmark in the "Automatically start new clip at scene break" checkbox.

Once you've turned off the automatic clip-creation feature, iMovie logs clips only when you click Import (or press Space) once at the beginning of the clip, and again at the end of the clip.

Tip: Tapping the Space bar is the same as clicking the Import button. In fact, if you tap Space when the camcorder is stopped, it begins to play *and* iMovie begins to capture the footage.

How much footage to capture

For best results, don't attempt to use the footage-importing process as a crude means of editing the footage on the fly. True, the ever-diminishing dark area of the Free Space graph (Figure 4-6) may put you under pressure to limit the amount of footage you import. But resist the temptation. You'll want to trim your clips in iMovie, using its frame-accurate snipping tools, not by "riding" the Import button in an effort to eliminate bad footage as it comes in.

This doesn't mean that you must transfer *everything* from your camcorder (although many people do, just for the convenience). But when you do find a scene you'll want to bring into iMovie, capture three to five seconds of footage before and after the interesting part. Later, when you're editing, that extra leading and trailing video (called *trim handles* by the pros) will give you the flexibility to choose exactly the right moment for the scene to begin and end. Furthermore, as you'll find out in Chapter 6, you need extra footage at the beginnings and ends of your clips if you want to use transitions, such as crossfades, between them.

The maximum clip length

The largest movie clip iMovie will capture is one that takes two gigabytes of disk space—which is 9 minutes, 28 seconds, and 17 frames long. At the end of that time, if the camcorder is still running, iMovie smoothly and automatically begins a second clip, placing another icon into your Shelf.

This limitation is nothing to panic over, however. After the importing, you can place the two clips side-by-side on the Clip Viewer; iMovie will play first one, then the next, *completely* seamlessly. No pop, blink, or dropped frame will give away the program's little secret: that during the importing, it had to split your very long clip into multiple parts.

If you follow this thought to its logical conclusion, you can see that as far as iMovie is concerned, there's really no maximum clip length. You can import an entire 60-minute DV cassette's worth of tape—if you've got 12.7 gigabytes of free hard drive space, of course—and iMovie will smoothly import all of it, even if it shows up on your Shelf in the form of seven different clip icons.

The Free Space graph

As noted earlier, the Free Space graph (Figure 4-6) updates itself as you capture your clips. It keeps track of how much space your hard drive has left—the one onto which you saved your project.

This graph includes a color-keyed early-warning system that lets you prepare for that awkward moment when your hard drive's full. At that moment, you won't be able to capture any more video. Look at the colored bar that grows out of the left side of the graph:

- If it's **green,** you're in good shape. Your hard drive has over 400 MB of free space—room for at least 90 seconds of additional footage.

- If the graph becomes **yellow,** your hard drive has between 200 and 400 MB of free space left. In less than 90 seconds of capturing, you'll be completely out of space.

- When the graph turns **red,** the situation is dire. Your hard drive has less than 200 MB of free space left—about one minute of capturing remains.

- When the Free Space indicator shows that you've got less than 50 MB of free space left, iMovie stops importing and refuses to capture any more video. At this point, you must make more free space on your hard drive, either by emptying your Project Trash (see page 120) or by quitting iMovie and throwing away some non-iMovie files from your hard drive. (Mac Disk Explorer, described on page 101, can be an invaluable assistant in this situation.)

Tip: If you know the secret, you can adjust the 50 MB warning threshold so that iMovie warns you when you've got 30 MB of hard drive space left, or 100, or any number you prefer. See page 382 for instructions.

How iMovie Organizes Its Files

Few computer programs are as compulsive about housekeeping as iMovie. Every time you save a project file, iMovie doesn't just create a document on your hard drive, as AppleWorks or Word would. Instead, it creates an entire *folder* bearing your project's name (see Figure 4-8).

The Media Folder

Inside this folder is indeed a document with the name you gave your movie. It shares its space with yet another folder, this one called Media. And in the Media folder are several, or dozens, or hundreds of individual QuickTime movies—digital movie files, one for each clip or special effect you used in your movie. Here, too, are any audio files or still images that you've imported into your movie.

Understanding how your project folder works can be useful. For example, it teaches you that the actual iMovie project file—called "The Cruise" at lower-left in Figure 4-8—occupies only a few kilobytes of space on the disk, even if it's a very long movie. Behind the scenes, this document contains nothing more than a list of internal *references* to the QuickTime clips in the Media folder. Even if you copy, chop, split, rearrange, rename, and otherwise spindle the clips *in iMovie,* the names and quantity of clips in the Media folder don't change; all of your iMovie editing, technically speaking, simply shuffles around your project file's internal *pointers* to different moments on the clips you originally captured from the camcorder.

The bottom line: If you copy the project document to a Zip disk and take it home to show the relatives for the holidays, you're in for a rude surprise, because it's nothing without its accompanying Media folder. (And that's why iMovie insists upon creating a folder that keeps the document and its media files together.)

Caution: *Never* rename or delete the files in the Media folder. iMovie will become cranky, display error messages, and forget how you had your movie the last time you opened it.

Do your deleting, renaming, and rearranging in *iMovie,* not in the Media folder. And above all, don't take the Media folder out of the folder the project document is in (or vice versa). Doing so will render your movie uneditable, at least until you put the Media folder and project document together again in the same folder.

Figure 4-8:
Every iMovie project gets its own folder (top left). Inside (lower left) is both a document bearing the same name and a Media folder that contains all the clips (right). They're always called Clip 01, Clip 02, and so on, even if you've renamed them in iMovie.

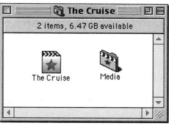
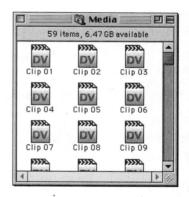

Figure 4-9:
iMovie has no traditional Save As command, but you can achieve the same effect manually. Suppose that, having finished half of your movie, you want to save it under a different name. Quit iMovie and duplicate the project folder on your hard drive (top). Give the duplicated project folder a different name; then, to help you keep your versions straight, also rename the actual project file inside it (bottom).

The Phantom "Save As" Command

Knowing about how iMovie stores its files also solves what some people consider an iMovie limitation: the fact that it has no Save As command. If iMovie did have a File→Save As command, you could save your project under a different name halfway through working on it. You could create midproject backups, for example. Or you could create multiple versions of the same movie—short and long versions. You could spin out an intermediate version just before making some radical editing decision that you might regret later, so that you'll have a safe version to return to.

You would also use up your hard drive's space fairly quickly, because each Save As process would duplicate all of the massive clip files in your project folder. But if you want to perform a Save As procedure, you can still do it—just not from within iMovie. Instead, follow the steps shown in Figure 4-9.

Sharing Clips among Projects

It's also worth noting that, if you want to use a certain clip in more than one project, you don't have to go to the trouble of downloading it again from your camcorder. Instead, just proceed like this:

1. **Find out the Finder clip number of the clip you want.**

   In other words, open the iMovie document that contains the clip you'd like to reuse. (Suppose it's in a project called Opening Night.) In the Clip Viewer (see Figure 4-4), double-click the clip. A dialog box appears, as shown in Figure 4-10, that identifies the clip's name as it appears in the Finder, in the Opening Night→Media folder. Remember this number (such as Clip 09) and click OK.

Tip: It's a good idea to choose File→Empty Trash at this point, too. Remember that cropping, splitting, or trimming clips doesn't actually eliminate any video footage from your hard drive; it simply makes your iMovie project *play* a shorter chunk of the full-length video clip that's still on your hard drive. Only when you empty the trash does iMovie actually delete data from the clips on your hard drive.

By emptying the trash, you ensure that the clip you're going to import is actually the same length as the one in its current project.

---

2. **Open the iMovie project into which you want to bring the clip.**

   See "Switching Files," below.

3. **Choose File→Import.**

   The standard Open File dialog box appears.

4. **Navigate to the Media folder inside the project folder that contains the clip you want to borrow.**

   In this example, you'd locate the Opening Night→Media folder. There you'll see all the clips that belong to that project.

5. **Double-click the clip you want.**

Having cleverly noted its number in step 1, you know exactly which of the clips (of which there could be dozens) is the scene you want. iMovie places the imported clip onto your Shelf.

Having cleverly noted its number in step 1, you know exactly which of the clips (of which there could be dozens) is the scene you want. iMovie places the imported clip onto your Shelf.

Switching Files

To open a different iMovie Project, choose File→Open Project. If you've worked on the current movie but haven't saved the changes yet, iMovie asks you whether you'd like to save them or not; click Save or Don't Save, as appropriate.

Tip: If you're a keyboard-shortcut fan, you can press ⌘-D instead of clicking Don't Save.

Figure 4-10:
When you double-click a clip, this dialog box appears. It identifies the clip's number as it appears in the Finder—a useful piece of information, because you may have renamed it in iMovie. Doing so never renames the clip in the Finder, however. (You shouldn't rename a clip in the Finder, either.)

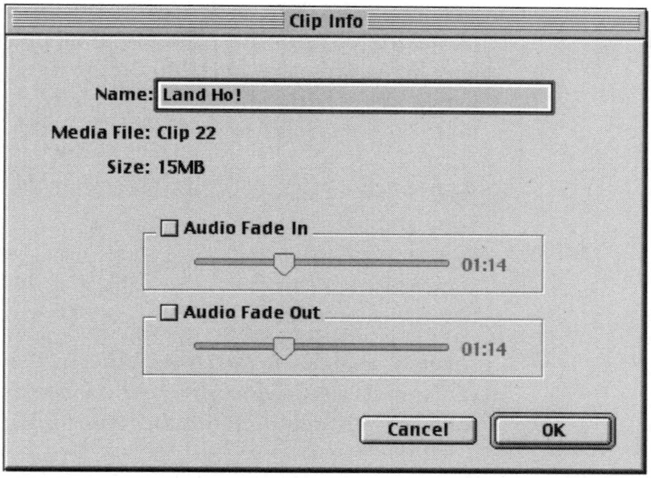

Clip Info / Name: Land Ho! / Media File: Clip 22 / Size: 15MB / Audio Fade In 01:14 / Audio Fade Out 01:14 / Cancel / OK

Now you're shown the contents of your hard drive. Navigate to the project folder that contains the next movie you want to edit. Double-click that project folder to open it, and then double-click the identically named iMovie *document* inside it. After a moment, the new movie's clips appear on the screen, and you're ready to go.

The Phantom "Revert to Saved" Command

Many Mac programs offer a Revert command in the File menu. After you've taken a few wrong turns in your editing, choosing File→Revert discards all the changes you've made to the file *since the last time you saved it.*

The iMovie File menu has no Revert command—at least, not in the File menu. You can achieve exactly the same effect, however, by choosing File→Open Project. When iMovie asks if you want to save changes to your project, click Don't Save. iMovie now shows the list of folders on your hard drive; all you have to do is open the *same* file you just had open a moment ago.

When it opens, you'll find it exactly as it was when you last used the Save command.

Starting a New Project

Starting a new project after you've been editing an older one works much the same way: Choose File→New Project; indicate whether or not you want to save the changes to your outgoing movie (if you haven't already saved them); and wait as iMovie opens a new, empty Shelf and Clip Viewer.

Importing Footage from Non-DV Tapes

We live in a transitional period. The huge majority of the world's existing camcorders and VCRs require VHS, VHS-C, or 8 mm cassettes.

The newer DV camcorders are rapidly catching up, and will soon outsell—and replace—the older formats. But for now, potential video editors face a very real problem: how to transfer, into iMovie, the footage they shot before the DV era. Fortunately, this is fairly easy to do if you have the right equipment. You can take any of these three approaches:

Approach 1: Use a Digital8 Camcorder

Sony Digital8 camcorders accommodate 8 mm, Hi-8, *and* Digital8 tapes (8 mm cassettes recorded digitally). Just insert your 8 mm or Hi-8 cassettes into the camcorder and proceed as described in this chapter. iMovie never needs to know that the camcorder doesn't contain a DV cassette.

Actually, a Digital8 camcorder grants you even more flexibility than that. Digital8 camcorders also have *analog inputs,* shown back in Figure 1-3, which let you import footage from your VCR or other tape formats. Read on:

Approach 2: Record onto Your DV Camcorder

Even if you don't have a Digital8 camcorder, the one you bought may well have analog inputs anyway. If so, your problem is solved.

1. **Unplug the FireWire cable from the DV camcorder.**

   Most camcorders' analog inputs switch off when a FireWire cable is hooked up.

2. **Connect RCA cables from the Audio Output and Video Output jacks on the side of your older camcorder or VCR. Connect the opposite ends to the analog inputs of your DV camcorder.**

   Figure 1-3 illustrates this arrangement. Put a blank DV tape into your DV camcorder.

Tip: If both your old camcorder and your DV camcorder have *S-video* connectors (a round, dime-sized jack), use them instead. S-video connections offer higher quality than RCA connections.

---

3. **Switch both camcorders into VTR or VCR mode.**

You're about to make a copy of the older tape by playing it into the camcorder.

If every fiber of your being is screaming, "But analog copies make the quality deteriorate!", relax. You're only making a single-generation copy. Actually, you're only making *half* an analog copy; it's being recorded digitally, so you lose only half as much quality as you would with a normal VCR-to-VCR duplicate. In other words, you probably won't be able to spot any picture deterioration. And you'll have the footage in digital format now forever, ready to make as many copies as you want with no further quality degradation.

4. **Press the Record button on the DV camcorder, and Play on the older camcorder or VCR.**

You can monitor your progress by watching the LCD screen of your camcorder. Remember that the DV cassette generally holds only 60 minutes of video, compared with two hours on many previous-format tapes. You may have to change DV cassettes halfway through the process.

When the transfer is finished, you can use the newly recorded DV cassette in the DV camcorder, exactly as described in this chapter and in the rest of the book.

Tip: Not all camcorders with analog inputs require you to dump the footage onto a DV *tape* as an intermediary. As described below, modern Sony camcorders can pour the analog signal into the Mac *as it plays,* eliminating several steps (and one hour of waiting per tape).

Approach 3: Use a Media Converter (Sony or Not)

If your DV camcorder doesn't have analog inputs, you can buy an *analog-to-digital converter*—a box that sits between your Mac and your VCR or older camcorder. It's an unassuming half-pound gray box, about 3 by 5 inches. Its primary features include analog audio and video (and S-video) inputs, which accommodate your older video gear, and a FireWire jack, whose cable you can plug into your Mac.

You can buy any of several different models. The Sony DVMC-DA1 has been discontinued; its successor, the DVMC-DA2, works fine with iMovie 2. (The DA2 model was incompatible with iMovie 1.0 without the purchase of a special LANC cable.) The Sony box costs about $400 at this writin; the very similar Hollywood-DV Bridge (*www.dazzle.com*) is $300.

Their rival is the less sleek but far more economical Director's Cut box from Power R (*www.powerr.com/pcproducts.html;* see Figure 4-11). At $290, it saves you a lot of money. Unlike the Sony boxes, it can handle either NTSC (North American) or PAL (European) video signals. And it's designed specifically for Macintosh video editing.

In either case, you'll be very pleased with the video quality. And when it comes to converting older footage, the media-converter approach has a dramatic advantage over DV camcorders with analog inputs: You have to sit through the footage only once. As your old VCR or camcorder plays the tape through the converter, the Mac records it simultaneously. (Contrast with Approaches 1 and 2, which require you to play the footage *twice*—once to the DV camcorder, and from there to the Mac.)

Unfortunately, you can't control these devices using iMovie's playback controls, as described in this chapter. Instead, you must transfer your footage manually by pressing Play on your VCR or old camcorder and then clicking Import on the iMovie screen. In that way, these converters aren't as convenient as an actual DV or Digital8 camcorder. (iMovie's onscreen controls can control the converter only if you have Sony's DVMC-DA2 Media Converter, a LANC cable, and a Sony analog camcorder.)

Tip: If you're truly strapped for cash, a media converter box may be the least expensive route to iMovie 2 editing happiness. You could, in theory, continue to use your old 8 mm, Hi-8, VHS, or VHS-C camcorder forever, pouring the raw video into the Mac through media converter, editing in iMovie, and then pouring the finished movie back out to your camcorder. The double signal conversion to and from DV format means you won't get the same heart-stopping color fidelity and picture quality, but you'll still be in the game for less than half the cost of a new DV camcorder.

Figure 4-11:
It's not fancy, but the Director's Cut box is a better value than Sony's Media Converter. For example, it requires no external power; it draws its juice from the Mac, via FireWire cable. It also offers double sets of inputs and outputs, so you can keep your TV and VCR hooked up simultaneously.

Approach 4: Use a Recent Sony Camcorder

All of Sony's current DV and Digital8 camcorders offer a spectacular solution to the "old tapes" problem: analog-to-digital *passthrough* conversion. In other words, the camcorder itself acts as one of the media converters described above. The footage never hits a DV tape; instead, it simply plays from your older VCR or camcorder directly into the Macintosh. (The models offering this feature are the TRV-11, TRV-20, TRV-900, PC5, PC100, and VX2000, plus the Digital8 models—the TRV-120, 320, 520, 525, 720, and 820.)

If you've got a drawer full of older tapes, such a camcorder is by far the most elegant and economical route, especially if you're shopping for a new camcorder anyway.

Building the Movie

W hether on your Mac or in a multimillion-dollar Hollywood professional studio, film editing boils down to three tiny tasks: selecting, trimming, and rearranging *clips.*

Of course, that's like saying that there's nothing more to painting than mixing various amounts of red, yellow, and blue. The art of video editing lies in your decisions about *which* clips you select, *how* you trim them, and which order you put them in.

At its simplest, iMovie editing works like this:

1. **Trim your clips until they contain exactly the footage you want.**

2. **Drag your clips from the Shelf to the Clip Viewer, where iMovie plays them in one seamless pass, from left to right.**

3. **Rearrange the scenes by dragging them around on the Clip Viewer (or its alter ego, the Timeline).**

4. **Add crossfades, titles (credits), effects, music, and sound effects.**

This chapter is dedicated to showing you the mechanics of the first three tasks. The following chapters cover the fourth step, and Chapter 10 offers tips for adding taste and artistry to these proceedings.

Navigating Your Clips

As you're building your movie, you can store your clips in either of two places: the Shelf or the strip at the bottom of the window. You put clips on the Shelf before deciding what to do with them, and drag them down to the storyboard area once you've decided where they fit into your movie.

This clip-assembly area at the bottom of the iMovie 2 screen can appear in either of two ways, depending on which of the two tabs you click (the eyeball or the clock):

- **Clip Viewer.** In this view, which should seem familiar if you've used iMovie 1, each clip appears as an icon, as though it's a slide on a slide viewer. Each is sized identically, even if one is eight minutes long and the next is only two seconds.

- **Timeline.** This view also shows a linear map of your movie. But in this case, each clip is represented by a horizontal bar that's as wide as the clip is long. Short clips have short bars; long clips stretch across your screen. Parallel bars below the clips indicate the sound tracks playing simultaneously.

Note: You can read much more about these two all-important views of your work at the end of this chapter. It's important now, however, to note that Apple hasn't given a name to this bottom-of-your-screen area as a *whole*. To prevent you from having to read about the "Clip Viewer/Timeline area" 47 times per chapter, this book uses the made-up term *Movie Track* to refer to this editing track, regardless of which view it's showing.

You can do several things to a clip, whether it's on the Shelf or the Movie Track:

Select It

When you click a clip—the picture, not the name—iMovie highlights it by making its border (the "cardboard" portion of the "slide") or its bar (in the Timeline) yellow. The first frame of the selected clip appears in the Monitor window. (If you're in Camera Mode at the time, busily controlling your camcorder by clicking the playback controls, iMovie immediately switches back into Edit Mode. The camcorder stops automatically.)

Once you've highlighted a clip (whether in the Shelf or the Movie Track), you get to see some very useful statistics about it, such as its name, duration, and, surprisingly enough, the date and time you originally filmed it. To see this information, study the top edge of the Movie Track, as shown in Figure 5-1.

Figure 5-1:
Thanks to the automatic date-stamping feature built into every DV camcorder, you even see the date and time a highlighted clip was originally recorded.

And to *de*select a clip (all clips, in fact), choose Edit→Select None (⌘-D, a keystroke familiar to Photoshop users). Alternatively, click anywhere *except* on a clip (such as on the striped iMovie background), or Shift-click the first or last in a series of highlighted clips.

Knowing how to deselect your clips will save you frustration; when several clips are highlighted in the Shelf, the entire *movie* plays back when you press the Space bar, which isn't always what you want.

Select Several

You can highlight several clips simultaneously using exactly the same techniques you'd use to select several desktop icons: either by Shift-clicking the ones you want or, if they're on the Shelf, by *drag-selecting* them. This technique involves positioning the cursor in the gray striped area between clips and dragging diagonally over the clips you want to select. As you drag, you create a dotted-line selection rectangle. Any clips touched by, or inside, this rectangle become highlighted.

After selecting several clips in this way, you can drag any *one* of them to the Movie Track, the Project Trash, or to another part of the Shelf; all others go along for the ride. You can also use the Cut, Copy, or Clear commands in the Edit menu to affect all of them at once.

Tip: Whenever you've selected more than one clip (either in the Shelf or the Movie Track), iMovie adds up their running times and displays the total at the top edge of the Movie Track in the "seconds:frames" format. It says, for example, "<Multiple> Time: 12:01."

Figure 5-2:
While a clip plays, the Playhead (the down-pointing triangle) slides across the Scrubber Bar. If you can catch it, you can drag the Playhead using the mouse, thus jumping around in the movie. Or you can simply click anywhere in the Scrubber Bar. Either way, the playback continues at the new spot in the clip.

Play It

You can play a highlighted clip in the Monitor window by pressing the Space bar (or clicking the Play button underneath the Monitor window).

You can stop the playback very easily: Press the Space bar a second time, or click anywhere else on the screen—on another clip, another control, the Monitor window, the striped iMovie background, and so on.

Jump Around in It

Whether the clip is playing or not, you can jump instantly to any other part of the clip in one of two ways:

- Drag the Playhead handle to any other part of the Scrubber bar (see Figure 5-2).
- Click directly in the Scrubber bar to jump to a particular spot in the footage. Doing so while the movie is playing saves you the difficulty of trying to grab the tiny Playhead as it moves across the screen.

Tip: To play back a section repeatedly for analysis, just keep clicking at the same spot in the Scrubber bar while the clip plays.

FREQUENTLY ASKED QUESTION

The Little Ruler Lines

When I click a clip, I see little tick marks under the Scrubber Bar. But I'll be darned if I can figure out what they represent. Not frames, not seconds…What are they?

If your clip is longer than 2 seconds, 20 frames (at low monitor resolution) or 4 seconds, 3 frames (at high resolution), you have a right to be bewildered. As it turns out, iMovie can only cram so many tick marks into the length of that Scrubber Bar—80 tick marks at 800 x 600 resolution, 123 tick marks at 1024 x 768. (Figure 5-2 shows these

tick marks.) In longer clips, therefore, the tick marks represent nothing.

When the clip gets shorter, however, the tick marks become more meaningful. At below 2:20 (low resolution) or 4:03 (high resolution), each tick mark represents one frame. Pressing the right or left arrow key makes the Playhead jump from one tick mark to the next—one frame to the next—which gives you much more precision in trimming or splitting your clips.

Step Through It

By pressing the right and left arrow keys, you can view your clip one frame at a time, as though you're watching the world's least interesting slide show. Hold down these arrow keys steadily to make the frame-by-frame parade go by faster.

Adding the Shift key to your arrow-key presses is often more useful—it lets you jump *ten* frames at a time. In time, you can get extremely good at finding an exact frame in a particular piece of footage just by mastering the arrow-key and Shift-arrow-key shortcuts. (These shortcuts work only when the clip isn't playing.)

Note: to iMovie veterans: In iMovie 2, you can arrow-key-step all the way to the last frame of a clip. iMovie no longer stops at the second-to-last frame, as it did in iMovie 1.

Scan Through It

The Rewind and Fast Forward buttons let you zoom through your footage faster, just as they do when you're controlling your camcorder. Click once to start, again to stop. But when you're playing footage you've already imported, these buttons offer some extra features.

For example, you don't have to click Play first. The Rewind and Fast Forward buttons start your clip playing at double speed even from a dead stop.

The keyboard shortcuts ⌘-left bracket and ⌘-right bracket (the [and] keys) have the same function as clicking the Rewind and Fast Forward buttons. Here again, press the keystroke once to start, a second time to stop.

Note: The Rewind and Fast Forward buttons, and their related keystrokes, are no longer *variable-speed* functions. In iMovie 1, the more times you clicked them, the faster iMovie sped through your footage; in iMovie 2, you get a single speed.

Rename It

When iMovie imports your clips, it gives them such creative names as *Clip 01, Clip 02,* and so on. Fortunately, renaming a clip on the Shelf or Clip Viewer is very easy; just click directly on its name ("Clip 11") to highlight it, and then type the new name. All the usual Macintosh editing techniques work inside this little highlighted renaming rectangle, including the Delete key and the Cut, Copy, Paste, and Select All commands in the Edit menu.

You can also rename a clip by double-clicking its icon. The Clip Info dialog box appears (see Figure 4-10), where you can edit the name. This is the *only* way to change a clip's name in the Timeline Viewer, by the way.

You have much more flexibility when naming clips than when you name Macintosh file icons. An iMovie clip's name can be 127 letters and spaces long. Be aware, however, that only about the first eleven letters of it actually show up under the clip icon. (The easiest way to see the whole clip name is to double-click the clip icon—and then to drag your cursor through the Name field in the resulting dialog box.)

The clip renaming you do in iMovie doesn't affect the names of the files in your project's Media folder on the hard drive (see page 108). Files there remain forever with their original names: Clip 01, Clip 02, and so on. That's why, in times of troubleshooting or file administration, the Clip Info box that appears when you double-click a clip can be especially useful. It's the only way to find out how a clip that you've renamed in iMovie corresponds to a matching clip on your hard drive.

Tip: Because you can only see the first few letters of a clip's name when it's on the Shelf, adopt clever naming conventions to help you remember what's in each clip. Use prefix codes like CU (for "close-up"), ES ("establishing shot"), MS ("medium shot"), WS ("wide shot"), and so on, followed by useful keywords ("wild laughter," "sad melon," and so on). If the clip contains recorded speech, clue yourself in by including a quotation as part of the clip's name.

Reorganize It

You can drag clips from cubbyhole to empty cubbyhole on the Shelf. Doing so not only helps you organize the clips in your head before committing them to the Movie Track, but it also affects the order in which they appear on the Movie Track if you drag several simultaneously, as explained later in this chapter.

The freedom to drag clips around in the Shelf offers you a miniature storyboard feature. That is, you can construct a *sequence* by arranging several clips in the Shelf. When they seem to be in a good order for your finished scene, drag the whole batch to the Movie Track at once.

If the Shelf appears full or mostly full, don't worry; you can install a clip onto the Shelf even if you don't see any empty cubbyholes. Drag and drop a clip (or even a mass of highlighted clips) anywhere on the Shelf, even onto an occupied cubbyhole. iMovie automatically creates enough new cubbyholes to hold them all.

Put It in the Project Trash Can

You can get rid of a clip by dragging it directly onto the project Trash icon (see Figure 4-4).

At first glance, you might assume that this Trash works like the standard Mac Trash. After all, the icon looks similar, and there's an Empty Trash command in the File menu.

In fact, the project Trash is different in a number of ways. It doesn't bulge when something's in it, and you can't double-click it to open a window revealing its contents. Furthermore, the MB counter underneath tells you exactly how much footage is inside.

You're entitled to wonder, however: if you can't open the project Trash window, and therefore can't retrieve the footage inside, what good is it?

The answer is that the Trash can is primarily intended to serve as a mechanism that lets you delay committing to your editing decisions. There are several ways to recover the footage in the Trash after deleting or cropping clips: quit iMovie without saving changes, using the Advanced→Restore Clip Media command (see page 122), or pasting something you've cut.

The Trash is also the key to iMovie's ten-level Undo command. Whenever you delete some footage (either by dragging a clip to the Trash can or by using one of the trimming commands, described later in this chapter), iMovie stores it in this Trash can. Then, if you decide to use the Undo command, even ten times in a row, iMovie will be able to restore the footage you had cut—by pulling it, behind the scenes, out of the project Trash.

That's why, whenever you choose File→Empty Trash, you *lose* your ability to undo the last ten steps you took. (And why would you ever choose File→Empty Trash, especially when doing so can take several long minutes? Under one circumstance only: when you need more disk space, such as when you want to import more footage from the camcorder.)

The Trash is also the key to the Advanced→Restore Clip Media command. As described on page 122, this command lets you restore a clip to its freshly dumped-from-the-camcorder condition, the way it was before you chopped it up or trimmed it down. As long as you haven't emptied the Trash, this command remains at your disposal.

Tip: As you work in iMovie, remember to choose File→Save (or press ⌘-S) frequently, just as you would with any kind of document. iMovie is an extremely stable program, but things happen. Fortunately, saving in iMovie is instantaneous; it doesn't require the long, disk-intensive wait that you might expect from a video-editing program. You're saving only your Project file, and not making any changes to the large, underlying DV files in your Media folder.

FREQUENTLY ASKED QUESTION

Time for Emptying the Trash

Sometimes the Trash seems to empty really quickly. Other times, it takes forever. What's up with that?

This one's technical, but good.

Behind the scenes, a computer knows where each file begins as it lies on your hard drive's surface. It knows where the *end* of each file is, however, only by measuring a certain distance from the *beginning*.

If you've chopped off the *end* of a clip, therefore, iMovie needs only a fraction of a second to empty the Project Trash. All the Mac has to do is adjust its internal file pointers to remove the end of the file, even if you've cut a few gigabytes of information.

But if you cut just *one frame* off the beginning of a clip,

emptying the Project Trash makes the Mac *copy* all of the remaining frames, shifting them toward the beginning of the file, to fill up the hole you created.

That's why you can crop 300 MB off the end of a clip and the Trash empties very quickly; but editing just one 120 K frame off the beginning may make the Mac copy up to 2 GB of data, which can take several minutes.

The time estimate iMovie shows you when emptying the Trash is fairly accurate. The program computes it by adding up the amount of data that will have to be moved. Its calculations assume that your hard drive can transfer 3.6 MB per second—a fairly conservative assumption. If your disk is faster than that, your Project Trash will empty faster than the estimate indicates.

Three Ways to Trim a Clip

Most of the time, you'll want to trim out the deadwood from your clips before you put them onto the Movie Track, so that you're left with only the very best shots from the very best scenes. This process is the heart of iMovie—and of video editing.

Tip: All of the techniques described in this section are what digital video editors call *destructive* ones—each technique chops up pieces of footage. If, just after performing one of these trimming techniques, you tap the Space bar and discover, during the playback, that you trimmed the wrong thing, choose Edit→Undo to restore the clip as it was before your trim.

And if even the Undo command (or ten Undo commands in a row) can't restore the clip to its original condition, you can always highlight the chopped-up clip using the Restore Clip Media command described on page 122.

POWER USERS' CLINIC

Beyond Undo: Restore Clip Media

As programs go, iMovie is a forgiving one. Not only does it have an Undo command—it's a *ten-step* Undo command, meaning that you can undo the last ten editing steps you took. (The Undo command can even unimport a clip from your camcorder.)

Still, a ten-level Undo isn't always ideal. If you made a mistake eight steps ago, you can undo that step, but only by undoing the seven successful editing steps you took thereafter.

The new Advanced→Restore Clip Media command can be perfect in such situations. Remember that every time you cut or crop a clip, iMovie doesn't actually disturb the clip itself—the file on your hard drive. Instead, it simply shifts around its own internal *pointers* to the portion of the clip that you want to use. As a result, it's a piece of cake for iMovie to say, "Oh, you want me to throw away those pointers and give you back the original clip as it came from the camcorder? No problem."

In the iMovie 2 era of slow motion, fast motion, and reverse motion clips, the Restore Clip Media command gives you a convenient safety net, a chance to start with a clean slate on a clip-by-clip basis.

When you use the command, iMovie displays a dialog box that lets you know what's about to happen, as shown here. If you click Restore, iMovie returns the clip to its original, precut, precrop condition, even if you've already placed it into the Movie Track. In that case, the clip's bar in the

Timeline Viewer grows correspondingly wider, shoving other clips to the right to make room.

Note that if you've emptied the Project Trash, as described on page 120, forget it—both the ten-level Undo and the Restore Clip Media command are unavailable. (Emptying the Project Trash empties iMovie's Undo and Restore Clip Media memory.)

That's why some iMovie veterans are in the habit of duplicating clips before trimming and splitting them. After clicking a clip in either the Shelf or the Movie Track, choose Edit→Copy, followed immediately by Edit→Paste; you'll see a perfect duplicate of the clip appear.

When you do so, you're not actually duplicating any files on your hard drive; copying and pasting clips doesn't eat away at your remaining free space. Even if you whittle away at one of these copies by trimming it or splitting it, your original is safe in its full-length, freshly imported condition. If it turns out that you trimmed too much of your clip, you can return to the copy—your backup—without sacrificing the other editing work you've done since you made the copy.

If you decide to adopt this technique, be prepared for one other twist: As you cut or crop footage, your Project Trash will always remain empty. That's because any frames you're cutting from one clip are still required by the other clip, so iMovie can't afford to put anything into the Trash in readiness for permanent deletion.

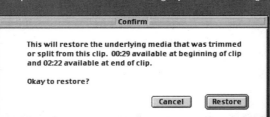

Confirm

This will restore the underlying media that was trimmed or split from this clip. 00:29 available at beginning of clip and 02:22 available at end of clip.

Okay to restore?

[Cancel] [Restore]

Highlighting Footage in iMovie 2

Unlike the expensive big-gun DV editing programs, iMovie works just like other Mac programs: You highlight some footage, then use the Cut, Copy, or Paste commands to move it around. All three of the footage-trimming techniques described in this chapter, for example, begin with *highlighting,* or selecting, a portion of your footage; here's how you go about it.

1. **Click a clip to select it.**

   The clip can be either in the Shelf or the Movie Track.

2. **Position your cursor just underneath the tick marks of the Scrubber bar, as shown in Figure 5-3.**

   If you've done it right, the ghosts of two triangle handles appear, side-by-side. As you move your cursor horizontally without clicking, homing in on the beginning trim point, the ghost handles follow it around.

Figure 5-3:
Top: When you point just underneath the Scrubber bar, two faint, transparent triangular handles appear face-to-face.

Bottom: Carefully drag horizontally until they enclose only the scene you want to keep. Finally, when you choose the Edit→Crop command, everything outside of these handles is trimmed away and put into the project Trash.

3. **Drag horizontally until the triangle handles surround the footage you want to keep.**

   As soon as you push the mouse button down, the ghost handles become real triangle handles. One remains where you clicked; the other follows your cursor as you drag.

   The Monitor window behaves as though you're scrolling the movie, so that you can see where you are as you drag the movable triangle. Also as you drag, the portion of the Scrubber bar between your handles turns yellow to show that it's highlighted. Whatever Edit menu command you use now (such as Cut, Copy, Clear, or Crop) affects only the yellow portion.

After you've just dragged or clicked a handle, the arrow-key skills you picked up on page 118 come in extremely handy. You can let go of the mouse and, just by pressing the left and right arrow keys, fine-tune the position of the triangle handle on a frame-by-frame basis. (You can tell which triangle handle you'll be moving. It's the one marked by the Playhead, as shown in Figure 5-3. To move the *other* triangle handle, click it first.) Continue tapping the left and right arrow keys until the Monitor shows the precise frame you want—the first or last frame you'll want to keep in the clip.

Remember, too, that if you press *Shift*-right or -left arrow, you move the triangle handle ten frames at a time. Between the ten-frame and one-frame keystrokes, you should find it fairly easy to home in on the exact frame where you want to trim the clip.

Tip: After you've highlighted a stretch of the Scrubber bar, you can *extend* the selected portion just by dragging again beneath any un-highlighted portion of the Scrubber bar (to the right or left of the selected region). Conversely, you can drag beneath the highlighted portion to make the selection *smaller*. Either way, the end of the yellow bar jumps to your cursor as though attracted by a magnet. And either way, you avoid having to redo the entire selection; one of your two endpoints remains in place.

Simply clicking doesn't do the trick; your mouse must actually move to make the yellow bar grow or shrink.

WORKAROUND WORKSHOP

Chasing the Elusive Ghost Handles

If you're used to editing in iMovie 1, the ghost handles are something new. It's easy to see why Apple made the change; in the olden days, most people clicked once to make the handles appear, then again to drag the handles apart. In iMovie 2, a single click-and-drag does the trick.

That's all well and good—*if* you can get the ghost handles to appear at all. Unfortunately, they have a tendency to vanish, and you may find yourself frustrated at your inability to make them appear.

The secret: The ghost handles vanish whenever your arrow cursor *touches the Scrubber bar from below.* When that happens, iMovie assumes that you don't intend to do any cropping at all—that instead, you simply intend to click in the Scrubber bar to move the Playhead—and it politely

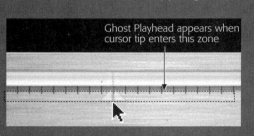

Ghost Playhead appears when cursor tip enters this zone

hides the ghost handles to get them out of your way.

Once the ghost handles disappear, you can't bring them back by putting the cursor back below the Scrubber bar. You must start over again, moving your cursor well clear of the Scrubber bar—clear up into the Monitor window, for example—and then back down to the handle area. Only then do the ghost handles reappear.

On the other hand, you can highlight footage even when the ghost handles have disappeared—if you know where to click. Be sure to drag *under* the tick marks, not on them. If your cursor ventures even more than slightly into the tick-mark zone, you'll simply drag the Playhead instead of highlighting anything. To highlight footage, the tip of the cursor must fall in the area shown by the dotted lines in this illustration.

As you drag the triangle handles, a special readout appears on the top edge of the Movie Track that identifies the clip you're editing and, more importantly, the amount of footage between the handles. It might say, for example, "**Clip Selection:** Judy Laughing, **Time:** 02:15" (which means two seconds, fifteen frames).

Being able to see exactly how much footage you're about to cut (or preserve) can be extremely useful when the timing of your movie is important, as when editing it to accompany a music track or when creating a movie that must be, for example, exactly 30 seconds long.

Snipping Off One End of a Clip

Having mastered the art of selecting a portion of a clip, as described in the previous section, you're ready to put it to work. Suppose, for example, that you want to shave off some footage from only one end of your clip:

1. **Highlight the footage you want to delete (at the beginning or end of the Scrubber bar).**

    The arrangement should look like Figure 5-4.

Tip: There's a quick trick for highlighting the beginning or end of a clip. Start by positioning the Playhead at the spot where you'd like the selection to start (or end). Then just Shift-click at the beginning (or end) of the clip.

This Shift-click doesn't have to be very precise; it can even be directly to the right or left of the Scrubber bar itself (it doesn't have to be under the tick marks). Instantly, iMovie highlights everything from the Playhead to the end you clicked.

---

2. **Choose Edit→Cut.**

    iMovie promptly trims away whatever was highlighted between the triangles. As a bonus, your invisible Clipboard now contains the snipped piece, which you're

Figure 5-4:
To trim footage from one end of the clip, just highlight that much, using the triangle handles. The Monitor window shows you where you are in the footage as you drag the triangles. And once again, you can use the arrow keys to fine-tune the position of the triangle you've most recently clicked.

welcome to paste right back into the Shelf or Movie Track using the Edit→Paste command, in case you might need it again.

Tip: You can also press the Delete key, or choose Edit→Clear, to perform exactly the same function as Edit→Cut. The difference is that the Delete key and Clear command don't put the cut material onto your invisible Clipboard, ready for pasting, as the Cut command does. Similarly, the Delete/Clear command doesn't replace what's *already* on the Clipboard, unlike the Cut command.

Cropping Out the Ends of a Clip

If you want to trim some footage off of *both* ends of a clip, you may prefer to begin by highlighting the part in the middle that you want to *keep:*

1. **Select the footage you want to keep.**

   Use any of the techniques described on page 123.

2. **Choose Edit→Crop (or press ⌘-K).**

   When you use this command, all of your signposts disappear, including the two triangle handles and the yellow part of the Scrubber bar. What used to be the yellow part of the Scrubber bar has now, in effect, expanded to fill the *entire* Scrubber bar. Your clip is shorter now, as a tap on the Space bar will prove to you.

Note: After you use the Crop command, the MB number underneath your project Trash icon usually increases. That's because, behind the scenes, iMovie hasn't actually thrown away the footage pieces you've just carved off. It's hanging onto them in case you decide to use the Edit→Undo command or the Advanced→Restore Clip Media command.

Chopping Out the Middle of a Clip

In this technique, you *eliminate* the middle part of a clip, leaving only the ends of it in your project.

At first, you might not expect to encounter this situation very often, but in time, you might be surprised. The flexibility offered by this technique means that you can be less fussy when you're importing clips. You can import longer chunks of footage, for example, secure in the knowledge that you can always hack out the boring stuff that happens to fall in between two priceless moments.

1. **Select the footage you want to delete.**

   Again, you can use any of the tricks described on page 123.

2. **Choose Edit→Cut (or Edit→Clear), or press the Delete key.**

   If you're not prepared for it, the results of this technique can be startling—and yet it's perfectly logical. If you cut a chunk out of the middle of the clip, iMovie has no choice but to throw back at you the *two end pieces*—as two separate clips, side-by-side on the Shelf or the Movie Track.

Either way, the name of the newly created clip will help you identify it. If the original clip was called "Cut Me Out," the new, split-off clip is called "Cut Me Out/1."

Tip: Whenever you cut material out of a clip, iMovie stores the cut material in the Project Trash can—at least for a while. See "Put It in the Project Trash Can," earlier in this chapter, for details. Now you know why the MB counter underneath the Trash can goes up every time you cut footage from a clip.

Splitting a Clip

The techniques described in the previous section work well when you want to re-move some footage from a clip. Sometimes, however, it can be useful to split a clip into two separate clips *without* deleting footage in the process. For example, suppose you want the title of your movie to appear five seconds into a certain piece of footage. In iMovie, the only way to accomplish that feat is to split the clip into three pieces—the first one five seconds long—and put the title credit on the middle piece. (More on titles in Chapter 7.)

Figure 5-5:
After you split a clip, iMovie cuts your clip in two (Scrubber bar, top) and highlights both of the resulting clip icons (Clip Viewer, bottom). If the clip started out in the Movie Track, the Monitor window still lets you scroll all the way through the original clip. Only the telltale cut mark on the Scrubber bar lets you know that you're actually looking at two different clips side-by-side.

The Split Clip at Playhead command is exactly what you need for these situations.

1. **Click the clip to select it, whether in the Shelf or the Movie Track.**

   This time, you'll click above the Scrubber bar, not below it.

2. **Drag the Playhead along the top of the Scrubber bar until you find the spot where you want to split the clip.**

   You can press the right or left arrow keys to nudge the Playhead one frame at a time to the right or left (or Shift-arrow keys for *ten*-frame jumps).

3. **Choose Edit→Split Clip at Playhead (or press ⌘-T).**

   As shown in Figure 5-5, you wind up with two different clips, both highlighted. If the original was called "Split Me Up," iMovie calls the resultant clips "Split Me Up" and "Split Me Up/1." (To remove the highlighting, click anywhere else on the screen, or choose Edit→Select None.)

The Movie Track: Your Storyboard

When you're not trimming or splitting your clips, most of your iMovie time will be spent in the Movie Track—the horizontal strip at the bottom of the screen (see Figure 5-6). The idea is that you'll drag the edited clips out of the Shelf and into the correct order on the Movie Track, exactly as though you're building a storyboard or timeline.

As noted at the beginning of this chapter, the Movie Track offers two different views: the Clip Viewer and the Timeline Viewer. Both are illustrated in Figure 5-6.

Note: The following discussion covers the *mechanics* of using the Movie Track. See Chapter 10 for an overview of the *artistic* elements of film and video editing.

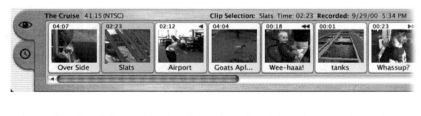

Figure 5-6:
Top: When you click the eyeball "tab" at the left edge, you see your camcorder footage.

Bottom: Click the clock icon to see the Timeline Viewer, which reveals your audio tracks (Chapter 8).

But you shouldn't consider your Movie Track arrangement cut in stone; in the Clip Viewer, you can freely rearrange clips by dragging them horizontally. Moreover, you can freely drag clips back and forth between the Shelf and the Clip Viewer. (You can drag clips into the Timeline Viewer, too, but not out again.)

Readouts in the Movie Track

iMovie doesn't use standard Macintosh windows, and it therefore has no standard title bar where, in any normal program, you'd see the name of your document.

Instead, iMovie identifies the name of your movie in bold type at the upper-left edge of the Movie Track (see Figure 5-6). There you'll also find a Time display that shows the total running time of the video.

Dragging in the Movie Track

There's not much to using the Movie Track—just drag a clip from the Shelf directly onto it. For your visual pleasure, iMovie shows you a ghosted, translucent image of the clip's first frame as you drag. Here are a few tips for making the most of this Shelf-to-Movie-Track procedure:

- If you want your former Shelf clip placed at the *end* of the clips in the Movie Track, drop it in the grayish empty area off to the right. If you want to put it *between* two clips on the Movie Track, drag your cursor between those clips, and watch as iMovie makes room by shoving existing clips to the right.

- You can also drag clips from the Clip Viewer *back* onto the Shelf. You can take advantage of this feature whenever you decide that a sequence of clips isn't quite working, and you're going to postpone placing them into the movie.

Tip: Even though you can't drag clips from the Timeline Viewer to the Shelf, you can achieve the same effect by cutting and pasting them.)

- In the Clip Viewer, you can rearrange clips by dragging their icons horizontally. Once again, iMovie makes room between existing clips when your cursor passes between them.

- In the Timeline Viewer, you can drag a clip only one way: to the right. When you do so, iMovie creates a pure black "clip," as described on page 134.

Dragging Several Clips Simultaneously

You don't have to drag one clip at a time; it's often more efficient to drag several clips simultaneously. For example, you might arrange several clips on your Shelf into a mini-sequence that you then drop into your Clip Viewer as a unit.

To highlight several clips in your Shelf, press Shift as you click them in sequence, or drag-select them, as described earlier in this chapter. Each sprouts a yellow border to indicate that it's been selected. Now drag any *one* of them; the others go along for the ride.

iMovie places the multiple selection on the Movie Track as a series of consecutive clips, but you may wonder how it determines the order in which they appear. It's not alphabetical, in length order, or even the order in which you selected them. Instead, iMovie matches the order in which they appeared on the *Shelf,* working from upper-left to lower-right.

You can drag multiple clips simultaneously from the Clip Viewer back up to the Shelf, too, but you have less flexibility. You can't select, for example, clips 1, 3, and 5; you can highlight only clips that sit next to each other on the Clip Viewer.

On the other hand, highlighting them for transport takes less effort: Just click the first one in the chain, and then Shift-click the last one. The two you clicked, and all the clips between them, are now all highlighted. (You can't Shift-click a clip to re-move it from the selection, as you can when working with the Shelf. Instead, to change your selection, you must de-select all of the clips—by choosing Edit→Select None, for example—and then build your selection again.)

Finally, drag any one of them up to the Shelf.

Tip: As you're building your film on the Movie Track, think in terms of *sequences* of shots. By Shift-clicking, you can select, say, six or seven clips that constitute one finished sequence, and drag it (or cut-and-paste it) into a new location in the Movie Track to suit your artistic intentions.

Copying and Pasting Clips

Dragging isn't the only way to move footage around in iMovie; the Copy, Cut, and Paste commands are sometimes more convenient, if only because they let you work from the keyboard instead of having to use the mouse.

For example, you can move a clip from the Shelf to the Clip Viewer by clicking it, pressing ⌘-X, clicking the Clip Viewer, and then pressing ⌘-V. (You can also *copy* the clip by beginning that sequence with ⌘-C instead.) You can move clips around within the Movie Track in the same way.

Tip: In a word processor, pasting can be dangerous: If you're not careful, pasting might *replace* some text that's already in the document. In iMovie, you have no such worries. Pasting *never* pastes over anything; it only inserts new clips.

You may wonder how you're supposed to know where your cut or copied footage will appear when pasted. Unlike a word processor, there's no blinking insertion point to tell you.

The scheme is actually fairly simple:

- If there's a *highlighted clip* in the Shelf, the pasted clips appear in the Shelf. They occupy the first available cubbyholes (as "read" from top left, across each row). If you want to paste into the Shelf, in other words, click a clip there first.

- If there's a highlighted clip in the Clip Viewer or Timeline Viewer, the pasted clip or clips appear *just to the right* of it. Here again, therefore, it's a good idea to click a Movie Track clip before pasting to show iMovie *where* to paste.

- If no clip is highlighted anywhere, iMovie pastes the cut or copied clips in the Movie Track, just to the right of whichever clip contains the Playhead.

Playing Clips Backward

When you hear that iMovie 2 can play clips backward, you might assume that this feature is a gimmick that's primarily useful for applying to footage of people jumping into swimming pools or jumping off of walls. To be sure, iMovie 2 does a great job at creating these comic effects, even if their novelty does wear off quickly.

But in adding reverse motion to iMovie's bag of tricks, Apple gave the serious filmmaker an important new tool that can be used in much less obvious situations—cases where your original footage needs some help. For example, you can use this feature to create a zoom out when all you'd filmed was a zoom in, or a pan to the right when you'd shot a pan to the left. You can make your star's head look away from the camera instead of toward it. Even reversing the playback of a slow-motion eye blink can make all the difference in the emotional impact of a certain shot.

To make a clip play backwards, select it (anywhere—Shelf, Clip Viewer, or Timeline Viewer). Choose Advanced→Reverse Clip Direction (or press ⌘-R).

WORKAROUND WORKSHOP

Fast, Slow, Reverse Motion—and Transitions

If you change a clip's speed or direction, as described on these pages, iMovie doesn't bat an eye. In fact, it creates these effects instantaneously, without making you wait for any kind of rendering or processing.

If you've already placed the clip into the Movie Track and added transitions (see Chapter 6), however, the dialog box shown here pops up every time you change a clip's speed or direction.

> That operation will invalidate one or more transitions. Do you want to re-render with the existing settings?
>
> ☐ Don't Ask Again   [Cancel]   [OK]

The point is clear: The crossfade into the next (or previous) clip will have to be updated, too. Otherwise, it won't match the clip's new speed or direction.

Unfortunately, this dialog box doesn't give you much of a

choice. If you click OK, iMovie proceeds to re-render the transition. If you click Cancel, iMovie ignores your request to change the clip's speed or direction. If you turn on Don't Ask Again, then iMovie will, henceforth, *always* re-render affected transitions when you adjust a clip's speed or direction, without showing the dialog box pictured here.

None of these options, in other words, means "Please change the clip's speed or direction, but don't worry about the transition; just get rid of it." If that's what you want, do it manually by clicking Cancel, clicking the transition icon, deleting it (page 148), and then adjusting the clip's speed or direction all over again.

The video in a reverse-motion clip plays back beautifully; even the audio gets reversed, offering hours of fun to people who look for secret messages in Beatles albums. (Of course, you can always turn off the clip's sound, if that backward-audio effect isn't what you want; see page 210.)

In fact, if you apply the Reverse Clip Direction command to several highlighted clips (or the whole movie!) at once, iMovie is smart enough to reverse the clips *and* reorder them, so the segment of the movie you've selected still plays in the correct sequence.

To help you remember that you've reversed a clip, iMovie stamps it with a left-pointing arrow, as shown in Figure 5-8.

ON LOCATION

The Secret of Time-Lapse Video

You can see iMovie: The Missing Manual *reader Pat McCourt's homemade—and very effective—attempt at time-lapse photography at the results at* http://homepage.mac.com/patrickmccourt/iMovieTheater1.html. *Here's how he did it:*

It probably goes without saying, but you need a tripod to do time-lapse video. You could rest your camera on a solid surface and hope for the best, but even the slightest movement of the camera might ruin the ultimate result. It's also worth mentioning that you should set up where people won't be walking in front of the camera. In my "Half Dome Sunset" movie, I thought it might be interesting to see the heads of tourists, scurrying back and forth in the foreground, so I included them on purpose. (To protect my setup, I made a "Do not touch" sign and hovered nervously near the tripod. Even so, at one point, a kid actually crouched in front of the camera for a second, but the result is not as disastrous as I thought it would be.)

To capture my footage, I simply set the camera up on the tripod, composed the shot and pressed the red button. My camera is a Sony Digital8 model; it uses Hi-8 tapes with a one-hour capacity, so I got about an hour's worth of video.

Back home, I set about the task of distilling this 60 minutes of footage down to one minute. My first attempts, using iMovie 1, went nowhere fast. I had thought it might not be too difficult to delete all but one frame in sixty, but boy, was I wrong.

So I downloaded iMovie 2, intending to use its clip-speed control. The maximum length of an iMovie clip is about 9 minutes and 28 seconds, so I wound up with seven clips from my hour of footage. As it turns out, the ratio of the fastest setting on the speed control is 6 to 1. So it would take three rounds of acceleration to bring the movie in under a minute (60/6=10; 10/6=1.66; 1.66/6=0.28).

I sped up each clip, exported it to tape, and then reimported the faster version—and repeated the process. When I had done this three times to all seven clips, the resulting film was shorter than I had hoped (about 30 seconds). I considered slowing it to the desired one-minute duration using the speed control, but it then occurred to me that I might be losing frames in the process of slowing down the shortened clips.

So I went back to the previous generation of clips and sped them up them one notch less than I had on the other passes. This yielded the one-minute movie I was looking for.

After that, it was a simple matter to add titles and music. Ever since, as a kid, I saw the time-lapse sequence of a blooming flower on the opening credits of the *Wonderful World of Disney,* I've harbored a keen interest in time-lapse images. Now, thanks to iMovie, I can make my own time-lapse movies; I'm happy to say that it's easy and fun.

Tip: If you need to crop a reversed clip, first un-reverse it (by choosing Advanced→Reverse Clip Direction a second time). A bug in iMovie 2.0.1 makes the Edit→Crop command crop the clip as though it *weren't* reversed, meaning that the material you've selected with the crop handles *isn't* the material you'll get after the crop. Un-reversing the clip, cropping, and then re-reversing it solves the problem.

Tricks of the Timeline Viewer

Everything you've read in the preceding pages has to do with the Movie Track in general; most of the features described so far are available in either of the Movie Track's incarnations—the Clip Viewer or the Timeline Viewer.

In iMovie 2, however, the Timeline Viewer is more than just another pretty interface. It's far more useful (and complex) than the Clip Viewer.

Many of the Timeline's super powers have to do with audio. Sound tracks, narration, music tracks, and sound effects all appear here as horizontal colored bars that play simultaneously with your video. You can read about these features in Chapter 8.

Some of the Timeline's features, however, are useful for everyday video editing—that is, if you consider playing footage in slow motion or fast motion everyday effects.

Figure 5-7:
Top: The Views tab of the Preferences dialog box, which contains the on/off switches for thumbnails and "details."

Bottom: Four arrangements of the same Timeline: The standard display, where a thumbnail frame identifies each clip; the barren no-thumbnails look; no thumbnails, but details turned on; and thumbnails with details.

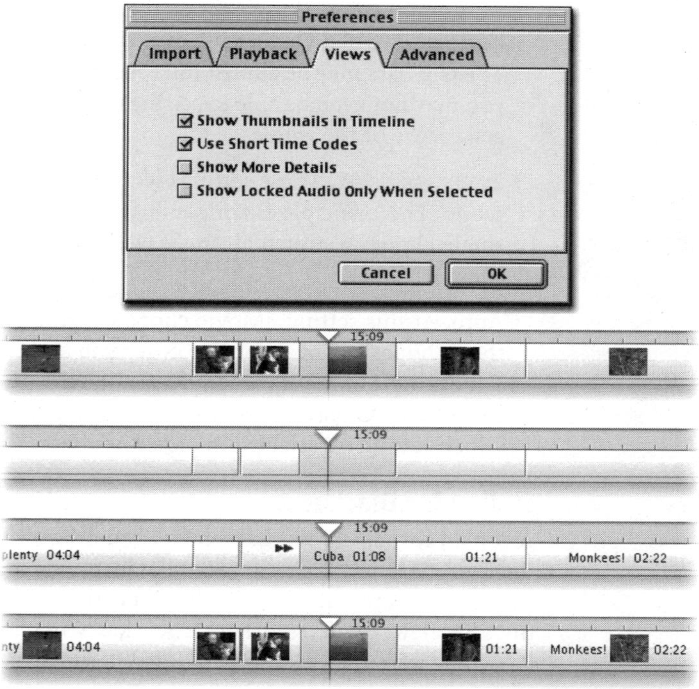

What the Bars Show

When you first install iMovie 2, your Timeline Viewer bars appear as shown at top in Figure 5-7. The first frame of the clip appears in the center of the bar, but otherwise you see very little clip information.

By choosing Edit→Preferences and clicking the Views tab, you can experiment with various settings that affect the Timeline view. For example, "Show Thumbnails in Timeline" is the on/off switch for the small photo that helps you identify a clip at a glance (see Figure 5-8). Turning this checkbox off makes your Timeline Viewer less attractive, but makes scrolling much smoother and faster.

You can also turn on Show More Details, if you like; it adds clip names and clip timing information to the clip bars. Both of these alternatives are illustrated in Figure 5-7.

Zooming

The Timeline Viewer has a scroll bar, whose handle appears to be made of blue tooth gel, that lets you bring different parts of your movie into view. But depending on the length and complexity of your movie, you may wish you could zoom in for a more detailed view, or zoom out for a bird's-eye view of the whole project.

That's the purpose of the "1x" pop-up menu shown at lower left in Figure 5-6. It adjusts the relative sizes of the bars that represent your clips like this:

- **1x.** At this setting, iMovie shows the entire movie in a single screen, without your having to scroll. (This setting may give iMovie 1 fans a distinct sense of déja vu.) The clip bars may be almost microscopic—if it's a long movie with short scenes, you may not even be able to see the thumbnail picture on each—but at least you get a sense of the whole.

- **2x, 3x, 4x...50x.** These settings work like the magnification power on a microscope. The principle is simple: *bigger numbers make bigger clip bars*. At 50x, a single clip may stretch all the way across the screen, filling the entire Timeline Viewer.

- **Auto.** At this setting, iMovie chooses a zoom setting on its own—a zoom level that it hopes will be comfortable for you and appropriate to your movie's length. For example, it makes the smallest clip wide enough for you to see its thumbnail image and still have some margin that you can grab with your mouse. It tells you which setting it's selected in parentheses, such as "Auto (5x)."

Sliding for Blackness

As noted earlier in this chapter, you can drag a clip in the Timeline Viewer only to the right. When you do so, you introduce a gap between the clip and the one to its left; iMovie automatically fills the gap with blackness and silence. If you flip back to the Clip Viewer, you'll see that iMovie has actually created a new clip, represented by its own icon in the Clip Viewer, called Black.

What you do with this gap is your business. You can leave it black, creating a very effective "bookend" between scenes. You can switch to the Clip Viewer and drag the Black clip up onto your Shelf for future reuse. Or you can precisely fill it with video from elsewhere in your project (see page 219).

Note: If there's a transition to the left of a clip (Chapter 6), you can't drag the clip to the right.

Slow Motion, Fast Motion

The fans spoke, and Apple listened: iMovie 2 lets you create perfect, pristine, glorious slow-motion and fast-motion effects.

Slow motion is extremely effective when you're going for an emotional, nostalgic, warm feeling, especially when you delete the original soundtrack and replace it with music (see Chapter 8). On the more pragmatic side, it's also useful when analyzing your tennis swing, golf stroke, or sleight-of-hand technique.

Fast motion is generally useful only for comic effects—kids wrasslin' on the living-room floor is a sure winner—but can also help with time-lapse effects, as described on page 132.

When you click a clip—anywhere, even in the Shelf—the Faster/Slower slider at the bottom edge of the Timeline Viewer lights up (shown at the bottom edge in Figure 5-6). You can drag this slider to the left or right to make the clip play faster or slower.

The five Faster notches on the slider make your clip play two, three, four, or five times its original speed; the five Slower notches make it take two, three, four, or five times as long to play. Unfortunately, you can't make a clip play just *slightly* faster; you can park the little blue handle only on the slider notches, not anywhere between.

When you adjust this slider, a few things happen:

- The clip's yellow bar grows or shrinks in the Timeline to indicate its new playback duration.

- A special icon appears in the corner of the clip (in the Shelf or Clip Viewer), indicating that you've toyed with its playback speed. (See Figure 5-8.)

- iMovie does its best to stretch or compress the audio along with the video. But instead of raising or lowering the pitch, as you'd hear if you sped up or slowed down a tape, iMovie chops the sound up into tiny snippets, which it plays se-

Figure 5-8:
The tiny black symbols at the upper-right corner of a clip reminds you that you've messed with its playback speed or direction, as indicated by these clips' names.

quentially at their original pitch. As a result, the audio takes on an electronic, quivery aspect that may not be quite as smooth-sounding as you might like.

Tip: If the distortion of slow- or fast-motion audio bothers you, you may find it wise to split the audio from the video *before* applying a fast- or slow-motion effect, so that the sound will be unaffected. Of course, the sound will no longer match the length of the video clip, but you may be able to solve this by cropping some of the audio or video.

Ultra-Fast, Ultra-Slow Motion

I want to speed up my banana-slug footage beyond the scope of the speed slider—really fast. How can I do it?

Crank up the speed of the clip to its highest setting, and then export the clip to tape on your camera, as described in Chapter 11.

Then reimport the same clip into iMovie, which considers the reimported clip to be at "normal" speed. Now you can use the speed slider again on the same clip—and repeat the whole procedure as necessary—until you get the extreme speed changes you want.

Figure 5-9:
When the Movie Track is ready to play, the Scrubber bar shows many different segments, one for each of the clips in it. The relative lengths of the segments show you the relative lengths of the clips. You can use all of the navigating and editing techniques described in this chapter, including pressing the arrow keys, splitting or trimming clips, and so on.

Playing the Movie Track

The Monitor isn't limited to playing clips; it can also play the Movie Track. That's handy, because one of iMovie's best features is its ability to show your movie-in-progress whenever you like, without having to *compile* or *render* anything, as you sometimes do in more expensive editing programs.

Playing the Whole Movie

To play back your *entire* Movie Track, make sure that no clip is selected in the Shelf. You can accomplish this feat in any of several ways:

- Click anywhere on the screen except on a clip.

- Choose Edit→Select None, or press ⌘-D.

- Press the Home key, which in iMovie means "Rewind to beginning." As a time-saving bonus, the Home key (which is above the number keypad on most modern Macs) *also* deselects all clips, as though it knows that you want to play back the entire Clip Viewer now.

- Click the Home *button,* which is beneath the Monitor just to the left of the Play button. Once again, iMovie deselects all clips in the process of rewinding.

You can tell at a glance when you've succeeded in preparing the Movie Track for playback by the appearance of subdivisions in the Scrubber bar (see Figure 5-9). When you tap the Space bar, iMovie plays your complete movie so far from the location indicated by the Playhead in the Scrubber bar. (If you press Home, you play the movie from the beginning.) iMovie plays one clip after another, seamlessly, from left to right as they appear in the Clip Viewer.

Playing your movie back is the best way to get a feeling for how your clips are working together. You may discover that, in the context of the whole movie, some are too long, too short, in the wrong order, and so on.

Playing a Segment of the Movie

You don't have to play the entire Movie Track. You can play only a chunk of it by first selecting only the clips you want (and transition icons, as described in Chapter 6). To do that, click the first clip you'll want to play, and then Shift-click the final one.

Now click the Play button or press the Space bar; iMovie plays only the clips you highlighted.

While the Movie is Playing

As the Movie Track plays, three simultaneous indicators show your position in the film. First, of course, the Playhead slides along the subdivided-looking Scrubber bar.

If the Timeline Viewer is visible, a duplicate Playhead slides along *it.* If the Clip Viewer is visible, on the other hand, a bright red, inverted T cursor slides along the faces of the clips themselves, which lets you know at a glance which clip you're seeing on the Monitor window—and how much of it you've seen (see Figure 5-10). You can't drag this cursor like a true scroll-bar handle; it's purely an indicator.

While the movie is playing, you can take control in several ways:

• Use the playback controls beneath the Monitor (or their keystroke equivalents) to pause, stop, rewind, and so on.

• Navigate the whole movie by clicking in the Scrubber bar or dragging the Playhead, exactly as when navigating a clip.

• Adjust the volume by pressing the up-arrow or down-arrow key.

• Jump into Play Full Screen mode by clicking the Play Full Screen button.

• Stop the playback by pressing the Space bar.

• Stop the playback *and* rewind to the beginning by pressing the Home key.

Figure 5-10:
Because every clip icon is the same size, but not every clip is the same length, the T indicator speeds up or slows down as it arrives at the left edge of each clip. (You can see it in the center clip here, approaching the right side of the frame.) Feel like hacking? You can turn off the T indicator if you like; see page 377.

Editing Clips in the Movie Track

Fortunately, all of the editing tricks for trimming and splitting clips described in this chapter also work in the Movie Track. In other words, just because you see the segmented Scrubber bar (Figure 5-9) doesn't mean you can't click below it to produce the triangle handles, or click above it in readiness to use the Split Clip at Playhead command.

You can also perform many of the same clip-editing operations that you read about in their Shelf context, earlier in this chapter. For example, you can rename a clip, delete it from the project, or use the Edit-menu commands on it, exactly as you operate on Shelf clips.

Full-Screen Playback Mode

Whenever you're tempted to play your movie in progress, consider clicking the Play Full Screen button, shown in Figure 5-9. It makes the playback—even if it's already under way—fill the entire computer screen.

To interrupt the movie showing, click the mouse or press any key on the keyboard. (The usual Macintosh "cancel" keystroke, ⌘-period, ironically, *doesn't* work in this context.)

Note: The quality of the full-screen playback isn't the same pristine, crystal-clear playback you'll get when you transfer your finished movie back to your camcorder for TV playback. In fact, it's little more than a blown-up version of what you see in the Monitor window while editing your movie. If it's grainy there, it's enlarged-grainy in full-screen playback.

Figure 5-11:
In iMovie 2, the Play Full Screen function plays from wherever the Playhead happens to be; if you've highlighted part of a clip or part of your whole movie, you see only that segment.

---

iMedicine

I am a clinical psychologist working at the Uppsala University Hospital in Sweden with children suffering from different kinds of psychiatric problems.

Some time ago, a patient (girl, nine years old) with severe injection phobia was referred to me. She had developed her very strong fear/avoidance behaviors for receiving injections during the treatment for a somatic disorder. She also had a history of unsuccessful psychological treatment for the injection fear. Together with an assistant, I treated her with exposure techniques, and at the same time, documenting the treatment process with a DV camcorder.

After every session, I quickly put together movie samples, which she brought home to look at during the week in order to provide further training. The samples consisted of scenes showing her taking part in different kinds of exercises, such as slowly, and under controlled circumstances, getting closer to sharp items, needles and hypodermic syringes while ex-periencing that she habituated to the fear. The video samples also included instructions for the homework assignments she had to perform between treatment sessions.

After six treatment sessions, she was completely cured from her fear—that is, she was able to receive injections and have blood samples taken without fear/avoidance or fainting.

I think the add-on procedure of the movie made a big difference; it boosted her motivation for taking an active part in the treatment. We also had great fun during the process. We're now planning extended use of this technique with patients who suffer from other kinds of problems.

I used an iMac DV Special Edition and a Panasonic DV camcorder. The video clips were transferred to a regular VHS-format videocassette for the patient to bring home.

—Kenneth Nilsson
Uppsala, Sweden

Transitions and Effects

This chapter is about two iMovie 2 tools—Transitions and Effects—that can make your raw footage look even better than it is. Both of these tools are represented by buttons on the Shelf/Effects/Sound palette that occupies the right side of your screen. This chapter covers both of these powerful moviemaking techniques.

About Transitions

What happens when one clip ends and the next one begins? In about 99.99 percent of all movies, music videos, and commercials—and in 100 percent of camcorder movies before the Macintosh era—you get a *cut.* That's the technical term for "nothing special happens at all"; one scene ends, and the next one begins immediately.

Professional film and video editors, however, have at their disposal a wide range of *transitions*—special effects that smooth the juncture between one clip and the next. For example, the world's most popular transition is the *crossfade* or *dissolve,* in which the end of one clip gradually fades away as the next one fades in (see Figure 6-1). The crossfade is so popular because it's so effective. It gives a feeling of softness and

Figure 6-1:
The world's most popular and effective transition effect: a Cross Dissolve.

grace to the transition, and yet it's so subtle that the viewer might not even be conscious of its presence.

Like all DV editing programs, iMovie 2 offers a long list of transitions, of which crossfades are only the beginning. You'll find an illustrated catalog of them starting on page 159. But unlike other DV editing software, iMovie makes adding such effects incredibly easy, and the results look awesomely assured and professional.

When to Use Transitions

When the Macintosh debuted in 1984, one of its most exciting features was its *fonts*. Without having to buy those self-adhesive lettering sets from art stores, you could make posters, flyers, and newsletters using any typefaces you wanted. In fact, if you weren't particularly concerned with being tasteful, you could even combine lots of typefaces on the same page—and thousands of first-time desktop publishers did exactly that. They thought it was exciting to harness the world of typography right on the computer screen.

You may even remember the result: a proliferation of homemade graphic design that rated very low on the artistic-taste scale. Instead of making their documents look more professional, the wild explosion of mixed typefaces made them look amateurish in a whole new way.

In video, transitions present exactly the same temptation: If you use too many, you risk telegraphing that you're a beginner at work. When you begin to polish your movie by adding transitions, consider these questions:

- **Does it really need a transition?** Sometimes a simple cut is the most effective transition from one shot to the next. Remember, the crossfade lends a feeling of softness and smoothness to the movie; is that really what you want? If it's a sweet video of your kids growing up over time, absolutely yes. But if it's a hard-hitting issue documentary, then probably not; those soft edges would dull the impact of your footage.

  Remember, too, that transitions often suggest the *passage of time*. In movies and commercials, consecutive shots in the same scene never include such effects; plain old cuts tell the viewer that one shot is following the next in real time. But suppose one scene ends with the beleaguered hero saying, "Well, at least I still have my job at the law firm!"…and the next shot shows him operating a lemonade stand. (Now *that's* comedy!) In this case, a transition would be especially effective, because it would tell the audience that we've just jumped a couple of days.

  In other words, learning to have taste in transitions is a lot like learning to have taste in zooming, as described in Chapter 2. Transitions should be done *for a reason*.

- **Is it consistent?** Once you've chosen a transitional-effect style for your movie, stick to that transition style for the entire film (unless, as always, you have an artistic reason to do otherwise). Using one consistent style of effect lends unity to your work. That's why interior designers choose only one dominant color for each room.

- **Which effect is most appropriate?** As noted earlier, the crossfade is almost always the least intrusive, most effective, and best-looking transition. But each of the other iMovie transitions can be appropriate in certain situations. For example, the Radial wipe, which looks like the hand of a clock wiping around the screen, replacing the old scene with the new one as it goes, can be a useful passage-of-time or meanwhile-back-at-the-ranch effect.

The catalog of transitions at the end of this chapter gives you an example of when each might be appropriate. Remember, though, that many of them are useful primarily in music videos and other situations when wild stylistic flights of fancy are more readily accepted by viewers.

Tip: The Fade In and Fade Out "transitions" in iMovie are exempt from the stern advice above. Use a Fade In at the beginning of *every* movie, if you like, and a Fade Out at the end. Doing so adds a professional feeling to your film; but it's so subtle, your audience will notice it subconsciously, if at all.

Creating a Transition

To see the list of transitions iMovie offers, click the Transitions button, as shown in Figure 6-2. The Shelf disappears, only to be replaced, in the blink of an eye, by a completely different set of controls.

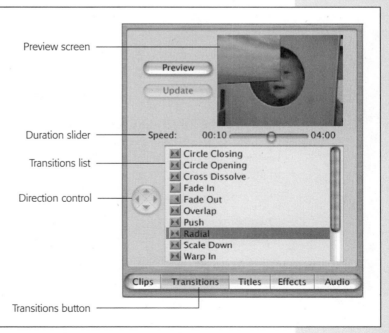

Figure 6-2:
When you click the Transitions button, a list of the transitions available in iMovie appears. (If you have only six transitions listed, it's because you haven't downloaded the free Plug-In Pack described on page 150.) When you click a transition's name, the preview screen above the list shows a fairly jerky simulation of what this effect will look like.

Preview screen

Duration slider

Transitions list

Direction control

Transitions button

Previewing the Effect

Like most video-editing software, iMovie has to do a lot of computation to produce transitions; without special add-on circuitry, no computer can show an instantaneous, full-speed, full-smoothness preview. Therefore, iMovie offers a choice of lower-quality (but instantaneous) previews:

- **The Preview window.** For a very small preview, shown in the tiny screen above the transitions list, just click the name of a transition.

  This preview plays in real time; it tries to make transition preview last exactly as long as the finished transition will. On slower Macs, you don't see all the frames in this little Preview window, making the transition appear jerky, but rest assured that the finished transition will be extremely smooth.

- **The Monitor window.** To see a preview in a much larger format—big enough to fill the Monitor window—click the Preview button.

Either way, you can drag the Speed slider just above the list to experiment with the length of each transition as you're previewing it. The numbers on this slider—*00:10* (ten frames) at the left side, *04:00* (four seconds) at the right side—let you know the least and greatest amount of time that a transition can last. When you release the slider, you'll see another quick preview in the miniature screen above it, and you'll also see, in the lower-right corner of the preview screen, the actual length of the transition you've specified.

Tip: The program doesn't yet know which clips you'll want to "transish." Therefore, iMovie uses, for the purposes of this preview, whichever clip is currently highlighted in the Movie Track, into which it crossfades from the previous clip. If the very first clip is highlighted, iMovie demonstrates by transitioning that clip into the second clip.

If no clip is highlighted, iMovie 2 is smart enough to seek out the "clip boundary" that's closest to the Playhead's current position; it uses the clips on both sides of that boundary for the preview (if it is a two-clip transition; if it's a one-clip transition, iMovie uses the clip to the right or left).

Applying the Effect—and Rendering

Once you've selected an effect and dragged the slider to specify how much time you want it to take, you can place it into the Movie Track (Clip Viewer or Timeline Viewer) in one of two ways:

- Drag the preview screen itself (Figure 6-2) directly down into the Movie Track.

- Drag the *name or icon* of the effect out of the transitions list and down onto the Movie Track.

Either way, drag until your cursor is between the two clips that you want joined by this transition; iMovie pushes the right-hand clips out of the way to make room. (Most transitions must go *between* two clips, and so they can't go at the beginning or end of your Movie Track. The exceptions are the Fade and Wash effects.) Then a slidelike icon (or, in the Timeline, triangle-branded bar) appears between the clips, as shown in Figure 6-3.

Tip: The tiny triangles on a transition icon or bar let you know what kind of transition it is without actually having to click it. A pair of inward-facing triangles is a standard transition that melds the end of one clip with the beginning of the next. A single, right-facing triangle indicates a transition that applies to the *beginning* of a clip, such as a fade in from black (or wash in from white); a single, left-facing triangle indicates a transition that applies to the *end* of a clip (such as a fade or wash *out*).

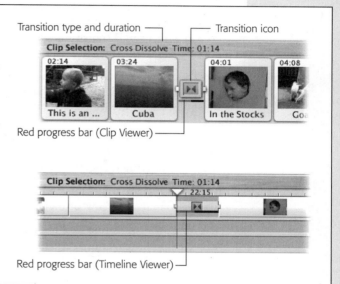

Figure 6-3:
Top: In the Clip Viewer, a transition shows up as a slide-like icon.

Bottom: In the Timeline Viewer, you get a bar whose width indicates its duration. Each transition has its own red progress bar that creeps along the bottom edge of the icon. After the clip has been fully rendered, this added strip beneath the icon disappears, and the transition is ready to play. (The Movie Track's top edge identifies the transition type and its duration when the transition icon is highlighted.)

Almost immediately, a tiny red line begins to crawl, progress-bar-like, along the lower edge of this icon (see Figure 6-3). In the terminology of digital-video editors everywhere, the Mac has begun to *render* this transition: to perform the thousands of individual calculations necessary to blend the outgoing clip into the incoming, pixel by pixel, frame by frame.

Whether it's an iMovie transition or a special effect in *Star Wars Episode I: The Phantom Menace,* rendering always takes a lot of time. In iMovie, the longer the transition you've specified, the longer it takes to render. You should feel grateful, however, that iMovie renders its transitions in a matter of minutes, not days (which complex Hollywood computer-generated effects often require).

Furthermore, iMovie lets you *continue working* as this rendering takes place. You can work on the other pieces of your movie, import new footage from your camcorder, or even *play* your movie while transitions are still rendering. (If the transitions haven't finished rendering, iMovie shows you its preview version.)

In fact, you can even switch out of iMovie to work in other Mac programs. (This last trick makes the rendering even slower, but at least it's in the background; you can check your email or work on your screenplay in the meantime.)

The convenience of this feature can't be overstated: In most "serious" video-editing programs, the computer locks you out completely while it renders.

Rendering simultaneous clips

You can even make iMovie render several transition effects, or even dozens, simultaneously; in iMovie 2, doing so no longer makes the program grind to a halt. In fact, if you give iMovie a little more memory (see page 370), you could easily set *hundreds* of transitions rendering simultaneously, with no more Mac slowdown than you'd get with a single transition rendering. They take longer to complete if they're rendering simultaneously, but they don't slow you down.

Insert more than that, and you may even get the error message shown at bottom right in Figure 6-6, which tells you that iMovie is out of memory and that you should wait until some of the transitions are finished rendering before continuing to add more.

When rendering is complete

When the rendering is complete, you can look over the result very easily.

- To watch just the transition itself, click the transition's icon or bar in the Movie Track (to make it yellow, or highlighted) and then press the Space bar.

- To watch the transition *and* the clips that it joins together, Shift-click the two clips in question. Doing so also highlights the transition between them. Press the Space bar to play the three clips you've highlighted.

- It's a good idea to watch your transition by "rewinding" a few seconds into the preceding footage, so that you get a sense of how the effect fits in the context of the existing footage. To give yourself some of this "preroll," choose Edit→Select None (or just click anywhere but on a clip) to deselect all the clips. Then click a spot on the Scrubber bar somewhere in the clip before the transition, and press the Space bar to play the movie from that point.

- If you don't care for what you've done, you can always choose Edit→Undo.

- If it's too late for the Undo command, you can return to the transition at any time, highlight its icon, and press the Delete key. Your original clips return instantly, exactly as they were before you added the transition.

How Transitions Affect the Length of Your Movie

As you can see by the example in Figure 6-4, most transitions make your movie shorter. To superimpose the ends of two adjacent clips, iMovie is forced to slide the right-hand clip leftward, making the overall movie end sooner.

Under most circumstances, there's nothing wrong with that. After all, that's why you wisely avoided trimming off *all* of the excess "leader" and "trailer" footage (known as *trim handles)* from the ends of your clips. By leaving trim handles on each clip—which will be sacrificed to the transition—you'll have some fade in or fade out footage to play with.

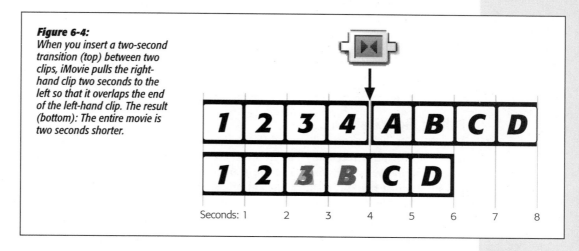

Figure 6-4:
When you insert a two-second transition (top) between two clips, iMovie pulls the right-hand clip two seconds to the left so that it overlaps the end of the left-hand clip. The result (bottom): The entire movie is two seconds shorter.

Sometimes, however, having your overall project shortened is a serious problem, especially when you've been "cutting to sound," or synchronizing your footage to an existing music track, as described in Chapter 8. Suppose you've spent hours putting your clips into the Movie Track, carefully trimming them so that they perfectly match the soundtrack. And now, as a final touch, you decide to put in transitions. Clearly, having these transitions slide all of your clips to the left would result in chaos, throwing off the synchronization work you had done.

Now you can appreciate the importance of iMovie 2's new Advanced→Lock Audio Clip at Playhead command, which marries a piece of music or sound to a particular spot in the video. If all of your added music and sound elements are attached in this way, adding transitions won't disturb their synchronization. See page 214 for details on locking audio into position.

Tip: Certain transitions, including Overlap, Fade In, Fade Out, Wash In, and Wash Out, don't shorten the movie. As described at the end of this chapter, each of these four special transitions affects only *one* clip, not two. They're meant to begin or end your movie, fading in or out from black or white.

How Transitions Chop Up Clips

After your transition has been rendered, you'll notice something peculiar about your Scrubber bar: The transition has now become, in effect, a clip of its own. (If you switch to the Finder and look in your project folder's Media folder, you'll even see the newly created clip file represented there, bearing the name of the transition you applied.)

If you click the first clip and play it, you'll find that the playback now stops sooner than it once did—just where the transition takes over. Likewise, the clip that follows the transition has also had frames shaven away at the front end. Both clips, in other words, have sacrificed a second or two to the newly created transition/clip between them. Figure 6-4 illustrates this phenomenon.

Tip: You can rename a transition icon, if it helps you to remember what you were thinking when you created it. To do so, double-click its icon or bar; the Clip Info dialog box appears, in which you can change the name the transition icon displays in your Movie Track.

Editing the Transition

You can edit the transition in several ways: You can change its length, its type, its direction (certain effects only), or all three. To do so, click the transition icon, and then click the Transitions *button* (if the Transitions palette isn't already open). You can now adjust the Speed slider, click another transition in the list, or both. (You may also be able to change the direction of the effect, depending on the transition; at this writing, the Push effect is the only one that offers this option.)

When you click Update—a button that's available *only* when a transition icon is highlighted in the Movie Track—iMovie automatically re-renders the transition.

Deleting a Transition

If you decide that you don't need a transition effect between two clips after all, you can delete it just as you would delete any Movie Track clip—by clicking it once and then pressing the Delete key on your keyboard (or by choosing Edit→Clear). Deleting a transition clip does more than eliminate the icon—it also restores the clips on either side to their original conditions. (If you change your mind, Edit→Undo Clear brings back the transition.)

Transition Error Messages

Transitions can be fussy. They like plenty of clip footage to chew on, and once they've begun rendering, they like to be left alone. Here are some of the error messages you may encounter when working with transitions.

When you delete a clip

For example, if, in the process of editing your movie, you delete a clip from the Movie Track that's part of a transition, a message appears (Figure 6-5) that says: "This action will invalidate at least one transition in the project. Invalid transitions will be deleted from the project. Do you want to proceed?"

iMovie is simply telling you that if you delete the clip, you'll also delete the transition attached to it (which is probably just what you'd expect). Click OK. If you first click Don't Ask Again, iMovie will henceforth delete such clips without bothering you to ask your permission.

When the transition is longer than the clip

If you try to add a five-second crossfade between two three-second clips, iMovie throws up its hands with various similarly worded error messages (Figure 6-5, left). In all cases, the point is clear: The two clips on either side of a transition must *each* be longer than the transition itself.

Put another way, iMovie can't make your transition stretch across more than two clips (or more than one clip, in the case of the Fade and Wash effects).

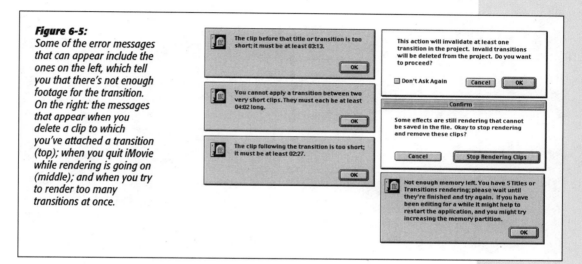

Figure 6-5:
Some of the error messages that can appear include the ones on the left, which tell you that there's not enough footage for the transition. On the right: the messages that appear when you delete a clip to which you've attached a transition (top); when you quit iMovie while rendering is going on (middle); and when you try to render too many transitions at once.

When you quit while rendering

If you quit iMovie while the rendering process is still under way, you get the message shown at middle right in Figure 6-5. The program is warning you that you're about to lose the partly rendered transitions. When you reopen the project file, the transition icons will be missing from the Movie Track, as though you'd never put them there.

When you get too ambitious

As noted earlier, too many transitions added too fast can bring iMovie to its knees, as shown in Figure 6-5 at bottom right. Wait until some of the transitions have finished rendering—or give iMovie more memory, as directed in Appendix B.

Transitions: The iMovie Catalog

The copy of iMovie 2 provided with your Mac (or your Web download) comes with only six transitions—the ones in the following list identified by the "(Built-In)" notation.

The selection was then more than doubled with the arrival of the iMovie 2 Plug-in Pack—a free download from *www.apple.com/imovie*, and a very worthy download at that. It includes not only seven additional transitions, but several additional text and video effects, too (see the end of this chapter and Chapter 7).

Here, for your reference, is a visual representation of each transition, and what editing circumstances might call for it. In each example, "first clip" refers to the clip that comes before the transition, and "second clip" is the clip that follows.

Downloading the iMovie Plug-in Pack 2

Using your Web browser, visit *www.apple.com/imovie*. On that page, you'll find a link to the iMovie Plug-in Pack 2. (Apple may release additional plug-in packs; on the other hand, note that this particular plug-in pack is incompatible with the plug-in packs for iMovie 1, and vice versa.)

Once you've downloaded the file (called iMovie_Plugin_Pack_2.sit) and decompressed it if necessary (using StuffIt Expander, the program in the Internet folder of every Mac), you wind up with a folder called iMovie Plug-in Pack 2. Inside is *another* folder bearing almost

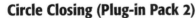

exactly the same name (iMovie Plugin Pack 2).

Quit iMovie, if it's running. Open your iMovie folder so that you can see the Resources folder inside it. Drag the inner iMovie Plugin Pack 2 folder directly into the Resources folder, as shown here. (You can also drag it into the Plugins folder within the Resources folder, if you like.)

That's all there is to it—when you launch iMovie again, you'll enjoy all of the additional transitions and text effects installed by the Plug-in Pack.

Circle Closing (Plug-in Pack 2)

This effect, called "Iris Close" or "Iris In" in professional editing programs, is a holdover from the silent film days, when, in the days before zoom lenses, directors used the effect to highlight a detail in a scene.

It creates an ever-closing circle with the first clip inside and the second clip outside. It's useful primarily at the end of the movie, when the second clip is solid black and the subject of the first clip is centered in the frame. When you meet all those conditions, the movie ends with an ever-shrinking picture that fades away to a little dot. (If the subject in the center waves goodbye just before being blinked out of view, this trick is especially effective.)

Circle Closing

Circle Opening (Plug-in Pack 2)

This effect is much like Circle Closing, except it's been turned inside out. Now the circle grows from the center of the first clip, with the second clip playing inside it, and expands until it fills the frame. (This effect would be called Iris Open or Iris Out in professional editing programs.)

Here again, this effect is especially useful at the beginning of a movie, particularly if the subject of the second clip is at the center of the frame. If the first clip in your movie is a solid black frame (see page 134), your film begins as though the camera's sleepy eye is opening to reveal the scene.

Citcle Opening

Cross Dissolve (Built-In)

The crossfade, or dissolve, is the world's most popular, subtle, and effective transition. The first clip gradually disappears, superimposed on the beginning of the second clip, which fades in. If you must use a transition at all, you can't go wrong with this one.

Tip: You can use a very short cross dissolve to create what editors call a "soft cut." When the footage would jump too abruptly if you made a regular cut, put in a ten-frame cross dissolve, which makes the junction of clips *slightly* smoother than just cutting.

Soft cuts are very common in interviews where the editors have deleted sections from a continuous shot of a person talking.

Cross Dissolve

Fade In (Built-In)

Use this effect at the beginning of your movie, or the beginning of a scene that begins in a new place or time. Unlike most transition effects, this one makes no attempt to smooth the transition between two clips. The fade in overlaps only the clip *to its right,* creating a fade in from complete blackness.

Because this transition affects only the clip that follows it, it doesn't shorten your movie or throw subsequent clips out of alignment, unlike genuine crossfade-style transitions.

Tip: In general, iMovie doesn't let you place one transition effect next to another. You can't transition into a transition, in other words.

Among the built-in transitions, the exceptions are the Fade (In and Out) and Wash (In and Out) transitions. Each of these affects only one clip, not two. (If you study the transition list carefully, you'll see a Fade or Wash icon has only one triangle, not two.) By placing an In immediately after an Out, you create an elegant fade out, then in to the next shot—a very popular effect in movies and commercials.

Placing an Out just after an In isn't quite as useful, because it reveals only a fleeting glance of the footage in between. But when you're trying to represent somebody's life flashing before his eyes, this trick may be just the ticket.

Fade In

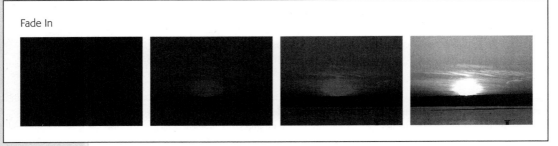

Fade Out (Built-In)

This effect, conversely, is best used at the *end* of a movie, or the end of a scene that requires a feeling of finality. Like its sister, the Fade In, this one doesn't involve two clips at all; it affects only the end of the clip to its left. As a result, it doesn't affect the length or synchronization of your movie.

It's worth noting, by the way, that a fade out is almost always followed by a fade *in,* or by the closing credits. You'll blast your audience's eyeballs if you fade out, sweetly and gracefully—and then cut directly into a bright new clip.

Both Fade In and Fade Out are very useful, and frequently used, effects. (Check out the final shot before the credits of almost every episode of, say, *The X-Files.)* But iMovie offers you an elegant, graceful, smooth fade to blackness, and then, unfortunately, the movie ends abruptly, instead of *holding* on the black screen for a moment.

That behavior is easy to fix, however: Just add a few seconds of blackness after the fade. To do so, switch to the Timeline Viewer and create a pure black clip, as described on page 134. Switch to the Clip Viewer, cut the black clip to the Clipboard, and paste it at the end of the movie. Now iMovie will fade out to black—and hold on that blackness.

Fade Out

Overlap (Built-In)

Overlap is almost exactly the same as the Cross Dissolve, illustrated earlier. The sole difference: The outgoing clip freezes on its last frame as the new clip fades in. (In a Cross Dissolve, the action continues during the simultaneous fades.) Use it in situations where you might normally use a Cross Dissolve, but want to draw the eye to the second clip right away.

Tip: Unlike the Cross Dissolve, the Overlap transition doesn't change the duration of your movie, which makes it a good choice for movies where you've spent a lot of time synchronizing audio and video; in those cases, a Cross Dissolve might knock things out of sync.

Push (Built-In)

In this transition, the first clip is shoved off the frame by the aggressive first frame of the second clip. This offbeat transition effect draws a lot of attention to itself, so use it extremely sparingly. For example, you could use it to simulate an old-style projector changing slides, or when filming a clever, self-aware documentary in which the host (who first appears in the second clip) "pushes" his way onto the screen.

Push Right

When you select this transition in the list, the four directional arrows—which are dimmed for most transition types—become available. Click one to indicate how you want the incoming clip to push its way onscreen: up, down, to the left, or to the right.

Radial (Plug-in Pack 2)

You probably saw this one in a few movies of the seventies. What looks like the sweep-second hand on a watch rotates around the screen, wiping away the first clip and revealing the second clip underneath. This transition suggests the passage of time even more than most transitions; it clues the audience in that the scene about to begin takes place in a new location or on a different day.

Radial

Scale Down (Built-In)

Scale Down, known to pro editors as the *picture zoom* effect, is a peculiar effect, whereby the end of the first clip simply shrinks away. Its rectangle gets smaller and smaller until it disappears, falling endlessly away into the beginning of the second clip, which lies beneath it. The rectangle seems to fly away into the upper-left corner of the second clip, not into dead center.

This kind of effect occasionally shows up on TV news, in documentaries, and so on, after you've been watching a close-up of some important document or photograph. By showing the close-up flying away from the camera, the film editor seems to say: "Enough of that. Meanwhile, back in real life..."

Scale Down

Warp In (Plug-in Pack 2)

This effect is very similar to Scale Down, except that as the first clip flies away, it seems to fold in on itself instead of remaining rectangular. That characteristic, combined with the fact that it flies away into dead center of the second clip's frame, makes it look as though the first clip is getting sucked out of the center of the picture by a giant video vacuum cleaner.

It's hard to think of *any* circumstance where this effect would feel natural, except when you're deliberately trying to be weird.

Warp In

  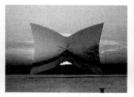 

Warp Out (Plug-in Pack 2)

You might think that this effect would be the flip side of the Warp In effect, but it's quite different. This time, the second clip intrudes on the first by pushing its way, as an ever-growing sphere, into the frame. What's left of the first clip gets smashed outward, bizarrely distorting, until it's shoved off the outer edges of the picture.

Warp Out

  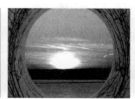 

Wash In, Wash Out (Plug-in Pack 2)

These two effects work exactly like Fade In an Fade Out, described earlier, with one big difference: They fade in from, and out to, *white* instead of black.

Fading in and out to white, an effect first popularized by Infiniti car commercials in the early eighties, lends a very specific feeling to the movie. It's something ethereal, ghostly, nostalgic. In today's Hollywood movies (including *The Sixth Sense),* a fade to white is often an indication that the character you've been watching has just died.

Fading out to white and then in from white—that is, putting two of these transitions side by side in your Movie Track—is an extremely popular technique in today's TV commercials, when the advertiser wants to show you a series of charming, brightly colored images. By fading out to white between shots, the editor inserts the video equivalent of an ellipsis (…like this…), and keeps the mood happy and bright. (Similar fade outs to black seem to stop the flow with more finality.)

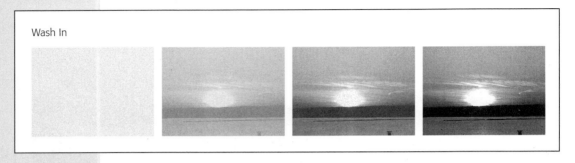

Wash In

Wash Out

The Effects Palette

The original iMovie offered two kinds of effects: Transitions and Text Effects. But neither could accurately be described *special* effects, things that make you say, "Cool!"

iMovie 2 addresses that limitation with a vengeance. As noted in Chapter 5, you can now play clips in slow motion, fast motion, or backward. But that's just the beginning; the new Effects button summons a panel full of additional visual effects that you can apply directly to your footage.

Some are designed to adjust the brightness, contrast, or color tints in less-than-perfect footage. Others fall into the same category as some of the transition effects described earlier in this chapter: "Nice to have in the toolkit, but pretty out-there; save for special situations." (The effects that simulate flashbulbs, pond reflections, and bleary-eyed bad LSD trips fall squarely in this category.)

Tip: The iMovie Plug-in Pack 2 described on page 150 offers five more effects than the ones included with your original copy of the program; see the catalog on page 159. They're a free download; go get 'em.

Selecting the Footage

Before you apply an effect, specify which lucky region of footage you want to be affected:

- **One clip.** Click a clip in the Movie Track or Shelf; the effect will apply to the entire clip.

- **Multiple clips.** If you highlight several clips in the Movie Track, your selected effect will apply to all of them, treating them as one giant clip. When you click the Apply button, you'll see multiple progress bars marching across the faces of the affected clips in the Movie Track.

- **Part of a clip.** If you use the Scrubber bar's selection handles to highlight only a portion of a clip, iMovie will split the clips at the endpoints of the selection, and then apply the effect to the central clip. (iMovie can apply effects only to *entire* clips, which is why this automatic splitting takes place.)

- **Parts of multiple clips.** If you choose Edit→Select None, you can use the Scrubber bar's selection handles to enclose any stretch of clips (or portions of clips) you like. If necessary, iMovie will again split the end clips at the location of your handles.

Figure 6-6:
Several of the effects in the Effects panel offer additional controls, which take the form of sliders beneath the list. You can drag the small blue handle of such sliders, or simply click anywhere in its track. The numbers in the corners of the Preview pane reflect the times you've selected by dragging the Effect In and Out sliders.

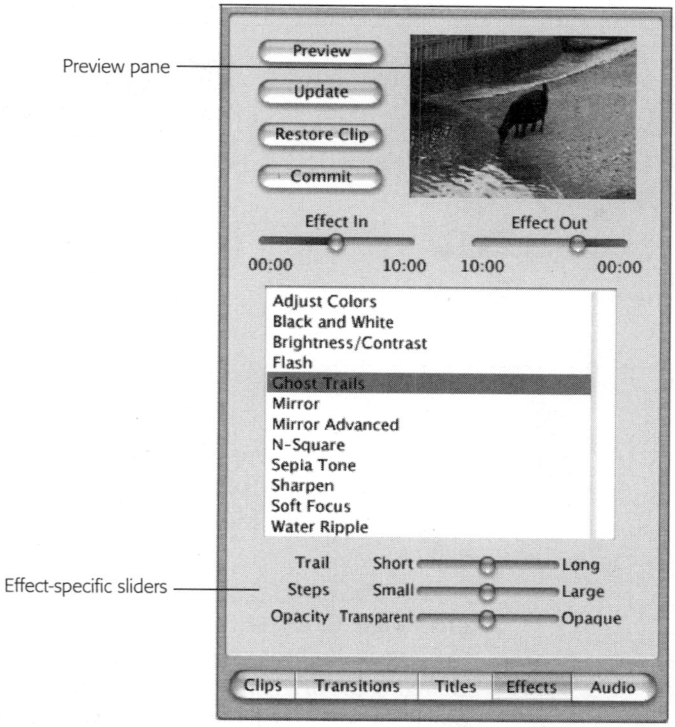

Surveying Your Options

Now click the Effects button. Portions of this panel (Figure 6-6) should look familiar; the list of effects, the Preview button, and the Preview pane all work exactly as they do for transitions. (For example, when you click an effect name, the small Preview pane shows a crude, jerky representation of what it will look like; if you click the Preview *button,* you see the same preview in the Monitor window.)

But you'll also find several other buttons and controls that don't exist anywhere else in iMovie:

- **Apply.** When you click Apply, iMovie begins to render the selected clip: to perform the massive numbers of calculations necessary to bring each pixel into compliance with the effect you've specified. As with transitions, effect rendering telegraphs its progress with a subtle red line, a miniature progress bar, that crawls from left to right beneath the selected clip (see Figure 6-7).

  Rendering effects works exactly like rendering transitions: You can continue working on other parts of your movie, but things can bog down if you've got several effects rendering at once. (You'll probably find that rendering effects takes much longer than rendering transitions, however, in part because you apply each effect to an entire clip instead of just the last couple of seconds.) Press ⌘-period to cancel the rendering.

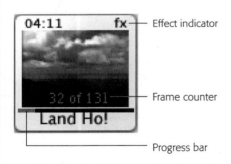

Effect indicator

Frame counter

Progress bar

Figure 6-7:
Both the thin red progress bar and the frame counter let you know how much longer you have to wait. You can tell at a glance that a clip has had an effect applied, thanks to the "fx" brand in the upper right.

It's important to note, by the way, that iMovie 2 actually applies the selected effect to a *duplicate* copy of the clip's DV file on your hard drive. (If you're curious, switch to the Finder; open your project folder, then its Media folder. Inside, you'll find a new clip called, for example, Water Ripple 01, which represents the modified clip.)

Now you've used up twice the amount of disk space for that clip: one version is unaffected, the other has the special effect applied. iMovie creates the behind-the-scenes duplicate as a safety net for you; these effects are *destructive,* forever changing the original footage. By using this duplicate-clip system, iMovie can be much more forgiving; it can give you the option of removing or adjusting the effect at any time.

- **Restore Clip.** Clicking this button means: "Throw away the effect. Bring back my original, unmodified clip." (When you empty the trash, or close the project file and save changes, iMovie deletes the modified-clip file from your hard drive, restoring the disk space it had been using.)

- **Commit.** When you click Commit, however, you're saying: "Apply this effect permanently; *don't* use up disk space by creating a copy of the original. I promise that I'll never want to change my mind. I understand that the Restore Clip button will no longer work on this clip."

  Clicking Commit also tells iMovie 2 to delete the *original* clip from your hard drive. (This deletion won't take place until you empty the Trash or close the project file and save changes.)

Tip: Ironically, you actually can undo a Commit—a safety net, an apparent contradiction in terms, that's all too absent from real life.

- **Effect In, Effect Out.** If you want the chosen effect to start and end exactly at the boundaries of your selection, leave these sliders at their zero points (the far left for Effect In, the far right for Effect Out).

  If you like, however, you can make these effects kick in (and kick out) gradually, after the clip has already begun (and before it has ended). That's the purpose of these two sliders: to give you control over when they begin or end.

  For example, if you drag the Effect In slider for a Black and White effect to 5:00, the clip will begin playing in full color. After playing for five seconds, however, the color will begin to leach out, leaving the rest of the clip to play in black-and-white (a useful effect if you're trying to depict someone slowly going colorblind). You can set the Effect In and Out points no more than ten seconds from the beginning or ending of a clip.

Tip: Here's how to make a knockout, professional-looking effect to open your film: Create a still clip from the first frame of a movie, as described on page 238. Split it in half. Convert the first half to black and white, then create a Cross Dissolve between it and the second half. The result: What appears to be a black-and-white photograph "coming to life" as it fades into color and then begins to play normally.

- **Effect-specific controls.** As you click the name of each effect in the list, additional sliders may appear at the bottom of the Effects panel. They're described in the following sections.

Effects: The iMovie Catalog

iMovie 2 comes with seven built-in effects; the iMovie 2 Plug-in Pack (page 150) gives you five more. The following illustrated list of the iMovie effects describes them all.

Adjust Colors (Built-In)

This powerful effect adjusts the actual color palette used in your clip footage. If your footage has an unfortunate greenish tint, you can color-correct it; if you're hoping for a sunset look, you can bring out the oranges and reds; if it's a sci-fi flick taking place on Uranus, you can make it look blue and spooky.

The special sliders for this effect affect the hue, saturation, and brightness of your footage. Hue, saturation, and brightness are cornerstones of color theory; you can read much more about them on the Web, or in books and articles about photo editing. In the meantime, here's a brief summary:

- **Hue Shift (Left—Right).** Adjusts the overall color tint of the clip. What iMovie is actually doing is rotating the hue around the hue circle, either to the left or the right. In practice, this effect doesn't do anything predictable to an image; you're meant to play with it until you find something you like.

- **Color (B&W—Vivid).** This slider lets you control the intensity of a color, or its *saturation*. If it's blue, you control *how* blue it is: increasing toward Vivid makes the blue more intense.

- **Lightness (Dark—Bright).** Use this slider to adjust the overall brightness or darkness of the *colors* in your clip. There's only a subtle difference between these effects and the Brightness/Contrast effect described below; this slider adjusts the brightness of the colors, rather than the overall brightness.

FREQUENTLY ASKED QUESTION

Multiple Effects, One Clip

I can't seem to apply more than one effect to a single clip. How is it done?

It's perfectly possible—and useful—to combine effects by applying first one, then another. For example, after using the Black and White effect, you may want to use Brightness/Contrast control to adjust its gray tones. You can even apply a single effect repeatedly, intensifying its effect.

The trick is that you must *commit* to the first effect—that is, you must click the clip and then click the Commit button on the Effects panel—before applying the second. You've just thrown away your chance of restoring the clip to its original, effect-free condition.

If this tradeoff concerns you, don't forget that you have a ten-step Undo command at your disposal; it can even undo

a click on the Commit button. If you use the Undo command repeatedly, you can even take back *repeated* Commit clicks.

If you're worried about running out of Undos, on the other hand, you can always use the principle described on page 109. Before clicking Commit, you could conceivably return to your project's Media folder in the Finder and Option-drag the appropriate effect clip (called, for example, Black and White 01) to the desktop, where it will serve as a worst-case backup. If you really make a mess of your clip, you can always drag this backup clip back into the Media folder. Upon relaunching iMovie, the program will invite you to have this clip placed back on the Shelf, ready for placing back into your Movie Track to replace the over-effected copy.

Black and White (Built-In)

This effect does one thing very well: It turns your clip into a black-and-white piece of footage, suitable for simulating security-camera footage or TV from the 1950s.

Brightness/Contrast (Built-In)

Footage that's too dark is one of the most common hallmarks of amateur camcorder work (see page 53). If you're filming indoors without extra lights, you may as well accept the fact that your clip will be too dark.

The Brightness/Contrast controls can help, but they're no substitute for good lighting in the original footage. When you drag the Brightness and Contrast sliders in very small amounts, you may be able to rescue footage that's slightly murky or washed out. Dragging the sliders a lot, however, may make the too-dark footage grainy and weird-looking.

Tip: Using the Effect In and Out sliders, you can control which *parts* of the clip are affected by the Adjust Colors and Brightness/Contrast effects. If you need the colors or brightness to shift several times over the course of a clip, consider chopping up the clip into several smaller clips, each of which is an opportunity to reset the effect settings and timings.

Flash (Plug-in Pack 2)

This effect simulates flash bulbs going off. You won't have much call for this effect in everyday filmmaking; but when that day arrives that you're trying to depict a movie star arriving at opening night—or somebody getting electrocuted—iMovie 2 stands ready.

- **Count (One—Max).** This slider controls how many flashes will go off in the scene. (The maximum number depends on your Speed slider setting and the length of the clip, but the most you'll get is about one every seven frames, or about four per second.)

- **Brightness (Min—Max).** Controls the intensity of each flash. For true flash-bulb effects, you'll want the slider at, or close to, its Max; for storm lightning or nuclear-bomb-watching effects, use lower settings.

- **Speed (Fast—Slow).** Governs how far apart the flashes appear.

Tip: You can use this effect to create a convincing newsreel (or school science film) look. First, turn your clip into black-and-white using the Black and White effect; then click Commit. Now apply the Flash effect with the sliders set to Max, Min, and Fast, respectively.

Ghost Trails (Plug-in Pack 2)

This effect (see Figure 6-8) makes moving portions of the video leave behind "visual echos," as shown below; in addition to blurry-vision effects, it can also be handy when you're trying to depict a runner as a superhero with blinding speed.

On clips without much motion, this effect does nothing at all.

The sliders let you control the intensity of the effect:

- **Trail (Short—Long).** Governs the length of the ghost images that follow a rapidly moving object in your scene.

- **Steps (Small—Large).** Controls how closely the ghost image follows the moving object.

- **Opacity (Transparent—Opaque).** Lets you specify the transparency of the ghost image.

Mirror (Plug-in Pack 2)

This completely freaky effect makes iMovie split the video picture in half down the middle; it then fills the left half of the screen with a mirror image of the right half. As shown in Figure 6-8, there's no seam to indicate what's going on; the result is an Alice-in-Wonderland hybrid.

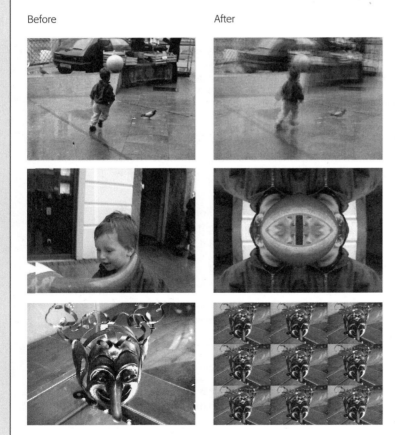

Before   After

Figure 6-8:
Top: The Ghost Trails effect, which might be better named "Bad drug trip," "Hangover," or "After the surgery."

Middle: The Advanced Mirror effect, which turns any footage into a wild, living kaleidoscope.

Bottom: The N Square effect at a low setting. Higher settings make the video look like "Hollywood Squares" gone berserk.

The Horizontal (Left—Right) slider moves the "mirror" left and right across the frame. At far left, the footage doesn't look any different. At far right, you've flipped the entire frame right-for-left. (While the Mirror effect in general doesn't seem to be very practical for most filmmaking, the ability to flip the frame horizontally can be terrifically useful. It can turn a sunrise into a sunset, make the fire engine drive west instead of east, and otherwise fix continuity problems.)

Tip: Be careful of *signs* (such as road signs) in footage you've mirrored. Their reverse-image type is a dead giveaway that you've rewritten history.

Mirror Advanced (Plug-in Pack 2)

While the Mirror effect places a virtual mirror that reflects the right or left half of the video images, Mirror Advanced can reflect vertically as well as horizontally—or both. At the default setting, all four quadrants of the picture are, in fact, upside-down and/or horizontally flipped copies of the lower-right quadrant of the original footage. (Figure 6-8 may make this clear, or maybe not.)

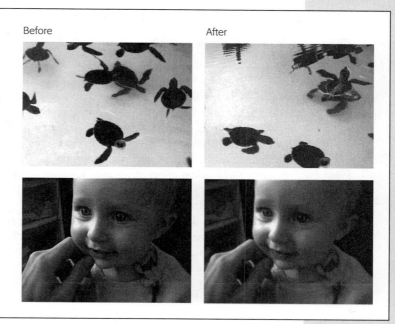

Figure 6-9:
Top: The Water Ripple in progress (it always starts at the upper-left corner of the frame). The still photo here doesn't do justice to the realism of the spreading pond ripples. Bottom: The Soft Focus effect.

Before   After

- **Vertical (Top—Bottom).** The position of this slider determines where the horizontal "mirror" should be placed: closer to the top of the frame or to the bottom. At the Top position you get no vertical reflections at all, effectively turning the Mirror Advanced effect into the Mirror effect described above.

Tip: If you drag the Vertical slider all the way to Bottom, and the Horizontal slider to Left, you neatly flip your clip upside-down–an iMovie first.

- **Horizontal (Left—Right).** This slider positions the second, vertical mirror from left to right across the frame. As with the Mirror effect, pushing this slider all the way to Left removes the horizontal reflections altogether.

The Effect In and Effect Out sliders make the mirrors fly in from the top and side of the frame as the clip plays. Memo to music-video makers: The effect can be truly creepy.

N-Square (Plug-in Pack 2)

If you've been secretly burning to remake *The Fly* from the insect's point of view, this is your effect (see Figure 6-8).

The Squares (Min—Max) controls how many panes the frame contains, each showing the same image. At the Min position, you get four copies; at Max, you get literally hundreds.

Tip: If you use the Effect In and Effect Out sliders, you get an interesting variation on the N-Square effect. The clip starts out looking normal; as it plays, the grid of duplicates flies in from the lower-right, sliding into its final matrix.

Sepia Tone (Built-In)

You might think of this effect as a more nostalgic version of the Black and White effect. Once again, the color drains out of your clip; but instead of black-and-white, you get brown-and-white, which conveys the feeling of memory (thanks to its resemblance to the look of antique photographs). Don't forget to follow up with the Brightness/Contrast effect, if necessary, to fine-tune the effect.

Sharpen (Built-In)

You might guess that this effect could help to repair out-of-focus scenes; in practice, however, the Sharpen effect isn't very effective in that role. Instead, it adds a fine grain to your footage, often creating a "solarized" color-banding effect, to the degree you specify using the Amount slider.

Soft Focus (Built-In)

Soft-focus lenses are often used when filming TV commercials that feature aging movie stars, because the fine netting or Vaseline coating on such lenses blur fine wrinkles. (Soft-focus lenses also give everything a faintly blurry, fuzzy-edged look, but that's the price the stars pay for wrinkle obfuscation.)

Now you, too, can hide your subjects' wrinkles, by applying this soft-focus effect after the filming is complete. This effect is also good for suggestion dreams, memory, or other hazy situations. Use the Amount slider to adjust the amount of blurriness.

Water Ripple

This effect makes the footage look as though seen in a rippling pond of perfectly reflective mercury; a gentle breeze seems to blow across the surface of the footage from upper-left. It would be hard to imagine when Water Ripple would be precisely the effect you're looking for—in a pinch, it could stand in for a David Letterman-esque "I remember it as though it were yesterday" lead-in to a flashback—but it certainly is beautiful.

Tip: The effects, transitions, and titles in iMovie 2 (and its Plug-in Pack) aren't the only ones available. $30 buys you 40 additional transitions (page curls, rotation, barn-door opening, zoom, spin, and others) and 16 more footage "filters" (mosaic, emboss, X-ray, and so on); this kit is a download from *www.geethree.com*. After you install it (just as you would the Plug-in Pack described earlier), the effects show up in the Transitions and Effects palettes just as though they'd been born there.

Another source of iMovie 2 add-ons is the consulting Web site of Glenn Reid, iMovie's lead engineer. He plans to stock the site with additional iMovie 2 plug-ins, tips, and tricks; check it out at *www.rightbrain.com*.

ON LOCATION

The 80-Year-Old Filmmaker

An 80-year-old man came into my shop one morning and told me that he finally retired. He said he would like to resume his old hobby from 60 years ago: making movies.

He asked for "Film cameras" and film editing gear. When I told him that such gear is complex and very expensive, he got very upset.

I asked him to consider a DV camcorder and an NLE editing program (*nonlinear editing,* such as iMovie, Premiere, and Final Cut). He bought the camera but didn't even want to see a Premiere demo. He had never used a computer in his life!

Two weeks later, the first iMac DV units came in.

I asked this customer to come back to the shop. This time he agreed to sit in front of the iMac and make few clicks on the iMovie buttons. After two more visits—and after I promised him unlimited support and training—he bought an iMac DV with iMovie.

He called every day the following week. And then stopped.

I called him to see how he was doing. He was very excited. He told me that he already made two five-minute nature movies, and was now searching for the right music for his sound track.

After few more days, he came in and proudly gave me a VHS cassette with his first completed movie: a five-minute short, featuring blooming flowers. With nice cross dissolves and a Vivaldi music track.

He proudly told me that:

1. His wife had teamed up with him as his "Sound Track designer."

2. He and his younger son, a computer engineer, at last have something in common.

3. They are both working now on sharing Web movies with the older son and his children, who live in the US.

4. He is happy like he was 60 years ago.

—*Danny Natovich*
Tel Aviv, Israel

Titles, Captions, and Credits

T ext superimposed over footage is incredibly common in the film and video worlds. You'd be hard-pressed to find a single movie, TV show, or commercial that doesn't have titles, captions, or credits. In fact, it's the *absence* of superimposed text helps identify most camcorder videos as amateur efforts.

In iMovie, the term *title* refers to any kind of text: credits, titles, subtitles, copyright notices, and so on. You use them almost exactly the way you use the transitions or effects described in Chapter 6: by choosing a text-animation style from a list, adjusting its duration using a slider, dragging it into your Movie Track, and waiting while iMovie renders the effect.

But you don't need to be nearly as economical in your use of titles as you are with transitions. Transitional effects and visual effects interfere with something that stands perfectly well on its own—the footage. Transitions and special effects that aren't purposeful and important to the film may well annoy or distract your audience. When you superimpose text, on the other hand, the audience is much more likely to accept your intrusion. You're introducing this new element for its benefit, to convey information you couldn't transmit otherwise.

Moreover, as you'll soon see, most of iMovie's text effects are far more focused in purpose than its transition and effect selections; you'll have little trouble choosing the optimum text effect for a particular editing situation. For example, the Scrolling Credits effect rolls a list of names slowly up the screen—an obvious candidate for the close of your movie. Another puts several consecutive lines of text in a little block at the lower-left corner of the screen—exactly the way the text in MTV music videos appears.

Tip: Using the Titles feature described in this chapter isn't the only way to create text effects. Using a graphics program like AppleWorks or Photoshop, you can create text "slides" with far more flexibility than you can in the Titles feature. For example, the built-in Titles feature offers you a choice of only sixteen limited colors and limited choice of type size. But using a "title card" that you import as a graphic, you're free to use any text color and any font size. You can even dress up such titles with clip art, three-dimensional effects, and whatever other features your graphics software offers.

Credits that you import as still graphics in this way can't do much more than fade in and fade out. When you bypass iMovie's built-in titles feature, you give up the ability to use the fancy animations. Still, the flexibility you gain in the look, color, and size of your type may be worth the sacrifice. For details on this technique, see Chapter 9.

Setting Up a Title

Adding some text to your movie requires several setup steps:

1. **Choose a title effect.**

2. **Type the text.**

3. **Specify the duration and timing.**

4. **Choose a font.**

5. **Specify the size of the lettering.**

6. **Choose an animation direction.**

7. **Turn on the Over Black checkbox, if desired.**

8. **Choose a color for the lettering.**

9. **Add a backdrop.**

Here are these same steps in more detail:

Choose a Title Effect

Start by clicking the Titles button. The effects list, and the other elements of the Titles palette, appear, as shown in Figure 7-1.

When you click an effect's name, you see a short preview in the Preview screen. (Use the catalog at the end of this chapter to guide you in choosing a text effect.) To see the same preview on the full-size Monitor, click the Preview button.

Tip: When showing you the preview, iMovie superimposes the text over whatever Movie Track clip is currently showing in the Monitor window. Drag the Playhead anywhere you like to specify which footage you'd like to see behind this preview. (If you haven't put any clips into the Movie Track, your preview shows only a black background, as though you'd turned on the Over Black checkbox.)

Type the Text

Beneath the list of text effects, you'll find a place to type the actual text you want to appear in this credit, caption, or title. Just click the box once to highlight the proposed text and then begin typing. (You don't have to backspace over the factory-installed dummy text first.)

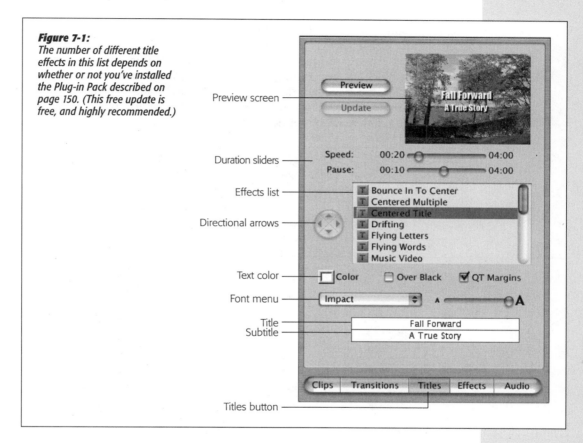

Figure 7-1:
The number of different title effects in this list depends on whether or not you've installed the Plug-in Pack described on page 150. (This free update is free, and highly recommended.)

Preview screen

Duration sliders

Effects list

Directional arrows

Text color

Font menu

Title
Subtitle

Titles button

Tip: The first time you run iMovie, the proposed title and subtitle aren't very stimulating: The first title is "My Great Movie," and its subtitle is your name (or whatever you've typed into the Owner Name blank in the File Sharing control panel). The second title is "Starring," and its subtitle is "Me." You get the idea.

iMovie has a knack for hanging on to title text. Once you change the text in the title and subtitle boxes, you've changed the starter text for *all* iMovie projects. You can also change this default—and the defaults of all text pairs in the Titles palette—using the secret iMovie Preferences document described on page 377.

The way this text box looks and acts depends on the kind of title you've selected in the list. They fall into three categories (see Figure 7-2):

Text blocks

When you choose the Music Video or Scrolling Block text effects, you get a simple text box, into which you can type any text you want. At the end of each line, you can press Return to create a new line, or press Return twice to create a blank line, exactly as you would in a word processor. (You can use the Cut, Copy, and Paste commands in the Edit menu to edit this text, too.)

Technically, the maximum amount of text you can type or paste here is 32 K—the standard Mac OS text-field limit you've enjoyed in SimpleText for years. The Music Video effect, furthermore, limits you to amount of text that fits on one screen. But the Scrolling Block effect is far more accommodating; as you paste more and more text into its box, the maximum setting of the Speed slider keeps changing as it approaches four minutes. (See "Music Video" and "Scrolling Block" in the catalog section at the end of this chapter for details.)

Tip: You don't have to settle for the proposed placement of the text when you choose one of the animation styles described below. By adding spaces before your text, or Returns after it, you get much more flexibility over where the text appears in the frame.

For example, if you add enough spaces and Returns to your text in the Music Video effect, you can place your text virtually anywhere on the screen.

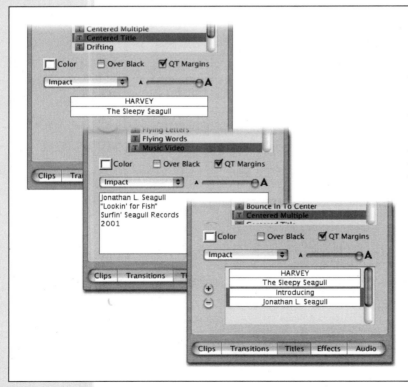

Figure 7-2:
The area into which you can type your text depends on the kind of text effect you've selected. You'll be offered either two lines for a title and subtitle (top left), one big text box (middle), or a virtually unlimited number of two-line pairs (bottom right), suitable for credit sequences at the end of your movie.

Title/Subtitle pairs

When you click the names of most effects, you're shown only two narrow boxes into which you can type text, as shown in Figure 7-2 at center. Whatever you type into the top box often appears in the larger typeface than the one in the bottom box.

Such effects as Bounce In To Center, Centered Title, Flying Letters, Flying Words, Scroll with Pause, Stripe Subtitle, Subtitle, Typewriter, and Zoom fall into this category.

Tip: You don't have to type text into both of these boxes. In fact, *most* of the time you'll probably type into only the top box. The subtitle box underneath is there solely for your convenience, for those occasions when you need a second, usually smaller, line of type underneath the larger credit.

Pair sequences

When you're creating the credits for the end of a movie, you usually want two columns of text: on the left, the list of roles; on the right, the actors who portrayed them. In these situations, you need iMovie to offer *pairs* of slots—enough to accommodate the names of everybody who worked on your movie. It's easy to spot the text effects that offer these two-line pairs; they're the ones with the words "Multiple" or "Rolling" in their names.

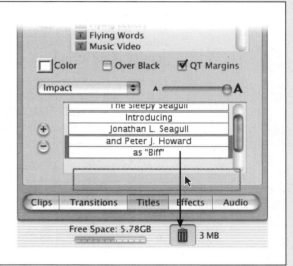

Figure 7-3:
You can rearrange the credits in your sequence by dragging the edge of a credit pair up or down in the list, and waiting patiently as iMovie scrolls the list (arrow). You can also remove a credit by clicking the – button or by dragging the text box directly to the project Trash can (lower arrow). But don't choose File→Empty Trash as your next step. Doing so wipes out your ability to use the Undo command for your last ten editing steps.

After clicking one of these title effects, you see not one but two different text-box pairs. The window offers a scroll bar, plus an Add button, so that you can add more pairs and scroll through them.

Start by clicking the top box and typing the first character's name (*Raymond,* for example). Press Tab to highlight the lower box, and then type the actor's name (*Dustin*

Hoffman, for example). If there's another empty pair of boxes beneath the one you've just filled, press Tab again, and fill in those boxes, too.

You'll know when you've filled up all the available boxes: You'll either discover that you can't scroll down any more, or when you press Tab, you'll circle around and wind up in the *first* box you filled in. At that point, click the Add button beneath the text boxes to add another pair of boxes. Keep going this way—clicking Add, typing a pair of names, clicking Add again—until you've typed in the names of everybody you want added to the list of credits.

Specify the Timing

In iMovie 1, you could specify how long your text hung around on the screen. Each text effect came with a different preset minimum and maximum time; for example, the Centered Large Tile couldn't be shorter than 1 second or longer than 4 seconds, 20 frames.

In iMovie 2, you have more control over the timing of your titles' animation—and more complexity to understand. Most of the iMovie 2 title styles offer two sliders just below the Preview screen:

- The **Speed** slider has different results with different titles; setting a faster Speed setting makes the Centered Title fade in/out faster, Flying Words fly faster, Typewriter type faster, and so on. For title styles involving motion, it controls the text speed; for title styles that remain still (such as Centered Title), it controls the amount of time the text spends on the screen. The catalog of title styles at the end of this chapter identifies the Speed slider's effect for each style.

- The **Pause** effect depends on the style, too. For titles that fade in and out, it controls the amount of time the text will be fully manifested on the screen, readable and at full size and brightness, between its fade in and fade out segments. For titles whose text flies or rolls into place (such as Typewriter or Flying Words), Pause controls how long the finished title hangs around after it's complete.

Once you've grasped the purpose of these sliders, their inclusion in iMovie 2 is a very good thing. For example, if you're putting together an action film, the slow, leisurely, canned fade ins of the old iMovie 1 titles could kill the excitement you're trying to build.

As you adjust these sliders, the readout in the lower-right corner of the preview screen shows you, in "seconds:frames" format, the time settings you've specified. (You have to wait until the preview is finished playing before these numbers appear.) For example, if it says "05:20 + 01:08 = 6:28," iMovie is trying to tell you, in its way:

"You've set the Speed slider to 5:20, which is 170 frames. So I'll make the text fade in over half of that time: 2 seconds, 15 frames. Then you've set the Pause slider to 1:08, so I'll make the text sit there on the screen for 1 second, 8 frames. Finally, I'll take another 2 seconds, 15 frames to fade out."

Note: Not all of the effects offer a Pause slider. Drifting, Music Video, the Rolling Credits effects, and the Subtitle effects have no motion/pause sequence to speak of. Either they move steadily or they don't move at all.

In these cases, the time readout is affected only by the Speed slider and simply means "Total time on the screen."

Take into account your viewers' reading speed. There's only one thing more frustrating than titles that fly by too quickly to read, and that's titles that sit there on the screen forever, boring the audience silly. In professional video editing, a rule of thumb is: Leave the words on the screen long enough for somebody to read them out loud twice.

Preview the effect

As with the transitions described in the previous chapter, a standard computer these days doesn't have the oomph to show you a living, real-time preview of the title as it's superimposed on your video. Therefore, iMovie offers two kinds of preview:

- **Preview box.** If you click a title style's name, you see a real-time preview of your title animation in the small Preview box above the list of titles. It's jerky and rough, but it lasts as long as the finished title will last, giving you a good idea of your title's readability. (The Speed and Pause sliders affect these previews.)

- **Monitor window.** If you click the Preview *button,* iMovie shows another kind of preview in the Monitor window. This time, you get to see every single frame of the animation, no matter how long it takes your Mac to spew out these images. Of course, this means that you won't see the animation play at real-world speed; you're getting, in essence, a slow-motion version of the full effect.

Choose a Font

Using the pop-up menu just below the list of effects, you can choose a typeface for your text. Consider these guidelines:

- **Use only TrueType or PostScript fonts.** Mac OS 9 no longer needs Adobe Type Manager (ATM) installed in your Control Panels folder in order to display smooth, gorgeous *PostScript* fonts on the screen. Just don't use *bitmapped* fonts.

  And if you have no idea what these terms mean, don't worry. *All* the fonts that came preinstalled on your Mac are TrueType fonts, and will look terrific in your iMovie production. (The new fonts installed by programs like Internet Explorer and AppleWorks are also in TrueType format, and also look great in iMovie.) You need to worry about the font type only if you've manually installed some additional ones onto your Mac.

Note: The beauty of iMovie's titling feature is that the fonts you choose become embedded into the actual digital picture. In other words, when you distribute your movie as a QuickTime file, you don't have to worry that your recipients might not have the same fonts you used to create the file; they'll see on their screens exactly what you see on yours.

- **Be consistent.** Using the same typeface for all of the titles in your movie lends consistency and professionalism to the project.

- **Remember the QuickTime effect.** If you plan to distribute your finished movie as a QuickTime file—an electronic movie file that you can distribute by email, network, CD, disk, or Web page—use the biggest, boldest, cleanest fonts you have. Avoid spindly delicate fonts, or script fonts; when your movie is compressed down to a 3-inch square, what looks terrific in your Monitor window will be so small it may become completely illegible. (Look at each illustration in the catalog discussion at the end of this chapter. If the text is hard to read there, you won't be able to read it in a small QuickTime movie, either.)

If your movie will be a QuickTime movie, turn on the QT Margins checkbox, too. Doing so increases the maximum font size you're allowed to select using the text-size slider described below. (See the sidebar "Making Your Titles 'TV-Safe'" for the explanation.)

UP TO SPEED

The "TV-Safe" Area, Overscanning, and You

Millions of TV viewers every day are blissfully unaware that they're missing the big picture.

In its early days, the little cathode-ray guns inside the TV worked by painting one line of the TV picture, then turning around and heading back the opposite direction. To make sure that the screen was painted edge to edge, these early TVs were programmed to overshoot the edges of the screen—or, to use the technical term, to *overscan* the screen.

TV technology is much better now, but even modern TVs exhibit overscanning. The amount varies, but you may be missing as much as 10 percent of the picture beyond the left and right edges (and often the top and bottom, too).

TV producers are careful to keep the action and titles in the part of the frame that's least likely to be lost in overscan. But as a film editor, the *TV-safe area* is suddenly your concern, too. The overscanning effect means that when you show your iMovie productions on a TV, you'll lose any-

TV-safe area   Lost when viewed on TV

A Big Dog Story
Life in the Flea Circus

thing that's very close to the edges of the frame.

Most of the time, that's no problem; only when you're adding titles does the overscanning effect become a worry. Unfortunately, in iMovie 1, a few of iMovie's built-in title effects began or ended squarely in the no-man's land outside the TV-safe area.

Avoiding text-chopping problems in iMovie 2, however, is supremely easy: Just turn *off* the QT Margins checkbox. Doing so makes iMovie shrink the text enough so that it won't get chopped off on a TV—guaranteed.

This business of the TV-safe area *isn't an issue* if you plan to convert your iMovie work into QuickTime movies, which have no such complications. That's why this checkbox is worded as it is; "QT Margins" means "Assume that this movie will be shown as a QuickTime movie, and therefore won't have chopped-off margins." When the QT Margins checkbox is turned *on,* the text-size slider lets you crank your font sizes a few notches higher.

Come to think of it, you might want to choose big, bold, clean fonts even if you're going to play the finished movie on a TV, whose resolution is far lower than that of your computer screen. Be especially careful when using one of the text effects that includes a subtitle; iMovie subtitles often use an even smaller typeface than the primary title font, and may lose legibility if the font has too much filigree.

Finally, favor *sans serif* fonts—typefaces that don't have the tiny *serifs*, or "hats and feet," at the end of the character strokes. The typeface you're reading now is a serif font, one that's less likely to remain legible in a QuickTime movie. The typeface used in the next (Tip) paragraph is a sans serif font.

Tip: Some of the standard Mac fonts that look especially good as iMovie fonts are Arial Black, Capitals, Charcoal, Chicago, Gadget, Helvetica, Impact, Sand, Techno, and Textile.

Some of the fonts whose delicate nature may be harder to read are Monaco, Courier, Old English, Swing, Trebuchet, Times, Palatino, and Verdana.

Specify the Size of the Lettering

In iMovie 2, you no longer have to contend with two sets of text effects, such as "Center Title" and "Centered Title Large." There's only one kind of each effect—and a new text-size slider. The odds of creating type that shrinks to illegibility when converted to QuickTime movies are greatly lessened.

Don't get too excited, however; iMovie 2 is still extremely conservative with its font-size choices. Even with the slider at the far right and "QT Margins" turned on, iMovie doesn't let you make titles that fill the screen. (Keeping your text short may help; if the phrase is very long, iMovie further reduces the point size enough to fit the entire line on the screen, even if the type-size slider is at its maximum. In other words, you can make the font for the credit *PIGGY* much larger than you can *ONE HAM'S ADVENTURES IN MANHATTAN.*)

If you feel hemmed in by the font-size limitations, consider using a still-image "title card" with text as large as you like, as described on page 237.

Choose an Animation Direction

Most of iMovie's text effects are animated. They feature words flying across the screen, sliding from one edge of the frame to the other, and so on. Some feature directional arrows (seen in Figure 7-1, for example) that let you control which direction the text flies or slides in. By clicking the appropriate arrow, you can specify which direction the text should fly. (The directional controls are dimmed and unavailable for other text effects.)

Note: In the case of the Music Video effect, the arrow specifies which *corner* the text block should sit in, motionless.

The catalog of text effects at the end of this chapter identifies those that offer a direction control, and what it does in each case.

The "Over Black" Checkbox

Under normal circumstances, the text you've specified gets superimposed over the video picture. Particularly when you're creating opening or closing credits, however, you may want the lettering to appear on a black screen—a striking and professional-looking effect. In those cases, turn on the Over Black checkbox.

It's important to note that when you do so, you *add* to the total length of your movie. Adding the Over Black title is like inserting a new clip; you force the clips to the right of your text effect to slide further rightward to accommodate the credit you just inserted. (When the Over Black checkbox *isn't* turned on, by contrast, adding a text effect doesn't change the overall length of your movie.)

Tip: The Over Black option is attractive for three reasons. First, it looks extremely professional; it's something people who don't have an editing program like iMovie can't even do. Second, the high contrast of white against black makes the text very legible. Third, the audience will *read* it, instead of being distracted by the video behind it.

Choose a Color for the Lettering

By clicking the tiny square beside the word Color, you get a little pop-up menu that offers 24 text colors. Click the one you want for the letters in your text. Above all, choose a color that *contrasts* with the footage behind the lettering: white against black, black against white, yellow against blue, and so on.

Fortunately, iMovie 2 gives you many more color choices—and much brighter ones—than the original iMovie. They're still "TV safe," however. (If colors are too bright [saturated], the edges of the letters can smear and tear when played back on a TV. All of the colors in Apple's text-color palette are safe from that kind of problem.)

Unfortunately, not every iMovie production is destined for playback on a TV. What if you want to turn your film into a QuickTime movie? What if you want a text color that's brighter or more saturated than the iMovie 2 collection of 24?

In such cases, you can work around Apple's palette shackles in either of two un-documented ways:

- As mentioned at the beginning of this chapter, you can create your titles as still images, using any colors you like, as described in Chapter 9.

- You can *change* iMovie's default set of colors using free add-on software, as described in the box on page 177.

Add a Backdrop

If you left your education to the Apple online help, you might assume that there are only two kinds of images that can underlie your titles: video footage or a solid black frame. Fortunately, there's a third option that greatly expands your creative possibilities: superimposing your text on a still image, such as a photo or some gradient fill you've created in, say, AppleWorks.

WORKAROUND WORKSHOP

Changing iMovie's Text-Color Palette

If the muted pastel shades in the Titles palette aren't quite what your hard-hitting sci-fi drama calls for, you're not completely out of luck. With a few quick clicks in ResEdit, the free editing program available at *www.missingmanual.com,* you can choose new colors for the iMovie text-color palette.

Note: ResEdit changes the actual code in your software. Use ResEdit only when you've got a "cookbook" to follow, such as this one:

Quit iMovie. Launch ResEdit. Click the jack-in-the-box to make it go away.

When the Open File dialog box appears, navigate to, and open, your iMovie program (inside the iMovie *folder* on your hard drive).

What appears next is a screenful of icons only programmers could love. Double-click the icon called *clut,* which stands for Color Look-Up Table and looks like—hey!—a pop-up palette of colors. The resulting window contains a single phrase: "Safe Color Palette"; double-click it to open the window shown here at top.

Each of the tiny colored squares at the top of this window represents one of the colored squares in the iMovie title-color palette. Double-click a square to change its color; the Apple Color Picker dialog box appears. You can specify a different color by clicking the color displays in this special dialog box. (Hint: Click the Crayons icon at the left side of

the window; that's the simplest way to choose a new color.)

When you're finished in the Color Picker, click OK. The tiny square palette icon shows the new color you've selected for it.

Choose File→Quit. When you're asked if you want to save your changes, click Yes.

Now open iMovie. Sure enough, you've installed a new color into the iMovie title-color palette.

But for heaven's sake, don't stop reading now—the best is yet to come. As it turns out, iMovie's color palette is not only tame, it's also *tiny.* Who can live a life in the visual arts with a color palette of only 24 shades? Using ResEdit, you can also add *more* colors to this palette—*lots* more.

To bring about this delightful arrangement, quit iMovie; open ResEdit again. Use it, once again, to open iMovie and the *clut* icon, and the "Title Colors" item. This time, however, choose Resource→ Insert New Color. Like magic, a new square appears in the row of title colors shown in the ResEdit window.

As before, double-click it to specify a hue for it in the Color Picker. When you close the Color Picker, choose Resource→Insert New Color again, and begin the cycle anew. Continue until every shade of text you'll ever want in a movie is represented here. Then quit ResEdit, save changes, open iMovie, and enjoy your newfound color freedom.

In fact, the iMovie Web site offers a set of stunning, ready-to-download, perfectly proportioned backdrop graphics just for this purpose. (At this writing, you can find them at *www.apple.com/imovie/freestuff.*) Figure 7-4 shows the effect.

Tip: One of the still backgrounds you can download from the Apple Web site—part of the Video collection—is called Color Bars. It lets you begin and end your movie with the standard, broadcast-TV color bar chart like the one shown (in shades of gray) at lower right in Figure 7-4. In professional video work, about 20 seconds of color bars are always recorded at the beginning of a tape. They give the technicians a point of color reference for adjusting their monitors and other reproduction equipment to ensure that the footage looks the same on their gear as it did on yours. Their goal is to adjust the knobs until the white bars look white, not pink, and the black ones don't look gray.

If you intend your movie to be used for TV broadcast, the color bars may actually be required by the station. If not, the color bars make your homemade production look and feel as though you edited it in a $600-per-hour New York editing facility.

To use one of these backdrops, import it into your project as you would any graphics file, as described on page 237. That discussion also shows you how to control how long a still image should last when it appears in your movie. From there, you should have little difficulty superimposing titles as described in this chapter.

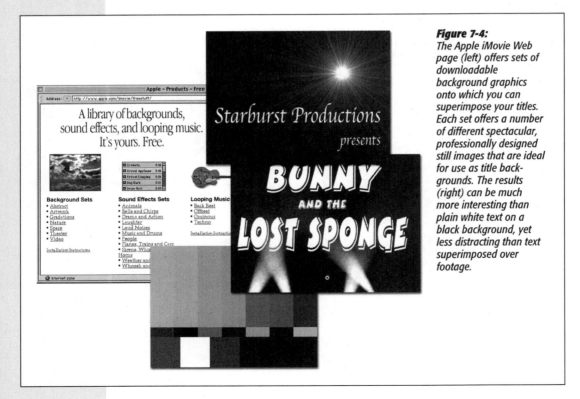

Figure 7-4:
The Apple iMovie Web page (left) offers sets of downloadable background graphics onto which you can superimpose your titles. Each set offers a number of different spectacular, professionally designed still images that are ideal for use as title backgrounds. The results (right) can be much more interesting than plain white text on a black background, yet less distracting than text superimposed over footage.

Inserting and Rendering a Title

When you've taken into consideration all the options described so far in this chapter, you probably have a good feel for how this title is going to look once it's inserted into your movie. Now it's time to commit it to digital film.

Dragging the Title into the Movie Track

To place the title you've selected into Movie Track, proceed as follows:

1. **Decide where you want the title to begin.**

   Begin by pressing the Home key on your keyboard, which simultaneously deselects all clips and rewinds the Playhead to the beginning of the Movie Track. Now you can drag the playhead along the Scrubber bar, as shown on page 117. As you do so, a bright red, inverted T cursor slides along your Clip Viewer (or a duplicate Playhead slides along your Timeline Viewer) to indicate your position.

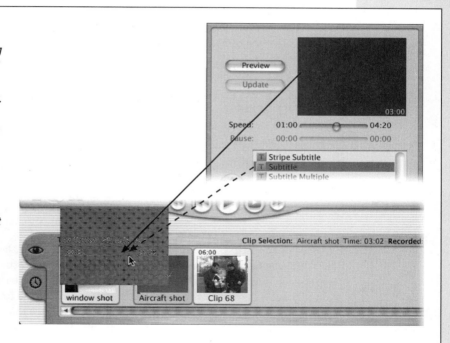

Figure 7-5:
The Apple instructions tell you to drag the name of the title you want out of the Titles list directly into the Movie Track. That method works, too, but if you drag the Preview window instead, your cursor has a much bigger target. Furthermore, dragging the preview window forces you to confirm that you've had a look at the preview of the title you're about to install. Either way, the clips in the Clip Viewer or Timeline Viewer scoot to the right to make room for the title you're inserting.

Consider the location of your title carefully. If you're superimposing it on a black background or a still image, no problem. But if you're planning to superimpose it on moving video, choose a scene that's relatively still, so that the video doesn't distract the audience from the words on screen. Be particularly careful not to superimpose your titles on an unsteady shot; the contrast between the jiggling picture and the rock-steady lettering on the screen will make your audience uncomfortable.

Sometimes, such as when you've selected a title style that fades in from nothing, it's OK to put the title squarely at the beginning of a clip. At other times, you'll want to position the title a few seconds into the clip.

2. **If you've selected a starting point for a title that's in the middle of the clip, position the Playhead there and then choose Edit→Split Video Clip at Playhead.**

It's a fact of iMovie life: A title can begin only at the *beginning* of a clip, never the middle. To make the title seem as though it's starting partway through a clip, therefore, you must *turn* that spot into the beginning of a new clip by chopping the clip in half.

This is not the only time the title feature will be chopping your clips into smaller clips, as Figure 7-6 will make clear.

3. **Drag the Preview window from above the list of titles directly onto the Movie Track, as shown in Figure 7-5.**

Drag it just to the left of the clip you'll want to play underneath the title text. All clips to the right scoot rightward to make room for your cursor.

Rendering Begins

Now iMovie begins to *render* the title effect: to create a new clip that incorporates both the original footage and the text you're superimposing.

In some ways, this title-rendering process resembles the transition- or effect-rendering process described in the previous chapter. For example, you can stop it by pressing ⌘-period. (You also temporarily suspend all rendering if you click inside the Title palette's text boxes—a courteous gesture on iMovie 2's part; it doesn't want the background rendering to make your text editing feel sluggish.)

The longer the title is to remain on the screen, the longer the rendering process takes. But exactly as when rendering transitions, you can continue to do other work in iMovie (or even in other programs) while the title is rendering. In fact, you can even play titles before they're fully baked, to see what they'll look like in your final movie (even full screen)—another handy preview feature that doesn't require you to wait until the rendering is finished. You can even have several titles rendering simultaneously, although iMovie slows down quite a bit if you have more than, say, three titles rendering at once.

This time, however, the bright red progress bar creeps along in the very skinny bar just below the clip itself, as shown in Figure 7-6. In other words, a title in the Movie Track doesn't have its own icon, as a transition does. Instead, you get to see a miniature illustration of what it's going to look like. (Tiny lettering appears directly *on* the superimposed clip icon to help you identify it as a title clip.)

While the rendering is proceeding, you get a digital readout that also keeps you apprised of the rendering's progress, as shown in Figure 7-6. It shows you how many frames long the newly created title clip is going to be, and how many of these frames iMovie has already computed. For example, "30 of 150" indicates that iMovie has finished creating one second of this five-second title credit. (As noted in the Introduction, there are 30 frames of video per second in NTSC format; 25 in PAL.)

Finally, as soon as you've finished dragging a title into the Movie Track, the affected clip's name instantly changes. It takes on the first words of your actual title. If the clip was called, for example, "slow zoom down alley," iMovie renames it "Shoestring Productions presents," or whatever your title says. (You can see this effect, too, in Figure 7-6.) As a bonus, a tiny letter T appears in the upper-right corner of the "slide" in the Clip Viewer, a friendly reminder that you've applied a title to it.

Figure 7-6:
If you want a title to begin partway into a clip (top), instead of at the very beginning, you must first chop the clip into two pieces (middle). During rendering, a counter shows you how many frames iMovie has already rendered, and a progress bar keeps track of the rendering progress (bottom).

After the title has finished rendering, you'll find that iMovie has automatically made yet another clip split—at the ending point of the title (bottom). The result: After you're done inserting a title, that portion of your movie occupied by the title has become a clip unto itself.

Inverted "T" shows where clip will be split

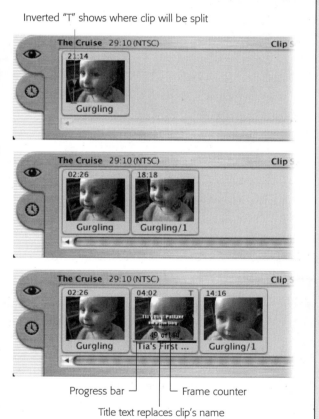

Progress bar — Frame counter

Title text replaces clip's name

How Titles Chop up Your Clips

As Figure 7-6 illustrates, it's not enough that you split your clip if you want the title to begin part way into the footage. iMovie may chop up your clips on its own, according to this scheme:

- If the title you've specified is shorter than the clip, iMovie splits the clip in two. The first portion gets the title text embedded into it; the second portion is left alone.

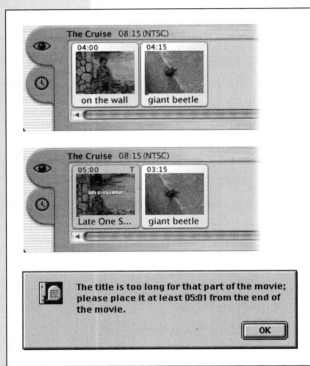

Figure 7-7:
If your title is longer than its clip, iMovie steals however many seconds of footage it needs from the next clip and incorporates it into the first clip. If you look carefully at the durations of these two clips before (top) and after the title has been applied, you'll see that the second clip has been shortened by two seconds, and the first clip lengthened, when the stealing process is over (middle). If you try to apply your title to a too-short clip when there's no subsequent clip from which iMovie can steal frames, on the other hand, you get the error message shown at bottom.

- If the title is *longer* than the clip, iMovie *steals footage* from the next clip to the right (see Figure 7-7). In fact, it continues to eat up as many additional clips as necessary to fulfill the duration you've specified for it. This powerful feature means that you can make a single title sequence extend across series of short clips, still images, transitions, and so on. (Contrast with the Transitions and Effects described in Chapter 6, which limit their appetites to single clips.)

iMovie may still chop up the final clip in the sequence, however, to accommodate the tail end of the title sequence.

Checking the Result

When the rendering process is complete—or even before it's complete—check out the effect. Click the title clip in the Movie Track and press the Space bar to view the title clip, or shift-click the clips before and after the title clip (and then press the Space bar) to see how the title looks in the context of the clips around it. Or just drag the Playhead back and forth across the title to see how it looks.

If the title isn't quite what you wanted—if it's the wrong length, style, or font, or if there's a typo, for example—you can change its settings as described in the next section. If the title wasn't *at all* what you wanted—if it's in the wrong place, for example—you can undo the entire insertion-and-rendering process by highlighting the title clip and pressing the Delete key (or choose Edit→Undo, if you added the title recently). The original footage returns, textless and intact.

POWER USERS' CLINIC

Multiple Simultaneous Superimposed Titles

If you've read this chapter carefully, you may have discovered an intriguing aspect of titles: After iMovie creates one, you don't wind up with a special TV icon in your Movie Track, as you do when you create a transition (see Chapter 6). Instead, the clip that now has your superimposed title is just an ordinary clip—one that you can treat like any other clip; you can move it around in the movie, put it back onto the Shelf, and so on.

As a result, there's nothing to stop you from applying *another* title to the same clip…and another, and another. Each can have its own style, animation, duration, color, font, and text. By carefully splitting each title clip in the Movie Track before applying the next title to it, you can stagger the entrance of each title, so that your words fly onto the screen exactly when, and how, you specify.

Furthermore, by combining these titles so that they don't crash into each other—or *do* crash into each other in artistic ways—you can come up with extremely complex title sequences that rival some of the fanciest opening-credit sequences Hollywood has ever dreamed up.

Editing a Title

Editing a title is easy. Click the title clip's icon in the Movie Track. Click the Titles button, if the list of titles isn't already open.

Now you can adjust the title style, the text of the title itself, the title's timing, the direction of the motion, or any other parameters described in the first part of the chapter. When you're finished, click the Update button just above the duration slider. iMovie begins the rendering process again, putting in place a brand-new title, and splitting the superimposed footage in a different place, if necessary.

Note: The good news is that your ability to edit the title isn't subject to the ten-level Undo limitation. In other words, you can revise the settings for a title at any time, even if it's too late to use Undo.

But if you've applied *multiple* superimposed titles, as described in the box on page 183, you can revise only the most recent title you've applied to a particular clip.

Deleting a Title

As noted above, a title clip is just a clip. You might wonder, therefore, how you can remove a title without also deleting the footage it affects.

Yet sure enough, iMovie remembers what your clips looked like before you overlaid them with a title (see the sidebar box below). That's why you can click a title clip at any time, press the Delete key, and see it restore the original footage that it consumed to make the title. True, pressing Delete on a conventional clip deletes it; but pressing Delete on a title clip simply deletes its "titleness." The clip to its right merges back into its formerly text-overlaid portion, leaving you with only one clip instead of two.

Note: If you've *moved* the clip that follows the title clip, and you *then* delete the title clip, iMovie will still put back the underlying footage that it consumed, but it may no longer be where you expect it to be. The program can't "splice" the footage back onto the beginning of a clip from which it was split, because iMovie doesn't know where that clip is (you might even have deleted it). If you move the clips back into their original sequence after deleting the title, the footage will still be continuous, but there might now be a cut or break where the title ended, as if you had split the clip at that point.

POWER USERS' CLINIC

Behind-the-Scenes Undo Magic

As noted above, iMovie can restore an original clip when you delete a title that you've superimposed on it, even weeks later.

Yet as noted in this chapter, iMovie creates titles by *modifying* the original clips—by changing the actual pixels that compose the image. So where is iMovie storing a copy of the original clip, for use when you decide to delete the title?

In the project's Media folder (see page 108). There you'll find the original clip from the camcorder (called "Clip 1," for example), untouched. There you'll *also* find a new clip (called "Typewriter 1," for example), bearing the name of the title style you used. *This* clip contains the modified portion of your original clip.

The iMovie Titles Catalog

This discussion describes and illustrates each of the title effects available in iMovie 2, as enhanced by the free Plug-in Pack (see page 150). Along the way, you'll find out several useful pieces of information about each title:

- Where this title style comes from—either Built-In or the Plug-in Pack 2.

- Limitations on the number of seconds it can appear on the screen, including both the Speed (fade in + fade out durations) and Pause duration.

- How the Speed slider affects the effect.

- Which text-block category it falls in (as described on page 170): text-block, title/subtitle pair, or scrolling pair sequence.

- Which directions you can make the text move, if any.

- When you might find each effect useful.

Note: Despite the smooth, professional look of iMovie's text effects, many of them may become tiny and illegible when you export your finished movie as a QuickTime movie (see Chapter 12). They may look terrific in your Monitor window or when played on your TV; however, in a small QuickTime movie frame, especially the kind you might post on a Web page or send by email, the text may shrink away to almost nothing.

If you have time to experiment with different versions of your movie, exporting each to a QuickTime movie until you find a text effect that's legible, great. If not, use the notations in this section as a guide; they assume you've set the text slider to its maximum and turn on the QT Margins checkbox.

Bounce In To Center (Built-In)

Duration minimum/maximum: *28 frames/10 seconds*
Speed slider: *Controls flying-on speed*
Category: *Title/subtitle pair*
QuickTime text size: *OK*

Bounce In To Center

In this animated effect, the title slides down from the top of the frame and comes to rest, with a little springy bounce, in the center; if you've specified a subtitle, it floats upward simultaneously from the bottom of the frame. Use it for quirky or comic opening credits—it's not very subtle.

Centered Multiple (Built-In)

Duration minimum/maximum: *1 second/8 seconds*
Speed slider: *Controls fade in/fade out speed*
Category: *Pair sequence*
QuickTime text size: *OK*

Centered Mutliple

 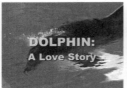  

The Center Multiple is one of the most useful of all the iMovie text effects. It's ideal for opening credits, because each name (along with an optional subtitle) fades professionally onto the screen, remains there for a moment, and then fades away again. The next name fades in to repeat the cycle. (If you haven't seen this particular opening-credit style used at the beginning of a million TV shows and movies, you haven't watched enough TV.)

What's especially nice about this effect is that the type is large enough to see no matter what you intend to do with your movie—exporting it back to tape or saving it as a QuickTime movie.

Centered Title (Built-In)

Duration minimum/maximum: *1 second/4 seconds, 20 frames*
Speed slider: *Controls fade in/fade out speed*
Category: *Title/subtitle pair*
QuickTime text size: *OK*

This kind of title has the same virtues as its multiple-pair sibling described above: It creates big, bold type. This time, however, iMovie shows only a single line of text (or two lines, if you take advantage of the subtitle option), fading in, leaving it on the screen for a moment, then fading out, making this effect ideal for displaying the title of your movie.

Tip: By using several consecutive Centered Titles, you achieve exactly the same effect as the Centered Multiple sequence described above, except with individual control over the timing of each text pair.

Drifting (Built-In)

Duration minimum/maximum: *20 frames/8 seconds*
Speed slider: *Controls total time on screen*
Category: *Title/subtitle pair*
QuickTime text size: *OK*

Drifting

This effect, the only new title effect in iMovie 2, duplicates the opening credits of many a recent Hollywood movie, not to mention TV commercials for the *New York Times* and various over-the-counter drugs. Your two text lines appear at center screen and gracefully float in opposite directions. The effect is extremely eye-catching, although it can be annoying to try to read lines of text that are slipping apart.

Flying Letters (Built-In)

Duration minimum/maximum: *4 seconds, 12 frames/37 seconds, 5 frames*
Speed slider: *Controls flying-on speed*
Category: *Title/subtitle pair*
QuickTime text size: *OK*
Direction control: *Up or down*

Flying Letters

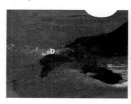

In this effect, the letters of your title (and subtitle, if you've specified one) fly onto the screen one at a time from the upper-right or lower-right corner of the frame (depending on the directional arrow you click), gradually assembling the phrase you've specified. If nothing else, this effect is certainly offbeat; it can quickly get boring if you use it more than once, however.

Flying Words (Built-In)

Duration minimum/maximum: *14 frames/7 seconds*
Speed slider: *Controls flying-on speed*
Category: *Title/subtitle pair*
QuickTime text size: *OK*
Direction control: *Up or down*

Flying Words

 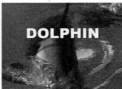  

Imagine the Flying Letters effect just described, but with entire words flying onto the screen instead of letters. You should still use it sparingly, but it may be less tedious for your audience to watch.

Music Video (Built-In)

Duration minimum/maximum: *15 frames/10 seconds*
Speed slider: *Controls total time on screen*
Category: *Text block*
QuickTime text size: *Too small to read*
Direction control: *Left or right*

Music Video

If you've ever seen a music video on MTV or VH-1, you'll recognize this effect instantly. It places the block of text you've typed—four or five short lines of it, for example—into the lower-left or lower-right corner of the screen, depending on which directional arrow you select.

The authenticity of this effect is unassailable. It looks *exactly* like the credits that appear at the beginning of actual music videos. Even with the type-size slider all the way to the right, however, the type is extremely small—too small for videos you intend to distribute by email or on the Web.

Tip: The Music Video title is one of the most useful text styles; it's the only iMovie text style that gives you complete freedom over placement of your text. You can make your title appear off-center, in any corner of the frame, and so on.

The trick is to use "white space" to position the text. By pressing the Space bar before typing each line, you can push your text to the middle or right side of the frame; by pressing Return after the text, you can force the text upward to the middle or top of the frame.

Combine these techniques with the left/right directional buttons for various wacky-placement effects.

Rolling Centered Credits, Rolling Credits (Built-In)

Duration minimum/maximum: *3 seconds/45 seconds, 1 frame*
Speed slider: *Controls total time on screen*
Category: *Pair sequence*
QuickTime text size: *Barely legible*
Direction control: *Up or down*

Rolling Centered Credits

 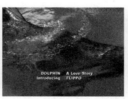  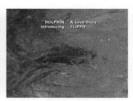

Rolling Credits

Here it is: the closing-credits effect that wraps up every Hollywood movie you've ever seen. It creates what the pros call a *roll*—text that slides up the screen from the bottom, as though on an endless roll of clear plastic, showing the names of the characters and the actors who played them. (A *crawl*, on the other hand, slides onto the screen from side to side, like the tornado-warning notices that sometimes appear during a TV show. At this writing, iMovie offers no method for creating crawls, much to the disappointment of TV stations in Iowa; but future plug-in packs may include one.)

Be careful when using this effect for two reasons: first, remember that 45 seconds is the longest crawl you can create, and iMovie automatically adjusts the speed of scrolling to fit all the names you've typed into the duration you've specified. You couldn't fit even 10 percent of the closing credits of *Titanic* into 45 seconds, at least not without scrolling them too fast to read. (On the other hand, you can always use multiple *sets* of Rolling Credits titles, as described on page 190.)

Second, the type is very small. Once again, this can be a problem if you intend to save your movie as a QuickTime file.

The Rolling Credits effect is identical to the Rolling Centered Credits except for the formatting—instead of straddling an invisible "gutter" of empty space, the two columns (of character names and actor names) are separated by a dotted line.

Scroll with Pause (Built-In)

Duration minimum/maximum: *7 seconds, 6 frames/1 minute, 24 seconds, 22 frames*
Speed slider: *Controls scroll-in/scroll-off speed*
Category: *Title/subtitle pair*
QuickTime text size: *OK*
Direction control: *Up, down, left, right*

Scrolling With Pause

The title and subtitle (if you've specified one) slide, as a pair, from the edge of the screen you've specified (by clicking the directional arrows); pause at the center of the screen for the audience to read it; and then continue sliding on their merry way off the screen.

This isn't an effect you're likely to use often. But it can look quirky and charming if the speed and the typeface are right. For example, when your credits slide from left to right, you suggest an old-time slide projector changing slides.

Scrolling Block (Built-In)

Duration minimum/maximum: *20 frames/4 minutes or more*
Speed slider: *Controls total time on screen*
Category: *Pair sequence*
QuickTime text size: *Very small*
Direction control: *Up or down*

Scrolling Block

iMovie isn't quite flexible enough to simulate the opening credits of *Star Wars,* where a long block of introductory text scrolls slowly upward from the bottom of the screen, shrinking as it recedes into the distance. But using this effect, you can get almost all the way there; you can have a long block of text, pages and pages long if you so desire, scroll slowly up from the bottom of the screen. (It just doesn't shrink into a triangle).

This roll effect is extremely common in commercial theatrical movies. You can use it at the beginning of your movie, to explain the plot setup. At the end of the movie, you can use it to provide a postscript or update to the events the audience has just witnessed (like the postscripts at the end *of A Civil Action, October Sky,* or *Bugsy*). You can also tack one of these scrolling text blocks onto the end of one of the other iMovie scrolling-text effects (it can follow the Rolling Credits effect, for example) to provide some neatly centered copyright, an "in memoriam," or disclaimer information. As far as the audience is concerned, it will be just one more part of the same smooth scroll. (Nor do you have to begin this follow-up scrolling block after the regular credits have completely disappeared off the top of the screen. You can make the additional scrolling block appear at any moment, even while the previous crawl is still finishing up its movement, using the tip in the sidebar on page 183.)

The directional arrows let you control whether this roll proceeds downward from the top or upward from the bottom. You're welcome to make your text block scroll down from the top, but do so with the knowledge that you're doing something unconventional, even unheard-of, in the world of filmmaking.

This effect is unique in that its maximum time on screen depends upon how much text you've pasted or typed into its text box. The more text you paste, the higher the Max setting on the Speed slider rises. As you approach the 32 K maximum text limit, you'll notice two important side effects. First, the Speed slider's maximum rises to four minutes or more. Second, you'll bore your audience silly.

Stripe Subtitle (Built-In)

Duration minimum/maximum: *1 second/10 seconds*
Speed slider: *Controls total time on screen*
Category: *Title/subtitle pair*
QuickTime text size: *OK*

Stripe Subtitle

This effect lets you create what the pros call a "lower third"—a stripe across the bottom of the picture where the text identifies, for example, the name and affiliation of the person being interviewed. The tinted background is an unusual touch, but it's attractive.

Oddly enough, the Color pop-up menu here *doesn't* change the color of the text, as it usually does. (Text in the Stripe Subtitle effect must always be white.) Instead, it affects the color of the stripe itself, which is a *gradient*—a shaded blend that proceeds from the most opaque color at the left side to nearly transparent at the right.

Subtitle (Plug-in Pack 2)

Duration minimum/maximum: *1 second/4 seconds, 20 frames*
Speed slider: *Controls total time on screen*
Category: *Title/subtitle pair*
QuickTime text size: *OK*

Subtitle

This effect gives you the more traditional look for a "lower third" title, one that identifies the person or place being shown in the footage: The text quietly fades in, white lettering centered at the bottom of the screen, and then fades out again. As the name implies, you can also use this effect to provide captions to translate, say, an opera performance, although that's probably going to be a less frequent requirement in your moviemaking career.

Subtitle Multiple (Plug-in Pack 2)

Duration minimum/maximum: *3 seconds/14 seconds*
Speed slider: *Controls total time on screen*
Category: *Pair sequence*
QuickTime text size: *Too small*

Subtitle Multiple

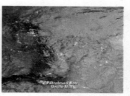

This effect is identical to Subtitle, with one difference: it provides spaces for multiple title/subtitle pairs. In other words, you can use this effect for closing credits (as shown here), when you want memorable footage of each person to play above his name and character.

Typewriter (Built-In)

Duration minimum/maximum: *1 second, 12 frames/14 seconds, 20 frames*
Speed slider: *Controls time for text to fully appear*
Category: *Title/subtitle pair*
QuickTime text size: *OK in bold fonts*

Typewriter

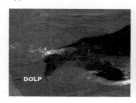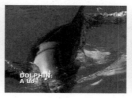

You occasionally see this effect used in the credits of TV police dramas (especially *JAG* and *Homicide*): The letters spill across the screen from left to right, as though being rapidly typed in a word processor. (For some inexplicable reason, Hollywood movies generally depict text appearing on *any* computer screen using this effect, even if it's just a dialog box or error message popping up. The chattering teletype sound that accompanies this phenomenon makes Hollywood computers seen even less like real-world computers.)

Tip: When this title style was under development at Apple, it was called *X-Files*—a reference to the animated titles in *The X-Files* that establish the time and date of each new scene. Before iMovie was officially unveiled, the name was changed to Typewriter for obvious reasons (obvious to lawyers, anyway).

ON LOCATION

Everything Old is New Again

I'd only used iMovie for about 20 minutes before I decided to make the Big One: A 30-minute family-history movie that I planned to show the whole family tree at Easter.

I had ten different small reels of 8 mm film that ran about 40 minutes total. (Not 8 mm *videocassettes*—8 mm *reels.*) I had the old movies transferred directly to DV by these guys: *www.thetransferstation.com.* They did a great job, and even returned the tapes ahead of schedule, all cleaned and color-corrected.

I also had many still photos from the family "archives." These I scanned on my desktop scanner and saved as PICT files, and later imported them into iMovie.

For opening titles, I exported several frames from some of the movies. I took the resulting PICT files into Photoshop, where I used the hue/saturation commands to turn them into sepia stills. I then darkened them around the edges for a vignette effect.

I imported these stills back into iMovie and ran the titles on top of them. They gave the viewer a foreshadowing of the movie ahead, and really set a nostalgic tone.

Because this was a personal job, I knew I could use any music I wanted—no ASCAP issues here! I used Frank

Sinatra's "It Was a Very Good Year" over the titles, giving my father billing ahead of the title, of course. He was the primary camera operator in those days (most of these films were shot before I was born), so he also got the Director of Photography credit. The monochromatic opening sequence and the nostalgic opening music worked great when I contrasted the first scenes in color. Given that the only color material they had back then was Kodachrome, the stills from slides and the 8 mm color was wild-looking, like Technicolor. Which only reinforced the nostalgic theme.

Eventually, I plan to set both my parents on a couch or big comfortable chair, *When Harry Met Sally*-style, and cut in their comments shot today. I'll set up my DV camcorder, show them a section of my family movie, then tape them commenting about the segment they just watched, reflecting back on their feelings about that point in their lives.

The finished product aired at Easter, as planned. It was very well received, but few heard all the audio and sound effects because of all the laughing and comments. (Dontcha hate movie talkers?) But I'll give VHS copies to all the family later, and I'm sure they will appreciate the work then.

—Paul M. Bowers
San Diego, CA

Zoom (Plug-in Pack 2)

Duration minimum/maximum: *1 second/7 seconds, 6 frames*
Speed slider: *Controls zoom-in speed*
Category: *Title/subtitle pair*
QuickTime text size: *OK*

Zoom

When you select this effect, your text flies out of the center of the screen, growing larger as it approaches, from a tiny dot to very large, bold type (if the typed phrase is short). It holds for a moment, then fades out gracefully.

This effect is dramatic and punchy. Use it to get attention when the name of your movie finally appears on the screen, and to differentiate it from the opening credits that may have preceded it.

Zoom Multiple (Plug-in Pack 2)

Duration minimum/maximum: *1 second/7 seconds, 6 frames*
Speed slider: *Controls zoom-in speed*
Category: *Pair sequence*
QuickTime text size: *Excellent if text is short*

Zoom Multiple

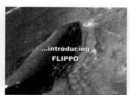

Use this variation on the Zoom effect described above for opening credits, especially those that are accompanied by rock music and exciting footage shot through the windshield of a fast-moving car. (If you know what's good for you, don't use either Zoom effect to introduce soft, sweet, or nostalgic flicks.)

Narration, Music, and Sound

I f you get lucky, you may someday get a chance to watch a movie whose soundtrack isn't finished yet. You'll be scanning channels and stumble across a special about how movies are made, or you'll see a tribute to a film composer, or you'll rent a DVD of some movie that includes a "making of" documentary. Such TV shows or DVDs sometimes include a couple of minutes from the finished movie as it looked *before* the musical soundtrack and sound effects were added.

At that moment, your understanding of the film medium will take an enormous leap forward. "Jeez," you'll say, "without music and sound effects, this $100 million Hollywood film has no more emotional impact than…my home movies!"

And you'll be right. It's true that in our society, the *visual* component of film is the most, well, visible. The household names are the directors and movie stars, not the sound editors, composers, *foley* (sound effects) artists, and others who devote their careers to the audio experience of film.

But without music, sound effects (called SFX for short), and sound editing, even the best Hollywood movie will leave you cold and unimpressed.

Audio in iMovie 2

More than anything else, the second version of iMovie is about the power of audio. Where iMovie 1 was frequently accused of being underpowered in the audio-editing department, iMovie 2 has some of the most useful and cleverly designed audio features imaginable. Now you can separate the audio and video from a certain clip, gaining the freedom to add new audio to existing video—or vice versa. You can also glue a piece of audio to a particular spot on a video clip, ensuring that they'll stay synchronized no matter how much the Movie Track's clips slide left and right in the course of editing. And audio clips are now first-class citizens when it comes to editing; you can crop or split them just as you can with video clips.

You access all of these new audio features in the redesigned Timeline Viewer, where your soundtracks are given visual form.

The Two iMovie Soundtracks

Much like traditional film cameras, iMovie separates the audio and video into separate tracks, which you can view and edit independently. In iMovie, you can view the contents of your soundtracks with a single click—on the clock icon shown in Figure 8-1.

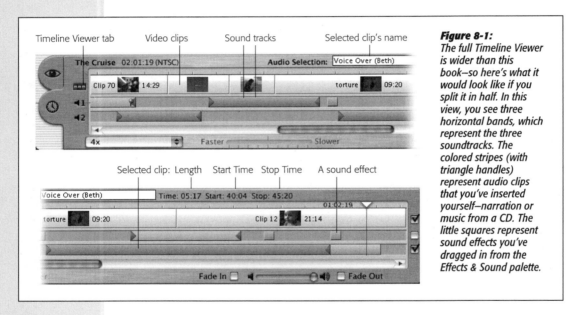

Figure 8-1:
The full Timeline Viewer is wider than this book—so here's what it would look like if you split it in half. In this view, you see three horizontal bands, which represent the three soundtracks. The colored stripes (with triangle handles) represent audio clips that you've inserted yourself—narration or music from a CD. The little squares represent sound effects you've dragged in from the Effects & Sound palette.

As noted in Chapter 5, the top horizontal band of the Timeline Viewer is dedicated to the *video* component of your movie. It shows tiny thumbnails that help you identify which clips you've placed in which order. For the most part, you won't do much with this strip when you're editing audio; its primary purpose is to help you see where you are in the movie.

The two skinnier horizontal strips underneath it, labeled 1 and 2, are your playground for audio clips. In iMovie 1, you could put only certain kinds of audio into each of these two tracks. For example, Track 1 held sound that you recorded from your Mac's microphone (such as narration). Track 2 held music imported from an audio CD.

In iMovie 2, however, the two audio tracks are equivalent. Each of them can hold sound from any of these sources, which you're free to drag between the two tracks at any time:

- **MP3 files.** iMovie 2 can import files in this popular music format directly.

- **Narration,** or anything else that you record with your microphone.

- **Sound effects.** Choose these from iMovie 2's Audio palette (gunshots, glass breaking, applause, and so on).

- **AIFF audio files.** You can bring these into iMovie using its File→Import File command.

- **Music from a CD.** You can insert a standard audio CD and transfer part or all of a song into iMovie to serve as the music for a scene.

- **Your camcorder audio.** Using a new iMovie command, you can turn the ordinarily invisible audio portion of a video clip into an independent sound clip, which you can manipulate just as though it were any other kind of sound clip.

This chapter covers all of these sound varieties.

Tip: Ordinarily, when playing your movie, iMovie plays the sound in both audio tracks simultaneously. But you can use the three checkboxes at the right end of these tracks to control which ones play back. When you want to isolate and listen to only one track, turn off the other two checkboxes. These checkboxes also govern which soundtracks are exported when you send your finished iMovie production back to tape or to a QuickTime movie.

Audio Clips

In many regards, working with sound files is much like working with video clips. For example, each piece of sound appears as a horizontal colored bar in the Timeline Viewer. You can move a clip around in the movie by dragging horizontally; cut, copy, and paste it; delete one by selecting it and then pressing the Delete key; and so on.

As you work, remember to use the zoom control (the pop-up menu at the lower-left corner of the Timeline Viewer) to magnify or shrink your audio clips as necessary; details are on page 134.

Renaming sound clips

When you click an audio clip, iMovie intensifies its color to show that it's highlighted, as shown in Figure 8-1 (middle). (CD music is purple, camcorder sound and microphone narration are orange, and sound effects are blue.) The top edge of the Timeline Viewer shows you the audio clip's name, duration, and start and stop times (in "minutes:seconds:frames" format) relative to the entire movie.

To rename a selected audio clip, simply click its name in the box at the top edge of the Timeline Viewer and retype. Alternatively, double-click the clip to summon the Clip Info window, where the clip's name appears at the top, already highlighted.

Note: You can't rename *video* clips in the Timeline Viewer by using the little rename box. In the Timeline Viewer, the only way to rename a video clip is to double-click it and type a new name for it in the Clip Info box..

Listening to a sound clip

Unfortunately, iMovie doesn't show you any sound waves or other visual indication of what's in each sound. The only way to isolate and listen to a particular audio clip is to proceed as shown in Figure 8-2.

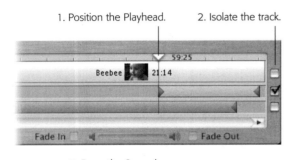

1. Position the Playhead.   2. Isolate the track.

Figure 8-2:
A view of the right end of the Timeline Viewer. Drag the Playhead so that the vertical lines beneath it strike the piece of sound you want to listen to. Then turn off the Track On/Off checkboxes to isolate the track you want. Press the Space bar to begin listening.

3. Press the Space bar.

Recording Narration

If anyone ever belittles iMovie 2 for being underpowered, point out an iMovie feature that isn't available at *all* in the expensive video editing programs: the ability to record narration while you watch your movie play. If your Mac has a microphone, you can easily create any of these effects:

- **Create a reminiscence.** As the footage shows children playing, we hear you (but don't see you) saying, "It was the year 2000. It was a time of innocence. Of sunlight. Of happy children at play. In the years before the Great Asteroid, nobody imagined that one six-year-old child would become a goddess to her people. This, then, is her story."

  This technique of superimposing an unseen narrator's voice over video is called a *voice-over.* It's incredibly popular in movies (such as *Saving Private Ryan, Chinatown,* and, of course, the *Look Who's Talking* movies), TV (especially *The Wonder Years*), and commercials. (A typical effect: We're shown footage of a young boy, but we're hearing his adult voice as he narrates a story that took place a long time ago.)

- **Identify the scene.** Even if your movie isn't one with a story line, iMovie's narration feature offers an extremely convenient method of identifying your home movies. Think about it: When you get photos back from the drugstore, the date is stamped across the back of each photo. In years to come, you'll know when the photos were taken.

Video cameras offer an optional date-stamp feature, too—a crude, fantastically ugly digital readout that permanently mars your footage. But otherwise, as they view their deteriorating VHS cassettes in 2020, most of the world's camcorder owners will never know where, why, or when their footage was shot. Few people are compulsive enough to film, before each new shot, somebody saying, "It's Halloween 2001, and little Chrissie is going out for her very first trick-or-treating. Mommy made the costume out of some fishnet stockings and a melon," or whatever.

But using iMovie, it's easy to add a few words of shot-identification narration over your establishing shot, especially because the time and date when the footage was shot is staring you at the face (see Figure 8-1).

- **Provide new information.** For professional work, the narration feature is an excellent way to add another continuous information stream to whatever videos or still pictures are appearing on the screen. Doctors use iMovie to create narrated slide shows, having created a Movie Track filled with still images (see Chapter 9) of scanned slides. Realtors feature camcorder footage of the houses under consideration, while narrating the key features that can't be seen ("Built in 1869, this house was extensively renovated in 1880..."). And it doesn't take much imagination to see how *lawyers* can exploit iMovie.

Preparing to record

Your Mac's microphone takes one of two forms: built-in or external. The built-in mike, a tiny hole in the plastic just above the screen of the iMac or PowerBook, couldn't be much more convenient—it's always with you, and always turned on. The built-in mike on an iMac DV works very well because the computer doesn't have a fan inside; it's completely silent. On the PowerBook, however, use the built-in mike only in a pinch; unfortunately, it picks up the sound of the computer's fan. The only way to avoid this additional background noise is to plug in an external microphone.

If you have an iBook or Cube, you can plug in an external USB microphone (the Apple Products Guide at *www.guide.apple.com* offers a list) or use an adapter (such as the iMic, *www.griffintechnology.com)* that accommodates a standard microphone. If you have a desktop Power Mac, it probably came with a gray, half-cone-shaped microphone called the PlainTalk microphone. You'll find a corresponding miniplug jack for it on the back.

Note: The PlainTalk mike's pin is slightly longer than a standard miniplug. Standard microphones don't work in a Mac without an adapter like the NE Mic from *www.griffintechnology.com.*

Once you've figured out which microphone you're going to use, quit iMovie. Show your Mac which microphone you want to use, as instructed in Figure 8-3.

Tip: If the Sound control panel doesn't let you make a choice here, it's probably because some piece of software has already seized control of your sound circuitry. Try quitting all of your sound-using programs and turning off any extensions, such as the ViaVoice extension, that rely on your microphone.

Once you've launched iMovie, you'll experience the same problem in reverse: You won't be able to change the sound input because *iMovie* has seized the sound circuitry. You must quit *all* sound-capable programs before changing inputs.

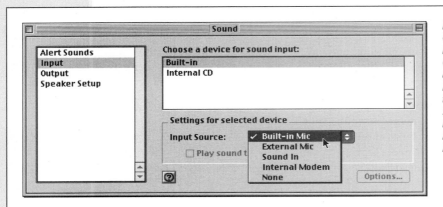

Figure 8-3:
Choose ⬛ →*Control Panels*→*Sound. Click Input in the list at the left; click Built-in; and ensure that the Input Source pop-up menu says "Built-in Mic" or "External Mic."*

Making the recording

Once you've specified the microphone you want to use, open your iMovie project. Here's how you record narration:

1. **Click the musical-note tab so that you're looking at the Timeline Viewer.**

   Figure 8-1 shows this tab.

2. **Drag the Playhead to a spot just before you want the narration to begin.**

   You can use all the usual navigational techniques to line up the Playhead: Press the Space bar to play the movie, press the right and left arrow keys to move the Playhead one frame at a time, press Shift-arrow keys to make the playhead jump ten frames at a time, and so on.

3. **Open the Audio palette, if it's not already open.**

   You do so by clicking the Audio button, shown in Figure 8-4.

4. **Click Record Voice and begin to speak.**

   You can watch the video play as you narrate.

   If the level meter isn't regularly reaching three-quarters of the way across its graph (see Figure 8-4), then your narration isn't loud enough. On playback, it will probably be drowned out by the camcorder audio track.

Unfortunately, iMovie offers no Input Volume control. If the level meter seems too low (as it is on many iMac models), your only options are to lean closer to the microphone, speak louder, or use an external microphone. (Of course, you can also make the other audio tracks softer during the editing process, but then your entire movie volume level is likely to be too low.)

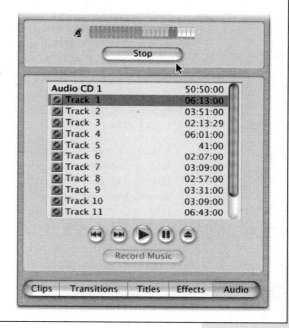

Figure 8-4:
To summon the Record Voice controls, click the Audio button. If your microphone is correctly hooked up, the Record Voice button is available. (Otherwise, it's dimmed.) Just above the button is a live "VU" level meter. Test your setup by speaking into the microphone; if this meter twitches in response, you're ready to record.

5. **Click Stop to complete the recording.**

Now a new stripe appears in the upper sound track, orange and highlighted, like those shown in Figure 8-1. Drag the Playhead to the left—to the beginning of the new recording—and then press the Space bar to listen to your voice-over work.

If the narration wasn't everything you hoped for, it's easy enough to record another "take." Just click the stripe representing your new recording and then press Delete to get rid of it. Then repeat the process.

Tip: If you're still recording narration after five minutes, iMovie hits the Stop button automatically. If your narration is very long, you'll have to record it in separate chunks.

According to Apple, this feature was introduced because sound files are fairly big (they take about 10 MB of hard drive space per minute). If you were to forget that you'd started recording, you could fill up your hard drive with recorded silence. You might even wander off to dinner, returning the next morning to find your hard drive completely full.

Well, it *could* happen.

Recording and choosing from separate takes

If you like what you recorded, but think that you might be able to do better, you don't have to delete the first one forever. You can record the new take and then compare the two. In fact, iMovie offers three different ways to do so:

- **Use a temporary "shelf."** Drag the newly recorded audio clip (the stripe) to another spot in the Timeline Viewer. For example, if you drag it far to the right, beyond any other existing sound clips, you've just stashed it on a makeshift "shelf." Now move the Playhead back to the correct spot and re-record the narration. By dragging the two resulting sound clips around, or by using the Cut and Paste commands, you can try out one, then the other.

- **Use Cut and Paste.** Alternatively, after recording the first take, click its clip and then choose Edit→Cut. Record the new take; if you don't like it, you can always delete it and then paste the original one—which has been on the invisible Clipboard all this time—back into place.

- **Use the Undo command.** Finally, don't forget that you can always use the Edit→Undo command several times in succession. If you delete the first take, re-record, then decide that you preferred the original take, just choose Edit→"Undo Record from Microphone" and then "Undo Clear." In fact, if you can keep your takes straight, you can use this method to try *several* different takes; you have a ten-level Undo command at your disposal.

You can edit and adjust the resulting sound clip just as you can other sounds in iMovie. See "Editing Audio Clips" later in this chapter for details.

Importing CD Music

Absolutely nothing adds emotional impact to a piece of video like music. Slow, romantic music makes the difference between a sad story and a one that actually makes viewers cry. Fast, driving music makes viewers' hearts beat faster (scientists have proven it). Music is so integral to movies these days that, as you walk out of the theater, you may not even be aware that a movie *had* music—but virtually every movie does, and you were emotionally manipulated by it.

Home movies are no exception. Music adds a new dimension to your movie—so much so that some iMovie fans *edit to music.* They choose a song, lay down in the Music Track, and then cut the video footage to fit the beats, words, or sections of the music.

Tip: Even if you don't synchronize your video to the music in this way, you might still want to experiment with a music-only soundtrack. That is, *turn off* the camcorder sound, so that your movie is silent except for the music. The effect is haunting, powerful, and often used in Hollywood movies during montage sequences.

In any case, iMovie makes it extremely easy to add professional-sounding music tracks to your movies. You just insert your favorite music CD (Carly Simon, Rolling Stones, the Cleveland Orchestra, or whatever), choose the track you want to swipe, and the deed is done.

FREQUENTLY ASKED QUESTION

Fun with Copyright Law

Don't I break some kind of law when I copy music from a commercial CD?

Absolutely. Stealing music from a commercial, copyrighted CD breaks a number of interesting laws. That's why some iMovie fans hesitate to distribute their iMovie films in places where lawyers might see them—such as the Internet.

But frankly, record company lawyers have bigger fish to fry than small-time amateur operations like you. You're perfectly safe showing your movies to family and friends, your user group, and other smaller circles of viewers. You get into real trouble only if your movie becomes popular—or starts making money.

Still, if your conscience nags you, the world is filled with CDs of royalty-free music—music that has been composed and recorded expressly for the purpose of letting filmmakers add music to their work without having to pay a licensing fee every time they do so. (The prices vary, but you might spend $40 for a CD, or $10 for an individual track.)

Visit a search page like *www.google.com,* search for *music library* or *royalty-free music,* and start clicking your way to the hundreds of Web sites that offer information about, and listenable samples of, the music you're about to buy. (Many of these sites require the *RealAudio plug-in,* an add-on for your Web browser that you can download and install from *www.real.com.)*

Here's the procedure for grabbing some music off a favorite CD:

1. **Open the Audio palette, if it isn't already open.**

   Do so by clicking the Audio button shown in Figure 8-5.

2. **Insert the music CD into your CD-ROM drive.**

   After a moment, its list of songs on the CD shows up in the list. (To avoid confusion with the iMovie audio *tracks,* this chapter refers to the CD selections as *songs.)*

   Unfortunately, they're probably called Track 1, Track 2, and so on. If you'd rather see the songs' actual names, see the Power Users' Clinic sidebar on page 207.

   The music may begin to play automatically. If it does, you can stop it by clicking the Stop button. And to prevent it from auto-starting in the future, choose →Control Panels→QuickTime Settings; choose AutoPlay from the pop-up menu at the top of the window; and turn off Enable Audio CD AutoPlay.

3. **Find the song you want.**

   To do so, click one of the songs in the scrolling list, and then click the Play button. Unfortunately, there's no way to fast-forward. What looks like Rewind and Fast Forward buttons in the Music palette are actually Previous Track and Next Track buttons.

Tip: The playback controls in the Audio palette are independent of the playback controls in the Monitor window. You may find it useful, therefore, to play your movie in progress *as* you listen to the different songs on your CD, so that you can preview how the music might sound when played simultaneously with the video.

The easiest way to experiment in this way is to click the Play button in the Audio palette at precisely the same instant that you press the Space bar to begin the movie playback.

GEM IN THE ROUGH

MP3 Meets iMovie

Music CDs aren't the only good source of music to accompany your video productions. The Internet is running over with great-sounding music, much of it free, in the form of *MP3 files.*

You can find these files by the tens of thousands on the Internet at, for example, *www.mp3.com* or *www.listen.com,* neatly organized by category. (If you've never downloaded

MP3 files before, you may have to poke and click around for awhile, and maybe even provide your email address for the benefit of the sites' junk email lists, before you figure out how to download actual MP3 files.)

Once you've found and downloaded a music file that you like, you can import it into your project exactly as you would an AIFF file, as described on page 208.

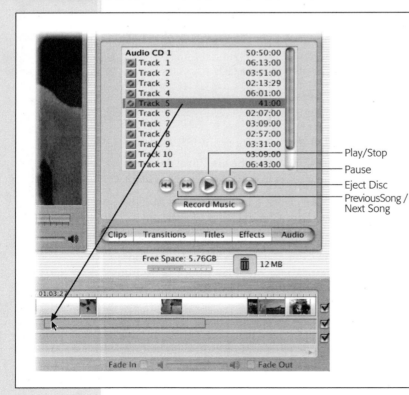

Figure 8-5:
The list in the Audio palette identifies the different songs (tracks) on your CD, along with the play length of each one. Drag an entire song into your movie, as shown here by the big arrow, or excerpt only a part of it by clicking Record Music while the playback continues.

4. **If you want to incorporate an entire song from a CD, drag its name out of the Audio palette and onto one of your audio tracks, as shown in Figure 8-5.**

iMovie pays attention to the location of your cursor when you release it in the Timeline Viewer, so that you can specify exactly where you want the music to begin. (On the other hand, you can always adjust the starting point of the music after you've placed it, by dragging its audio-clip stripe horizontally.)

Depending on the length of the song you've selected, this importing process can take 30 seconds or more. That's how long it takes for iMovie to turn the CD song into a new, multimegabyte audio file on your hard drive (in your project's Media folder).

5. **If you'd rather use only an *excerpt* from one of your CD songs, use the Record Music button.**

You can use this button in either of two ways. If the music isn't playing, click Record Music to start the CD playing *and* begin recording from it. You can also click Record Music when the music is already playing; iMovie begins capturing the sound into your Timeline Viewer.

Tip: You can click the Pause button as often as you like; each time, both the playback and the importing process freezes so you can get your bearings, making it easier for you to gauge when to stop importing. The Pause button doesn't introduce any kind of glitch or pop in the resulting recording.

Either way, a new purple stripe appears at the location of your Playhead in the lower audio track. The stripe grows longer as the music continues to play. As a bonus, iMovie plays the video in your Monitor window simultaneously, giving

---

POWER USERS' CLINIC

The End of "Track 1," "Track 2"...

Whenever you insert a music CD into iMovie, the list of songs (as shown in Figure 8-5) isn't wonderfully helpful: The song names are listed as Track 1, Track 2, Track 3, and so on. Clearly, it would be a lot easier to find the music you want if you could see the *actual names* of the songs on the CD.

You can. The free program called NetCD Player (available from *www.missingmanual .com,* among other places) automatically downloads the

Electric Light Orchestra Gr...	50:50:00
Out of the Blue	06:13:00
Turn to Stone	03:51:00
Telephone Line	02:13:29
Tightrope	06:01:00
Petrified	41:00
Late One Night	02:07:00
Nobody's Fool	03:09:00
Don't Bring Me Down	02:57:00
Up in the Air	03:31:00
Who Said It	03:09:00
Guitar Man	06:43:00

list of songs on each of your CDs from one of the Internet's giant CD databases. The track names—and the name of the CD itself—thereafter appear automatically in the iMovie list.

As a bonus, these names also appear in the AppleCD Audio Player program, the program (on your hard drive in the Applications folder or menu) that serves as the "front panel" for the Mac's built-in CD player.

---

you a good idea of how the music fits with the footage, both in length and in feeling.

To stop importing the music, click the Stop button shown in Figure 8-5.

When you're finished importing music, you're free to eject the CD (by clicking the Eject button shown in Figure 8-5), insert another one, and nab another selection of music; iMovie no longer requires the first CD. iMovie has converted the stolen music into an independent sound file on your hard drive.

Note: If you recorded only portions of songs, iMovie names these files in your project's Media folder— *Music 01, Music 02,* and so on. If you drag an entire CD Track into your movie, iMovie identifies it by CD name, track number, and excerpt-from-that-track number, such as *Audio CD 1. Track 19 01.* (If you've used NetCD Player to fill in the actual names of your CDs and tracks, as described in the following sidebar box, you get the name of the CD and the song name instead of these generic numbers.)

AIFF Files and Sound Effects

The files iMovie creates when it imports music from your CD are called *AIFF (Audio Interchange File Format)* files. Most Mac fans who aren't heavily into audio may not have encountered AIFF files before; these aren't the sound files that play when double-clicked (System 7 sounds). But AIFF sounds are extremely popular among professionals. All kinds of computers can read them; the sound quality can be extremely high—CD quality, in fact; and the Internet is filled with downloadable AIFF files that you can use in your iMovie projects.

iMovie itself comes with quite a number of sound effects in the form of AIFF files, suitable for dropping into your movies. Here are a few of the ones that show up in the Audio palette (see Figure 8-4):

Cat Meow	Horse Whinny
Crickets	Kid Laugh
Crowd Applause	People Laugh
Crowd Clapping	Thunder
Dog Bark	Trumpets Fanfare
Drum Roll	Wagon Crash
Footsteps	Water Lapping
Forest Rain	Whistle up
Glass Breaking	Wild Laugh
Horn Honk	

Across from each sound's name, you see its length, expressed in "minutes:seconds" format.

Adding a Sound Effect

You can drag a sound effect from the audio palette into either of the audio tracks in the Timeline Viewer; as your cursor moves over a track, a yellow insertion-point bar helps you see precisely where the sound will begin. Once placed there, the sound effect appears as two tiny squares separated by a fine horizontal line, as shown in Figures 8-1 and 8-5. (If the sound is short, or if your Timeline Viewer is zoomed out quite a bit, iMovie may not bother to show both squares *and* their connecting line. If there isn't room to show a horizontal line that's at least a couple of inches wide, you see only a single square.)

A sound-effect clip behaves much like any other sound clip, in that you can edit its volume in any of the ways described in "Editing Audio Clips," later in this chapter. You can also double-click one of its squares to open the Clip Info dialog box in order to rename the effect. You can slide it from side to side in the track to adjust where it *begins,* but you can't shorten, crop, or split it, as you can any other sound clip.

Creating Your Own Sound Effects

It's important to remember that the list of sound effects in the Sounds palette isn't magical. It's simply a listing of the AIFF files that were sitting in your iMovie→Resources→Sound Effects folder at the moment you launched iMovie. By all means, open that folder and delete, or move out, any sound effects you can't imagine ever needing.

Similarly, any AIFF file that you download from the Internet, copy from a sound-effects CD, create using a shareware sound-editing program, or save out of a QuickTime movie can also become an iMovie "sound effect." Just drop it into the iMovie→Resources→Sound Effects folder and relaunch iMovie; the new files show up in the Sounds palette automatically.

Tip: Apple offers hundreds of free, downloadable music recordings and sound effects in AIFF format. They're ideal for use in your movies because they have extremely high quality, and they encompass a broad array of effects: animal sounds, bells, chirps, doors, explosions, short musical flourishes, thunder, rain, spaceship sounds, comedy sounds, wind, and much more. At this writing, the Web addresses for these goodies are *www.apple.com/imovie/freestuff* and *www.apple.com/imovie/freestuff/audio.html.*

Just remember that, as noted on the Web page, iMovie takes longer to start up the more of these files you put into your iMovie→Resources→Sound Effects folder. For best speed, load only the ones you need.

Editing Audio Clips

Fortunately, you can do more with your audio clips than just insert them into the Timeline Viewer. You can lengthen them or shorten them, make them fade in or out, adjust their volume relative to the rest of the movie, shift them to play earlier or later in time, and even superimpose them.

Making Clip-by-Clip Volume Adjustments

To make a particular clip quieter, relative to the other tracks, click its representation in the Timeline Viewer to select it. (In the case of sound effects, click one of its blue squares.) The clip (or square) darkens to show that it's highlighted.

Having selected an audio (or video) clip in this way, you can affect its volume level in one of two ways: either by dragging the volume slider shown in Figure 8-6 or by adding a fade in or out, as described in the next section.

If you drag the volume slider all the way to the left, you mute the sound completely— for *this clip only.* The ability to mute selected clips can be very useful. Suppose, for example, that the last second of a clip caught the unseemly off-camera belch of a relative at the dinner table. In a flash, you can edit it out. *Split the clip* just before the belch (see page 127); you'll see absolutely no visual difference in your movie. But in your Timeline Viewer, you'll see that the belch has now been relegated to its own miniclip, which you can mute by setting its volume to zero (or just delete it).

Tip: Although the volume slider lets you adjust the overall volume of a particular clip, you can't ever make it *louder* than the original recording. Every audio clip you record or import is considered at "100 percent" when it first arrives in iMovie; you can only make it softer than its original incarnation.

If you do find yourself with an audio clip that was recorded too softly, the best solution is to export it to a shareware program like SndSampler (which is available at *www.missingmanual.com*). SndSampler and similar programs offer a powerful and convenient Amplitude command that lets you boost the volume of any sound file—or even part of one.

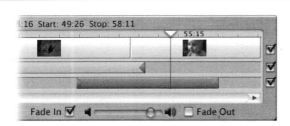

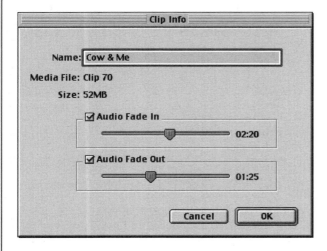

Figure 8-6:
Top: To create a short, gradual fade in or fade out for a highlighted audio clip, click one, or both, of the Fade checkboxes shown here. You can also make the entire clip softer or louder—relative to the other audio clips—by dragging the handle on the Volume slider to the left or right.

Bottom: You have more control over the timing of audio fades in the Clip Info dialog box.

Fading In and Out

Most people just use the Fade checkboxes shown in Figure 8-6 and call it a day. These boxes add a canned amount of fade to the beginning or end of the high-lighted audio clip.

But you gain far more flexibility if you *double-click* an audio clip (or highlight it and then choose File→Get Clip Info, or press ⌘-Shift-I). In that case, you get the Clip Info dialog box, which contains Fade In and Fade Out sliders. Using these controls, you can specify a much faster or slower fade than iMovie might create with its Fade checkboxes.

Tip: iMovie stores your Fade checkbox and Volume slider settings independently for every audio clip. That's why the position of the Volume slider, for example, may jump around as you click different audio clips.

WORKAROUND WORKSHOP

Faking Volume Adjustments within a Clip

In professional video-editing programs, you can draw, right onto the audio-clip icons on the screen, a line that looks like a graph of the stock market. It controls the clip's play-back volume over time. It's an extremely attractive feature, as even one evening of TV viewing will show you. It's a rare documentary or news show, in fact, that doesn't begin a story with a full-volume, at-tention-getting shot (protesters shouting, band playing, airplane landing, and so on), whose audio fades to half volume after a few seconds, just in time for the reporter to begin speaking.

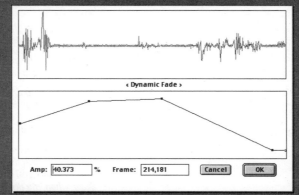

As you've probably dis-covered, iMovie offers no such feature. You can audio fade into or out of silence at the beginning or end of the clip, and you can make the *entire* clip softer or louder—but you can't adjust *part* of a clip.

That's what you might think, anyway. In fact, creating midclip volume fades and surges is incredibly easy—just chop up the clip. By dividing a sound clip into several smaller chunks, you gain the ability to set the overall-vol-ume slider independently for each one. With a little ex-perimentation, you'll find it fairly easy to bring out a cer-tain phrase, to make another section fade to half volume, and so on. You can even perform this kind of magic to the original camcorder au-dio; just split the video clip and then apply in-dependent volume ad-justments.

Furthermore, it's easy enough to add smooth volume changes to clips in the lower two tracks using a shareware program like SndSampler (available at *www.missingmanual.com,* among other places). Just use SndSampler to open the AIFF files in your project's Media folder; use the Transform→Dynamic Fade command, as shown here; and edit away.

Adjusting Many Clips at Once

You can adjust the volume levels of more than one clip simultaneously—a technique that comes in handy more often than you might think. For example, you may decide that *all* of the music excerpts you've grabbed from a CD are too loud relative to the camcorder audio. In one fell swoop, you can make them all softer.

Start by selecting the clips you want to affect. You can select as many as you want, even if they're on different audio tracks:

- To select several clips, shift-click them in any order. It's not like the equivalent maneuver in the Clip Viewer, where shift-clicking selects only *consecutive* clips. When editing audio, you can shift-click clip 1, clip 3, and so on.

- To select *all* of the clips in just one audio track, highlight *one* clip there. Then choose Edit→Select All.

- To unhighlight a selected clip, shift-click it.

Now when you drag the Volume slider, or even use the Fade In and Fade Out checkboxes, you're affecting all of the highlighted clips at once.

Note: When several clips are highlighted, you may see that the checkmark in the Fade box turns into a dash. That's your clue that some of the selected clips have been set to fade, and others haven't.

The Volume slider exhibits no such impartiality. It always shows the volume level of the *leftmost* selected clip.

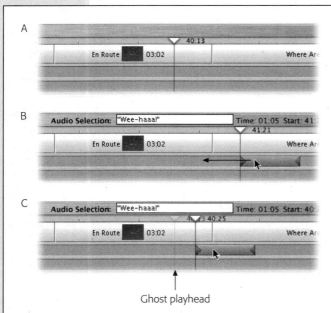

A

B

C

Ghost playhead

Figure 8-7:
If there were no ghost playhead, you'd have a very difficult time positioning audio clips.

A: You'd find the precise moment in the video where you wanted to begin.

B: You'd start to drag the audio clip—but clicking on an audio clip to drag it moves the regular Playhead, which means that your carefully marked spot disappears.

C: In iMovie 2, use the regular Playhead in conjunction with the arrow keys to precisely specify where you want the audio to begin. Now, when you drag the clip, the regular Playhead still jumps. But this time, iMovie leaves a faint line—the ghost playhead—where you were, serving as a target for your dragging operation.

Adjusting Playback Location: The Ghost Playhead

You can manipulate the playback timing for a particular clip—a great feature when you're trying to precisely position a sound effect so that it synchronizes with some action on the screen. The new iMovie 2 *ghost playhead* is a clever tool that helps you position audio clips with pinpoint precision. (Figure 8-7 illustrates why Apple created the ghost playhead in iMovie 2.)

Start by finding the spot where you want the audio clip to begin or end. Do that by dragging the Playhead in the Timeline Viewer, or by pressing the right and left arrow keys (to move one frame at a time) or Shift-arrow (ten frames at a time). When you've got the Playhead aligned, drag the audio clip's bar. As you do so, you'll notice that iMovie has marked your alignment point with a ghost playhead (Figure 8-7); as the beginning or end of the clip approaches this bookmark, the clip snaps neatly against it.

As long as the clip is highlighted, you can continue to fine-tune its position by pressing the right and left arrow keys (once again, add Shift to move the clip ten frames at a time).

Tip: Want to see a great example of sound-effects synchronization in iMovie? Visit *www.hoverground.com/ imovie/chungking.html.* The movie you'll see there was created with iMovie, and its humor and power stems almost exclusively from clever use of well-placed sound effects in the Timeline Viewer.

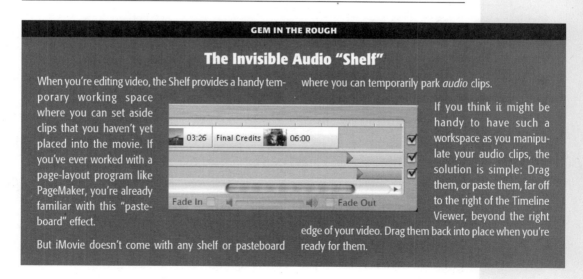

GEM IN THE ROUGH

The Invisible Audio "Shelf"

When you're editing video, the Shelf provides a handy temporary working space where you can set aside clips that you haven't yet placed into the movie. If you've ever worked with a page-layout program like PageMaker, you're already familiar with this "pasteboard" effect.

But iMovie doesn't come with any shelf or pasteboard where you can temporarily park *audio* clips.

If you think it might be handy to have such a workspace as you manipulate your audio clips, the solution is simple: Drag them, or paste them, far off to the right of the Timeline Viewer, beyond the right edge of your video. Drag them back into place when you're ready for them.

Locking Audio Clips to Video

Figure 8-8 illustrates a serious problem that results from trying to line up certain video moments (such as Bill-Gates-getting-hit-with-a-pie footage) with particular audio moments (such as a "Splat!" sound effect). In short, when you insert or delete some video footage *after* lining up audio clips with specific video moments, you shove everything out of alignment, sometimes without even realizing it. This syndrome can rear its ugly head in many video-editing programs (including iMovie 1).

You may wind up playing a frustrating game of find-the-frame, over and over again, all the way through the movie, as you try to redo all of your careful audio/visual alignments.

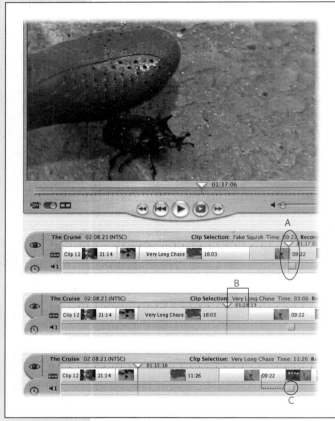

Figure 8-8:
Here's what would happen without iMovie 2's Lock Audio command.

A: You've carefully synchronized your audio and video, so that the dramatic moments occur during musical crescendos and the sound effects "hit" the right visual moments, such as this beetle-squishing (video) and crunching sound (audio).

B: Later, you decide to trim some unnecessary footage out of an earlier clip, indicated by the bracket.

C: Unfortunately, doing so makes all subsequent video clips slide to the left. The audio clips remain where they were; the result is chaos. The sound effect no longer aligns with the appropriate squish moment in the footage.

In iMovie 2, the solution is especially elegant. Whenever you place an audio clip that you'd like to remain aligned with a video moment, get it into position and then *lock* it by choosing Advanced→Lock Audio Clip at Playhead (or press ⌘-L). What happens next depends on how you've set things up:

• If you've dragged or nudged the Playhead to the frame you care most about, iMovie locks the audio to the video *at that frame,* as indicated by the little pushpin (see Figure 8-9). Even if you later trim away some footage from the beginning part of the video clip, the sync moment remains intact.

- If the Playhead isn't anywhere near the highlighted audio clip, iMovie simply locks the *beginning* of the highlighted audio clip to whatever video frame it's currently aligned with.

- If you've highlighted several audio clips, once again, iMovie "pushpins" the beginning of each clip at its present video location.

Figure 8-9:
Top: The pushpin marks the moment of audio/video marriage, where the Playhead was when you used the Lock Audio command.

Bottom: If you trim away so much footage from the beginning of the video clip that the pushpin point is no longer aligned within the video clip, the clip unlocks itself and floats freely in the audio track.

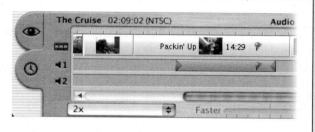

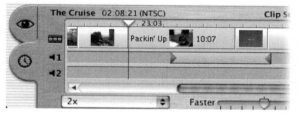

Once you've locked an audio clip to its video, you no longer have to worry that it might lose sync with its video when you edit your video clips. Nothing you do to the video clips to its left in the Timeline Viewer—add, delete, insert, or trim clips—will affect its synchronization.

It's important to understand, however, that locking an audio clip freezes its position *only relative to the video clip above it.* The audio clip isn't locked into a particular *time* in the movie (such as 5:23:12). Put another way, "Lock Audio" actually means "*Don't* Lock Audio (to one spot in the Movie Track); Let It Slide Around as Necessary."

Nor does locking an audio clip prevent *you* from shifting it; it's not as though dragging the audio clip will drag the "attached" video clip along with it. You're still welcome to slide the audio clip left or right in its track, independent of any other clips. Doing so simply makes iMovie realign the clip with a new video frame, lining up the pushpin accordingly. (If you *cut* the audio clip and then paste it into a new location, it forgets both its original video-clip spouse and the fact that it was ever "married" to begin with. When pasted, it's pushpin-free.)

To unlock an audio clip, highlight it and then choose Advanced→Unlock Audio Clip (or press ⌘-L again).

Cropping an Audio Clip

As you may remember from Chapter 5, the ability to *crop,* or chop off the ends of, a video clip is one of the key tools in video editing. In iMovie 2, you can adjust the beginning or ending points of any audio clip except sound effects—the ones represented by squares in the Timeline Viewer.

Tip: If you use the Extract Audio command described on page 220, you can even crop the original camcorder audio in this way, without cropping the actual video clip in the process. Doing so is a great way to trim out an audio glitch that appears at the beginning or the end of a shot without having to crop the actual video clip.

You can shorten one of your music or narration clips from either the beginning or the end. Drag the corresponding triangle handle inward, as shown in Figure 8-10.

For finer adjustments, click one of the triangles. (The triangle doesn't change color to indicate that you've highlighted it, but the Playhead snaps to its straight edge to let you know your click was successful.) Then press the right or left arrow key to move the handle in one-frame increments, or, if you press Shift as you do so, in *ten*-frame increments.

Tip: When your Timeline Viewer is zoomed out quite a bit, it can sometimes be extremely difficult to see the effects of cropping maneuvers. Very often, nudging one of the triangular handles only a frame or two produces no visible change in the Timeline Viewer at all.

You can zoom in, of course, or you can just watch the "Stop:" number shown at the upper-right of the Timeline Viewer. iMovie updates this number with each press of the arrow key, making it clear that you are, in fact, moving the handle you're trying to move.

Figure 8-10:
You can drag the leftmost handle inward (top, middle) to chop out the beginning of the clip, or the rightmost handle (bottom) to chop out the end of it. As you drag, the portion of the sound clip that will actually play is the usual orange or purple color; the light-colored excess, visible outside the dark portion, indicates how long the clip once was—and can be again.

Temporary vs. permanent cropping

When you drag an audio clip's triangles inward, you're not actually trimming the actual clip, moving the excess to the Trash; you're simply shortening the audible portion of the full-length clip. At any time in your project's lifetime, if you decide that you've overshot, you can always slide the handles back outward again. The very light orange or purple portion of each audio clip lets you know how much more of the original clip is still hanging around.

Note: As you drag the audio-clip crop handles inward or outward, it's reassuring to note that your audio clip will still fade in or fade out, according to your selection of the checkboxes at the bottom of the screen. iMovie is smart enough to adjust the location of the fade in or fade out when you crop your clip.

However, you may have good reason to make the cropped-clip arrangement permanent. First, in complex audio tracks, your clips can become cluttered and difficult to "read," thanks to the duplicate clip ends (the rectangular clip ends, plus the inward-pointing crop triangles). Second, dragging the crop handles doesn't reduce the amount of disk space that your audio file uses; iMovie hangs onto the full original clip in case you decide to un-crop it.

Fortunately, iMovie 2 offers a logical and simple way to make your crop permanent: Just choose Edit→Crop (or press ⌘-K. iMovie throws away whatever sound was beyond the boundaries of your crop triangles, exactly as though you'd just used the Crop command on a video clip (page 126).

Splitting an Audio Clip

On page 127, you can read about the power of the Edit→Split Clip at Playhead command, which uses the current Playhead location as a razor blade that chops a video clip in two. In the Timeline Viewer, however, you get a new command called Split Selected *Audio* Clip at Playhead. This new iMovie 2 command breaks the audio clip beneath the Playhead into two independent clips, exactly as you'd expect.

Tip: If your Edit menu doesn't list a command called Split Selected Audio Clip at Playhead, it's because your Playhead isn't in the middle part of a *highlighted* audio clip. If no audio clip is selected, or if the Playhead's vertical insertion point isn't running through it, the command says Split Video Clip instead (and has a very different effect).

Being able to split an audio clip is useful in a number of ways. For example:

- You can use it as another form of Crop command. Split off the unwanted end of some imported CD music, for example, and then delete the segment you don't need.

- You can separate statements in a voice-over (narration by an unseen speaker)—an extremely common requirement in professional editing.

 Suppose, for example, that you've got a voice recording of a guy recounting his days at the beginning of Apple Computer. One line goes, "We lived in a run-down tenement on the Lower East Side of Cupertino, but nobody cared. We loved what we were doing."

 Now suppose you've also got a couple terrific still photos of the original Apple building, plus a photo of the original Apple team, grinning like fools in their grungy T-shirts and beards. After using the Split Audio Clip command, you can place the first part of the recording ("We lived in a run-down tenement on the Lower East Side of Cupertino") beneath the campus photos, and then *delay* the second utterance ("But nobody cared. We loved what we were doing") until you're ready to introduce the group photo.

- In a crude sort of way, you can make the volume of a sound clip rise and fall over time—loud during the opening credits, but softer as the dialog begins, for example. Just keep chopping up the audio clip into as many segments as you'll want volume fluctuations. (You'll have to move the Playhead by hand before each split; pressing the arrow or Shift-arrow keys makes the whole clip shift in its track instead of moving the Playhead.)

Then choose Edit→Select None. Now use the Volume slider at the bottom of the screen to set the level for each chunk independently. If you spread out a volume increase across several different pieces, for example, the result is a fairly smooth crescendo. Unfortunately, a tiny hesitation or pop at each new clip chunk may tarnish the effect, but this trick works well under dialog, for example, which masks the transitions.

Tip: You can't split a clip and then immediately drag one of the halves to a new location. After the Split command, both clips remain in position, side-by-side, both highlighted; whatever you do will affect both pieces, as though you'd never split them at all. Shift-click the piece you *don't* want before trying to drag or cut anything.

Superimposing Audio Clips

iMovie may seem to offer only two parallel audio tracks, but that doesn't mean you can't have more layers of simultaneous soundtrack material. There may be only two horizontal strips on the screen, but there's nothing to stop you from putting audio clips *on top of each other*. By all means, drag a sound effect onto your already re-

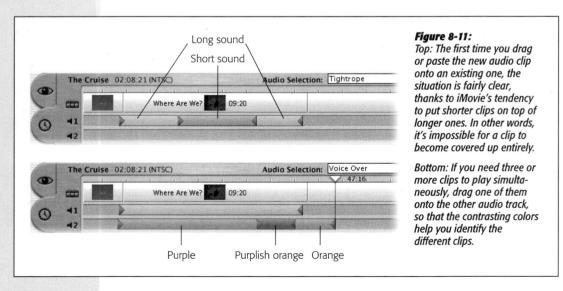

Figure 8-11:
Top: The first time you drag or paste the new audio clip onto an existing one, the situation is fairly clear, thanks to iMovie's tendency to put shorter clips on top of longer ones. In other words, it's impossible for a clip to become covered up entirely.

Bottom: If you need three or more clips to play simultaneously, drag one of them onto the other audio track, so that the contrasting colors help you identify the different clips.

corded narration clip, or superimpose two or more different CD music recordings, if that's the cacophonous effect you want. When playing back your project, iMovie plays all of the sound simultaneously, mixing them automatically.

In iMovie 2, the color coding can help a great deal in letting you identify what's going on when clips overlap. For example, the two colors (purple for CD audio, orange for camcorder or narration audio) can be a helpful clue, especially when they're superimposed—the overlapping portion is a perfect blend of the two colors (see Figure 8-11). When you must overlap audio clips, you'd be wise to drag orange clips on top of purple ones, or vice versa, instead of superimposing like-colored clips.

But if you're having trouble sorting out several overlapping sound clips, consider dragging one onto the far right end of your Timeline Viewer—your "pasteboard," as described on page 213. Often, just moving one clip out of the way is enough for you to understand what's going on in its original location. And remember to glance at the top of the Timeline Viewer as you click each audio clip; you'll be shown its name, which is another helpful clue when clips collide.

POWER USER'S CLINIC

The Elusive Split Edit

I want to do a split edit, or a J-edit. You know, where the dialogue from the next scene begins while we're still looking at the final seconds of the previous scene. Can you do that in iMovie 2?

Absolutely; in fact, you can easily make either a J-edit (where the audio starts before the video) or an L-edit (where the video starts before the audio).

Here's how you make the J-edit. Start by highlighting the tail portion of the outgoing scene, which we'll call Clip A, corresponding to the interval during which you'll want the

next scene's audio to play. (Use the Scrubber bar and crop handles for this, as described on page 123.) Choose Edit→Cut.

Now position the Playhead precisely at the beginning of the second scene. Choose Advanced→Paste Over at Playhead (see page 219).

That's all there is to it. You'll continue watching the *video* of the first scene, even though the *audio* of the second scene begins before the first one is finished.

Overlaying Video Over Sound

One of the most popular editing techniques—both with editors and audiences—is the *video overlay*. (On the Internet, you may hear this technique called an *insert edit,* which actually has nothing to do with pasting video over audio.)

As shown in Figure 8-12, a video overlay is where the video cuts away to a new picture, but you continue to hear the audio from the original clip.

Suppose, for example, that you've got footage of an old man describing his first love. As he gets to the part where he describes meeting her, you want to cut to a close-up of her portrait on his mantelpiece.

Veterans of iMovie 1 remember with great pain that program's inability to perform a video overlay. Moviemakers (and book authors) devoted many hours (and pages) to workarounds that involved exporting audio tracks to a different program, making the edit, and then importing them back into iMovie.

Figure 8-12:
When you overlay video over sound, you can illustrate what the speaker is saying without losing her train of voice.

"What did I love about Edenville? Well, not the odor, that's for sure. And not the plant. No, what I loved most was the old canoe lake. Oh, sure, it was all foamed up with nitrates, and you didn't dare touch the water. But without a doubt, those were some of the happiest days of my life. I'd give almost anything to take one more look at that old lake."

The "Extract Audio in Paste Over" Checkbox

In iMovie 2, all of that has changed; it's a piece of cake to paste a piece of video over an existing audio track. In fact, pasting video *without* replacing the sound track is exactly like pasting video the usual way (see page 130); only a single checkbox makes the difference:

1. **Choose Edit→Preferences.**

   The Preferences dialog box appears.

2. **Click the Advanced tab. Make sure "Extract Audio in Paste Over" is selected.**

   If this checkbox is *on*, you'll paste only the video, preserving whatever audio is already on your audio tracks. If the checkbox is *off*, you'll wipe out both the audio and the video in the spot where you paste.

3. **Click OK.**

Performing the Overlay

To perform the video overlay, follow these steps:

1. **Select the footage you'll want to paste.**

   If it's a complete clip, just highlight its icon on the Shelf or in the Movie Track. If it's a portion of a clip, use the crop markers to specify the part you want, as described on page 123.

2. **Cut or copy the selected footage.**

   Use the Edit→Cut or Edit→Copy commands as described on page 130.

Now you have to make an important decision. You're about to paste some copied video *over* some existing video. But how much of it do you want to paste? You can either "paste to fit" so that the pasted video begins and ends at precise frames, filling a "hole" in the existing footage of a particular length; or you can paste it all without worrying about where the end of the pasted material falls. In this second scenario, you don't want to have to specify a cutoff point (where the existing video cuts in again).

These two cases are illustrated in Figure 8-13.

3. **If you want to paste the entire copied chunk, position the Playhead in the Timeline Viewer exactly where you'll want the insert to appear. Then choose Advanced→Paste Over at Playhead (or press ⌘-Shift-V).**

The video you've pasted wipes out whatever was already there, even if it replaces multiple clips (or parts of clips). If the "Extract Audio in Paste Over" checkbox is turned on, as described on page 220, your edit is complete; you've got a cutaway to new video as the original audio track continues.

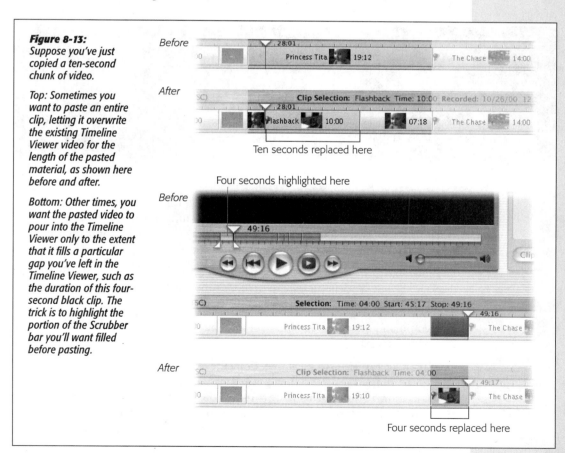

Figure 8-13:
Suppose you've just copied a ten-second chunk of video.

Top: Sometimes you want to paste an entire clip, letting it overwrite the existing Timeline Viewer video for the length of the pasted material, as shown here before and after.

Bottom: Other times, you want the pasted video to pour into the Timeline Viewer only to the extent that it fills a particular gap you've left in the Timeline Viewer, such as the duration of this four-second black clip. The trick is to highlight the portion of the Scrubber bar you'll want filled before pasting.

4. If you want to "paste to fit," highlight the portion of the movie that you'll want the pasted video to replace. Then choose Advanced→Paste Over.

To select the region that your paste will replace, you can use any of the techniques described in Chapter 4. If you want to knock out only a portion of a single clip, for example, click the clip in the Movie Track and then use the Scrubber bar crop handles (page 123) to isolate the section that will be replaced. If you want to paste into a segment that spans multiple clips (or parts of clips), choose Edit→Select None, and then use the cropping handles on the entire Scrubber-bar map of your movie.

When you paste, one of three things may happen. If the pasted material is *precisely* the same length as the region you've highlighted, great; the pasted chunk drops perfectly into the hole. If the pasted material is longer than the highlighted region, however, iMovie chops off the pasted portion, using as much of the first portion as possible to fit the area you've designated. And if the pasted material is too *short* to fill the reserved space, iMovie creates a "Black" clip (see page 134) to fill the remaining highlighted area.

FREQUENTLY ASKED QUESTION

The Audio Pop in Paste-Overs

When I paste video over existing audio, I sometimes hear a little pop, or I lose part of a word. What's going on?

As of iMovie 2.01, there's an unfortunate bug that causes this problem. Apple says it's a doozie of a bug, and that a substantial rewrite of the program would be required to fix it. There's no solution except to perform your paste-overs during momentary silences in the underlying audio track (pauses in the speech, for example), or to add very short audio fades at the ends of the affected clips.).

Extracting Audio from Video

iMovie 2 is perfectly capable of splitting apart the audio portion of your camcorder video. All you have to do is click the video clip in question and then choose Advanced→Extract Audio.

As shown in Figure 8-14, the recorded audio suddenly shows up in your first audio track as an independent audio clip; its "pushpins" indicate that it's been locked to the original video, as described on page 214.

This command unleashes all kinds of useful new tricks that weren't possible in the first version of iMovie:

• **Make an echo.** This is a great one. Copy the extracted clip and paste it right back into the audio track—and then position it a few frames to the right of the original, as shown at bottom in Figure 8-14. Use the slider at the bottom of the Timeline Viewer to make it slightly quieter than the original. Repeat a couple more times, until you've got a realistic echo or reverb sound.

- **Reuse the sound.** You can copy and paste the extracted audio elsewhere in the movie. (You've probably seen this technique used in dozens of Hollywood movies: About 15 minutes before the end of the movie, the main character, lying beaten and defeated in an alley, suddenly pieces together the solution to the central plot mystery, as snippets of dialogue we've already heard in the movie float through his brain, finally adding up.)

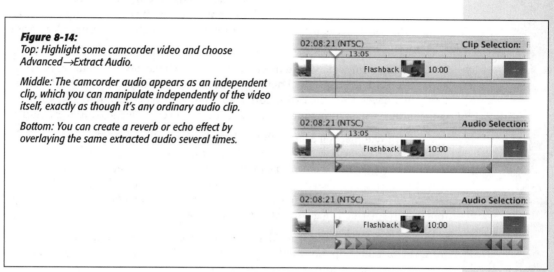

Figure 8-14:
Top: Highlight some camcorder video and choose Advanced→Extract Audio.

Middle: The camcorder audio appears as an independent clip, which you can manipulate independently of the video itself, exactly as though it's any ordinary audio clip.

Bottom: You can create a reverb or echo effect by overlaying the same extracted audio several times.

- **Crop the scene's audio.** Trim out an unfortunate cough, belch, or background car honk by cropping the audio, as described on page 216. Now the video can begin (or end) in silence, with the audio kicking in (or out) only when required. (Of course, *silence* isn't generally what you actually want, as described next.)

- **Grab some ambient sound.** In real movie editing suites, it happens all the time: A perfect take is ruined by the sound of a passing bus just during the tender kiss moment—and you don't discover it until you're in the editing room, long after the actors and crew have moved on to other projects.

You can eliminate the final seconds of sound from the scene by cropping or splitting the clip, of course. But that won't result in a satisfying solution; now you'll have three seconds of *silence* during the kiss. The real world isn't truly silent, even when there's no talking; the air is always filled with *ambient sound,* such as breeze, distant traffic, the hum of fluorescent lights, and so on. Even inside in a perfectly still room, there's *room tone.* When you want to replace a portion of the audio track with "silence," you usually want, in fact, to replace it with ambient sound.

Professionals always record about 30 seconds of room tone or ambient sound just so that they'll have material to use in case of emergency. You may not need to go to that extreme; you may well be able to grab some sound from a different part of the same shot. The point is that by importing that few seconds of scene into iMovie, extracting the audio, and then *deleting* the leftover video clip, you've got yourself a useful piece of ambient-sound "footage" that you can use to patch over unwanted portions of the originally recorded audio.

- **Add narration.** The technique described on page 200 is great for narration that you record at one sitting, in a quiet room. But you can add narration via camcorder, too; record yourself speaking, import the footage into iMovie, extract the audio, and throw away the video. You might want to do this if you're editing on a mike-less Mac, or if you want the new narration to better match the camcorder's original sound.

It's fascinating, important, and useful to note that iMovie never actually *removes* the audio from a video clip. You'll never be placed into the frantic situation of wishing that you'd never done the extraction at all, unable to sync the audio and video together again (which sometimes happens in "more powerful" video editing programs).

Instead, iMovie places a *copy* of the audio into the audio track. The original video clip actually remains married to its original audio—but iMovie sets its volume slider to zero, therefore muting it. You can, if you wish, extract audio from the same clip over and over again; iMovie simply spins out another copy of the audio each time. (When you extract audio, the video clip, too, sprouts a pushpin, but don't let that fool you. It's perfectly legal to extract the audio again.)

If you intend to use the extracted audio elsewhere in the movie *without* deleting it from the original clip, no problem; just click the video clip and then drag the volume slider at the bottom of the Timeline Viewer fully to the right once again.

ON LOCATION

iMovie vs. the Big Guns

I produce a local TV show called *Capital Magic Tonight*. I also work in the video/television field and have worked on many nonlinear editing systems. I'm very impressed with iMovie! Some people I know in the industry have knocked iMovie because it's limited; after all, how can it be any good without a $10,000 price tag?

I have a great story with iMovie concerning a TV station I worked for. They just bought a full-blown Power Macintosh with all the works. They were going to use it as a nonlinear editor using Adobe Premiere. A few months later, I bought an iMac DV Special Edition solely for iMovie. Using my Canon GL-1, moments after turning my new computer on, I was editing video!

Anyway, I came back to the station a few days later with my first show, produced with iMovie, to convert it to 3/4-inch tape, for broadcast at that station. One of the guys came over and started knocking iMovie, giving the speech about iMovie not being "professional," and so on. When he was finished with his talk, I looked him in the eye and said, "In my hand, I have a finished video that's ready to roll. I've had iMovie for five days. You've had that G3 with Premiere for over a month—do you have any outputted DV video?"

The answer was no, of course.

—Michael P. Howard

Still Pictures and QuickTime Movies

The DV camcorder is the source of iMovie material you'll probably use the most often, but it's not the only source; you can also bring in still images and existing QuickTime movies from your hard drive. You can also *export* still frames from your movie, a much more direct method of producing still images than having to use your camcorder's own built-in "digital camera" feature.

Importing Still Images

You might want to import a graphics file into iMovie for any number of reasons. For example:

- You can use a graphic, a digital photo, or another still image as a backdrop for iMovie's titling feature (Chapter 7). A still image behind your text is less distracting than moving footage.

- You can use a graphics file *instead* of using the iMovie titling feature. As noted in Chapter 7, iMovie's titling feature offers a number of powerful features, including animation—but also a number of serious limitations. For example, you can't specify any type size you like, enjoy full freedom of text color, or control the title's placement in the frame. (Each text effect locks the text in dead center, flush left, or flush right. If you want a title to appear off center, you're out of luck.)

  Preparing your own title "slides" in, say, Photoshop or AppleWorks gives you a lot of flexibility that the iMovie titles feature lacks; you get complete control the type size, color, and placement, for starters. You can also add graphic touches to your text or to the "slide" on which it appears (see Figure 9 -1).

- One of the most compelling new uses of video is the *video photo album:* a smoothly integrated succession of photos (from your scanner or digital camera), joined by crossfades, enhanced by titles, and accompanied by music. (Nothing, but *nothing,* makes a better and more cherished Christmas, birthday, or anniversary gift.) Thanks to iMovie's ability to import photos directly, creating this kind of video show is a piece of cake.

As your life with iMovie proceeds, you may encounter other uses for the picture-importing feature. Maybe, when editing a home movie of your kids tussling in the living room, you think it would be hilarious to insert some *Batman*-type fight-sound title cards ("BAM!") into the footage. Maybe you need an establishing shot of, say, a storefront or apartment building, and realize that you could save production money by inserting a still photo that passes for live video in which there's nothing moving in the shot. And maybe you want to end your movie with a fade out—not to black, but to maroon (an effect described later in this chapter).

Figure 9-1:
Preparing your "title cards" in a graphics program gives you far more typographical and design flexibility than iMovie's own titles feature gives you. Using separate graphics software, for example, you can enhance your titles with drop shadows, a three-dimensional look, or clip art adorning the frame.

The Dimensions of an iMovie Graphic

To prepare the pictures you'll import into iMovie, you need a graphics program. Some of the most popular are Adobe Photoshop (expensive professional software), AppleWorks (which comes with every iMac and iBook), PhotoDeluxe (which comes with most inexpensive Macintosh scanners), GraphicConverter (shareware available from, for example, *www.missingmanual.com),* and so on.

If you want your imported graphic to completely fill the screen when it's part of your movie, make its dimensions exactly *640 pixels wide, 480 high.* (That's for NTSC [North American] equipment. If you live in Europe or another region that uses PAL systems, as described on page 5, substitute 768 x 576 everywhere in this chapter where dimensions are provided.)

Otherwise, you'll get one of the side effects shown in Figure 9-2.

Tip: If your graphic is wider than it is tall, and you *don't* reshape it according to the instructions in this section, you'll get black bands above and below it when it's inserted into iMovie. In other words, the result is the *letterboxed* look of some movie-theatre movies that are adapted to the smaller screen of a TV. (A movie screen, if you hadn't noticed, is much wider than a TV; movies you watch on TV usually have the right and left sides of the picture cropped out. True movie buffs and discerning directors often prefer the letterbox approach, which adds black bands but doesn't chop off the picture.)

Often, only the opening credits of these movies are letterboxed, so that TV viewers can read all the credits and view the opening panoramas in all their splendor. The bulk of the movie is instead cropped at the sides. By *deliberately* making your title-card graphics too wide—say, 640 x 380—you can force iMovie to display them in letterbox format, much to the awe of your friends.

Figure 9-2:
Top: Make the dimensions of your graphic exactly 640 x 480. Anything larger won't improve the quality of the picture; iMovie will automatically scale it down to 640 x 480, and meanwhile that graphics file will take up more memory and disk space.

Middle: Anything smaller will have a black border around it when it appears in your movie.

Bottom: And anything whose dimensions aren't in that exact 4:3 ratio will develop black borders either at the top and bottom or on both sides.

Getting your picture into this precise size and shape usually requires some manipulation in the graphics program. In this discussion, you'll find instructions for doing so in Photoshop, AppleWorks 6, PhotoDeluxe, and GraphicConverter.

Creating a Graphic from Scratch

Suppose you intend to design a graphic from scratch. Maybe it's going to be a simple black square, which you'll use to add a moment of blackness after the final fade out of your movie. Maybe it's going to be a title card that you intend to dress up using your graphics program. Regardless, the key is the same: to create a graphic that's exactly 640 pixels wide and 480 pixels tall.

- **Adobe Photoshop.** Choose File→New. In the resulting dialog box, specify a width of *640,* height of *480,* resolution of *72,* and mode of *RGB Color.* Click OK.

- **AppleWorks.** If you have AppleWorks 6, choose File→New→Painting. If you have AppleWorks 5, double-click Painting in the list of document types.

  When your new document appears, choose Format→Document. Specify margins of *0* on all four sides. In the Pixels Across box, type *640,* and in the Pixels Down box, type *480.* Click OK.

- **PhotoDeluxe.** Click the On Your Own button. Choose File→New; in the resulting dialog box, specify a width and height of 640 x 480 *pixels* (not inches), and a resolution of 72 pixels/inch.

- **GraphicConverter.** Choose file→New→Image. In the resulting dialog box, confirm that the settings are Width: 640, Height: 480, Resolution: 72. Change the Depth to one of the last two choices on the pop-up menu, unless you intend to create a fairly simple slide with no photos. Click OK.

Now you're ready to begin dressing up your empty, 640 x 480 graphic. When you're finished, see "Saving Your Still Image," later in this chapter.

Preparing a Scan or Digital Photo

Suppose that, as a person with limited time or artistic ability, you'd rather not draw something from scratch. You'd rather adapt an image that came from a scanner, digital still camera, or Internet download. Your primary challenge, then, is to convert your file into a 640 x 480 frame without losing much quality or chopping out too much of the image. (Fortunately, most digital cameras take pictures that are in the proper width-to-height *ratio,* so you won't have to do much cropping—but you'll still have to scale the resolution way down.)

Here are the steps.

Note: These instructions turn your graphic into a 640 x 480 image regardless of whether it started out being too small or too large. If it was *smaller* than 640 x 480, the graphics program will enlarge the image. However, just as you lose quality when you use an enlarging copying machine, enlarging a graphic on the Mac decreases its quality. When the image appears in your movie, it may look grainy or coarse if you've had to enlarge it in this way. Your only alternative is *not* to enlarge it, and to accept the black borders that will appear around it, as shown in Figure 9-2.

In Photoshop, you'll use the Image Size and Canvas Size commands to manipulate your image. These steps assume that you *don't* want iMovie to add black borders to your graphic, as shown in Figure 9-2, and that you instead want your graphic to completely fill the movie frame.

1. **Choose Image→Image Size.**

   The Image Size dialog box appears (see Figure 9-3).

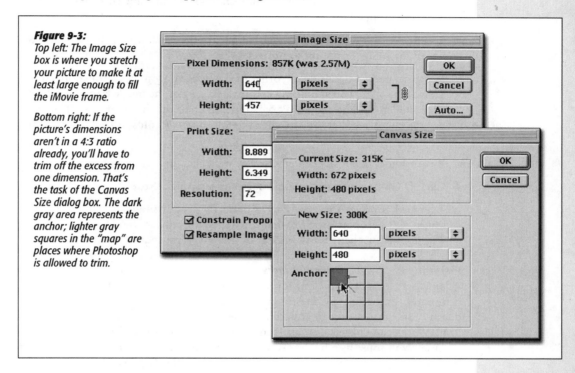

Figure 9-3:
Top left: The Image Size box is where you stretch your picture to make it at least large enough to fill the iMovie frame.

Bottom right: If the picture's dimensions aren't in a 4:3 ratio already, you'll have to trim off the excess from one dimension. That's the task of the Canvas Size dialog box. The dark gray area represents the anchor; lighter gray squares in the "map" are places where Photoshop is allowed to trim.

2. **Change the resolution to 72, then change the width to 640 pixels.**

   If the Constrain Proportions checkbox is turned on, the Height box changes automatically to retain the same dimensions as the original image. Now you have a decision to make.

   If the number in the Height box is now precisely 480 pixels, great—your work is done here. The graphic was correctly proportioned to begin with. Click OK and see "Saving Your Still Images," later in this chapter.

   But if the number in the Height box is *more* than 480, skip to step 4. If it's less than 480, as shown in Figure 9-3, proceed like this:

3. **Change the number in the Height box to 480.**

   In other words, your graphic was too short for the TV screen. You've now specified that you want the graphic to be at *least* 480 pixels tall. However, Photoshop automatically changes the Width number to a proportionate amount, making your graphic too wide (more than 640) now. You'll fix this problem in the next step.

4. **Click OK. Choose Image→Canvas Size.**

The Canvas Size dialog box now appears, also as shown in Figure 9-3. If you're still reading these instructions, it's because your graphic isn't perfectly proportioned to fit the TV screen. Therefore, you'll now have to chop off part of the image to make it fit. Fortunately, Photoshop gives you some control over which part gets chopped off.

5. **Specify a width of 640 and a height of 480. In the Anchor display, click the corner of the image you want to protect.**

In other words, which side or corner of the image do you *not* want chopped off? That's the square you should click. If the best part of the image is on the left side, click the left middle square; Photoshop will chop off the right side. If the best part of the image is at the top, click the top square; Photoshop will chop off the excess from the bottom.

If your image is already centered pretty well, click the center box.

6. **Click OK. When the warning message appears, click Proceed.**

The deed is done: You now have a perfectly proportioned, 640 x 480 graphic image. If the cropping wasn't what you hoped for, choose Undo—or close the file without saving changes to back out of this entire procedure.

Preparing the graphic in AppleWorks

AppleWorks can cut a large image down to 640 x 480 using the Format→Document command. Unfortunately, the program chops off pieces of the image to do so (it doesn't offer the option to scale down the image first, as Photoshop does). And AppleWorks can enlarge a smaller image to 640 x 480—but offers no way to do it precisely; you must use the Transform→Resize command and drag the corners of your image by hand. (Doing so is easier if you make the AppleWorks rulers visible, set their units of measurement to *points,* and zoom in to 200 percent.)

If you'd like better control, download the shareware program GraphicConverter and follow the instructions for it, described on page 232.

Preparing the Graphic in Adobe PhotoDeluxe

If you, like thousands before you, have equipped your Mac with a scanner, chances are good that it came with PhotoDeluxe, a surprisingly competent graphics program. Here's how you'd go about using it to adapt a graphic file for use in iMovie.

Note: The instructions here are almost identical to the ones provided for Photoshop earlier. Forgive the copy-and-paste job; as two graphics programs from the same software company, Photoshop and PhotoDeluxe work nearly identically.

---

1. **Click On Your Own; choose File→Open File. Open your graphics file.**

The picture appears on your screen.

2. **Click the Modify button at the upper-left corner of the screen.**

Now a row of icons appears at the top of the window.

3. **Click the Size tab. Click Photo Size.**

The Photo Size dialog box appears. It looks a lot like the dialog box shown at top in Figure 9-3.

4. **Change the resolution to 72. Then change the width to 640 pixels.**

The Height box changes automatically to retain the same dimensions as the original image (if the Constrain Proportions checkbox is turned on, that is).

If the number in the Height box is now precisely 480, then you lucked out; the graphic was correctly proportioned to begin with. Click OK, and see "Saving Your Still Images," later in this chapter.

But if the number in the Height box is *more* than 480, skip to step 6. If it's less than 480, proceed like this:

5. **Change the number in the Height box to 480.**

In other words, your graphic was too short for the TV screen. You've now specified that you want the graphic to be at *least* 480 pixels tall. PhotoDeluxe automatically changes the Width number to a proportionate amount, making your graphic too wide (more than 640) now. You'll fix this problem in the next step.

6. **Click OK. Click the Canvas Size button.**

The Canvas Size dialog box now appears, like the other box shown in Figure 9-3. You'll now have to chop off part of the image to make it fit. Fortunately, PhotoDeluxe lets you control which part gets chopped off.

7. **Specify a Width of 640 pixels, and a height of 480 pixels. In the Anchor display, click the corner of the image you want to protect.**

In other words, which side or corner of the image do you *not* want chopped off? That's the square you should click. If the best part of the image is on the left side, click the left middle square; PhotoDeluxe will chop off the right side. If the best part of the image is at the top, click the top square; PhotoDeluxe will chop off the excess from the bottom.

If your image is already centered pretty well, click the center box.

8. **Click OK. When the warning message appears, click Proceed.**

The deed is done: You now have a perfectly proportioned, 640 x 480 graphic image. If the cropping wasn't what you hoped for, choose Undo—or close the file without saving changes to back out of this entire procedure.

GraphicConverter

This handy software is *shareware*—that is, it works fine even if you haven't paid for it. But if you use it regularly, the honor system, your conscience, and the nagging reminder messages that appear whenever you open the program should compel you to send the requested payment to the author.

In any case, here's how to proceed:

1. **Choose Picture→Resolution. In the resulting dialog box, type *72* into both boxes, and then click OK.**

   This step ensures that, if your image came from a scanner, its "dpi" setting matches what iMovie expects.

2. **Choose Picture→Size→Scale.**

   The Scale dialog box appears, as shown in Figure 9-4.

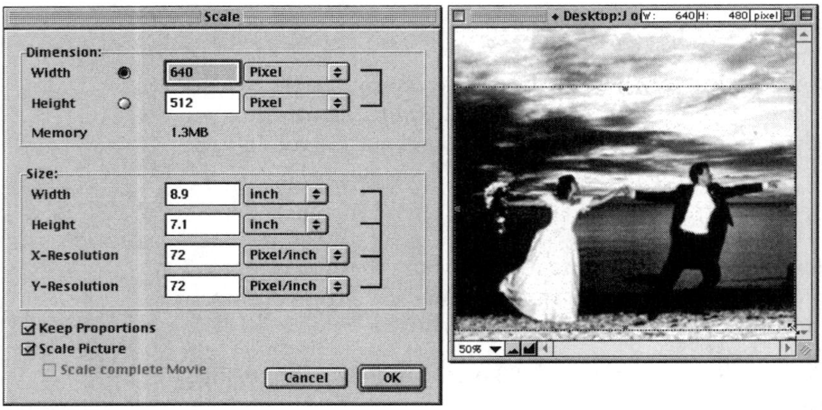

Figure 9-4:
Left: Use the Scale dialog box to make your graphic either 640 pixels wide or 480 tall.

Right: Then drag a diagonal line so that the numbers in the upper-right corner say X: 640 and Y: 480. (The rect-angle must stretch either from top to bottom or from side to side.)

3. **In the bottom two boxes, change the number to 72. From each of the two top pop-up menus, choose Pixel. Specify a width of 640 in the top Width box.**

   After a few seconds, you'll see the Height box change, too. What you do next depends on what number it changes to.

   If it's exactly 480, your work is done; click OK. If it's more than 480, skip to step 5. If it's less than 480, read on:

4. **Change the number in the Height box to 480.**

   After a few seconds, the Width box changes, too, now showing the number that's higher than 640. You'll fix this problem in the next step.

5. **Click OK.**

You return to your image, which may look larger or smaller.

6. **Drag diagonally across the image, carefully watching the numbers in the title bar until they say W: 640 and H: 480, as shown in Figure 9-4 at right.**

In essence, you're enclosing the part of the image that you'll want to *keep* after GraphicConverter chops out the part that's too big for the movie frame. If the rectangle you create doesn't reflect the portion of the image you want to keep, release the mouse. Drag the small box handles at the corners of the dotted-line rectangle to adjust the box's size. (You can always choose Edit→Undo: Selection and try dragging again, too.)

7. **When you've got the rectangle around the part of the image you want to keep, choose Edit→Trim Selection.**

Your graphic is ready to save.

FREQUENTLY ASKED QUESTIONS

The Case of the Rectangular Pixels

Why should I save my graphic at 640 x 480? I read on the Internet that each DV frame is actually 720 x 480. For best resolution, therefore, shouldn't I make my still pictures that size?

All right, Mr. Does-His-Homework. You want the technical explanation, and you shall have it.

It's true that each frame of digital video is actually 720 pixels wide, not 640. The explanation lies in an uncomfortable fact that iMovie carefully hides from you: The pixels that compose a digital video frame *aren't square*—they're actually rectangular. They're skinny, standing-up little rectangles.

When you see the image in iMovie or on TV, it's compressed so that it *appears* to be 640 x 480. In other words, techni-

cally speaking, an iMovie image is 12.5 percent stretched from what you're seeing on the screen. With certain add-on graphics programs, you might even be able to see the picture the way iMovie really thinks of it. (When those skinny rectangles are made square again, your subjects would all appear short and fat.)

As an additional favor to you, iMovie automatically converts these stretched pixels into square ones whenever you import or export graphics or QuickTime movies. The program thinks, "Well, whenever this final movie is viewed on TV or in a QuickTime movie, its dimensions will look like they're in a 4:3 ratio anyway, so I may as well request 640 x 480 still images and do the conversion behind the scenes, in my head."

Saving Your Still Image

After you've succeeded in massaging your graphic into the proper size and shape, the remaining steps are much easier.

If you're using Photoshop, AppleWorks, or GraphicConverter, choose File→Save As. If you're in PhotoDeluxe, choose File→Export→File Formats.

Either way, in the resulting dialog box, choose Format→PICT. Press ⌘-D (so that you'll save this graphic onto your desktop), type a name for it, and finally, click Save.

Tip: Technically, iMovie can import graphics in any format that QuickTime can understand, which includes PICT, JPEG, GIF, and even full-fledged Photoshop files. Avoid the GIF format, which limits the number of colors available to the image. But otherwise, it makes very little difference which graphics format you choose. Apple suggests PICT because in theory, it uses less image-altering compression than the JPEG format; in practice, you won't be able to see any difference.

When you quit your graphics program, you'll find your newly saved graphics file on the desktop.

Importing the Picture into iMovie

To bring your saved graphics file into iMovie, open the project into which you want it incorporated, and then choose File→Import File (or just press ⌘-I). When the standard Open File dialog box opens, navigate your way to the desktop (or wherever you put your graphics file), and double-click the file itself. Its icon shows up instantly in the Shelf or the Movie Track (depending on the setting you made by choosing Edit→Preferences→Import).

Tip: The factory duration setting for newly imported still images is five seconds. Once you've dragged a graphic into your Movie Track, you can always change its allotment of screen time, as described below.

But if you're creating a lot of still images, you'll find it annoying to have to change the playback duration of every single one to, for example, two seconds. The solution appears when you choose Edit→Preferences. In the Preferences dialog box, change the number in the "Still Clips are ___ seconds by default" box, and then click OK. From now on, newly created or imported clips appear in the Shelf with this new duration.

From now on, the picture you imported behaves exactly like a standard movie clip. You can rename it, drag it around, click it to view it in the Monitor window, drag it back and forth from the Clip Viewer and Shelf, delete it, incorporate it into titles or transitions, and so on.

Tip: After you've imported a graphics file into your iMovie project, it's OK to delete, rename, or move the graphics file you imported. iMovie doesn't need it anymore.

And if you've been lying awake at night, wondering *how* iMovie can display your graphic even after the original file is gone, look no farther than the Media folder inside your movie's project folder. There you'll find clip icons called Still 01, Still 02, Still 03, and so on. When you import a still image into a project, iMovie does itself the favor of making a *copy* of your original graphics file, which it stashes in this Media folder.

Specifying the timing of the picture

Because the image you imported is a still image, it doesn't have a *duration,* as a movie clip might. (Asking "How many seconds long is a photograph?" is like asking, "What is the sound of one hand clapping?")

Still, it's a clip, so iMovie has to assign it *some* duration; it uses five seconds as the starting point (unless you've changed this proposed value as described in the tip above). But you can make your graphic appear on the screen for as little as a single frame (a favorite of subliminal advertisers) all the way up to one minute (a favorite of all other advertisers). Changing this number is easy enough, using a special box that appears in iMovie only when you've highlighted a still-image clip, as shown in Figure 9-5.

This little duration box is both an indicator and a control. By changing the numbers in this box, you change the length of the still image's appearance. These tips should make doing so easier:

- You can use the standard Macintosh editing techniques within this tiny box. Press the arrow keys to walk your cursor from one number to the next, for example. Press the Delete key to backspace over the number to the left of the insertion point, or the forward-delete (Del) key, if your keyboard has one, to delete the number to the right of it.

Figure 9-5:
To edit the duration of a still image, click the clip to make this duration box appear. It illustrates the amount of time the picture will appear or on the screen, in "minutes: seconds:frames" format. Edit the clip's duration by changing these numbers.

- Double-click the *portion* of the number you want to change. For example, if a clip's duration box says 00:10:00 (ten seconds), double-click the 10 to highlight it, type the new number (such as *7)*, and press Enter. (You don't have to type a leading zero in front of a single-digit number.)

  In other words, when efficiency counts, *don't* waste your time deleting the numbers that are already in the duration box. Instead, double-click only the portion of it you want to change, and then type right over the highlighted digits.

- Similarly, if you want to change both the seconds and the frames, drag directly across the right pair of numbers of the box. (Whether or not you include the first colon in your drag makes no difference.) Type the new duration—seconds, a colon, and then frames—and then press Enter. Once again, you don't have to type any leading zeroes.

- If you highlight the entire duration box (by pressing ⌘-A, for example, or by choosing Edit→Select All), you can rapidly specify the new duration without having to type colons. The trick is to specify the grand total number of *frames,* keeping in mind that there are 30 frames per second (or 25 in PAL countries).

For example, the fastest way to specify a five-second clip (if you're right-handed) is to click the duration box as you hold the mouse in your right hand. With your left hand, press ⌘-A to highlight the numbers. With your right hand on the numeric keypad, type 150 (that's 5 seconds, at 30 frames per second) and press Enter. iMovie automatically converts the 150 into the appropriate notation: *00:05:00.*

If you use still images in your movies only occasionally, you might find this attention to efficiency and keyboard use a bit excessive. But if you process many still graphics, as you would in, say, cartoon animation (described later in this chapter), the tiny bits of time and effort you save using the speed techniques get multiplied by hundreds of repetitions.

Using Still Images as Titles

As noted at the beginning of this chapter, one of the best reasons to get to know the still-image importing feature is so that you can supplement, or replace, iMovie's built-in titling feature. By using still images as your titles, you gain the freedom to use any colors, type sizes, and positions you want.

The only disadvantage to this approach is that you sacrifice the professional-looking animation styles built into the iMovie titles feature. Even so, imported graphic title cards don't have to be still and static by any means. Consider these tricks, for example:

POWER USERS' CLINIC

The Fade-to-Black (or Fade-to-Puce) Secret

As noted in Chapter 6, it's very easy to create a professional-looking fade out at the end of your movie. Unfortunately, while iMovie does a great job at taking your film from the final footage to a black frame, it ruins the mood created by its own effect, by *ending the movie.* Unlike professional movies, which fade to black *and then hold* for a moment, iMovie fades to black at the end of the movie and then *stops playing,* sending your viewers back to iMovie, your desktop, the football game, or whatever was on the computer or TV screen before you played your movie.

The solution is very simple, and well worth making a part of your regular iMovie repertoire. Just after the final fade out, create a black rectangle, as described on page 134. (Recap: Paste a random clip after the final shot of your movie, drag it rightward in the Timeline Viewer to make a black clip appear, and then delete the random clip, leaving the freshly minted black clip behind.)

Then, instead of using the Fade Out transition effect described in Chapter 6, use the Cross Dissolve. iMovie responds by fading smoothly from the final footage of the clip into your black box.

As noted in Chapter 6, whenever you use a transition, iMovie splits the clip into two pieces—one that includes the transition animation, and the unaffected half. Change the duration of the unaffected half of your black square to make the moment of blackness as long as you desire.

Nor should you be content to fade to *black.* In fact, you can fade out to whatever color you desire—white, blue, gray, anything. Just import a 640 x 480 rectangle of the appropriate color at the end of your movie, and use the Cross Dissolve effect to fade into it.

The Freeze-Frame Effect

If you were a fan of 1970s action shows like *Emergency!,* you may remember how the opening credits looked: You'd be watching one of the starring characters frantically at work in some life-saving situation. As she looked up from her work just for a moment, the picture would freeze, catching her by lucky happenstance at her most flattering angle. At that instant, you'd see her credit flashed onto the screen: "JULIE LONDON (as Dixie McCall, RN)."

That's an easy one to simulate—and nobody will guess that it was created using a still image. To pull this off, you must first export the still frame from your footage that you'll want to use as the freeze-frame. (You'll find instructions for exporting a still frame in the next section.) Import the frozen shot into your graphics program, such as AppleWorks or Photoshop. Add the text you want.

Finally, import this touched-up image into iMovie as a still image. Place it at the precise frame in your footage from which you exported the still frame to begin with, and you've got your freeze-frame title effect.

INFREQUENTLY ASKED QUESTION

iMovie's Loopy Math?

Is iMovie buggy? I can't get the math to work out right when I want to specify a one-minute still frame. You know what I'm talking about, don't you?

The trick of typing in the total number of frames, and letting iMovie convert it to "minutes:seconds" format, works great—for low numbers, anyway.

But iMovie's math may appear to become loopy if you type in any number over 1,018 (which is 33 seconds, 28 frames). If you type in 1,019, for example, iMovie, a bit unsure of its math, comes up with 34 seconds even, apparently throwing in a free frame for good luck.

This apparent example of off-by-one math persists all the way to the maximum duration; if you type in 1,800 frames (which should come out to exactly one minute, iMovie's max), you get the error message telling you that the number you typed is too high. (Note to the Olympics Committee: Don't let iMovie do your finish-line timing calculations for you.)

Which brings us back to the original question. Is all of this iMovie's way of telling you: "Hey, pal—59 seconds of staring at a still image in your movie is already too long"?

Not at all; as it turns out, iMovie's math is fine. The problem is our using 30 frames per second as the multiplier. As described on page 286, standard NTSC video isn't 30 frames per second; for some almost embarrassing technical reasons, the correct number of frames per second, since the early days of TV, has been *29.97* frames per second. And when you use *that* factor for your multiplication, iMovie turns out to be 100% accurate.

This curious phenomenon was even more pronounced in iMovie 1, where the maximum time on-screen for a still image was a full *hour.* (A more interesting, and possibly more frequently asked question, then, might be: What inspired the iMovie team to lower the still-image time limit from one hour to one minute?)

And now, back to the book already in progress.

Tip: If you don't need the added typographical flexibility of your graphics program, you can simplify this procedure by simply creating a freeze-frame, as described on page 238, and then using iMovie's built-in title feature to add the text over it.

The Layered Effect

In many cases, the most creative use of still-image titles comes from using several of them, each building on the last. For example, you can make the main title appear, hold for a moment, and then transition into a second still graphic on which a subtitle appears (see Figure 9-6).

If you have more time on your hands, you can use this trick to create simple animations. Suppose you were to create ten different title cards, all superimposed on the same background, but each with the words in a different size or position. If you were to place each title card on the screen for only half a second (15 frames), joined by very fast crossfades, you'd have a striking visual effect. Similarly, you might consider making the *color* of the lettering shift over time. To do that, create two or three different title cards, each with the text in a different color. Insert them into your movie, join them with slow crossfades, and you've got a striking, color-shifting title sequence.

Figure 9-6:
If you place two still-image titles side-by-side, you can create simple animations. Here, the main title appears on a freeze-frame of the incoming footage. Then the subtitle fades in, superimposed on a different freeze-frame.

Creating Still Images from Your Footage

Not only can iMovie import images, but it can also grab selected frames from your footage, either for use as frozen frames in your movie or for export as graphics files.

Creating a Freeze-Frame

One of the juiciest fruits in the cornucopia of new iMovie 2 features is its Edit→Create Still Frame command. It creates a still image, in the Shelf, of the frame currently indicated by the Playhead. When you want a frozen frame created from your footage, you're spared the iMovie 1 hassle of exporting a frame to your hard drive and then reimporting it.

You can use the resulting still clip just as you would any still clip: Drag it into your Movie Track, apply effects or transitions to it, change its name or duration, and so on.

One of the most obvious uses of this feature is the *freeze-frame* effect, in which the movie holds on the final frame of a shot. It's a terrifically effective way to end a movie, particularly if the final shot depicts the shy, unpopular hero in a moment of triumph, arms in the air, hoisted onto the shoulders of the crowd. (Fade to black; bring up the music; roll credits.)

Here's how you do it:

1. **Position the Playhead on the frame you'll want frozen.**

   If it's the last shot of a clip, use the right and left arrow keys to make sure you're seeing the absolute final frame.

2. **Choose Edit→Create Still Frame.**

   iMovie places a new clip on your Shelf. It's a still image, set to play for whatever duration you've specified (see the tip on page 234).

   If you created this still clip from the *final frame* of a clip, proceed to the next step. If you created this clip from the *middle* of a clip, however, you should now choose Edit→Split Clip at Playhead. You've just chopped up the clip at the precise source of the still clip, resulting in two side-by-side clips in your Movie Track. Delete the right-hand clip.

3. **Drag the still clip from the Shelf into the Movie Track, just to the right of the original clip (Figure 9-7).**

   Adjust its playback duration, if necessary, as described on page 234.

If you play back the result, you'll be impressed at how smoothly and professionally iMovie joins the frozen frame onto the moving footage; there's not even a hint of a seam as the Playhead slides from clip to still.

Figuring out how to handle the *audio* in such situations is up to you; a still frame has no sound. That's a good argument for starting your closing-credits music *during* the final clip and making it build to a crescendo for the final freeze-frame.

Figure 9-7:
A great way to end a movie: Chop up the final clip and slow down each piece, finally coming to rest on your still image.

Exporting a Still Frame

While it's convenient to be able to grab a frame from your footage for use in the same movie (as a freeze-frame, for example), you may sometimes find it useful to be able to export a frame to your hard drive as a graphics file. You can use such exported images in any way you use graphics—for emailing to friends, installing on your desktop as a background picture, posting on a Web page, printing out and taping to the fridge, and so on. This feature is, after all, the reason that iMovie fans generally don't really care about the built-in still-photo features of DV camcorders; iMovie can create still images from *any* frame of regular video footage.

The quality caveat

It's worth noting, however, that the maximum *resolution* for a digital video frame—the number of dots that compose the image—is 640 across, 480 down. (By this time in the chapter, these numbers have probably become engraved into your cerebellum). As digital photos go, that's pretty pathetic, on a par with the photos taken by the cheapest digital *still* camera you can buy. (Most digital still cameras these days capture pictures at 1024 x 768 resolution and up—way, way up.)

The standard DV resolution is probably good enough for viewing your captured frames on the screen—that is, for use in Web pages and sending by email. But printing is a different story. Unless you first increase the resolution (dots per inch) of the image in, say, Photoshop, PhotoDeluxe, or GraphicConverter, you'll notice a distinct graininess to the printouts of frames you export from iMovie (see Figure 9-8). Unfortunately, when you increase the resolution, you shrink the photo because you're making each dot smaller. Doubling the resolution to 144 dpi, for example, shrinks a 4 x 4 photo down to 2 inches square.

Figure 9-8:
Digital still frames you export from your DV footage suffers from two disadvantages. First, the resolution is comparatively low. Second, the image is composed of only one set of interlaced scan lines, creating the jagged horizontal-line problem illustrated here.

But the low resolution of the video frame is only half the reason your captured pictures look so bad. Most camcorders capture images the same way television *displays* images: as hundreds of fine horizontal stripes, or *scan lines*. You don't actually see all of the scan lines at any one instant; you see odd-numbered lines in one frame, even-numbered lines in the next. Because the frames flash by your eyes so quickly, your brain smoothes the lines together so that you perceive one continuous image.

This system of *interlacing* may work OK for moving video images, but presents an unpleasant problem when you capture just one frame. Capturing a still image from this footage gives you, in essence, only half of the scan lines that compose the image. iMovie does what it can to fill in the missing information. But as shown in Figure 9-8, there's still a jaggedness problem involving the horizontal scan lines.

Tip: The only camcorders exempt from the interlacing problem are those with *progressive-scan* circuitry, such as the Canon Elura and Optura Pi. These camcorders don't see the world as being composed of interlaced scan lines; instead, they capture the whole picture at once, the frame in its entirety. As a result, you can get much better still frames out of progressive-scan camcorders (although they're still limited to 640 x 480 pixel resolution).

Exporting a frame

Now that your expectations have been duly lowered, here's how you capture a frame in iMovie.

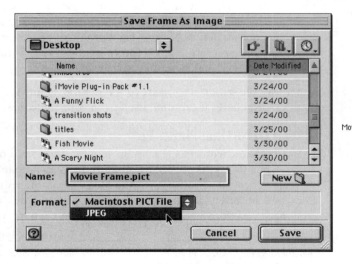

Figure 9-9:
The Save Frame dialog box (left) lets you name the picture you're saving. iMovie proposes the name "Movie Frame .pict" or "Movie Frame .jpg," depending on the format you choose—but those suffixes aren't necessary unless you intend to exchange the graphics with Windows users or post them on a Web page. When the process is over, the saved frames appear with their own icons on your desktop (right).

Open the project from which you want to grab a still photo. Press the Home key to make sure that no individual clips are selected, and then locate the frame you want to capture. Drag the Playhead along the Scrubber bar, for example. Remember that you can press the left and right arrow keys to step through the Movie one frame at a time, or Shift-arrow keys to jump ten frames at a time, in your quest for the precise moment you want to preserve as a still image.

When the image you want appears in the Monitor window, choose File→Save Frame As (or press ⌘-F). The Save Frame As Image dialog box appears (Figure 9-9). Use the Format menu to specify the file format you want for your exported graphic: PICT if you intend to use it as a desktop picture, JPEG if you intend to email it to someone or use it on a Web page. Navigate to the folder into which you want this graphic saved (or press ⌘-D to save it onto the desktop). Click Save.

Tip: You no longer have to worry about exporting a still frame as a PICT file from iMovie and then reimporting it without first changing it to JPEG format. The iMovie 1 problem that gave an exported, then reimported PICT file a jittery, annoying shimmer when viewed on a TV has been fixed in iMovie 2.

Then again, there's no *reason* to export a frame and then import it again. The Create Still Frame command described on page 238 is far more efficient, and dodges the PICT/JPEG issue completely.

Importing QuickTime Movies

When it comes to movies, iMovie can't just dish it out—it can also take it. You can bring any existing QuickTime movies into iMovie and incorporate them into your footage almost as easily as you can import still images.

Maybe you've created such QuickTime movies yourself, using other Macs or other software. Maybe you've grabbed a QuickTime movie from a CD-ROM or Web site, and you're not worried about copyright problems because you don't intend to show the finished product in public. (You *can't* grab video from DVDs, which are programmed to block such potential legal violations.)

Either way, the trick is to convert your older Movie into a *DV stream*—a movie clip that iMovie believes it captured itself from your camcorder.

Getting QuickTime Player Pro

This conversion requires the assistance of another piece of software: QuickTime Player, which is on every Macintosh hard drive, usually in the QuickTime folder. The free version that comes with the Mac doesn't offer the necessary conversion command, however. Only by upgrading your copy of QuickTime Player to the "Pro" version, at a cost of $30, do you gain the required Export command.

Tip: The upgrade to QuickTime Player Pro is useful to iMovie makers in dozens of ways; the ability to convert older QuickTime movies into DV format is only one of them. You can read about other useful QuickTime Player Pro features in Chapters 8, 14, and elsewhere in this book.

For instructions on making the upgrade (which you can do online), see the beginning of Chapter 14.

Saving the File

Converting your file is easy.

1. **Open the older QuickTime movie in QuickTime Player (the Pro version).**

   If you like, you can trim out the pieces you don't want to retain, as described in Chapter 14.

2. **Choose File→Export.**

   The Save File dialog box appears, as shown in Figure 9-10.

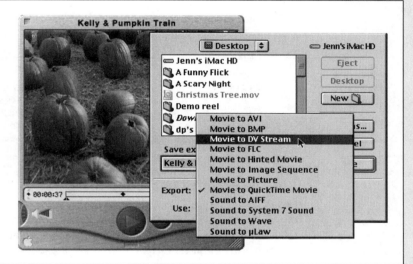

Figure 9-10:
Save your QuickTime movie as a DV Stream if you hope to import it into your iMovie project. (If your copy of QuickTime Player doesn't even have an Export command, then you haven't correctly updated it to the $30 Pro version.) The conversion to a DV stream takes quite a while, so be prepared to kill some time. (Go see a movie.)

3. **Using the Export pop-up menu at the bottom of the window, choose "Movie to DV Stream." Type a name for the converted version of your clip, navigate to your project's Media folder, and then click Save.**

   In other words, if you've been working on a film called *Dad Pays a Visit to the HMO,* save the newly created DV clip into the Dad Pays a Visit to the HMO→Media folder. You should accept QuickTime Player's proposal to add ".dv" to the end of the file's name to distinguish it from the original Movie.

   QuickTime Player now converts your Movie into a DV clip—a process that is neither quick nor stingy with hard drive space. For example, converting a one-minute QuickTime movie takes about fifteen minutes, and turns a 50 MB QuickTime file into a *300* MB DV QuickTime file.

4. **Open the iMovie project.**

   That is, open the Dad Pays a Visit to the HMO folder and double-click the document icon bearing the same name. (If that project was already open, quit iMovie first.)

Now you get the strange message shown in Figure 9-11. It's telling you that iMovie has found a new clip in its own Media folder that it doesn't remember putting there. If the message indicates that not all of the newly discovered clips will fit on your Shelf, see Figure 9-11.

Tip: If you didn't save the DV stream file into your project's Media folder in step 6, you can choose File→Import File at this point. Navigate to whatever folder *does* contain the DV stream file, and double-click it to import it into your project.

---

5. Click OK.

The QuickTime movie now appears in your Shelf as a clip that you can manipulate just as you would any movie clip.

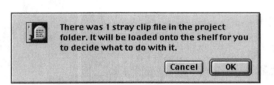

There was 1 stray clip file in the project folder. It will be loaded onto the shelf for you to decide what to do with it.

Cancel   OK

Figure 9-11:
When you open the project whose Media folder contains a new clip, you get this famous "stray clip" message. It lets you know that a clip, or several clips, have found their way into the project's Media folder that iMovie didn't put there.

Using the Imported QuickTime Clip

It's worth noting that most of the world's QuickTime movies aren't big enough, frame-size-wise, to fill your entire monitor. In fact, most of the world's QuickTime movies play in a window only a couple of inches square. (This business of iMovie, DV camcorders, and full-screen playback is a relatively new phenomenon.)

Therefore, when you play back an imported QuickTime movie, iMovie does what it hopes is the right thing: It blows up the QuickTime movie until the footage fills the entire iMovie playback screen (640 x 480 pixels).

As you probably know by now, however, enlarging *any* graphic on the computer usually winds up degrading its quality, because each pixel that composes the image must be enlarged. The bottom line: QuickTime movies you import into iMovie usually look coarse and blotchy unless they were at least 640 x 480 to begin with.

Fortunately, the era of small-size QuickTime movies is, for you, over. In the future, you can keep all your video on DV cassettes, always at full-screen size, and always at fantastic quality.

Grabbing Clips from Other Projects

One way to reuse clips among iMovie projects is to drag their Clip files among the projects' Media folders, as illustrated on page 108. But if you'd rather not switch to the Finder and muck around in folder windows, you can use a new iMovie 2 feature that simplifies the process: the File→Import File command.

When you choose it, the Import File dialog box appears. Navigate to the folder that contains the project whose footage you'd like to steal; open it; open the Media folder inside; and double-click the Clip file you want to import into the project that's open on the screen. After a moment—a *long* moment, as iMovie copies this enormous file into the current project's own Media folder—the imported clip appears on the Shelf.

Of course, these cheerful instructions overlook one massive roadblock: figuring out which of the dozens of clips in the raided project's Media folder *is* the one you want to import. After all, they don't have descriptive names, and you can't preview them. (There *is* a Show Preview button in the Import File dialog box, but it works only for still images.)

That's why the importing-a-clip-from-another-project routine generally involves a detour: Opening the *other* project, finding the clip (in the Shelf or Movie Track) that you're trying to reuse, double-clicking it, and reading its clip number in the Clip info dialog box that appears. Then you can return to your newer project and import the clip as directed above.

Tip: DV Stream files are the sole salvation of anyone who wants to convert an NTSC (North American) iMovie project to PAL (European) format, or vice versa. You'll have to export the entire movie as a DV Stream (see page 243), which can take many hours and gigabytes. When that's done, you can import the resulting DV Stream file into a newly created iMovie project as described in this chapter.

FREQUENTLY ASKED QUESTION

Capturing the Screen

I want to use iMovie to make a software training course. How do I make movies of what I'm doing on the Mac screen?

Use the remarkable shareware program called Snapz Pro 2 (available from *www.missingmanual.com*). It lets you specify which area of the screen you want to capture (or the whole screen). (For best use in iMovie, capture the entire screen, after first setting it to a resolution of 640 x 480 using the Monitors or Monitors & Sound control panel.)

Then, when you press a keystroke that you've specified, Snapz starts recording all the action on the screen: the movement of your cursor, windows and menus opening, and so on. All of it gets saved into a QuickTime movie, which you can then convert into a DV stream and import into iMovie, as described in this chapter.

IMOVIE 2: THE MISSING MANUAL

Professional Editing Techniques

The preceding chapters have covered the *technical* aspects of editing video in iMovie: where to click, what keys to press, and how iMovie's various controls operate. This chapter is about the *artistic* aspects of video editing: when to cut, what to cut to, and how to create the emotional impact you want.

Put another way, this chapter is a continuation of the film-theory crash course that began in the first three chapters of this book. Chapter 2, for example, describes filmmaking techniques that you must think about at the time you're *shooting*. This chapter offers some tricks in *editing*.

The Power of Editing

The editing process is crucial in any kind of movie, from a home movie to a Hollywood thriller. Clever editing can turn a troubled movie into a successful one, or a boring home movie into one that, for the first time, family members don't interrupt every three minutes by lapsing into conversation.

You, the editor, are free to jump from "camera" to "camera," angle to angle, to cut from one location or time to another, and so on. Today's audiences accept that you're telling a story; they don't stomp out in confusion because one minute, James Bond was in his London office, but showed up in Venice a split second later.

You can also compress time; that's one of editing's most common duties. (That's fortunate, because most movies tell stories that, in real life, take days, weeks, or years to unfold.) You can also *expand* time, making ten seconds stretch out to six minutes—a familiar effect to anyone who's ever watched a final sequence involving a bomb connected to a digital timer (and heroes racing to defuse it).

Editing boils down to choosing which shots you want to include, how long each one lasts, and in what order they should play.

Modern Film Theory

When you're creating a rock video or an experimental film, you can safely chuck all the advice in this chapter—and in this book.

But if you aspire to make good "normal" movies, ones that are designed to engage or delight your viewers rather than shock or mystify them, then you should become familiar with the fundamental principles of film editing that shape virtually every Hollywood movie (and even most student and independent films) of the last 75 years. For example:

Tell the story chronologically

Most movies tell the story from beginning to end. This part is probably instinct, even when you're making home movies. Arrange your clips roughly in chronological order, except when you're representing your characters' flashbacks and memories or deliberately playing a chronology game, as in *Pulp Fiction*.

Try to be invisible

These days, an expertly edited movie is one where the audience isn't even aware of the editing.

DV ETHICS

The Home-Movie Dilemma

As you edit your footage, you're altering reality; you're showing the audience only what you want it to see. When you create movies that have a story line, that's no problem—the audience knows perfectly well that what it's seeing didn't actually happen the way they're seeing it.

When you edit home movies, however, you have a dilemma. How true should you be to real life? If you followed the iMovie tutorial (see page 96), you worked with footage that showed a muddy dog being unsuccessfully washed by two noncommunicative children. In real life, those events might have constituted an unpleasant experience involving a ruined carpet and yelling parents. But with the help of a little sweet guitar music and some selective editing, the entire affair becomes a sunlit, nostalgic snapshot of idyllic childhood.

In a way, you've *already* pre-edited your life, simply in selecting what to film. Most people don't film the family bickering at dinnertime, the 20 minutes when the baby screams inconsolably, or the uneventful hours family members spend sleeping or watching TV. You're probably more likely to film the highlights—the laughter, the successes, the special events.

But when you edit this footage in iMovie, you'll probably weed out even more of the unpleasant, the boring, and the mundane. You may even be tempted to *rearrange* events, making the movie funnier, more entertaining, and more cohesive. When it's all over, you'll have a DV cassette filled with sunny, funny, exciting footage that may have come a long way from the much less interesting reality it was meant to capture—*especially* if you add music to your movies. (Music gives footage enormous emotional overtones that weren't there at all when the scene was originally filmed.)

All of this introduces a fascinating ethical challenge that's new to the iMovie era. In the past, few people could edit their home movies, so every home movie was pure documentary. With your DV camcorder and iMovie, you must decide whether you're a documentary maker, a storyteller, or both—and in what combination.

This principle has wide-ranging ramifications. For example, the desire to avoid making the editing noticeable is why the simple cut is by far the most common joint between film clips. Using, say, the Circle Opening transition between alternate lines of the vows at somebody's wedding would hardly qualify as invisible editing.

Within a single scene, use simple cuts and no transitions. Try to create the effect of seamless real time, making the audience feel as though it's witnessing the scene in its entirety, from beginning to end. This kind of editing is more likely to make your viewers less aware that they're watching a movie.

Develop a shot rhythm

Every movie has an editing *rhythm* that's established by the lengths of the shots in it. The prevailing rhythm of *Dances with Wolves,* for example, is extremely different from that of *Natural Born Killers.* Every *scene* in a movie has its own rhythm, too.

As a general rule, linger less on close-up shots, but give more time to establishing and wide shots. (After all, in an establishing shot, there are many more elements for the audience to study and notice.) Similarly, change the pacing of the shots according to the nature of the scene. Most action scenes feature very short clips and fast edits; most love scenes include longer clips and fewer changes of camera angle.

Maintaining Continuity

As a corollary to the notion that the audience should feel that they're part of the story, professional editors strive to maintain *continuity* during the editing process. This continuity business applies mostly to scripted films, not home movies; still, knowing what the pros worry about makes you a better editor no matter what kind of footage you're working with.

Continuity refers to consistency in:

- **The picture.** Suppose we watch a guy with wet hair say, "I'm going to have to break up with you." We cut to his girlfriend's horrified reaction—but when we cut back to the guy, his hair is dry.

  That's a continuity error, a frequent by-product of having spliced together footage that was filmed at different times. Every Hollywood movie, in fact, has a person whose sole job it is to watch out for errors like this during the filming process.

- **Direction of travel.** In the effort to make the editing as seamless as possible, film editors and directors try to maintain continuity of direction from shot to shot. That is, if the hero sets out crawling across the Sahara from right to left across the scene to be with his true love, you better believe that when we see him next, hours later, he'll still be crawling from right to left. This general rule even applies to much less dramatic circumstances, such as car chases, plane flights, and even people walking to the corner store. If you see her walk out of the frame from left to right in Shot A, you'll see her approach the corner store's doorway from left to right in Shot B.

- **The sound.** In an establishing shot, suppose we see hundreds of men in a battlefield trench, huddled for safety as bullets and bombs fly and explode all around them. Now we cut to a close-up of two these men talking—but the sounds of the explosions are missing.

  That's a sound continuity error. The audience is certain to notice that hundreds of soldiers on both sides were issued an immediate cease-fire just as these two guys started talking.

- **The camera setup.** In scenes of conversations between two people, you may notice that, even when the camera cuts from one person to the other, the degree of zoom, lighting, and positioning in the frame is roughly the same from shot to shot. It would look really bizarre to show one person speaking only in close-up, and his conversation partner filmed in a medium shot. (Unless, of course, the first person were filmed in *extreme* close-up—just the lips filling the screen—because the filmmaker is trying to protect his identity.)

- **Gesture and motion.** If one shot begins with a character reaching down to pick up the newspaper from her doorstep, the next shot—a close-up of her hand closing around the rolled-up paper, for example—should pick up from the exact moment where the previous shot ended. And as the rolled-up paper leaves our close-up field of view, the following shot should show her straightening into an upright position. Unless you've made the deliberate editing decision to skip over some time from one shot to the next (which should be clear to the audience), the action should seem continuous from one shot to the next.

Tip: For this reason, when filming scripted movies, directors always instruct their actors to begin each new scene's action with the same gesture or motion that *ended* the last shot. Having two copies of this gesture, action, or motion—one on each end of each take—gives the editor a lot of flexibility when it comes time to piece the movie together.

This principle explains why you'll find it extremely rare for an editor to cut from one shot of two people to another shot of the *same* two people (without inserting some other shot between them, such as a reaction shot or a close-up of one person or the other). The odds are small that, as the new shot begins, both actors will be in precisely the same body positions they were in as the previous shot ended.

When to Cut

Some Hollywood directors may tell their editors to make cuts just for the sake of making the cuts come faster, in an effort to pick up the pace.

The more seasoned director and editor, however, usually adopts a more classical view of editing: Cut to a different shot when it's *motivated*. That is, cut when you *need* to cut, so that you can convey new visual information by taking advantage of a different camera angle, switching to a different character, providing a reaction shot, and so on.

Editors look for a motivating event that suggests *where* they should make the cut, too, such as a movement, a look, the end of the sentence, or the intrusion of an off-camera sound that makes us *want* to look somewhere else in the scene.

Choosing the Next Shot

As you've read elsewhere in this book, the final piece of advice when it comes to choosing when and how to make a cut is this: Cut to a *different* shot. If you've been filming the husband, cut to the wife; if you've been in a close-up, cut to a medium or wide shot; if you've been showing someone looking off-camera, cut to what she's looking at.

Avoid cutting from one shot of somebody to a similar shot of the same person. Doing so creates a *jump cut,* a disturbing and seemingly unmotivated splice between shots of the same subject from the same angle. (Figure 3-3 shows a deliberate jump cut, used as a special effect.)

DV ETHICS

The Internet Continuity-Screwup Database

It's fine to say that the film editor's job is to attempt continuity of picture, sound, direction, and so on throughout a movie. The trouble is, that's not nearly as easy as it sounds. Remember that the editor works by piecing together individual clips from many different camera shots that may have been filmed on different days. When the production is as complicated as a Hollywood movie, where several different film crews may be shooting simultaneously in different parts of the world, a few continuity errors are bound to slip in—and sometimes they're hilarious.

Catching continuity errors in Hollywood movies has become a beloved pastime for thousands of movie fans. *Premiere* magazine, for example, carries a monthly feature called Gaffe Squad, in which readers point out continuity errors in popular commercial movies. An Internet search for *film continuity errors* yields hundreds of Web sites dedicated to picking apart the movies. Among these, the Internet Movie Database Goofs page *(http://us.imdb.com/Sections/Goofs*—capitals count) is Ground Zero; it's probably the largest collection of viewer-submitted movie errors ever assembled. They run along these lines:

Raiders of the Lost Ark: "During the firefight in Marion's bar, Indy's gun changes from a .38 revolver to the Colt .45, back to a .38, then back once again to a .45. This might be the reason that he is able to fire his gun seven times with every loading."

Back to the Future: "When talking to George at the clothesline, both of Marty's shirt pocket flaps are out, but in the next shot one of them is tucked in."

Pulp Fiction: "When young Butch is receiving the watch from the Army guy, the time changes twice as it is flipped over in his hand."

Jurassic Park: "As the helicopter lands on the island, we get a nice overhead view of the landing area, featuring a waterfall and two Jeeps waiting to take the passengers to the visitors' center. But when we see the ground-level view of the helicopter landing in the next shot, we see the Jeeps backing up to the position they were already in three seconds earlier."

Titanic: "When Capt. Smith orders, 'Take her to sea, Mr. Murdoch—let's stretch her legs,' they're standing to the right of the wheelhouse looking forward with the sun coming from their left. When Murdoch walks into the wheelhouse to carry out the order, the sun's behind him.'"

The Shining: "We see Jack Nicholson chop apart only one of the door's panels with his axe—and yet after we see him listen to the arrival of the Snow-Cat, both panels are chopped."

In other words, making a perfect movie is almost impossible. Of course, as an increasingly experienced film editor yourself, you already knew that.

Video editors sometimes have to swallow hard and perform jump cuts for the sake of compressing a long interview into a much shorter sound bite. Customer testimonials on TV commercials frequently illustrate this point. You'll see a woman saying, "Wonderglove changed… [cut] our lives, it really did… [cut] My husband used to be a drunk and a slob…[cut] but now we have Wonderglove." (Inevitably, a fast cross dissolve is applied to the cuts in a futile attempt to make them less noticeable.)

As you can probably attest if you've ever seen such an ad, however, that kind of editing is rarely convincing. As you watch it, you can't help wondering exactly *what* was cut out and why. (The editors of *60 Minutes* and other documentary-style shows edit the comments of their interview subjects just as heavily, but conceal it much better by cutting away to reaction shots—of the interviewer, for example—between edited shots.)

Popular Editing Techniques

Variety and pacing play a role in every decision the video editor makes. Here some common tricks and techniques professional editors use, which you can adopt for your use in iMovie editing.

Tight Editing

One of the first tasks you'll encounter when editing your footage is choosing how to trim and chop up your clips, as described in Chapter 5. Even when editing home movies, consider the Hollywood guideline for tight editing: Begin every scene as *late* as possible, and end it as *soon* as possible.

In other words, suppose the audience sees the heroine receiving the call that her husband has been in an accident, and then hanging up the phone in shock. We don't really need to see her putting on her coat, opening the apartment door, locking it behind her, taking the elevator to the ground floor, hailing a cab, driving frantically through the city, screeching to a stop in front of the hospital, and finally leaping out of the cab. In a tightly edited movie, she would hang up the phone—and then we'd see her leaping out of the cab (or even walking into her husband's hospital room).

You might keep this principle in mind even when editing your own, slice-of-life videos. For example, a very engaging account of your ski trip might begin with only three shots: an establishing shot of the airport; a shot of the kids piling on to the plane; and then the tumultuous, noisy trying-on-ski-boots shot the next morning. You get less reality with this kind of tight editing, but much more watchability.

Variety of Shots

As described in Chapter 2, variety is important in every aspect of filmmaking—variety of shots, locations, angles, and so on. Consider the lengths of your shots, too: In action sequences, you might prefer quick cutting, where each clip in your Movie Track is only a second or two long. In softer, more peaceful scenes, longer shots may set the mood more effectively.

Establishing shots

As noted in Chapter 2, almost every scene of every movie and every TV show—even the nightly news—begins with an *establishing shot:* a long-range, zoomed-out shot that shows the audience where the action is about to take place.

Now that you know something about film theory, you'll begin to notice how often TV and movie scenes begin with an establishing shot. It gives the audience a feeling of being there, and helps them understand the context for the medium shots or close-ups that follow. Furthermore, after a long series of close-ups, consider showing *another* wide shot, to remind the audience of where the characters are and what the world around them looks like.

As with every film editing guideline, this one is occasionally worth violating in special circumstances. For example, in comedies, a new scene may begin with a close-up instead of an establishing shot, so that the camera can then pull back to *make* the establishing shot the joke. (For example, close-up on main character looking uncomfortable; camera pulls back and flips over to reveal that we were looking at him upside down as he hangs, tied by his feet, over a pit of alligators.) In general, however, setting up any new scene with an establishing shot is the smart, and polite, thing to do for your audience's benefit.

Cutaways and Cut-ins

Also as described in Chapter 2, *cutaways* and *cut-ins* are extremely common and effective editing techniques. Not only do they add some variety to the movie, but they let you conceal enormous editing shenanigans. By the time your movie resumes after the cutaway shot, you can have deleted enormous amounts of material, switched to a different take of the same scene, and so on. Figure 10-1 shows the idea.

The *cut-in* is similar, but instead of showing a different person or a reaction shot, it usually features a close-up of what the speaker is holding or talking about—a very common technique in training tapes and cooking shows.

Reaction shots

One of the most common sequences in Hollywood history is a three-shot sequence that goes like this (Figure 10-1 again): First, we see the character looking off screen; then we see what he's looking at (a cutaway shot); then we see him again so that we can read his reaction. This sequence is repeated so frequently in commercial movies that you can feel it coming the moment the performer looks off the screen.

From the editor's standpoint, of course, the beauty of the three-shot reaction shot is that the middle shot can be anything from anywhere. That is, it can be footage shot on another day in another part of the world, or even from a different movie entirely. The ritual of character/action/reaction is so ingrained in our brains that the audience believes the actor was looking at the action, no matter what.

In home-movie footage, you may have been creating reaction shots without even knowing it. But you've probably been capturing them by panning from your kid's beaming face to the petting-zoo sheep and then back to the face. You can make this sequence look great in iMovie just by snipping out the pans, leaving you with crisp, professional-looking cuts.

Otherwise, it's safe to say that iMovie fans only rarely go to the trouble of creating the most common kind of reaction shot, in which we cut to a *listener's* reaction as the sound of the speaker's voice continues. Creating this effect requires that you separate the video from the soundtrack, which, in iMovie, is no picnic; it involves exporting your movie's sound track to another editing program, as described in Chapter 8.

Figure 10-1:
You've got a shot of your main character in action (top). We cut away to a shot of what he's looking at or reacting to (middle). When you cut back to the main character (bottom), you could use a different take on a different day, or dialog from a much later part of the scene (due to some cuts suggested by the editor). The audience will never know that the action wasn't continuous. The cutaway masks the fact that there was a discontinuity between the first and third shots.

Parallel cutting

When you're making a movie that tells a story, it's sometimes fun to use *parallel editing* or *intercutting*. That's when you show two trains of action simultaneously; you keep cutting back and forth to show the parallel simultaneous action. In *Fatal Attraction*, for example, the intercut climax shows main character Dan Gallagher (Michael Douglas) downstairs in the kitchen, trying to figure out why the ceiling is dripping, even as his psychotic mistress Alex (Glenn Close) is upstairs attempting to murder his wife in the bathtub.

You may not have much call for intercutting if you're just making home movies, especially because it's deliberately artificial. Everybody knows you've got only one camcorder, and therefore the events you're depicting couldn't have taken place simultaneously. But even if you're making movies that tell a story, you'll find this technique an exciting one when you're trying to build suspense.

Part Three:
Finding Your Audience

3

Back to the Camcorder

U nless you edit your movies keeping your eyes on the camcorder's screen (or a TV attached to your camcorder), as recommended on page 103, you've been editing your work-in-progress in the Monitor window. But as noted in Chapter 4, the Monitor window may not be able to provide a smooth, clear video image; you may have to make a compromise between smooth motion and crisp picture.

Fortunately, behind the scenes, every shred of crisp, clear, smooth-motioned video is intact on your hard drive. When you export the movie back to your DV camcorder, it appears in all its original, high-resolution glory.

Why Export to Tape

You might want to send your finished product back to the camcorder for any number of reasons. For example:

To Watch It on TV

Once your iMovie creations are back on the camcorder's DV tape, you can then pass it along to a television. To pull this off, you must connect the camcorder to your TV, using one of the following cables, listed here in order of preference:

- **S-video.** If both your camcorder and your VCR or TV have *S-video* connectors, use an S-video cable to join the two. (The camcorder shown at top in Figure 11-1 has an S-video connector; it's the large, round, black jack at the top of the connectors panel.)

  S-video transfer produces the best possible transfer quality between your DV camcorder and non-DV equipment.

• **RCA cables.** Most TVs and VCRs don't have S-video connectors, but almost all have *RCA phono* jacks, usually labeled Audio In and Video In. Connect them to the double- or triple-ended cable that came with the camcorder, like the one shown in Figure 11-1. (If it has *three* connectors at each end, the yellow one is for the video signal, and the red and white ends are for left and right stereo sound.)

Tip: If your TV is very old, it may not have auxiliary input jacks. In that case, plug your camcorder into the *VCR's* auxiliary inputs instead. It will patch the signal through to the TV.

Figure 11-1:
Top: Connect your camcorder's RCA jacks, shown here, to those of your VCR or TV. If your TV accepts only one sound cable (and not stereo inputs), plug the camcorder's left-channel connector (usually the red one) into the sole TV audio jack.

Bottom: Some camcorders, including most Canon and Sony models, come with a special, proprietary cable; the miniplug end goes into a special output jack on the camcorder; the far ends are RCA cables for your TV or VCR.

• **Coax inputs.** TVs of a certain era (or price) don't have the RCA-style cables shown in Figure 11-1, but do have a cable-TV (*coaxial*) input—a round connector about the size of a 24-point capital "O" with a single pin in the center. You can buy an adapter (at Radio Shack, for example) that lets you connect your camcorder's output cables to this kind of jack.

- **RF modulator.** If your TV doesn't even have that connector, it probably has two screws to which you can attach a "rabbit ears" antenna. You can buy an adapter called an *RF modulator* for this kind of connector, too.

- **Special patch cable.** Many DV camcorder models (including those from Sony and Canon) come with a special input/output cable with RCA connectors at one end, but a special miniplug at the camcorder end (see Figure 11-1, bottom). Plug this skinny end into the appropriate camcorder jack, often labeled "Audio/Video ID2" or "AV In/Out."

To Transfer It to Your VCR

The glorious thing about DV tape, of course, is that its picture quality and sound quality are sensational. Unfortunately, most of the world's citizens don't *have* DV camcorders or DV decks. They have standard VHS VCRs. If you want to show off your iMovie creations to the masses, you must first transfer your movies on to VHS cassettes. (Actually, you wouldn't want to distribute your creations on DV cassettes even if the masses *did* have DV camcorders; DV cassettes are just too expensive.)

You lose a lot of picture and sound quality when you transfer footage to a VHS cassette, whose lines-of-resolution capacity is lower than any other kind of reproduction (see page 16). Still, your viewers will most likely remark how *good* your movies look, not how bad. That's because most people are used to playing back VHS recordings they've made from *TV,* which (unless it's a satellite system) has its own low-resolution problems. The transfers you make from your Mac, even when played back on VHS, look terrific in comparison.

To make a transfer to your VCR, you have a choice: You can either copy the movie back onto a DV cassette in the camcorder, so that you'll have a high-quality DV copy, and then play it from the camcorder onto your VCR; or you can pour the video directly from the Mac, through the camcorder, into the VCR. Both of these techniques are described in the coming pages.

To Offload Footage from Your Mac

Another great reason to transfer your iMovie work back to the camcorder is simply to get it off of your hard drive. As you know, video files occupy an enormous amount of disk space. After you've made a couple of movies, your hard drive might be so full that you can't make any *more* iMovies.

Offloading the movie to your DV camcorder is the perfect solution, thanks to a key advantage of digital video: the ability to transfer footage back and forth between the camcorder and your Mac as many times as you like with *no deterioration in quality.* You can safely unlearn the years of experience you've had with VHS and 8 mm video; transferring video between the Macintosh and the DV camcorder is something that you can do casually and frequently.

Note: When you transfer an iMovie back to your camcorder, the footage remains in perfect, pristine condition. Remember, however, that there is a downside in doing so—once you've thrown away the digital video files from your Mac, you've lost the ability to adjust titles, effects, transitions, and soundtracks. For best results, therefore, transfer footage back to the camcorder only when you're finished editing the movie, or haven't edited it much at all.

Offloading video to reclaim disk space

After transferring the movie to a DV cassette in your camcorder, you can throw away the corresponding files on your hard drive, which frees up an enormous amount of disk space. The space-consuming digital-video clips themselves sit in the Media folder that lurks within the folder you've named for your project (see page 108). In other words, the Media folder is the one taking up all the disk space. Still, you may as well throw away the *entire* project folder (after "backing it up" onto the camcorder), because without the Media files, the actual iMovie document file is useless.

Offloading video to build a long movie

Your Mac's hard drive may be able to hold, say, 45 minutes of footage, but that doesn't necessarily mean that you can create a 45-minute *movie*. Almost always, your purpose in using iMovie is to *edit down* that raw footage, distilling it into a much shorter flick.

Yet you can indeed create a 45-minute finished movie (or even longer, depending on your hard drive size). The trick is to work on only one portion of it at a time, like this:

1. **Dump 45 minutes of raw footage from the camcorder onto the hard drive.**

   In this example, suppose you're using a Mac whose built-in hard drive holds about 45 minutes of footage.

2. **Edit down the footage to fifteen terrific minutes.**

   Polish it well, because you'll shortly be deleting the project file and won't be able to make any more changes to it.

3. **Eject the raw-footage cassette, and insert a new one called Finished Chunks. Play the finished 15-minute section from the Mac onto this new tape.**

   Use the instructions in the next section to do so. (It's an excellent idea to keep different DV tapes for raw footage and for finished iMovies. This lets you keep open the possibility that you may want to re-edit the original footage someday. It also minimizes the risk that you'll record over something important.)

4. **Delete the project folder from the hard drive. Reinsert the raw-footage tape into the camcorder.**

5. **Repeat steps 1 through 4 two more times.**

   At this point, then, you've got a second DV cassette called Finished Chunks that contains three 15-minute sections of polished movie.

6. Transfer all of the Finished Chunks footage onto the Mac. In iMovie, join the three 15-minute clips together with cuts or transitions.

That's all there is to it. Your 45-minute movie is complete, ready to play on the Mac, transfer back to a DV cassette, or even save as a 45-minute QuickTime movie (but don't attempt to email *this* baby). Yes, it would certainly be more convenient to work on a 76 GB hard drive, where such footage-shuffling isn't necessary. But this method doesn't require a several-hundred-dollar expenditure.

Transferring Footage to the Camcorder or VCR

The actual steps of transferring the project from iMovie back to the camcorder are fairly simple. The results are almost always satisfying, especially if you've had to look at your footage in its relatively coarse Mac rendition for hours or days; you finally get to see your masterpiece at full digital quality. Most people are particularly thrilled by the professional look of iMovie's transitions and titles when they see it on the actual TV (or camcorder LCD panel).

FREQUENTLY ASKED QUESTION

Splicing Together Movies on the Tape

I like your advice about creating a long movie by piecing together several shorter ones in iMovie. That works fine as long as the Mac is capable of holding the entire movie at one time. My problem is that I want to make a 90-minute movie, but my hard drive holds only 45 minutes. Now what?

If buying an additional hard drive is out of the question, you're still not out of luck: You can edit the segments of your grand epic on iMovie one at a time—and then record them in sequence onto the same tape.

You can combine movies onto a single tape much more seamlessly than you might imagine, provided that you use this trick before declaring each movie section complete: Add five seconds of blackness at the end of it. You can do so by using iMovie 2's "Add seconds of black at end of movie" option, described on page 265. If it's dramatically appropriate, create a fade out into this blackness at the end of the last shot in the segment, as described on page 152. Transfer your first movie segment, thus prepared, to tape A.

Now delete the project folder from your hard drive, which gives you space to edit the second segment of the movie. Insert your next raw-footage tape into the camcorder, trans-

fer the next batch of unedited footage to the Mac, and edit it in iMovie, once again adding a few seconds of blackness to the end of the segment.

Insert tape A into the camcorder again. Use iMovie's Camera mode to rewind the camcorder just to the beginning of the blackness (which concluded the first segment), as close as you dare to the end of the first segment's footage. Now you're ready to export the second segment of movie. When you do so, set the "Seconds of black" that appears *before* the movie to 0 (see Figure 11-2).

The extra seconds of blackness that you recorded at the end of the first segment provide a buffer that prevents the bursts of static and "video noise" that typically plague homemade video splices. When you record the second segment onto the same tape, you'll get a smooth, unnoticeable transition from the end of the first into the beginning of the second.

Repeat this procedure as many times as necessary to build your final movie onto tape A, one segment at a time. (And if your movie really is *90 minutes* long, use your camcorder's Long Play mode, as described at the end of this chapter. Otherwise, you'll run out of tape after 60 minutes.)

Why Export
to Tape

CHAPTER 11: BACK TO THE CAMCORDER

263

In iMovie 1, you had to begin the transfer process by sending your finished movie to a DV camcorder as a first step. In iMovie 2, however, a new possibility awaits: You can play the finished movie directly from the Mac to a VCR, using the camcorder only as a pass-through adapter that doesn't actually record anything. The following discussions offer both methods.

First to DV Tape, Then to VCR

If you'd like your finished movie on DV tape, preserving 100% of its original quality), proceed like this.

1. **Insert a blank cassette into your camcorder.**

   Confirm that the tape is unlocked (see page 270), and—*this is important*—that it's cued up to a part of the tape you're willing to record over.

   This may sound like an obvious step, but complacency on this point has led camcorder owners to the accidental erasure of many a precious piece of footage. Sooner or later, everyone finds out: A camcorder has no Undo command.

2. **Put the camcorder into VTR or VCR mode (refer back to Figure 2-1).**

   Confirm that its FireWire cable is plugged into your Mac. Unless you're willing to risk running out of battery power in midtransfer, plug your camcorder into a power outlet, too.

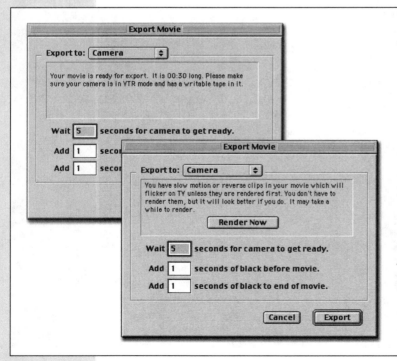

Figure 11-2:
Top: The Export Movie dialog box lets you specify whether you're sending your finished movie to tape or to a QuickTime movie, as described in Chapter 12.

Bottom: If you've applied slow-motion or Reverse Clip effects to your movie, a message at the top of the dialog box advises you that additional rendering will make the effect look smoother when the effect plays on a TV. (The additional rendering creates smoothed "in between frames" to fill in the "real" frames of your slowed-down footage.) The extra rendering takes even more time, but ensures a stunningly professional result.

Open your iMovie project on the Mac, if it isn't already open.

3. **Choose File→Export Movie.**

The Export Movie dialog box appears, as shown in Figure 11-2. Make sure that the pop-up menu at the top says Camera.

4. **Change the "Seconds of black" and "Seconds for camera to get ready" numbers in the dialog box, if necessary.**

The "Seconds of black" numbers specify how many seconds of blackness you want to appear on the tape before the movie begins or after it ends; three or four seconds is about right. Without a black "preroll," the movie would begin instantly. Your audience would be deprived of the customary "settle down and start paying attention" moment that precedes every TV show, movie, and commercial throughout the world. And without a moment of blackness at the end, the mood created by your movie might be shattered too soon.

The other number in this box, "Seconds for camera to get ready," is designed to account for the fact that no camcorder goes into Record mode instantly. Inside the camera, small wheels must first open the door of the cassette, extract the tape, and load it around the recording heads, all of which takes a moment or two. The number you enter in this box doesn't change what's recorded. In other words, your viewers won't have to wait this number of seconds; it's just a precaution to make sure that your camcorder is rolling to record when iMovie is playing.

Tip: As it turns out, iMovie needs a few seconds to get *itself* ready to send your movie back to the camcorder (during which a message says "Initializing"). Experiment with the "Seconds for camera to get ready" number, therefore; a setting of 1 or even 0 may work for your camcorder model.

iMovie will remember these settings for the next time you export a movie.

If you've applied slow-motion or reverse-motion effects to a clip (or clips), a Render button appears in the dialog box shown in Figure 11-2. It warns that unless you let iMovie take a few minutes to pad the slowed-down footage with in-between frames, the result may look jerky when played on TV. (The effect isn't very noticeable if you've only moved the Slower slider only one notch in the Timeline Viewer; but at greater degrees of slowdown, the jerkiness becomes more pronounced.)

If you've come this far in pursuit of quality—buying a Mac and a DV camcorder—this is no time to chicken out. You may as well click Render, so that iMovie can go all the way to the finish line with its quality obsession. (If you click Export without first clicking Render, you get yet another dialog box that offers one more chance to click the Render button.)

5. **Click Export.**

After a moment, iMovie commands the camcorder to begin recording, and then begins pumping your finished video over the FireWire cable to the tape (see Figure 11-3). While this process is taking place, you might want to open the LCD panel on the camcorder so that you can watch the transfer and listen to the audio. (iMovie plays the movie simultaneously in its Monitor window, but the camcorder screen's quality is generally superior.)

When the transfer is complete, the camcorder automatically stops recording. Your finished production is now safely on DV tape.

If you're having no luck making your camcorder record the iMovie footage, see Appendix B for troubleshooting instructions.

Tip: After the transfer is complete, slide the Camera/Edit switch on your iMovie screen (at the left edge of the screen, just below the Monitor) to its Camera position. Doing so puts iMovie into "I'm-controlling-your-camcorder-now" mode. Click Rewind, then Play to watch your newly transferred production.

Figure 11-3:
While iMovie sends your finished production back to the camcorder from whence it came, a progress bar shows how much longer you have to wait. You can interrupt the transfer process at any time by clicking the Stop button. The camcorder stops automatically, having recorded your movie up to the part where you stopped.

At this point, you can connect your camcorder to a VCR for transfer to a standard VHS (or other non-DV) cassette. Connect the camcorder to the Audio and Video input jacks on the VCR. (These jacks were once found exclusively on the *backs* of VCRs, but appear on the front panels of many recent VCR models for convenience in just such times as this.)

Make sure that the VHS tape is blank and not protected by its erase tab. If you're smart, you'll label it, too—*now,* before you even record it, so that you won't forget. Put it into the VCR and cue it up to the right spot. Cue up the camcorder, too.

Finally, put your camcorder into VCR or VTR mode, start the VCR recording, and then press Play on the camcorder. If your TV is on, you can watch the footage as it plays into your VCR. Press Stop on both the camcorder and VCR when the transfer is complete.

From Mac Directly to VCR

If your aim is to get your movie onto VHS tape, you don't have to transfer it to your camcorder first. Hook the camcorder to the Mac via FireWire cable, if it isn't already, and then hook the VCR to the camcorder as described above. Take the DV cassette *out* of the camcorder.

Make sure the "Video Play Through to Camera" option is turned on in the Preferences dialog box, as described on page 103.

Now choose File→Export Movie. A dialog box appears, saying: "Your camera appears to have no tape inserted, or may be a converter box. Okay to continue with Export?"

Tip: If the message instead says that "It is not possible to export to your camera," switch the camcorder into Camera mode and then back into VCR/VTR mode.

At this moment, you should press Record on your VCR—and then click Export on the Mac screen. Now iMovie 2 plays your finished movie directly through the camcorder to the VCR. Press Stop on the VCR when the movie is over.

Tip: If you have an analog-to-DV converter box like those described on page 113, use precisely the same steps; the converter replaces the camcorder in the setup described here.

Notes on DV Tapes

As noted in Chapter 1, DV cassettes present the promise of immortality for your video. Because you can transfer the footage nearly endlessly from camcorder to computer (or to camcorder) without ever losing quality, there's no reason your footage can't stick around forever.

The tapes themselves are not immortal, however. Although you can record and re-record them dozens of times, you can't do so indefinitely, as most people assume. You'll know when a particular cassette is starting to go when you begin to notice *dropouts* in the video—pops in the picture, tiny rectangular pixels of the wrong color. (More on dropouts on page 367.) At that point, it's time to retire that cassette.

Tip: Following the advice on the little set of label stickers that comes in each tiny DV cassette box will delay this cassette death as long as possible. It recommends that you keep the tapes in their boxes, away from dust, heat, magnets, electricity, marauding children, and so on.

Here are a few other cassette pointers that may surprise you:

The Two-Cassette System

Consider conceiving of each iMovie project as a two-cassette affair. Designate one cassette (or set of cassettes) as your raw-footage tapes, and a second set as the finished-movie tapes. (Video editors call these the *original* and *master* tapes, respectively.)

Doing so, and labeling the tapes carefully, makes it less likely that you'll accidentally record over some important movie that you slaved over for days. It also makes life simpler when friends come over and suddenly say, "Hey, let's see what you did with your Mac!" If you keep all of your iMovie creations on a single special cassette, you won't have to hunt for a particular tape to show them your prize-winning creations.

Labeling and Logging

DV cassettes are so tiny that you'll find it almost impossible to write more than a few words onto their little white labels. If you want to write down the list of finished movies you've recorded on such a cassette, you'll have to use the fold-out cardboard index card that comes inside the cassette's little plastic box.

Tip: As noted earlier, it's a good idea to label your DV cassettes *before* you record them, especially if you'll be filming an event that will require multiple tapes (such as weddings or shows). Your annotation doesn't have to be elaborate (*1, 2, 3,* and so on is fine), just something to prevent you from shoving an already-recorded cassette into the camcorder, forgetting, in the heat of the moment, that it's not a blank.

Figure 11-4:
You need a sharp fingernail, pocket knife blade, or other implement to slide this very small shutter (top right)—but at least you'll never need tape to cover the hole.

That's a real problem if you intend to create moves that are any more elaborate than simple home movies. While shooting, professional film and video makers keep careful track of which cassette contains which shots, and which *takes* of those shots were useful. In fact, they write "G" *(good)* or "NG" *(no good)* on the log sheet as they complete each shot.

This kind of logging is enormously useful even for the amateur. It can save you lots of time when you sit down to transfer the footage from camcorder to Mac, because you don't have to sit there watching the entire hour of tape. You already know that the first fifteen minutes were great, followed by fifteen minutes of lousy stuff that you can fast-forward past, and so on.

Long Play Mode

Most DV camcorders let you squeeze 90 minutes of video onto each 60-minute cassette by using Long Play (LP) mode, in which the tape travels more slowly through the camcorder electronics. On a DV camcorder, LP mode doesn't bear the same stigma of lousy picture quality that it does on VHS equipment; in fact, there's absolutely *no difference* in quality between LP and standard mode on a DV camcorder. The data is stored as a stream of numbers; the computer doesn't care how fast they're slipping through the camcorder innards.

You should, however, be aware of several LP side effects:

- You lose the ability to dub in a second soundtrack after having recorded some video. That's not much of a sacrifice, however, since you can do the same thing and more in iMovie.

- In theory, LP mode also increases the *chance* of getting dropouts (see page 367). Most people report no such occurrence, but it's more likely to occur when recording at LP speed. Experiment with your camcorder before recording some once-in-a-lifetime event in LP mode.

- Avoid recording LP and standard-speed footage on the *same cassette*. Camcorder makers warn that doing so is a recipe for scrambled footage.

- Use LP-recorded tapes only in the camcorder that recorded them. Swapping LP tapes among different camcorder models—or even different units in the same camcorder line—invites dropouts and other video noise, because the playback

---

ON LOCATION

iMovie as a Tech Tool

Most people probably use iMovie to create home movies, make home slide shows, and that kind of thing, but I use it to create video clips that I then incorporate into Macromedia Director presentations. I also know Adobe Premiere, but I wind up using iMovie to prepare these clips, just because it's so simple and quick.

I've also found that it's the most efficient tool for importing stills from my DV camera (a Canon ZR). I can just plug it in, start the import, and walk away for a while; iMovie knows to start a new clip at each scene (or picture) break. This is a *huge* time saver!

I have my share of complaints about iMovie. But even though I have access to more sophisticated tools, I'm just too lazy to use them.

I predict that my iMovie/Director project will have a tremendous impact, or at least it will impress my peers. (That's the most important thing.) Right now I'm preparing a presentation that will complete the requirements for my Certificate in Assistive Technology in Education. In a matter of days, I'll be wowing my class (at the Center for Accessible Technology in Berkeley) with my presentation. They'll be amazed at all the cool video clips that illustrate my points, not to mention the interactive nature of the Director interface.

If iMovie hadn't been so easy to use, I wouldn't have bothered with it. I'd have to show up at my presentation with a loud voice and a big poster.

—Jenna Jones
Petaluma, CA

---

heads in each camcorder are aligned differently. LP recordings use a much narrower stripe of tape to record video information (6.7 microns wide, instead of 10 microns wide in Standard Play mode), so even minor differences in the position of the heads in different camcorders can result in LP playback problems.

Clearly, LP recording is something of a black art. For the smoothest sailing in your DV career, avoid it except when getting 90 minutes in a single pass is crucial to your project.

The Protect-Tape Tab

In the old days of audiocassettes and VHS tapes, you could prevent an important recording from being accidentally erased by a clueless family member. You simply had to pry out or break off a tiny, plastic, square "protect" tab on the top edge of the cassette. Doing so left a hole that prevented the recorder from recording.

The trouble with that system, of course, is if you change your mind, the only way you can "unlock" the tape to permit recording again is to cover the little hole with a piece of tape. This is scarcely an elegant solution, and often a risky one, because a tape that peels off inside a VCR is a one-way ticket to the repair shop.

DV and Hi-8 cassettes (for Digital8 fans) are far more sophisticated. They have a sliding shutter that covers the "can't record" hole (see Figure 11-4), making it much easier to prevent recording on a particular tape and then to change your mind.

From iMovie to QuickTime

F or the best and most cinematic viewing experience, play your finished iMovie productions on TV, as described in the previous chapter. That way, your public gets to see the full DV quality that your camcorder captured.

But when you want to distribute your movies electronically, convert them into Quick-Time files instead. Both Mac and Windows machines can play these files right on the screen with little more than a double-click.

Your distribution options for QuickTime files are far greater than for videocassette. You can email a QuickTime file to somebody, or post it on the Web for all the world to see (see Chapter 13). You can put a QuickTime file onto a disk, such as a Zip disk, to transport it. If you have a CD-ROM burner (about $300), you can save your QuickTime movies onto CD-ROMs for inexpensive distribution of movies that are too big to post on the Internet. And with the aid of Apple's SuperDrive and iDVD software (see page 299), you can even make your own DVDs; just polish up your movies, burn them onto DVDs, and then call up the national buyer for Blockbuster.

This chapter covers all of these techniques, step by step (except calling Blockbuster).

Saving a QuickTime Movie

After you've finished editing your iMovie production, save it onto a DV cassette (as described in Chapter 11) as a backup, even if your primary goal in creating the movie is to save it as a QuickTime file. Relative to the time you probably spent editing your movie, the cost for making this backup is trivial, and it gives you flexibility if someday, somehow, you want to show that same movie on a TV or re-edit it in iMovie.

Once that's done, you're ready to proceed with the QuickTime creation process:

1. **Choose File→Export Movie.**

   The Export Movie dialog box appears, as shown in Figure 12-1. Choose Quick-Time Movie from the pop-up menu at the top.

2. **Using the Formats pop-up menu, choose one of the preset export formats (such as "Email Movie, Small" or "CD-ROM Movie, Medium")—or Expert.**

   This decision dramatically affects the picture quality, motion smoothness, file size, and window size of the finished QuickTime movie.

   Making a smart choice in this step requires some comprehension of the QuickTime technology itself; although "Understanding QuickTime" in the next section is many pages long, it's well worth absorbing. It's critical to your grasp of QuickTime movies, what they are, and what they can do.

   That section also contains item-by-item descriptions of the choices in this pop-up menu.

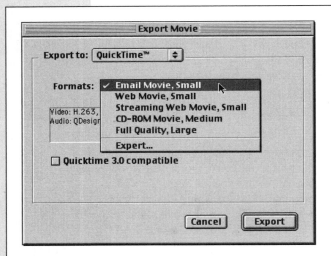

Figure 12-1:
Using the pop-up menu in this dialog box, you can indirectly specify how much compression you want applied to your movie, and what the dimensions of the finished movie frame will be. The small print below the pop-up menu gives the technical specifications for each option. They include which compression scheme it uses, how many frames per second you'll get, the dimensions of the movie, what kind of sound quality you can expect, and so on.

3. **Click Export.**

   Now the standard Save File dialog box appears.

4. **Type a name for your movie.**

   (Unless, of course, you really do want to call your movie "My Great Movie," as iMovie suggests.)

If your movie might be played on Windows computers, add the letters *.mov* to the end of its name—a requirement for machines who aren't savvy enough to know a movie file when they see one.

5. **Navigate to the folder where you'll want to store the resulting QuickTime file.**

You can just press ⌘-D if you want your QuickTime Movie saved onto the desktop, where it will be easy to find.

6. **Click Save.**

Now the time-consuming exporting and *compression* process begins. As you can read in the next section, compression can take a long time to complete; a 1-minute iMovie project can take 2 minutes, 20 minutes, or 2 hours to save and compress, depending on the settings you selected in Step 2.

A progress bar lets you know how much farther iMovie has to go. Meanwhile, the Monitor window and Scrubber bar show you which frame iMovie is currently crunching.

When the exporting is complete, the progress bar disappears. Switch to the Finder, where you'll find a new QuickTime movie icon (see Figure 12-2); double-click it to see the results.

Tip: You can click Stop at any time during the export process. Doing so doesn't undo the entire procedure; it simply stops the conversion. In other words, you still get a newly minted QuickTime file on your hard drive. It plays only as much of the movie as iMovie had been allowed to complete.

That's a terrific feature when you're trying to compare the effects of different codecs and export settings. You can export only a few seconds of your movie without having to sit through the entire conversion. Then you can check out the result, and make adjustments to your export settings, if necessary.

Figure 12-2:
When you double-click the resulting QuickTime movie on your hard drive (left), it opens into your copy of QuickTime Player, the movie-playing application described in Chapter 14. Press the Space bar to make the movie play back (right).

RediWhip.mov

Understanding QuickTime

A computer displays video by flashing many still images in rapid succession. But if you've ever worked with graphics, you know that color graphics files are data hogs. A full-screen photograph file might occupy 5 or 10 MB of space on your hard drive, and take several seconds to open up.

Unfortunately, most computers are far too slow to open up 30 full-screen, photographic-quality pictures per second. Even if they could, full-screen, full-quality QuickTime movies would still be mostly useless; each would consume hundreds of gigabytes of disk space, requiring days or weeks to download from the Web or by email—a guaranteed way to annoy citizens of the Internet and doom your moviemaking career to obscurity.

That's why most QuickTime movies *aren't* full-screen, photographic-quality films by any stretch of the imagination. In fact, most QuickTime movies are much "smaller"—in three different dimensions:

- **The window is much smaller.** It's rare to see a QuickTime movie that, when played back, fills the computer screen. Instead, most QuickTime movies today play in a much smaller window (see Figure 12-3), therefore requiring far less data, and resulting in far smaller files.

- **The frame rate is lower.** Instead of showing 30 frames per second, most QuickTime movies have far lower frame rates; even fifteen frames per second produces smooth motion. On the Web, especially during live QuickTime "broadcasts," still lower frame rates are common, such as two or five frames per second. This kind of movie is noticeably jerky, but sends so little data that people using regular telephone-line modems can watch live events in this format.

- **The video is *compressed*.** This is the big one—the technical aspect of QuickTime movies that gives you the most control over the resulting quality of your movie. In short, when iMovie uses QuickTime to compress your video, it discards color information that describes each frame. True, the picture deteriorates as a consequence, but the resulting QuickTime movie file is a tiny fraction of its original size. The following section describes this compression business in much greater detail.

The bottom line is that by combining these three techniques, iMovie can turn your ten-*gigabyte* DV movie into a three-*megabyte* file that's small enough to be emailed or posted on your Web page. The resulting movie won't play as smoothly, fill as much of the screen, or look as good as the original DV footage. But your viewers won't care. They'll be delighted to be able to watch your movies at all, and grateful that the files don't take hours to download. (And besides: Having already been exposed to QuickTime movies, most already know what to expect.)

Tip: The later the QuickTime version your System Folder contains, the better and faster the movie-exporting process becomes. If you don't have QuickTime 5, for example, download it from *apple.com* and install it as soon as possible.

A Crash Course in Video Compression

The following discussion explores some technical underpinnings of QuickTime technology. It may take you a few minutes to complete this behind-the-scenes tour of how a computer stores video. But without understanding the basics, iMovie's QuickTime-exporting options will seem utterly impenetrable.

Spatial compression

Suppose you overhear a woman telling her husband, "Would you mind running to the grocery? We need an eight-ounce box of Cajun Style Rice-A-Roni, and an eight-ounce box of Cajun Style Rice-A-Roni, and also an eight-ounce box of Cajun Style Rice-A-Roni." Why didn't she just tell him to pick up "three boxes" of it? You'd probably assume that she's a little loopy.

When it comes to storing video on a hard drive, your Macintosh faces the same issue. When storing a picture file, it must "write down" the precise color of *each pixel* of each frame. It could, of course, store this information like this:

- *Top row, pixel 1:* Beige

- *Top row, pixel 2:* Beige

- *Top row, pixel 3:* Beige

...and so on. Clearly, this much information would take a lot of space and a lot of time to reproduce.

Fortunately, when Apple engineers were designing QuickTime in the 1980s, it occurred to them that the individual dots in solid-colored areas of the picture don't need

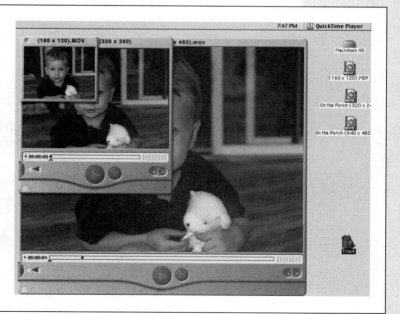

Figure 12-3:
This QuickTime movie is shown here in three standard playback sizes against the Macintosh desktop as a gauge of its size. The dimensions indicated in the title bars are in pixels. (A pixel is one tiny square dot.) Movies designed for playback from the hard drive are generally 320 pixels wide, 240 tall (320 x 240). Movies intended for the Web or sending by email are even smaller—sometimes only 160 x 120 pixels. The common denominator: Almost all QuickTime movies have the same relative dimensions—a 4:3 width-to-height ratio, which is exactly the same ratio as the picture produced by your TV and your camcorder.

to be described individually. That top row of pixels could be represented much more efficiently, and take up a lot less disk space, if the Mac were simply to write down:

- *Top row:* 60 consecutive pixels of beige

This simplified example illustrates the power of *compression software,* whose job it is to make graphics files smaller by recording their pixel colors more efficiently. This kind of compression explains why a JPEG file always takes up far less space on your hard drive (and less time to download by email) than, for example, the Photoshop or AppleWorks document that created it; the JPEG file has been compressed.

This form of file-size reduction is called *spatial* or *intraframe* compression. iMovie analyzes the picture on each individual frame and reduces the amount of information needed to describe it.

Temporal compression

But there's another way to reduce the size of a QuickTime file, too. Not only is there a lot of redundant color information from pixel to pixel on a single frame, but also from *frame to frame.*

Suppose, for example, that you've captured some footage of a man sitting behind a desk, talking about roofing materials. Picture the first pixel of the back wall in that piece of footage. Chances are good that this pixel's color remains absolutely consistent, frame after frame, for several seconds at least, especially if the footage was shot using a tripod. Same thing with the rug, the color of the desk, the fern in the pot beside it, and so on. These elements of the picture don't change at all from one frame to the next.

Here again, if it were your job to record what's on each frame, you could choose the slow and laborious method:

- *Frame 1:* The upper-left pixel is beige.

- *Frame 2:* The upper-left pixel is still beige.

- *Frame 3:* The upper-left pixel is *still* beige.

... and so on. This time, however, a clever QuickTime movie would record the details of only the *first frame.* "The upper-left pixel on the first frame is beige," it might begin. In filmmaker terminology, that first, completely memorized image is called the *key frame.*

Thereafter, rather than memorizing the status of every pixel on the second frame, the third frame, and so on, the Mac might just say, "On the next 60 frames, pixel #1 is exactly the same as on the first one." That more efficient description just made the resulting QuickTime file a *lot* smaller, as shown in Figure 12-4. (The subsequent, shorthand-recorded frames are often called *delta frames* by the geeks.)

This kind of shorthand is called *temporal* or *interframe* compression, because it refers to the way pixels change over time, from one frame to the next.

About Codecs

As shown in Figure 12-1, at the moment you save your QuickTime movie, iMovie asks you which of several schemes you want to use for compressing your footage. To use the technical terminology, it asks you to choose a *codec* from a long list. That term is short for compressor/decompressor, the software module that translates the pixel-by-pixel description of your DV footage into the more compact QuickTime format—and then *un*translates it during playback.

Each QuickTime codec works differently. Some provide spatial compression, some temporal, some both. Some are ideal for animations, and others for live action. Some work well on slower computers, others on faster ones. Some try to maintain excellent picture quality, but produce very large QuickTime files on the disk, and others make the opposite tradeoff. Later in this chapter, you can read about each of these codecs and when to use them.

Figure 12-4:
When iMovie saves a QuickTime movie, it doesn't bother writing down the description of every pixel on every frame. If there are a lot of areas that remain identical from frame to frame, the QuickTime movie doesn't remember anything more than, "Same as the previous frame."

In this example, the faded portions of the picture are the areas that the QuickTime movie data doesn't describe–because they're the same as on the first (key) frame. (At last you understand why, as you may have read in Chapter 2, using a tripod for your footage doesn't just give your movies a more professional look. By ensuring that most of the picture stays exactly the same from frame to frame, a tripod-shot video helps to produce smaller QuickTime files.)

In the meantime, all of this background information should help explain a few phenomena pertaining to converting DV movies into QuickTime files:

- **Saving a QuickTime movie takes a long time.** It's nothing like saving, say, a word-processing document. Comparing every pixel on every frame with every pixel on the next frame involves massive amounts of number crunching, which takes time. (Some codecs take longer than others, however.)

- **QuickTime movies don't look as good as the original DV.** Now you know why—in the act of shrinking your movie down to the file size that's reasonable for emailing, copying to a CD-ROM, and so on, a codec's job is to *throw away* some of the data that makes a movie look vivid and clear.

- **QuickTime is an exercise in compromise.** By choosing the appropriate codec and changing its settings appropriately, you can create a QuickTime movie with excellent picture and sound. Unfortunately, it will consume a lot of disk space. If you want a small file on the hard drive *and* excellent picture and sound, you can make the QuickTime movie play in a smaller window—160 x 120 pixels, for example, instead of 320 x 240 or something larger—or at a slower frame rate. The guide in this chapter, some experimentation, and the nature of the movie you're making all contribute to helping you make a codec decision.

The Canned Export Settings: What They Mean

iMovie offers several ready-to-use QuickTime compression settings that govern the quality, file size, and playback-window size of the movie you're exporting. Here's a guide to these presets to help you choose one that's appropriate for your movie-distribution plans.

Each of the descriptions below includes the following information:

- **Video codec.** As noted earlier, iMovie offers access to QuickTime's long list of codecs, each offering a different tradeoff in compression speed, file size, picture quality, and so on. These codecs are described in detail in the next section.

- **Size.** These dimensions, in pixels (of which there are 72 per inch on your computer screen), indicate how big the finished QuickTime movie "screen" window will be. Use Figure 12-3 to guide you.

- **Frame rate.** This number tells you how many frames (individual pictures) you'll see per second when the QuickTime Movie plays back. Thirty frames per second is standard NTSC television quality (in PAL countries, it's 25 per second); ten to fifteen frames per second begins to look less smooth; anything under ten yields a flickering, old-time movie effect.

Trivia: Old-time silent movies actually played at *18* frames per second.

- **Audio codec.** This statistic is the sonic equivalent of the frame rate, in that it tells you what kind of sound quality you'll get. At 44.1 kHz, the quality is exactly the same as that of a commercial music CD. At 22 kHz, it's half as good, but you won't hear any difference except when you listen through headphones or stereo speakers. When the sound plays through the *built-in* speaker on the standard Macintosh, most people can't tell the difference between 44.1 and 22 kHz.

Tip: All of the canned export presets preserve the stereo sound present in your original camcorder footage. Unfortunately, most computers don't *have* stereo speakers. (Among Mac models, the iMac and PowerBook are the only ones that do.) Meanwhile, saving two independent soundtracks makes your QuickTime file larger than it would be if it were saved in mono.

Therefore, if creating a compact QuickTime Movie file is important to you, consider using the Expert settings, described later in this chapter, to eliminate the duplicate soundtrack.

- **Time to compress one minute of video.** The "Time to Compress" statistic provided below indicates how long it took an iMac DV Special Edition to compress a standard sample movie that's exactly one minute long. (Compressing a ten-minute movie, of course, would take about ten times as long.) Of course, the time it will take your movie to get compressed and saved depends on the codec you've chosen, the length of the movie, and how much motion is visible on the screen, and your Mac's speed, but here's a rough guide.

- **File size.** The final statistic provided for each option shows you how big the resulting QuickTime file might be (in megabytes). These numbers, too, refer to the sample one-minute DV movie described in the previous paragraph.

Email Movie, Small
Video codec: *H.263*
Size: *160 x 120*
Frame rate: *10 per second*
Audio codec: *QDesign Music 2, mono, 22 kHz*
Time to compress one minute of video: *4 minutes, 20 seconds*
File size: *790 KB*

The movie you export with these settings is fairly blurry, and the size of the QuickTime "screen" is closer in size to a Wheat Thin than a Cineplex.

Still, the H.263 video codec has two important benefits. First, it makes the exporting much faster than if you used, say, the Sorenson codec (which takes nearly twice as long). Second, the resulting QuickTime file is relatively tiny; at under 800 K for a minute-long movie, it's actually within the realm of possibility that you could email this thing to somebody without incurring their wrath. (The Sorenson codec, the one iMovie 1 chose for "Email Movie, Small," produces a much better-looking movie. But its movies are 3.3 MB per minute—far too large for casual emailing.)

Web Movie, Small
Video codec: *H.263*
Size: *240 x 180*

Frame rate: *12 per second*
Audio codec: *QDesign Music 2, stereo, 22 kHz*
Time to compress one minute of video: *7 minutes, 18 seconds*
File size: *1.3 MB*

This kind of movie is much more satisfying to watch than the Email type. The image is over twice as big, and the higher frame rate gives much smoother motion.

Once again, the Sorenson video codec could provide far better image quality; but at 1.3 MB per minute, the product of the H.263 codec is small enough to download from a Web page without a high-speed Internet connection.

Streaming Web Movie, Small

In quality and size, this preset is identical to the "Web Movie, Small" preset described above. The only difference is that this kind of movie comes set up for *streaming* delivery from the Web: It's played on your audience's screens *as* it's being sent from the Web. In other words, your viewers don't have to download the entire movie before playing it.

Streaming means that your movies can be extremely long, even if they're therefore extremely large files. Only a tiny bit at a time is sent to your spectators' computers.

For details on putting your QuickTime movies on the Web, see Chapter 13.

CD-ROM Movie, Medium

Video codec: *H.263*
Size: *320 x 240*

FREQUENTLY ASKED QUESTION

"QuickTime 3.0 Compatible"

What does the "QuickTime 3.0 Compatible" checkbox mean, and why is it available for only some of the presets?

Most of iMovie's preset settings shrink your movie using compression schemes that were introduced in QuickTime 4. Anyone who wants to play your movies back, therefore, requires QuickTime 4 or later (a free download from *www.apple.com/QuickTime*). It's available for both Macintosh and Windows.

Turning on the QuickTime 3.0 Compatible checkbox changes only the codec iMovie uses to compress the *audio* track. If the checkbox is turned off, most iMovie presets use the QDesign Music 2 codec, an ultracompact compression scheme that requires QuickTime 4 or later. (If a

QuickTime 3 machine plays the movie, no sound comes out, although the video still plays.)

If you turn on the "QuickTime 3 Compatible" box, on the other hand, you get IMA compression instead, which makes the file bigger. (The larger iMovie 2 presets, such as the CD-ROM Movie presets, use IMA compression anyway [or no compression at all], which is why they don't offer the QuickTime 3.0 checkbox.)

Hundreds of thousands of computers are running the older version of QuickTime; movies created with this option can played back on *both* QuickTime 3 and 4 computers. Therefore, movies that are QuickTime 3 Compatible can be heard on far more computers.

Frame rate: *15 per second*
Audio codec: *IMA 4:1, Stereo, 44.1 kHz*
Time to compress one minute of video: *7 minutes, 20 seconds*
File size: *4.5 MB*

As you can see by the specs above, a "CD-ROM Movie" generally contains too much data to be suitable for live Web delivery. But saving your QuickTime productions into this kind of QuickTime file is ideal if you plan to play it from a hard drive or a CD-ROM that you record yourself, as described later this chapter. The high frame rate means that motion will seem smooth, and the 320 x 240 dimensions of the window mean that the movie will fill a decent fraction of the computer screen. That's big enough to see a good amount of detail.

Tip: If you're willing to endure more compressing time and a larger resulting file, you can give your CD-ROM movies a dramatic picture-quality upgrade by substituting the Sorenson Video codec for the H.263 codec. (Use the Expert settings described on the next page to do so; duplicate the settings described here, but choose the Sorenson Video codec instead of H.263.)

The only down side is that the resulting QuickTime movie contains too much data for older, slower CD-ROM drives, such as those rated below "12X," to deliver to the computer's brain. The movie will *play* on slower CD-ROM drives, but it will skip a lot.

Full Quality, Large
Video codec: *DV*
Size: *720 x 480*
Frame rate: *29.97 per second (for NTSC; 25 for PAL)*
Audio codec: *No compression; stereo, 48 kHz*
Time to compress one minute of video: *2 hours*
File size: *260 MB*

As the numbers (and the example in Figure 12-3) show you, this is the QuickTime format for people whose equipment doesn't mess around. The file size is massive—much too large for playback from a CD-ROM drive, or even from the average hard drive.

That's because this setting isn't intended for playback; it's intended to offer you a means of *storing* your iMovie production without sacrificing any video quality. The "Full Quality, Large" setting applies *no compression at all* to your audio or video.

Yet preserving your iMovie work as a giant, single DV clip on the hard drive is still a useful exercise. It can save hard drive space, for one thing; the resulting QuickTime file is still far smaller than the collection of DV clips in your project's Media folder from which it was made. After creating a "Full Quality, Large" movie, you could delete the project folder to free up some disk space, confident that you've got your entire movie safely preserved with 100 percent of its original DV quality intact.

The Expert Settings

As you can see by Figure 12-1, the canned presets aren't the only ways you can turn your iMovie project into a QuickTime movie. By choosing Expert from the pop-up menu shown here, you invoke the dialog box shown in Figure 12-5. Here you can control every aspect of the compression process, including which codec it uses, the degree of sound compression, how many frames per second you want, and so on.

For example:

Width and Height

These numbers let you specify the dimensions for the playback window of your Quick-Time movie. See Figure 12-3 for some examples of these different sizes. Of course, the larger the window you specify, the longer the movie will take to save, the slower it will be transmitted over the Internet, and the larger the resulting file will be.

Keeping the dimensions you specify here in a width-to-height ratio of 4:3 is extremely important. (In the business, they call the width-to-height ratio the *aspect ratio* of the picture.) The QuickTime software plays back most smoothly if your movie retains these relative proportions. Furthermore, if the width and height you specify *aren't* in a 4:3 ratio, iMovie will have to squish the picture accordingly, which may lend a funhouse-mirror distortion effect to your film.

The huge majority of QuickTime movies play in at one of several standard sizes, such as 160 x 120, 240 x 180, or 320 x 240. All of them maintain this 4:3 aspect ratio. Still, there are dozens of other possible sizes that maintain the correct proportions. iMovie makes it easy for you to find them; just turn on the "4:3" checkbox. Now, whenever you change the number in the Width or Height box, the other box changes automatically, so that the numbers in the boxes are always in the correct relationship.

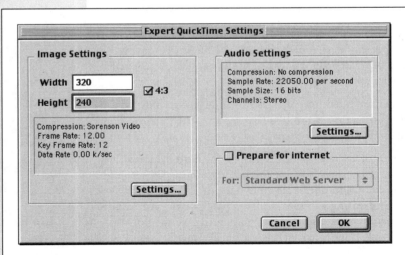

Figure 12-5:
The Expert QuickTime Settings dialog box appears when you choose the Expert setting from the dialog box shown in Figure 12-1. By clicking these two Settings buttons, you can adjust almost every aspect of the compression methods described in this chapter, manually making every tradeoff between file size, picture quality, playback window size, sound quality, and so on.

Image Settings

The Settings button in the lower half of the Expert QuickTime Settings dialog box takes you to the powerful Compression Settings dialog box (Figure 12-6), the heart of the entire Expert software suite. Here's what the controls do:

Compressor

This pop-up menu lets you choose one of the 18 codecs—or None, which means that iMovie won't compress your project at all. Each of these codecs is useful in a different situation; each compresses your footage using a different scheme that entails different compromises. You can read "iMovie Codecs: A Catalog" in the next section to read about the codecs listed in this pop-up menu; for now, it's enough to note that for live video that will be played on modern computers, the Sorenson Video codec almost always produces the highest quality at reasonably small file sizes.

"Colors" pop-up menu

The second pop-up menu in the Compression Settings dialog box lets you control the *color depth* of the movie you create—that is, the number of colors available for

---

FREQUENTLY ASKED QUESTION

Oddly Shaped Movies

I'm doing a project where I need my movie to be perfectly square, not in a 4:3 width-to-height ratio. But every time I try to specify these dimensions in the Expert QuickTime Settings dialog box, I get a distorted, squished iMovie movie. What can I do?

What you're really asking is how to *crop* your movie. Remember that iMovie creates DV movies, which have a 4:3 aspect ratio. If you want any other proportions without squishing the picture, you have no choice but to *trim off* some of the edges of the picture, thus cropping it.

Unfortunately, neither iMovie nor QuickTime Player Pro (Chapter 14) offers any simple method of cropping the pic-

ture. There are programs that can do so, however: Cleaner 5 (*www.terran.com*), the $500, professional Quick-Time-compression software, or MediaCleaner EZ, its $100, more streamlined sibling. As shown here, either one lets you draw a dotted-line rect-angle that indicates how you'd like the picture to be cropped.

If you're using iMovie for professional purposes, or if you make a lot of movies with it, a program like Media Cleaner is a worthwhile investment. Think of it as a much, much more powerful and flexible version of the Expert Quick–Time Settings dialog box shown in Figure 12-5. Its sole purpose in life is to compress movies, using much more efficient and intelligent software than that built into iMovie.

---

reproducing colors in your movies. Not every codec lets you control this aspect of your Movie. The Sorenson Video codec, for example, creates full-color movies, and that's that. Some of the other codecs, however, may let you choose from among some of these choices (see Figure 12-7):

- **Best Depth.** This setting means that, when played back, your movie will display the best possible color on the monitor it's on. The movie will automatically make a selection from the remaining choices described here.

- **Black and White.** This doesn't mean "black and white" like a black-and-white TV (which actually shows video in shades of gray, not just pure black and pure white). Instead, this option creates a movie like the one shown at lower-right in Figure 12-7—extremely stark and abstract. (As a bonus for your artistic daring, the resulting QuickTime file is extremely small, having discarded all of the color information.)

- **4 Grays, 4 Colors, 16 Grays, 16 Colors.** Don't use these options unless you're trying to create a special effect. The resulting QuickTime movie looks grainy and blocky, as though it's trying to paint a sunset with only four or sixteen shades (see Figure 12-7).

- **256 Grays, 256 Colors.** Movies that play in 256 shades of gray look pretty darned good for a movie in TV-style "black and white." It turns out that 256 shades of gray is just about as many gradations as the human eye can distinguish.

  256 *colors,* on the other hand, is a different story. The movie won't look good at all (better than 16 colors, for sure, but still very computerish looking).

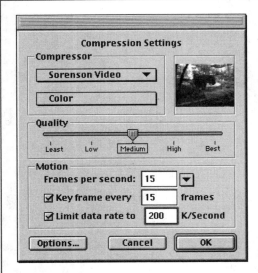

Figure 12-6:
This dialog box gives you point-by-point control over the look, size, and quality of the QuickTime movie you're exporting. Not all of these controls are available for all codecs—that is, depending on what you choose using the top pop-up menu, some of the controls here may be dimmed and unavailable. Furthermore, only some of the codecs offer an Options button at the lower-left corner of the dialog box.

- **Thousands of Colors.** Unless you're deliberately trying to simulate some bad-video special effect, this is almost always the option you want. It creates photographic-quality, full-color playback in a file that is nonetheless much smaller than one saved at the "Millions of Colors" setting. Moreover, the QuickTime software technology itself is fine-tuned to provide the smoothest playback at this setting.

Figure 12-7:
Top left: The original elephant movie, in "Thousands of Colors" mode. Because this book is printed in shades of gray, the remaining examples shown here are only simulations of the differences between the other choices in the Colors pop-up menu. At upper right: 256 colors.

Lower left: The "16 Colors" setting.

Lower right: Black-and-white. (Grayscale fans: Each corresponding gray level looks one step better than color—only in shades of gray, of course. For example, 256 grays has the same picture quality as the example at upper-left, 16 grays match the look at upper-right, and so on.)

- **Millions of Colors.** If you were comparing color photographs, it's conceivable that you could tell the difference between thousands and millions of colors. In a movie, however, there's little discernible difference—except in the file size, which is *much* larger at the Millions setting.

Quality slider

This slider offers yet another tradeoff between the size of the resulting QuickTime file and the quality of its picture. In general, the proposed value (usually Medium or High) offers the best balance between file size and picture quality. But on important projects, by all means experiment. Export the first few seconds of your movie several times, moving the slider each time, so that you can compare the results. (See the Tip on page 273 for instructions on exporting only the first few seconds.)

Frames per second

The number you specify here makes an enormous difference in the smoothness of the QuickTime movie's playback. As always, however, it's a tradeoff—the higher the number, the larger the QuickTime file, and the more difficult is to email, store, or transfer.

You can type any number between 1 and 29.97 in this box, or you can use the pop-up menu to the right of the "Frames per second" box. Here's what you can expect from these settings:

- **8, 10.** These movies are very compact, and make good candidates for transmitting over the Internet. They also look very jerky.

- **12,15.** These are by far the most common frame rates for today's QuickTime movies. By playing only half as many frames as you'd see on a TV show, the Quick-Time movie saves itself a lot of data, making it smaller on the disk and more likely to succeed when played on slower computers. And yet this many frames per second tricks the eye into perceiving satisfying, smooth motion; most people can sense that they aren't seeing quite the motion quality they'd see on TV, but don't miss the other fifteen frames each second.

- **24, 25.** An actual Hollywood movie plays 24 frames per second, and the European television signal (PAL) plays at 25. These settings, in other words, are provided for situations where you want excellent motion quality, without going all the way to the extreme of 29.97 frames per second of the American TV standard (NTSC). You save a little bit of disk space, while still showing as many frames as people are accustomed to seeing in motion pictures.

- **29.97.** If you're wondering how this oddball number got into the pop-up menu, you're not alone. As it turns out, every source that refers to television broadcasts as having 30 frames per second (including other chapters in this book) is rounding off the number for convenience. In fact, a true television broadcast plays at *29.97* frames per second. (iMovie can reproduce that rate for you, if it's important to do so. In fact, that's iMovie's top frame rate.)

RARELY ASKED QUESTION

30 fps Drop Frame

OK, I'll bite. Why on earth did the USA, which is supposed to be so technically advanced, settle on a TV standard that plays at such an oddball frame rate? Why is it 29.97— why couldn't it be rounded off to 30?

The 29.97 frame rate, known in the TV business as *30 fps drop-frame*, dates back to the dawn of color TV. As they prepared to launch color TV broadcasts in January 1954, network engineers wanted to make sure that the expensive black-and-white TV sets of the day could receive the color

shows, too. (Talk about backward-compatible software!)

Trouble was, when they tried to broadcast a color signal at the then-standard 30 frames per second, the extra color information wound up distorting the audio signal. Eventually, they hit upon a discovery: If they slowed down the frame rate just a hair, the distortion disappeared. The video, meanwhile, looked just as good at 29.97 frames per second as it did at 30.

A standard was born.

• **30.** Don't fall for it—this choice is for suckers. NTSC (North American) digital video itself is 29.97 frames per second, so asking it to save a QuickTime movie with an even *higher* rate is like thinking you'll be wealthier if you exchange your dollar bills for quarters.

If you *do* try choosing 30 from this pop-up menu, when you click OK, you'll be scolded, told you're out of line, and then returned to the dialog box to make another choice.

As described under "Quality slider" in the previous section, you don't have to sit there all day, exporting your movie in its entirety, just to see the effects of different frame-rate settings. Try exporting only a few seconds of the movie at each frame rate. Then play back the short QuickTime movies. You'll get a self-instruction course in the effects of different frames-per-second settings, as well as how many frames per second your particular Mac can keep up with.

Key frame every __ frames

You can read about *key frames* earlier this chapter—they're the full frames that get "memorized" in your QuickTime movie, so that the QuickTime file can store less data for subsequent frames (see Figure 12-4).

Key frames make your QuickTime file bigger, so you have an incentive to make them appear infrequently (that is, to type in a higher number in this box). But if the resulting QuickTime movie is something that your viewers might want to *skip around* in, key frames are very useful. Somebody might scroll back into the movie to a spot with no key frame. When playback begins at that point, the image might be scrambled for a fraction of a second, until the next key frame appears.

In most cases, one key frame per second is about right. In movies that will be played back only from beginning to end and never rewound or scrolled, it's safe to increase the number in this box.

Limit data rate

Each delivery mechanism—a CD-ROM, a cable modem, a 56K modem, and so on—delivers information at a different rate. If you want to ensure that no frame-skipping or jerkiness will occur when somebody plays your movie, turn this checkbox on and type a number into the box.

The precise number to type depends on your goals for the movie you're exporting—in other words, it depends on what kind of gadget will be playing the movie data. Here are some guidelines for the Sorenson codec:

If the movie will be played by:	Use this maximum data rate:
56K Modem	5 K/second
ISDN	12 K/second
T1 or cable modem	20 K/second
CD-ROM	100 K/second
Hard drive	250 K/second

iMovie automatically adjusts the picture quality as necessary, on a moment-by-moment basis, so that the QuickTime movie will never exceed this rate.

Options

When you choose the names of certain codecs from the Compressor pop-up menu—Motion JPEG, Photo-JPEG, PNG, Sorenson Video, or TIFF, to be precise—an Options button magically appears at the lower-left corner of the dialog box shown in Figure 12-6.

In general, you can ignore this button and the extremely technical dialog box that appears when you click it. The "options" for the Sorenson codec aren't options at all, as you can see in Figure 12-8.

The options that appear for the other codecs offer only one useful option—"Optimize for Streaming." You'd use this checkbox if you intended to prepare your movie for *streaming Internet video,* as described in the next chapter. Trouble is, you'd be foolish to use the JPEG, PNG, or TIFF codecs for this purpose to begin with. Codecs like Sorenson offer far better quality, smaller size, and better compatibility.

Audio Settings

On the lower-right corner of the dialog box shown in Figure 12-5 is a second button called Settings. This one lets you specify how—and how much—your soundtrack is compressed in the exported QuickTime movie (see Figure 12-9).

Figure 12-8:
When you click Options for the Sorenson option (the one most people use when exporting a QuickTime movie), the resulting dialog box does not, in fact, offer any options at all. Instead, it simply summarizes the settings that this codec is about to use. (As you can read later in this chapter, $500 buys you a more professional version of the Sorenson codec. If you had it, you'd be able to change these options.)

Compressor

Most people think of *video* compression when they think of codecs (those who've even *heard* of codecs, that is.) But iMovie offers a choice of audio codecs, too. This pop-up menu lets you specify which one you want to use.

Many of them aren't, in fact, appropriate for movie soundtracks. Remember that these codecs are provided by QuickTime, not by iMovie, and that QuickTime is designed to be an all-purpose multimedia format. It's supposed to be just as good at creating pictureless sound files as it is at creating movies. For best results in most movies, use the QDesign or IMA setting. For the benefit of trivia fans, here's the complete list:

- **24-bit Integer, 32-bit Floating Point, 32-bit Integer, 64-bit Floating Point.** If you don't already know what these are, then you're not a hardware or software engineer who traffics in this kind of audio file. These formats are high-quality, no-compression, sound-only file formats that aren't appropriate for movie soundtracks.

- **ALaw 2:1.** Use this low-quality, low-compression European standard only when requested, such as when you're exporting audio-only files with people who require ALaw as an exchange format.

- **IMA 4:1.** This codec was one of the first QuickTime movie audio compressors. It provides excellent audio quality—you *can't* change it to a sample size less than 16-bit—and plays back equally well on Windows and Macintosh.

  It's great for movies that will be played from a hard drive or CD-ROM. Be aware, however, that the resulting disk-space savings aren't very great. For example, the compression isn't good enough for QuickTime movies that will be played over the Internet.

- **MACE 3:1, MACE 6.1.** These options are included for people who want to swap sound files with very old Macs. They feature high compression, but very low quality. Playback works only on Macs.

Figure 12-9:
It probably goes without saying that the better the audio quality you specify, the larger your QuickTime movie will be. In any case, this is the dialog box where you make such decisions. Audio isn't nearly as data-greedy as video, so compressing it isn't nearly as urgent an issue (unless you intend for your movie to play over the Internet).

- **QDesign Music 2.** An engineering breakthrough, this is the sound codec to use. It maintains terrific audio quality, but compresses the sound a great deal, producing files small enough to deliver over the Internet. (Apple's favorite example: One minute of music from an audio CD requires 11 MB of disk space, but after compression by this codec, it consumes only 150 K and sounds almost as good.) The only disadvantage: Computers running versions of QuickTime before 4.0 can't play back the soundtrack.

- **Qualcomm PureVoice.** The good news is that this codec compresses the audio down to almost nothing, which makes it great for transmission over the Internet or including on a small disk, while still producing intelligible recordings of human speech. (The quality isn't quite as good as telephone quality). The very low data requirements make it great for Internet-bound movies, but the quality makes it lousy for music or anything else besides speech. (And no wonder—Qualcomm, who developed this codec, makes cell phones.)

- **ULaw 2:1.** Like ALaw, ULaw is a common format for exchanging sound files with Unix computers.

Rate, Size

A computer captures and plays back sound by capturing thousands of individual slices, or snapshots, of sound per second. Much as though they're describing somebody at a wine tasting, computer nerds call this process *sampling* the sound.

The two controls here let you specify how *many* samples you want the Mac to take per second (the sampling Rate) and how *much data* it's allowed to use to describe each sample (the sampling Size).

Even if that technical explanation means nothing to you, the principle is easy enough to absorb: The higher the Rate and Size settings (see Figure 12-9), the better the quality of the audio and the larger the size of the resulting QuickTime file. Here are a few examples of the kind of file-size increase you can expect for each of several popular rate and size settings. (Note that the information here is *per channel*. If you're going for stereo, double the KB ratings shown here.)

- **11 kHz, 8 bits.** Sounds like you're hearing the audio track over a bad telephone connection. Tinny. Use it only for speech. 662 K per minute.

- **11 kHz, 16 bits.** Sounds a lot better. Roughly the sound quality you get from the built-in Mac speaker. 1.3 MB per minute.

- **22 kHz, 16 bits.** Starting to sound very good, suitable for playing on a computer equipped with external speakers. 2.6 MB per minute.

- **44.1 kHz, 16 bits.** This is the real thing, the ultimate audio experience: CD-quality audio, suitable for listening to with headphones. The ultimate storage and transmission headache, too—this much data requires 5.3 MB per minute, mono. But of course, you'd never go this far without also including the stereo experience (make that 10.6 MB per minute in stereo).

Use: Mono/Stereo

These radio buttons let you specify whether or not your movie's soundtrack is in stereo.

As noted earlier in this chapter, exporting your QuickTime movie with a stereo format is often a waste of data. Most computers that might play back your movie, including tower Power Macs and iBooks, don't *have* stereo speakers.

Furthermore, even though most camcorders include a stereo microphone, there's virtually no separation between the right and left channels, thanks to the fact that the microphone is mounted directly on the tiny camcorder. Nor does iMovie let you edit the right and left audio channels independently. In other words, even if people are listening to your movie with stereo speakers, they'll hear essentially the same thing out of each.

Therefore, consider using the Mono setting when you're trying to minimize the amount of data required to play back the soundtrack.

The Video Codecs: A Catalog

When you decide to export your iMovie production as a QuickTime movie, you can get a great deal of control out of how the Mac produces the resulting movie file by choosing Expert from the dialog box shown in Figure 12-1. You get access, for example, to a long list of codecs.

As you can read in this listing, few of these codecs are very useful for everyday use. Many of them are designed for saving still frames (not movies), for storing your movies (not playing them), or for compatibility with very old versions of the QuickTime software. Most of the time, the Sorenson Video compressor (for CD or hard drive playback) or H.263 (for Internet playback) are the ones that will make you and your audience the happiest.

- **Animation.** This codec is significant because, at its Best quality setting, it maintains *all* of the original DV picture quality, while still managing to convert files so that they're smaller than files with no compression at all. The resulting file is therefore huge when compared with the other codecs described here, but not as huge as it would be if you used the None choice in this pop-up menu.

  As a result, the Animation codec is a popular format for storing or transferring QuickTime footage from one piece of video-editing software to another. Because the files are so huge, however, it's not so great as a finished movie-file format.

- **Cinepak.** This compressor does a sensational job of producing a very tiny QuickTime file; the sample movie described earlier becomes an impressively small 2 MB. Until the invention of the Sorenson codec described below, almost all CD-ROM-bound QuickTime movies were compressed using this codec. Unfortunately, the compromises are severe: The picture quality is often greatly degraded, and the compression and saving process takes a very long time.

- **BMP, PNG, Photo-JPEG, TIFF.** You may recognize these formats as popular *still image* graphics file formats. Remember that QuickTime is designed to be a Grand Central Station for multimedia files of all kinds—not just movies, but sound files and graphics files as well. These graphics-format options are largely irrelevant to movies. (They appear in your Compressor list because they're among QuickTime's master list of codecs, *all* of which are made available to QuickTime-savvy software programs like iMovie.)

- **Component Video.** In the era before digital video, you could convert footage from your camcorder into a digital file only if you had a *digitizing card,* an expensive circuit board for this purpose. Component Video is the format these digitizing cards used, because it could store video extremely quickly on your hard drive during the digitizing (capturing) process. It was designed for real-time recording speed, not for compression. The files it creates require huge tracts of disk space.

- **DV-NTSC, DV-PAL.** *DV,* of course, means digital video. (NTSC is the format used in the Western Hemisphere; PAL is used in Europe and Australia.) Suppose you've just completed a masterful DV movie, and the thought of compressing it to some much smaller, image-degraded QuickTime movie breaks your heart. You can use one of these two codecs to turn your finished, effect-enhanced, fully edited iMovie production into a new, raw DV clip, exactly like the DV clips in the Media folder in your project folder. You might do so if, for example, you wanted to import your entire movie into another DV editing program, such as Final Cut Pro (see Chapter 15), or if you wanted to turn it into a Video-CD or DVD, as described at the end of this chapter.

Tip: This option is the sneaky solution for anyone who wants to convert an iMovie project from NTSC *into* PAL format, or vice versa. For example, if you've shot your movie with a PAL camcorder, iMovie won't let you export the result to an NTSC camcorder. But if you export the PAL production as a DV stream using this codec, you can start a new iMovie project, import the converted (now NTSC-format) clip, and export the new project to an NTSC camcorder.

- **Graphics.** Uses a maximum of 256 colors to depict each frame. As you can tell by Figure 12-7, the result is grainy and blotchy. Use it only if your movie contains nothing but solid-colored images, such as cartoons, pie charts, or other computer-generated simple images. Even then, this aging codec doesn't compress the video very much.

- **H. 261, H. 263.** These codecs were designed for video teleconferencing, in which a tiny, jerky image of you is transmitted over a telephone line to somebody who's also equipped with a video telephone. The compression is extreme, so the picture suffers considerably—but the files are small enough to email or download from a Web page. These codecs work best in footage where very little is going on—like a person sitting in front of a video telephone.

- **Intel Indeo.** This compression format is very similar to Cinepak described earlier, in that it creates highly compressed movies that can play back from a CD-ROM. Indeo movies look slightly better than Cinepak ones, especially if not much is going on in the picture, and compress about 30 percent faster than Cinepak. Despite the word Intel in the name, this format doesn't play back on Windows computers, thanks to a format discrepancy between the Mac and Windows versions of Indeo.

- **Intel Raw.** This format is another older one that, in the pre-DV era, was used to exchange files between personal computers like Macs and professional editing machines like Avid.

- **Motion JPEG.** This code doesn't perform any temporal (frame-to-frame) compression. Each movie frame is saved as an individual, full-sized color picture. The disadvantage is, of course, that the resulting files are extremely large. In fact, you need to buy a special circuit board for your computer just to be able to play back this kind of movie. In other words, motion JPEG is occasionally useful when editing video, but never for distributing it.

So what good is it? Motion JPEG is the format used by many professional DV editing machines (such as those from Avid, Accom, and Discreet); because there's no key-frame business going on, editors can make cuts at any frame. (Doing so isn't always possible in a file created by a codec that stores only the *difference* between one frame and the next. A particular frame might contain data that describes only new information, as shown in Figure 12-4.)

Tip: Motion JPEG is *not* the same thing as MPEG, which is the format used to store movies on the DVD disks you can rent from Blockbuster. Despite the similarity of names, the differences are enormous. For example, MPEG uses temporal compression and requires special software to create, as described at the end of the chapter.

- **None.** If quality is everything to you, and disk space and Internet-ability is nothing, you can use this option, which (like the DV codecs) doesn't compress the video at all. The resulting QuickTime file may contain so much data that your computer can't even play it back smoothly. You can, however, put it in a cryogenic tank in anticipation of the day when superfast computers come your way.

Or, of course, you can simply use the Animation codec instead, which gives you some compression, while introducing little or no degradation of the picture quality.

- **Planar RGB.** This format is another one that's designed for use with still images, not with video. This one preserves the *alpha channel* of the graphic (a transparency feature), so that, if you owned a fancier editing program, you could superimpose a photo on top of video.

- **Sorenson Video.** Here it is—the codec that gives you very high quality with excellent compression, and files so small that you can play them from a CD-ROM or even over the Internet. Sorenson-compressed movies play back on either Macs or Windows computers, too.

- **Video.** You might think of this, one of the original QuickTime codecs, as the "fat Sorenson." The quality is very high, and it doesn't take very long to compress and save the movie in this format—but the compression is light. The resulting files aren't suitable, therefore, for transmitting on the Internet.

Tip: The Video compressor doesn't take very long to save a QuickTime file. For that reason, it's a great choice of format when you want to *test* your finished iMovie; to see how it will look as a QuickTime movie, to see how your transitions and titles will look, to experiment with different frame rates, and so on.

Burning QuickTime Movie CDs

As you may have read in the previous chapter, iMovie makes it easy to preserve your masterpiece on videotape, suitable for distribution to your admiring fans. You may

Secrets of the Sorenson Codec

Because the Sorenson Video codec offers such high quality at such small file sizes, getting the most out of it has become the subject of many a Web page and Internet discussion group. One of the best sources of information can be found at *www.terran-int.com,* the company that makes the Media Cleaner software described earlier in this chapter. The company's Web site offers a Sorenson Video tips page, which offers these pointers:

- The Sorenson codec requires fairly fast computers for playback, especially if the frame size is larger than 320 x 240.

- When you play back a Sorenson movie in QuickTime Player (see Chapter 14), you can use the Movie→Double Size command to enlarge the "movie screen" size. Technically speaking, all QuickTime Player does is to double the size of each pixel of each frame—but somehow, the result looks very good (at least, when compared with similarly enlarged movies prepared by other codecs).

- Don't create key frames any more often than one per second: They take up a lot of disk space and

degrade the movie quality. If your movie plays at 12 frames per second, therefore, use a number that's twelve or higher in the Key Frames box shown in Figure 12-6.

- If you're a professional, or soon to become one, $500 buys you something called the Sorenson Developer Edition codec. It offers a number of extremely technical added options that, in the right hands, lead to even better quality QuickTime movies. For example, the Developer Edition generates key frames automatically at the beginning of each new cut, and offers *variable bitrate encoding*—a compression scheme whereby frames filled with motion or transitions get the most "attention" by the data in the movie, and less active frames get correspondingly less. The result is more efficient use of the movie's data—and better visual quality.

If you've ever wondered why your iMovie films, when exported as QuickTime movies, don't look quite as good as the Hollywood movie ads on the Apple Web site, now you know part of the story.

sometimes find it useful, however, to preserve your QuickTime movie files (the ones you export from iMovie using the instructions in this chapter) on a CD.

Of course, in the world of video, what's meant by "CD" varies dramatically. There have been as many different incarnations of video disks as there have been of Madonna. These days, if you claim to have put video on a CD, you probably mean one of these three things:

- You took some ordinary QuickTime movies and burned them onto a CD-ROM, which you can play only on the computer. You insert the CD, see the icon for the QuickTime movie file, and double-click it; you then watch it in the QuickTime Player program (see Chapter 14).

- You created a *Video CD,* which isn't the same thing as a DVD. A Video CD is indeed a videodisk, and it can indeed be played by many DVD players. But the quality is no better than that of a VHS videocassette. Technically speaking, this disk contains an *MPEG-1* movie file.

- You created a *DVD videodisk,* exactly like the ones for rent or sale at the video store. The picture quality is gorgeous; the disk lets you navigate the movie using an on-screen menu system; and you may even have a choice of language soundtracks. (Technically, what you created is an *MPEG-2* file.) This is what Apple's iDVD is all about, as described on page 299.

The following discussion offers a road map for creating each of these three kinds of "videodisks." Be warned, however: All three require the purchase of additional equipment.

Burning a Recordable CD-ROM

Having exported a QuickTime movie as described in this chapter, it may be that you simply want to store it where it isn't eating up the space on your hard drive. Or maybe you want to distribute a few of these movies to friends—but because QuickTime movies are much too big to fit on floppies or Zip disks, a CD-ROM seems like a convenient and inexpensive way to go.

In these cases, you need to buy a *CD-R* or *CD-RW drive,* sometimes called a *CD burner*—a $300 gadget that plugs into one of your Mac's USB or FireWire ports. You can buy blank CDs, which you can fill with any files you like from your hard drive, whether they're QuickTime movies, spreadsheets, or computer games.

Tip: CD burners are available in two different types. The less expensive kind accepts *CD-R* (recordable) blank CD discs, which cost less than $1 apiece. You can record such CDs *once,* and that's that—you can't erase them or re-record them. This kind of CD burner is rapidly disappearing from the catalogs.

For almost the same $300 or so, you can buy a *rewritable* CD-ROM drive—a much more flexible gadget. It accepts both CD-R and CD-RW (rewritable) discs, which cost about $1 more apiece but can be erased and re-recorded over and over again.

Making a CD requires special CD-ROM-burning software, which is included with your burner; most CD-ROM burners come with a program called Toast, which is shown in Figure 12-10.

Burning a Video CD

It's important to understand that storing your QuickTime movies on a recordable CD-ROM (or even a DVD-*RAM*, an erasable disk that's an option on Power Mac G4 models) doesn't really create a videodisc. When you do this, you're simply copying a QuickTime *file* onto another disk, exactly as though it were a Zip disk or external hard drive. You can't play the resulting disk on a DVD player attached to your TV.

A Video CD, on the other hand, is the cheap, less talented sibling of DVD. A Video CD plays back your movies with roughly VHS-tape quality (352 x 240 pixels), which is not nearly as good as the original DV video.

Where you can play your Video CDs

Commercial Video CDs play back in any DVD player and laserdisc player. (As a bonus, they also play back on any modern computer, including the Mac.) Unfortunately, only certain DVD players—those with a *dual-wavelength laser*—can play back Video CDs that *you've* created. Most DVD players from Sony and Pioneer work well with homemade video CDs, but many models from Toshiba, Panasonic, Philips/Magnavox, and RCA don't recognize them.

Tip: DVD players are more likely to be able to play Video CDs you've created using a CD-*rewritable* (CD-RW) drive than a CD-*recordable* (CD-R) one.

Unfortunately, there's no sure way to know in advance whether a particular DVD player will play back your homemade Video CDs until you try it. That is, unless you

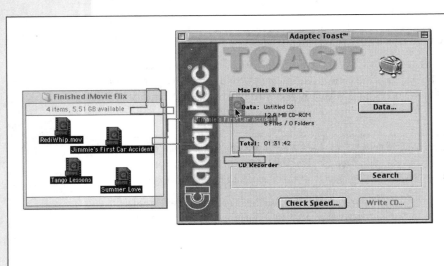

Figure 12-10:
Using Toast couldn't be easier. To create a Macintosh CD, choose Format→ "Mac Files & Folders." Then drag finished QuickTime movies from the Finder directly onto the Toast window, as shown here. Then, when you click Write CD, the program engraves your data onto a blank CD.

create a video CD as described here, and then take it to an electronics store to try it on the different DVD player models you're considering buying. (And if you already own a DVD player, insert your homemade CD and hope for the best.)

The basic steps involved in creating a Video CD go like this:

Phase 1: Export as a QuickTime movie

Use the steps described earlier in this chapter to save your finished iMovie project as a Full Quality QuickTime movie. At 29.97 frames per second and the full 720 x 480-pixel dimensions (on NTSC systems), the resulting QuickTime file isn't exactly gentle on your hard drive; a full-length, 74-minute Video CD requires 30 GB of hard drive space just for the movie itself.

Phase 2: Convert the QuickTime movie into an MPEG-1 file

At one time, the best-known MPEG-1 creation software was Astarte M.Pack. In early 2000, however, Apple bought Astarte and took M.Pack off the market, in order to use its technology for creating iDVD, described on page 299.

Fortunately, several other programs are already available for converting your Quick-Time movie to MPEG-1 format:

- **iDiscWriter.** The company's Web site *(www.netviewdisc.com)* lets you download the complete manual, which offers a fascinating course in Video CDs, and a fully operational five-day demo program, so that you can try the entire process for yourself. As a bonus, the Video CDs created by this $250 program begin movie playback automatically when inserted into a Mac or Windows PC; your audience doesn't have to launch or double-click anything.

- **VCDMaker Professional.** This $700 program, also from *www.netviewdisc.com,* is far more complex than iDiscWriter, but lets you create professional, "authored" Video CDs that let your viewers jump from one video segment to another, as on a DVD.

- **MPEG Power Professional.** This $500 program isn't the simplest Video CD-making program; as the stripped-down sibling of a much more expensive *DVD*-making program, its options go on for days. To get a feel for it, you can download a free, working demo from Heuris, *www.heuris.com.* (The demo version is fully functional, except that its MPEG files last only eight seconds.)

- **Cleaner 5.** At $600, this program from Terran *(www.terran.com)* isn't the least expensive MPEG-1 creator. It is, however, the easiest one to use. Just drag your exported QuickTime file's icon into Cleaner 5's Batch window, and then proceed as shown in Figure 12-11.

Tip: As this book went to press, Terran was contemplating the creation of a very inexpensive Lite version of Cleaner 5 that nonetheless includes Toast-compatible MPEG-1 conversion. Check at *www.terran.com* to see if this program is yet available.

The conversion (*encoding*) into MPEG-1 format can take quite a bit of time—several per *one* minute of your movie. When it's all over, you wind up with a Toast-compatible *Video CD image file* on your hard drive.

Phase 3: Burn the CD

The final step requires a CD burner and Toast Deluxe 4.0 or later. (The Video CDs made by CD-*RW* burners—rewritable ones—are more likely to play successfully in DVD players than discs made by CD-R burners.)

Launch Toast, and then drag the icon of your Video CD Image of your movie segments into the list window. (You can also click Data, click "Video CD image file," and then navigate to, and double-click, the image file.)

Finally, insert a blank CD into the CD burner. Click Write CD. In the following dialog box, click Write Disc.

Now Toast goes about the business of recording the video onto the CD. After about 20 or 45 minutes (depending on the speed of your burner and how it's connected to your Mac), the deed is done. Your disk pops out of the burner like toast from a toaster. (Get it?) Now the CD is ready to play, either on your Mac or in a DVD player attached to your TV.

Burning a DVD with iDVD

If your iMovie production is really good, you may have had visions of Tower Video dancing in your head. And, sure enough, it's perfectly possible to create professional-quality DVD disks just like the ones that come out of Hollywood.

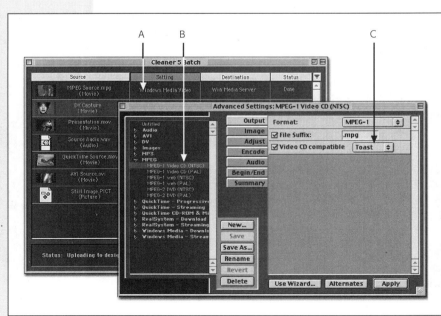

Figure 12-11:
To make a file ready for Toast using Cleaner 5.0.2 or later, double-click the Settings column next to your movie's name in the Batch window (A). When the Settings window appears, select "MPEG-1 Video CD" (B). Then turn on the "Video CD compatible" checkbox and, finally, choose Toast from the pop-up menu (C). Click Apply, then set Cleaner 5 to work.

A DVD is a complicated work of art, often featuring menus, alternate soundtracks, a choice of camera angles, and the other goodies that make rented or purchased DVDs so exciting. Until recently, it therefore required an equally complicated piece of software called a DVD authoring program, such as the $2,500 MPEG Power Professional DVD (*www.heuris.com*). Then, even after buying the software, you still needed a machine to burn the DVD discs: the Pioneer DVR-S201, which costs another $5,400. Blank DVDs used to cost about $40 each.

All of this changed explosively in January 2001, when Apple CEO Steve Jobs announced two new products: the SuperDrive and iDVD. The SuperDrive, available at first only in certain Power Macintosh G4 models, is a combination CD/DVD *player* and CD/DVD *recorder*. In other words, Apple has broken new ground; it's selling a $3,500 computer that includes an adaptation of the very same $5,400 Panasonic DVD burner described above.

iDVD, meanwhile, is the extremely easy to use, free software that comes with the SuperDrive. The steps for creating a DVD are simple: First, update your copy of iMovie to version 2.0.3 or later, using the free updater at *www.apple.com/imovie*. Then, when you're finished editing your project in iMovie, choose File→Export; in the Export dialog box, choose the "For iDVD" option. Save the file to your hard drive, keeping in mind that it will occupy a relatively enormous amount of space.

Next, drag your exported movies from your desktop into the iDVD window, as shown in Figure 12-12. Drag them around into a sequence you like; click their names to retitle them. Use the slider that appears when you click a thumbnail to choose the frame you'll want to represent that movie in this "table of contents" view. Use the Themes controls to specify a look for your main menu screen, or drag a graphics file from your desktop into the iDVD window to use it as the backdrop for you main menu.

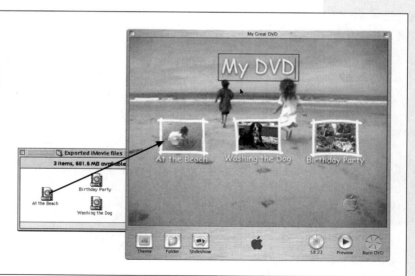

Figure 12-12:
In Apple's iDVD program, devising a menu system for a DVD you're about to burn is as simple as dragging the exported movie files from their Finder-folder window into the iDVD screen. Drag them into a pleasing sequence; click the disk's title, or one of the clip titles, to edit it, as shown here.

Click the Preview button in the lower-right corner to summon a virtual remote control, which you can use to hold a dress rehearsal for the finished DVD; for example, when you click one of the thumbnail images, the DVD player will play the corresponding movie.

Finally, click the Burn DVD button at the lower-right corner of the screen; insert a blank DVD (which Apple sells in five-packs for $50). Your SuperDrive does the rest. It takes about two hours to burn one hour of video (the maximum for iDVD), a far cry from the 12 or 24 hours required by previous DVD software. You can play the resulting disk in any standard DVD player; your audience will at last get to savor your digital video in its full glory.

Tip: If you can't justify buying a new Mac just to burn a couple of DVDs, you can hire a video service to do much of the work for you. For example, you can send the MPEG-2 files necessary for DVD mastering to a DVD mastering facility, who's already got the equipment. (Search the Web for *DVD mastering services;* you'll find plenty of them, including *www.digitalforce.com* and *www.flickfactory.com.)* The service costs about $300.

Putting Movies on the Web

A fter editing your iMovie to perfection, you'll want to show it to the world. Sure, you can preserve your work on videotape (Chapter 11) or CDs (Chapter 12); that's fine if you want to make a handful of copies for a few friends.

But the big time is the Internet. This 200-million-seat megaplex is where the action is, where unknown independent filmmakers get noticed, and where it doesn't cost you a penny to distribute your work to vast worldwide audiences.

Make the Big Screen Tiny

All of the techniques described in this chapter assume that you've exported your iMovie production as a QuickTime movie (see Chapter 12).

Now, you *could* post your 24-frames-per-second, 640 x 480, stereo-CD-quality sound motion picture on your Web page. But you'd have to include instructions that say, "Please download my movie! It's only 2 gigabytes—about five days of continuous downloading with a 56 K modem. But trust me, it's worth the wait!"

Most people on the Internet connect using an ordinary telephone-line modem, such as a 28.8 K or 56 K model. These modems receive data very slowly; they're not very well equipped for receiving video from the Internet.

If you expect anyone to actually watch your movies, therefore, you, like thousands of Internet moviemakers before you, will have to make your Web-based movies *tiny*. To make your movie watchable by people with regular telephone-line modems, use the Expert settings described on page 282 to specify:

- A frame size of 160 x 120

- The H.263 or Sorenson codec

- A frame rate of no more than 12 frames per second

- A monaural soundtrack, not stereo

If the need to downsize your movie like this doesn't crush your artistic pride, the worst is over. Here, then, is how you can make your videos available to the universe.

Free Movie-Posting Pages

By far the easiest way to post your movies on the Internet is to use a service specifically designed to showcase independent movies. It's easy to use these services; they make your movies available to anyone on the Internet; and they don't cost a penny. The combination of iMovie and the Internet makes the world of film *democratic* for the first time. Money doesn't matter anymore, only creativity. No wonder programs like iMovie make Hollywood movie studios excited…and a little nervous.

Once you've transferred your movie to these special Web sites, you'll be given a URL (Web address) that you can email to your friends. When they visit your page, they can watch your flick.

UP TO SPEED

Getting Ready for iTools

The most complicated part of using the Apple iTools services is setting them up. To do so, you need a Mac that already has an Internet account (America Online is OK). Some of the iTools features, including the HomePage feature described in this chapter, require Mac OS 9.

Go to *www.apple.com*. Click the iTools tab at the top of the window. Click the big Start button. You'll be guided through the process of downloading the iTools Installer. Eventually, you'll see its icon appear on your desktop. It looks like a red toolbox. If your Web browser window is covering up your desktop, choose Hide America Online, Hide Netscape Communicator, or Hide Internet Explorer from your Application menu.

Now double-click the iTools Installer and follow the instructions on screen. Switch back to your browser when the installation is over; you'll be asked to type in your name, address, phone number, and so on. Click Continue, and then Accept. Now you're supposed to make up a member

name (such as *alincoln* or *skibunny*) and password. You're also asked to make up a question and answer (such as, "First-grade teacher's name?" and "Smithers"). If you ever forget your password, the iTools software will help you, but only if it knows that you're you because you've answered this question correctly.

The next Web page asks if you want to configure your email program to get and send email for your new Mac.com email account. An account summary screen now appears (make sure to print it or save it), and then, finally, the system offers to send an email message to your friends letting them know about your new email address (which is *whatever-name-you-chose@mac.com*).

From now on, when you visit the Apple Web page and click the iTools tab, you'll see buttons for the four primary iTools services, including the two described in this section: iDisk and HomePage.

The Apple iTools Web Site

One of the most popular free movie-playing services is Apple's iTools Web site. (You can find it by going to *www.apple.com* and clicking the iTools tab.) As you'll read there, iTools is a collection of useful Internet features—ratings and reviews of Web pages, electronic greeting cards, a filtering program that prevents kids from seeing unauthorized Web sites, and so on. Among these free Web services is one called HomePage that lets you generate your own Web page and occupy it with an iMovie movie.

To take advantage of the HomePage feature, you must also become familiar with another a iTools feature: *iDisk,* an electronic, virtual "backup disk" on the Internet. The following tutorial walks you through placing your movie onto the iDisk disk and then creating a Web page that plays the movie. These instructions assume that, first of all, you've exported your iMovie masterpiece as a QuickTime movie (see Chapter 12), and that you've signed up for an iTools account.

Putting the movies on your iDisk

For many people, the crown jewel of the Apple iTools is iDisk. It creates a 20 MB phantom hard drive icon on your desktop. Anything you drag into the folders on this disk gets copied—apparently onto this miniature Zip disk on your desktop, but actually to Apple's secure servers on the Internet.

In other words, iDisk is a free backup disk. It's a clever solution for people whose Macs don't have floppy drives or Zip drives—and even a good idea for those who do, because this backup disk is off-site. If a fire or thief destroys your office *and* your backup disks, your iDisk is still safe.

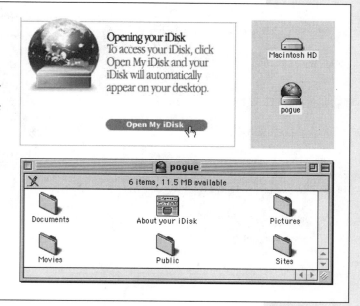

Figure 13-1:
On the Apple Web page, click Open My iDisk (top left). Now wait; even with a high-speed Internet connection, it takes about half a minute for your iDisk icon to appear on your desktop. At last, however, it does, bearing your member name (top right). Double-click it—and wait—to see its contents (bottom). Note that you can't create your own folders on this special disk, only within the folders provided here. (The Movies folder is the one you care about.)

Be warned—iDisk is very slow. Connecting to it, and transferring files, over a standard phone-line modem is a procedure measured in minutes, not seconds. Still, uploading your movies to *any* Internet site doesn't take place at what you'd call pulse-pounding speed.

To load your movies onto the iDisk—a prerequisite for posting them on the Apple Web site—pull the iDisk onto your screen, as shown in Figure 13-1. Now drag your QuickTime movies into the Movies folder. That's all there is to it—there's nothing left to do but wait for the long upload to complete.

Designing your Web page

The next step is to set up the Web page that will play your movie.

1. **In your Web browser, go to** *www.apple.com.* **Click the iTools tab. Type in your name and password; click Submit.**

   Capitalization counts in your name and password, by the way.

   Now you arrive at the main iTools screen.

2. **Click HomePage.**

   The HomePage screen appears.

3. **Click Add A Page.**

   Now you're offered several standard Web page templates, such as Photo Album, Baby Announcement, and so on (see Figure 13-2).

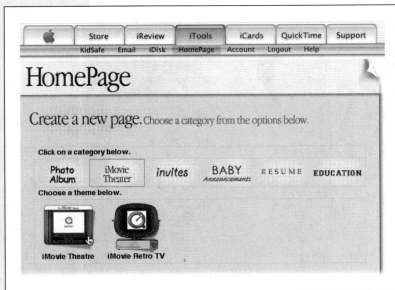

Figure 13-2:
The Apple HomePage system comes with prefab designs for several common personal Web-page purposes: party invitations, baby announcements, and so on. The one you want, of course, is iMovie Theater. Click it, then click one of the special playback "frames" below it.

4. **Click iMovie Theater, then click the "theater" style you prefer (Figure 13-2).**

   Next you arrive at the main iMovie Theater configuration page. Using the Edit buttons on this page, you'll specify the movie you want to play, the title you want to give it, and any notes or credits you want to appear underneath it.

5. **Click the Edit button just under the QuickTime logo; on the HomePage screen, click the movie you want.**

   If you know that you've added a movie to your iDisk, as described in the previous section, but the movie's name doesn't show up on the list here, click the Update iMovies button.

6. **Click Apply. Click the next two Edit buttons in turn; fill in the movie title and additional notes, and then click Apply each time.**

   If you'd like to omit one of the proposed pieces of information—if you don't have any particular directorial notes, for example—edit it anyway, if only to delete the dummy text that appears there (see Figure 13-3).

7. **Click Preview to see how the Web page will look.**

   Click the Play button, as shown in Figure 13-3, to try playing your movie over the Internet.

Figure 13-3:
The Preview function lets you see how your Web page is proceeding; the Play button is the triangle at the left end of the scroll bar. Don't forget to edit the text at the bottom of the window. Otherwise, your iMovie Web page will appear in final form with the words, "Write a sentence or two here about your movie. Who was the star? Who Directed? Where was the movie filmed?"

8. If everything looks good, click Publish.

When you click the Publish button at the top of the screen, three things happen. First, new Web-page (HTML) documents appear in the Sites folder of your iDisk. If you know how to use a Web-page creation program like PageMill, you can make changes to your Web page just by editing these documents. Second, the URL (Web address) for your Web page appears on your screen, which you can copy and then email to anyone who'd be interested. (Unfortunately, it's not particularly catchy; it's along the lines of *http://homepage.mac.com/YourMemberName /imovie.html).*

Finally, your Web page is now available for anyone on the Internet to see. Corporations and professional Web designers may sniff at the simplicity of the result, but it takes *them* a lot longer than ten minutes, and more than $0, to do the same thing.

You can create as many Web pages as you want (within the space constraints of your iDisk). When you return to the HomePage screen, a list of your existing Web pages appears (complete with Edit Page and Delete Page buttons). So does the Add A Page button, which you can click to start the process of building another Web page.

Other Internet "Film Festivals"

The iTools system is very simple, and it's the ideal place to post *home* movies—flicks for whom the target audience is friends and family.

It's not, however, the only place to post your movies on the Web. Fueled by the recent success of independent, low-budget movies, new Web sites are appearing whose sole purpose is to accept and show independent, student, and amateur movies. Most have rating systems that let visitors, as well as enterprising movie companies, see at a glance which movies are worth viewing.

Most of these sites don't accept porn or home movies. But if you've attempted anything more ambitious, you lose nothing by posting your work on the sites. There's no charge. You generally retain the rights to your movie. And if your work is great, it *will* be noticed.

You'll notice right away that all of these Web sites use *streaming* video. That means that you're saved the tiresome bother of having to download each enormous movie file before viewing it. Instead, you wait only for a few seconds, or at most a minute or two—long enough for only the beginning footage to arrive at your Mac. Then the movie starts to play automatically. QuickTime plays the part of the movie it's already received, even as later parts of the movie are still being downloaded.

Tip: Before posting your movies, watch a few of the featured movies already on these Web sites to get a feel for what people are doing and what kinds of movies each of these sites accepts. You may get more out of watching the movies that *other* people have posted than posting your own. The lessons you can learn from other amateurs and independents—both in the mistakes they make and in the clever techniques they adopt—make this book's teachings look like only Chapter 1.

Here are some of the most popular film festivals of this type, listed from most exclusive to least.

AtomFilms.com

Atom is the big time—the most commercial and professional Web site of its kind. The site specializes in short films and animations, from 30 seconds to 30 minutes long. Your stuff has to be good to make the cut, however, as Atom posts fewer than 10 percent of the movies it receives. Its explicit purpose is to get them sold to TV producers and Hollywood studios. (Unfortunately, very few of the movies here are available in QuickTime format; Atom isn't one of the most Mac-friendly movie sites.)

iFilm.com

iFilm is Atom's biggest rival. It's much less fussy about what gets posted; several hundred movies are available. The odds are pretty good, then, that some of its contributors will get picked up. As made famous by *Time* magazine, two guys who made the short black comedy *Sunday's Game,* for example, were offered a TV development deal from Fox.

iFilm provides a special Web page for each movie, complete with your synopsis, credits, and your feedback ratings. There's even a feature that automatically emails anyone you specify with a notice that you've posted a new movie. And the site is overflowing with special resources for filmmakers, such as news, reviews, lists of film festivals, and so on.

DigitalFridge

This Web site (*www.digitalfridge.com*) accepts both pictures and movies. In fact, at this writing, it's got far more pictures than movies. It also has a couple of handy features: For one thing, the editors post almost every movie, so you won't be filtered out by somebody who doesn't share your tastes. Second, you can designate your movie as either public (anyone can look at it) or private (a password is required to view it). It's also got a big limitation: Your movie can't be larger than 4 MB, which will certainly make it difficult for you to demonstrate your mastery of the medium.

Hoverground.com

This special site is just for iMovie productions, just for Mac people, and, when you get right down to it, just for readers of this book. It's designed to be a showcase of your iMovie work—that's all. There are no ads; nobody collects your email address; and nobody will get offered a Fox TV series (but you never know). On the other hand, it's a much more low-key, high-entertainment-value showcase.

Tip: Want to get your movie posted—and popularized—on some of these Internet film festivals? Then make a *spoof* of a popular commercial movie. No matter how poor the quality, nor how inexpensively done, clever satires rise to the top on these sites and get thousands of viewings. *Saving Ryan's Privates, Pies Wide Shut,* and *The Sick Scents,* for example, constantly top the iFilm.com "Most Viewed" list.

Posting a Movie on Your Own Web Site

Posting movies on other people's Web pages is one thing. In many cases, however, you might prefer the control and the freedom of putting movies onto your *own* Web page, designed the way you like it.

You'll quickly discover that this process is more technical than the ones described so far in this chapter. For example, the following discussion assumes that you do, in fact, already have a Web site.

UP TO SPEED

Getting a Web Site

If you want a Web site, you've got to get somebody to *host* it; somebody with a full-time, high-speed Internet connection who's willing to lend a few megs of hard drive space to hold your text, pictures, and movies. Fortunately, most Internet service providers—including America Online and EarthLink—offer such a service at no charge. Check your ISP's Web page (or, on America Online, keyword: *MyPlace*) for rudimentary instructions on creating a Web page and posting it online. (For more detailed instructions, consider reading a book on the topic.)

If the 5 MB or 10 MB of data space offered by your ISP isn't enough to hold the movies you'll be uploading, you may find it worthwhile to investigate one of the free Web-site posting services on the Internet. In exchange for a free Web site, technical help, and a generous chunk of hard-drive space for your movies, you agree to let the service slap an ad across the top of your Web page.

You might try, for example, FortuneCity (*http://fortunecity.co.uk*, 100 MB of free space), Dreamwater.com (50 MB of space), WebJump.com (25 MB of space), or NetFirms.com (25 MB). Several of these services, including Dreamwater and FreeServers.com, offer simple create-your-own-web-page "assistants," and get you a comparatively simple Web address for your page (it's along the lines of *http://YourName.freeservers.com*, where *YourName* is something that you specify).

Playing the Movie in a Pop-up Window

If you have a Web page, you're probably already familiar with the notion of *FTP* (file transfer protocol), the method you use to deposit new Web pages, graphics, and other elements onto your Web site. You do this using a program like Fetch (free), Anarchie (shareware), or even the Network Browser that's built into Mac OS 9 (see *Mac OS 9: The Missing Manual*). Figure 13-4 shows the idea.

Setting up streaming playback

QuickTime provides a feature called Fast Start, which means that when a Web page visitor clicks your movie, he can begin to watch it before it's downloaded in its entirety. His copy of QuickTime estimates when enough movie data has been downloaded so that the whole movie can play without having to pause for additional data. The effect is a lot like the *streaming video* feature described earlier, except that there's a considerable pause as the first portion of the movie is downloaded. (On the other hand, you save thousands of dollars on the cost of specialized hardware and software that's required for a true streaming-video system).

To take advantage of this feature, use the Expert Settings dialog box when you're creating your QuickTime movie from the iMovie project. As shown in Figure 12-5 (in the previous chapter), iMovie offers a checkbox called "Prepare for Internet." If you turn this checkbox on and choose Standard Web Server from the pop-up menu, iMovie automatically encodes some extra instructions into the resulting QuickTime file that permit your movie to do this "fast starting" when played back from your Web page.

Playing your movie

Once you've uploaded your iMovie, you—and everyone else on the Internet—can watch it just by typing in the correct address. If your Web site's usual address is *www.imovienut.com,* and the name of your movie file is *mymovie.mov,* then the URL (address) for your new movie is *www.imovienut.com/mymovie.mov.* (If you placed it into a folder within your Web site listing—called *flicks,* for example—then the address is *www.imovienut.com/flicks/mymovie.mov.)*

Tip: Mac and Windows computers consider capital and lowercase letters equivalent in Web addresses like these. The Unix machines that dish out Web pages by the millions, however, don't. Therefore, using only lowercase letters is a good precaution to avoid subjecting your visitors to "Web page not found" messages.

If one of your fans types this address into the Web browser or clicks a link that goes to this address, one of three things happens.

- If your visitor's computer has the *QuickTime plug-in* software installed (almost all modern Macs do), a new little movie window opens automatically. (See Figure 13-5.) As soon as a few seconds of the movie have downloaded, it begins to play automatically.

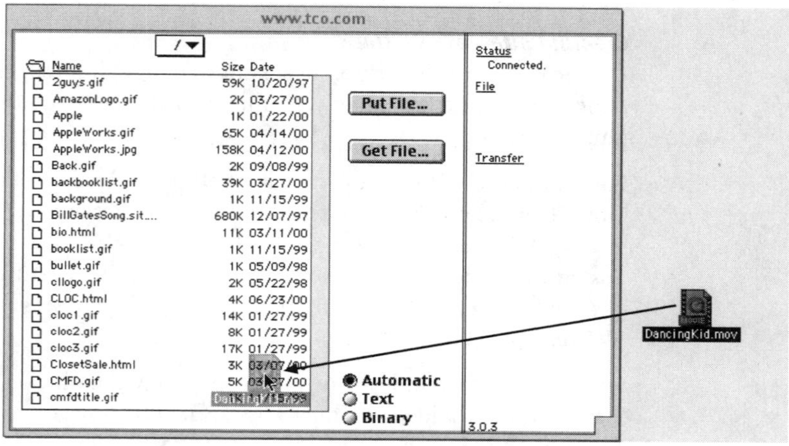

Figure 13-4:
You can use a program like Fetch (available from this book's page at www.missingmanual.com, among other places) to place your movies onto your Web site. You'll need a name, password, and FTP address, all of which are provided by your Web-hosting service or ISP. Then drag the icon of the movie from your desktop into the Fetch window.

• If your visitor doesn't have this QuickTime plug-in installed, which is likely if she's using a Windows computer, a message appears on the screen. It offers three choices: Track down the necessary plug-in, download the QuickTime movie to the hard drive, or choose another program to play the movie.

Tip: To make it easier for your Windows friends to download the plug-in necessary to watch QuickTime movies, create a link on your Web page that says something like: "To watch this movie, please download the free QuickTime plug-in at *http://www.apple.com/quicktime.*"

• Some browsers have been configured to hand off all downloadable files whose names end with *.mov* to a "helper application," such as QuickTime Player. In such cases, QuickTime Player now opens (independently from the browser), and the movie appears in its window.

Figure 13-5:
The easiest way to put a movie on your Web page is simply to upload it there. Then create a link to it. When clicked, the link makes the movie pop up in its own, separate window. Your viewers can use the Play, Stop, and scroll controls as they see fit.

Creating alternate versions

If your Web-hosting service makes enough hard drive space available, consider creating an alternate version of your movie for viewers who don't have the QuickTime plug-in.

For example, the Windows equivalent of QuickTime is called the *AVI* format. Using QuickTime Player Pro, described in the next chapter, you can convert your movie into an AVI file, which you can post on your Web page exactly the same way you posted the QuickTime movie. Then you can put two different links on your Web page: "Click here for the QuickTime version (Mac users)," and "Click here for the AVI version (Windows users)."

Of course, your Windows visitors won't enjoy the quicker gratification of the Fast Start feature provided by QuickTime. But you'll save them the trouble of having to download and install a special plug-in. (Creating a very tiny movie—no larger than 160 x 120 pixels, for example—is especially important when saving in AVI format.

Thanks to the lack of the Fast Start feature, Windows users who don't use the Quick-Time plug-in must wait for the entire movie to download before they can begin watching it.)

The HTML code

If you'd like to make the presentation of your movie a little bit more elegant, you can use the sample HTML code listed here as a template. Even if you've never programmed in the HTML language, you can simply type these codes anywhere fine Web pages are written—in Adobe PageMill, FileMaker Home Page, BBEdit, or whatever program you use to make your Web pages.

In a pinch, you can type the following directly into SimpleText and then drag the resulting document into your Web space exactly as shown in Figure 13-4. (Of course, you should change the italicized text to match the actual address and name of your movie.)

```
<HTML>
<HEAD>
<TITLE> Watch my iMovie here!</TITLE>
</HEAD>
<BODY>
<P> Click <A HREF="http://www.myserver.com/foldername/
mymovie.mov"
>here</A>
to watch my iMovie!</P>
<P>You'll need the free QuickTime plug-in to watch my movie in
your browser. You can also download it to your hard disk and
watch it with the free QuickTime Player.</P>
<P>You can get the QuickTime plug-in and QuickTime Player
for Mac and Windows at <A HREF="http://www.apple.com/
quicktime"> http://www.apple.com/quicktime</A>. </P>
<P>Thanks for watching!</P>
</BODY>
</HTML>
```

Embedding the Movie in Your Web Page

In the previous section, you read about how to create a link that makes your movie pop up in a separate window. But the really smooth operators on the Internet scoff at such an amateur hack. It's far more elegant to create a movie that plays in place, directly on your Web page—no pop-up window necessary.

Doing so requires yet further immersion in the HTML programming language—but only up to your ankles. If you're not afraid, proceed:

The <EMBED> command

Creating this effect requires a few more lines of HTML code. One of them is the <EMBED> tag, which instructs your visitor's Web browser on how to handle media types it doesn't ordinarily know how to display (in this case, a QuickTime file). It can learn to understand QuickTime movies, however, either by relying on a helper application or a plug-in. Following the <EMBED> tag, you'll want to type in a variety of *<EMBED> tag attributes*—additional HTML commands that give the browser further instructions on formatting and displaying the file.

You can string the <EMBED> tag and its attributes together on a single HTML line, like this:

```
<EMBED SRC="mymovie.mov" WIDTH=240 HEIGHT=196 AUTOPLAY=true
CONTROLLER=true LOOP=false PLUGINSPAGE="http://www.apple.com/
quicktime/">
```

Here's what each line means:

- **<EMBED SRC="mymovie.mov">.** This command instructs the browser to play the QuickTime file you've uploaded to your Web site, called, in this example, *mymovie.mov.* Upon reading this instruction, the visitor's browser will check its preferences file to see how she's configured it (using the Edit→Preferences command) to handle this particular media type. If the QuickTime plug-in is installed, the browser will use it to play your movie; if not, the browser will check to see which helper application (if any) she's specified to display .mov files, and then attempt to open the file with *it.*

  If no plug-in *or* designated helper program exists, the browser simply announces that it is unable to process the "mymovie.mov" file. The error message lets your visitor either manually choose a helper application on her hard drive, download the QuickTime plug-in, or download the QuickTime movie file to the hard disk.

- **<WIDTH=240 HEIGHT=196>.** These attributes tell the browser the dimensions of your movie—in this case, 240 pixels wide and 196 pixels high. (If you decide not to make the QuickTime scroll bar appear, as described below, make the height 180 [the actual movie height]. The additional sixteen pixels accommodate the scroll bar.)

- **<AUTOPLAY=true>.** You can set this action to either *true* or *false.* When you write *true,* the movie begins to play automatically once the browser has received enough data from the server. (As noted earlier, this feature works only when QuickTime 4 is installed on your visitor's computer, and when you've turned on the Fast Start option for the movie you saved.) If it's *false,* your visitor must click the Play button.

- **<CONTROLLER>=false.** This true/false command specifies whether or not the QuickTime scroll bar (controller bar) appears at the bottom of the movie picture.

Tip: If <AUTOPLAY> is set to *false,* you should have <CONTROLLER> set to *true;* otherwise, no one will be able to start your movie!

- **<LOOP=false>**. The <LOOP> attribute tells the plug-in to play the movie once ("false"), over and over continuously ("true"), or forwards to the end, then *backward* to the beginning, then forward to the end, and so on ("palindrome"). In most cases, you'll want to set this one to *false*. (Besides, if you've decided to make the QuickTime controller scroll bar appear as described in the previous paragraphs, your viewers can replay the movie themselves by clicking the Play button, if they really think they missed something the first time.)

- **<PLUGINSPAGE="http://www.apple.com/quicktime/">**. This handy attribute provides a hyperlink to the Web page where your visitors can download the necessary plug-in (in this case, QuickTime). It's by no means necessary to include this line of code, but it's a helpful thing to do, and can spare your viewers a lot of aggravation when they can't figure out why your movie doesn't show up on their screens.

More <embed> tag attributes

If you're kind of getting into this, here are a few more commands you can use to tweak the way your movie is presented:

- **<BGCOLOR>**. If you specified <WIDTH> and <HEIGHT> attributes that are larger than the dimensions of the movie itself, you can specify the color of this extra "background space" with this attribute. You can use either the *name* of the color (such as "silver" or "blue") or its *hexadecimal value* (such as "#C0C0C0" or "#0000FF"), if you know it.

- **<STARTTIME>** and **<ENDTIME>**. Using these commands, you can specify exactly which section of your movie should play, so that you don't have to subject your viewers to the entire thing. You can choose the exact start and end points for the movie, down to 1/30th of a second. Do so in the "minutes:seconds:frames" format that you know from using iMovie, like this:

```
<EMBED SRC="mymovie.mov" width="240" height="196"
STARTTIME=1:01:01 ENDTIME="2:15:07">
```

If you don't include these commands, the movie plays from beginning to end.

- **<HIDDEN>**. Use this attribute if you want the *video* part of the movie to be invisible, so that only the sound plays. You don't need to modify this command with any particular number or modifier. Just include the word in the HTML line, like this:

```
<EMBED SRC="mymovie.mov" WIDTH="240" HEIGHT="196" HIDDEN>
```

- **<HREF>**. This attribute creates a link to another Web page that opens when your Web page visitor clicks the movie itself. The link can open another Web page, a picture, or even another movie, which, in turn, opens the door for the creation of elaborate, interactive, you-control-the-action-on-my-movie projects. The HTML might look like this:

```
<EMBED SRC="mymovie.mov" WIDTH="240" HREF="http://
www.myserver.com/foldername/anotherpage.html HEIGHT="196"
HIDDEN>
```

- **<TARGET=QUICKTIMEPLAYER>.** This command makes the QuickTime plug-in launch the QuickTime Player program as a helper application, so that your movie will play within the QuickTime Player window instead of right there on your Web page. (If your movie opens in QuickTime Player, you give your viewers the option of enlarging the picture using the commands in the Movie menu, for example.)

This attribute works in conjunction with the <HREF> attribute, like this:

```
<HREF="mymovie.mov" TARGET=QUICKTIMEPLAYER>.
```

Making a "poster movie"

Using the <EMBED> tag in conjunction with the QuickTime plug-in is great, because it lets you embed a movie directly into your Web page. Trouble is, the data for your entire movie starts downloading to your visitors' Web browsers the instant they arrive at your page. (This downloading takes place even if you turned off the Autoplay option. It's true that the movie won't start *playing* instantly, but the data will nonetheless begin transferring, so that the movie will be ready to play when your visitor *does* click the Play button.)

This automatic downloading could annoy your visitors, both because it slows their Web browsers down substantially, and because some people have wireless connections where they're charged by the *amount of data* transferred. If your movie file is on the hefty side, or if you've got more than one movie on the Web page, this kind of unsolicited data-ramming could infuriate your visitors.

You can solve this problem easily enough by creating a *poster movie*, a separate movie file that contains only one single picture (see Figure 13-6). Rather than embedding the actual movie in your Web page, you can embed this poster movie, turning it into a button that downloads the real movie file—only when clicked.

This arrangement gives your viewers the ability to look over the Web page before deciding whether or not to download the movie in its entirety.

To make a poster movie, you can use a still image from the original iMovie file. (See Chapter 9 for instructions on exporting a single frame from your movie as a JPEG file.) Actually, any old graphic image will do, such as a JPEG or GIF file, as long as it's the right size (640 x 480 pixels, again as described in Chapter 9).

Note: In the following steps, you'll turn this still picture into a *one-frame movie*. The explanation is technical, but juicy: By turning a tiny QuickTime movie (instead of a plain JPEG or GIF file) into a poster frame, you'll force your visitors' QuickTime movie-playing plug-in to become activated as soon as they arrive at your Web page. When they then *click* your poster frame, the actual movie will begin playing promptly, having already loaded the QuickTime plug-in.

---

1. **Create a new iMovie document. Choose File→Import; navigate to the still image, and double-click it.**

   The image appears on your Shelf or Movie Track, depending on your iMovie Preferences setting.

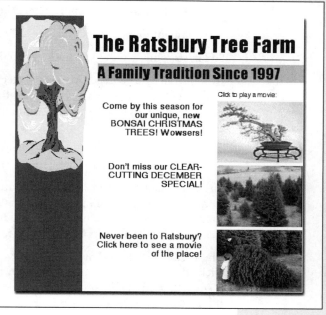

Figure 13-6:
Using poster movies is crucial if you are embedding more than one movie on a single Web page; otherwise, your audience has no way to choose which movie they want to see. As a bonus, the poster-movie scheme pre-loads the QuickTime plug-in software (if it's installed), which shortens the wait your visitors will experience when they finally decide to play the movie.

2. **Drag the graphic into your Movie Track, if it isn't already there; set its timing to play for only one frame.**

   Instructions for specifying how long a still image should play in your movie are on page 237.

3. **Choose File→Export Movie.**

   The Export Movie dialog box appears.

4. **Choose Export To→QuickTime; then choose Formats→Expert.**

   Now the Expert QuickTime Settings dialog box appears. (All of these dialog boxes and steps are described in greater depth in Chapter 12.)

5. **Specify a height and width to match that of the actual movie.**

   In other words, you want your poster frame to be exactly the same size as the movie itself.

6. **Click Settings.**

   Now the Compression Settings dialog box appears.

7. **From the top pop-up menu, choose Photo-JPEG. Specify one frame per second; click OK.**

In essence, you're creating a movie that's only one frame long. By specifying JPEG compression, you've ensured that this single frame will be as small, data-wise, as possible, for faster downloading.

8. **Click OK again, then Export; name the movie, and then click Save.**

You might name the picture "MoviePoster.mov," for example.

So far, so good—you've got a poster-movie frame on your hard drive.

Now you need to embed this new poster movie into your Web page. The process resembles the one where you embedded the movie into the Web page, but this time, you'll need a couple of additional commands:

```
<EMBED SRC="movieposter.mov" WIDTH=240 HEIGHT=180 AUTOPLAY=TRUE
CONTROLLER=FALSE LOOP=false HREF="mymovie.mov" TARGET="myself"
PLUGINSPAGE="http://www.apple.com/quicktime/">
```

First, note that the <CONTROLLER> attribute is set to "FALSE." Since the movie frame is just a single still picture, having a scroll bar underneath it would confuse the heck out of your visitors—and wouldn't even work. Without the controller bar, the poster movie appears as a still image, as it should be.

The attribute <HREF="mymovie.mov"> tells the browser that as soon as the visitor clicks the poster-movie image, the browser should load the "mymovie.mov" file. <TARGET="myself"> specifies that the new movie should load directly *in place of* the poster movie. Because the poster frame and the movie have the same <HEIGHT> and <WIDTH> attributes, the movie will seamlessly appear where the poster frame used to be.

POWER USERS' CLINIC

QuickTime Streaming Server

The Fast Start feature of QuickTime 4 is a great feature. Without it, your movie wouldn't begin to play until its entire multi-megabyte mass had been downloaded to your visitor's browser.

That's a good beginning. But in the professional world of Web video, the next step is *QuickTime streaming.* This relatively young technology lets many viewers simultaneously watch your movie in real time, live, as it's played from the host hard drive—without waiting for *anything* to download.

QuickTime streaming makes possible live "Webcasts," such as the occasional Steve Jobs keynote speeches and other historic events.

Serving up QuickTime streaming isn't something that the average Mac can do. It requires a Power Mac equipped with special streaming QuickTime software, a full-time, high-speed Internet connection, and a new operating system—Mac OS X Server. Apple's QuickTime Streaming Web site has the details at *www.apple.com/quicktime/servers.*

Tip: As with any graphic on any Web page, you or your Web-design software should remember to *upload* the newly created poster-frame graphic. You can use Fetch for this purpose, for example, as shown in Figure 13-4.

Optimizing Online Movies

This chapter covers the fundamentals of putting your iMovie on the Web, but there's a lot more to online video. The next step is tweaking the movie files *themselves* to optimize them for online viewing.

When you put your movie on the Web, millions of people can see it, which is wonderful. Unfortunately, some of those people connect to the Internet using dial-up modems, some use high-speed data lines like ISDN, while the luckiest connect through such ultrafast pipes as cable modems, DSL, or T3 circuits. If you had the time, hard drive space, and inclination, you could actually create *different versions* of your movie, one for each of these connection speeds. For instance, a cable-modem owner would see a high-resolution, 320 x 240 movie playing at fifteen frames per second; his neighbor, dialing in on a 56 K modem, would see a 240 x 180 version (an *alternate* version) playing ten frames per second. Each person would see an appropriately sized rendition that would be as large and beautiful as that kind of Internet connection would permit.

ON LOCATION

iMovie Goes to School

As the teacher of a class called "Writing & Media," I've been involved in basic video production for five years now. We produce a daily "B-TV" video news program and various special projects, including short documentaries and sports highlight videos. Having used analog equipment for five years, we were constantly frustrated by the time-consuming process of using VCRs to edit, and the low quality of the VHS tapes after two or three generations.

My class bought an iMac DV Special Edition with our fundraising revenue in February 2000 primarily for video editing. We already had a Sony Digital8 video camera with the FireWire connector, so we were very excited to enter the world of digital video. My students mastered the basic uses of the software in less than a week—three classes—and started making some amazing video projects.

The iMovie software saves us a lot of time and leads to a much better quality project! We dub in background music, add titles, and create credits for a professional look and feel. After editing, we put our final production back on tape via the camera, and then make a VHS copy to play over our school video system. The students are very excited about using iMovie; now we're swamped with requests from various student groups and classes to use it for various school projects.

—Michael Rio
Bellevue High School
Bellevue, MI

Tip: How does a Web page know which version of the movie to transmit? The answer lies in the ▸→Control Panels→QuickTime Settings control panel. If you choose Connection Speed from the pop-up menu at the top of this control panel, you'll see the list of different connection methods—modem, T1, and so on. You're supposed to click the one that connects you to the Internet.

When you click a movie on a Web page, the Web-page computer actually asks your Mac what kind of connection speed you've got. Your Mac responds with whatever setting you've made in the QuickTime Settings control panel.

Performing this kind of optimization is an elaborate field of study that, as you can imagine, gets massively complicated. It requires, among other things, a program like Cleaner 5 *(www.terran.com)*. The company's Web site is worth visiting if you're interested in pursuing this degree of customization. It's absolutely teeming with information about producing online video. Furthermore, Apple's own QuickTime Authoring Web site *(www.apple.com/quicktime/authoring)* has some excellent tutorials on these more advanced strategies. The Apple site also offers a downloadable free tool—MakeRefMovie—that can bundle the alternate-speed movies together with the master movie file, as well as some guidelines for creating the alternate movies themselves.

Part Four:
Beyond iMovie

4

QuickTime Player Pro

If iMovie is the program on your hard drive that's the master of *DV* files, its sibling software, the corresponding master of traditional *QuickTime* movies, is QuickTime Player, a small, free program that comes with every Macintosh. It usually comes filed in the Applications→QuickTime folder. And when you install a new operating system or buy a new Mac, there's an alias of it sitting on your desktop at the right side of the screen. It does three things very well: show pictures, play movies, and play sounds (Figure 14-1).

If you're willing to pay $30, you can upgrade your copy of QuickTime Player to the Pro version. Doing so grants you a long list of additional features, most notably the ability to *edit* your QuickTime movies (not just watch them).

There are two reasons QuickTime Player is worth knowing about. First, if you turn your iMovie projects into QuickTime movies (Chapter 12), QuickTime Player is the program you'll probably be using to play them on your screen. Second, the Pro version acts as an accessory toolkit for iMovie, offering you the chance to perform several tricky editing maneuvers you couldn't perform with iMovie alone.

This chapter covers both versions of the program; it uses QuickTime 5 for illustration purposes. (QuickTime 4 is very similar.)

QuickTime Player (Free Version)

The free version of QuickTime Player is designed exclusively to play movies. You can open a movie file either by dragging it onto the QuickTime Player icon, or by launching QuickTime Player and then choosing File→Open. As shown in Figure 14-1, a number of controls help you govern the movie's playback:

- **Close box.** Click to get rid of this movie window, exactly as you would any Mac window.

- **Audio level meters.** This little graph dances to indicate the relative strength of various frequencies in the soundtrack, like the VU meters on a stereo. If you don't see any animation here, then you've opened a movie that doesn't have a soundtrack.

- **Resize handle.** Drag diagonally to make the window bigger or smaller.

Tip: When you drag the resize handle, QuickTime Player strives to maintain the same *aspect ratio* (relative dimensions) of the original movie, so that you don't accidentally squish it while resizing the window. If you *want* to squish it, however, press the Shift key as you drag.

If you hold the Option key while dragging, meanwhile, you'll discover that the movie frame grows or shrinks in sudden jumping factors of two—twice as big, four times as big, and so on. On slower Macs, keeping a movie at an even multiple of its original size in this way ensures smoother playback.

- **QuickTime TV button.** Click here to open a window filled with icons of Quick-Time "TV stations," which you can watch if you have an Internet connection.

- **Scroll bar.** Drag the Playhead to jump to a different spot in the movie.

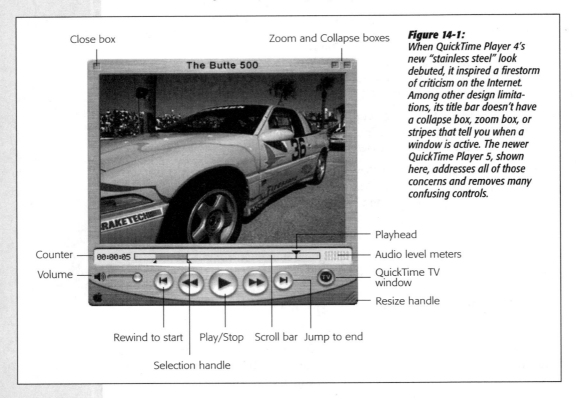

Close box

Zoom and Collapse boxes

The Butte 500

Figure 14-1:
When QuickTime Player 4's new "stainless steel" look debuted, it inspired a firestorm of criticism on the Internet. Among other design limitations, its title bar doesn't have a collapse box, zoom box, or stripes that tell you when a window is active. The newer QuickTime Player 5, shown here, addresses all of those concerns and removes many confusing controls.

Counter

Volume

Playhead

Audio level meters

QuickTime TV window

Resize handle

Rewind to start | Play/Stop | Scroll bar | Jump to end

Selection handle

Tip: You can also press the right and left arrow keys to step through the movie one frame at a time. If you press Option-right or -left arrow, you jump to the beginning or end of the movie. In the Pro version, Option-arrow also jumps to the beginning or end of the selected stretch of movie, if any.

- **Play/Stop button.** Click once to start, and again to stop. You can also press the Space bar, Return key, or ⌘-right arrow for this purpose. (Or avoid the buttons altogether and double-click the movie itself to start or stop playback.)

Tip: You can make any movie play automatically when opened, so that you don't have to click the Play button. To do so, choose Edit→Preferences→General, and turn on "Play movie from beginning when opened."

- **Selection handles.** These tiny black triangles appear only in the Pro version; you use them to select, or highlight, stretches of footage.

FREQUENTLY ASKED QUESTION

QuickTime Player vs. QuickTime Player Pro

Every time I launch QuickTime Player, I get this stupid ad about upgrading to QuickTime 4 Pro. How can I get rid of it?

Easy one. Quit Quick-Time Player. Choose ◆→Control Panels → Date & Time. Reset your Mac to a date far beyond its obsolescence point—the

year 2020, for example. Close the control panel.

Now open QuickTime Player. Click the Later button for the very last time. Quit the program, reset your clock to the correct date, and enjoy the fact that you've played a little trick on the program's calendar-watching feature. You'll never see the ad again (at least, not until 2020).

All of these shenanigans are only necessary, of course, if you've decided not to upgrade to QuickTime Player Pro, whose additional editing playback and exporting features are documented in this chapter.

To turn your copy of QuickTime Player into QuickTime Player Pro, call (888) 295-0648, or visit *www.apple.com/quicktime*. After providing your credit-card number, you'll be given a serial number that unlocks the Pro features lurking inside QuickTime Player.

After receiving the serial number, choose ◆→Control Panels →QuickTime Settings; choose Registration from the pop-up menu, and click Enter Registration. Your serial number gets stored in the System Folder→Preferences folder, in a file called QuickTime Settings; remember that fact when you upgrade your System Folder or your Mac. (The same password works for QuickTime 3, 4, and 5; you don't need a new serial number if you've ever paid for one.)

Once you've done so, you gain several immediate benefits, not the least of which is the permanent disappearance of the "upgrade now" advertisement. Still, you should remain vigilant, because new versions of QuickTime Player are always on the way. QuickTime Player's Help→Check for QuickTime Updates command will keep you up to date.

• **Volume.** In QuickTime Player 4, this sound-volume control is a knob. You can make the soundtrack louder or softer by dragging this thumbwheel up or down, by dragging *horizontally* across the small speaker design to its right, or by pressing the up or down arrow keys.

In QuickTime Player 5, it's been replaced—to the joy of interface design purists—by a slider. You can adjust the volume by dragging the handle, clicking in its "track," or pressing the up or down arrow keys; click the little speaker icon to mute the sound entirely.

• **Counter.** In "hours:minutes:seconds" format, this display shows how far your Playhead has moved into the movie.

If you have QuickTime Player Pro 4, and you've highlighted a stretch of movie by dragging the tiny triangles underneath the scroll bar, you can make this counter show the start and end times of the selection. To do so, click the tiny gray triangle above and to the left, or below and to the left, of the number display.

In QuickTime Player Pro 5, the counter shows the position of whichever selection handle you've most recently clicked (if any).

Hidden Controls

Don't miss the Movie→Show Sound Controls and Movie→Show Video Controls commands in QuickTime Player 5. As shown in Figure 14-2, they let you fine-tune the audio and video you're experiencing.

Fancy Playback Tricks

Nobody knows for sure what Apple was thinking when it created some of these additional features, but here they are. Really, exactly how often do you want your movie to play backward? Some of these features are available only in the unlocked Pro version of the QuickTime Player, as indicated below.

• **Change the screen size.** Using the Movie menu commands, such as Double Size and Fill Screen, you can enlarge or reduce the actual "movie screen" window. Making the window larger also makes the movie coarser, because QuickTime Player simply doubles the size of every dot that was present in the original. Still,

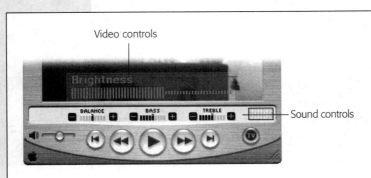

Video controls

Sound controls

Figure 14-2:
Click the word Brightness to summon the Contrast or Tint sliders; drag your mouse across the vertical bars to adjust the picture accordingly. The Sound controls replace the scroll bar; when you're finished adjusting the balance, bass, or treble, choose Movie→Hide Sound Controls to make the scroll bar return.

when you want to show a movie to a group of people more than a few feet back from the screen, these larger sizes are perfectly effective.

- **Play more than one movie.** You can open several movies at once and then run them simultaneously. (Of course, the more movies you try to play at once, the jerkier the playback gets.)

  As a sanity preserver, QuickTime Player plays only one soundtrack—that of the movie you most recently clicked. If you really want to hear the cacophony of all of the sound tracks being played simultaneously, choose Edit→Preferences→ General, and turn off "Only front movie plays sound." (The related checkbox here, "Play sound in background," controls what happens when you switch out of QuickTime Player and into another program.)

Tip: If you have Player Pro, you can use the Movie→Play All Movies command to begin playback of all open movies at the same instant.

- **Play the movie backward.** You can play the movie *backward,* but not always smoothly, by pressing ⌘-left arrow, or by Shift-double-clicking the movie itself. (You must keep the Shift button pressed to make the backward playback continue.) There's no better way to listen for secret subliminal messages.

- **Loop the movie (Pro only).** When you choose Movie→Loop and then click Play, the movie plays endlessly from beginning to end, repeating until you make it stop.

- **Play a selection (Pro only).** When you choose Movie→Loop Back and Forth and then click Play, the movie plays to the end, and then plays *backward,* from end to beginning. It repeats this cycle until you make it stop.

- **Play every frame (Pro only).** If you try to play a very large movie that incorporates a high frame rate (many frames per second) on a slow Mac, QuickTime Player skips individual frames of the movie. In other words, it sacrifices smooth motion in order to maintain synchronization with the soundtrack.

  But if you choose Movie→Play All Frames and then play the movie, QuickTime Player says, "OK, forget the soundtrack. I'll show you every single frame of the movie, even if it isn't at full speed." You get no sound at all, but you do get to see each frame of the movie.

QuickTime Player Pro

If you've spent the $30 to upgrade to the Pro version of QuickTime Player, you've unlocked a number of additional features. Some of these are playback tricks described in the previous section; others are especially useful for iMovie work. The remaining pages in this chapter document a few of the uses you'll find for QuickTime Player Pro.

Presenting Your Movies

After going to the trouble of editing down your footage (as described in Part 2) and exporting it as a QuickTime movie (as described in Chapter 12), what you may want to do most of all is to *show* the movie to other people. Even the non-Pro version of QuickTime Player can play movies, of course, but the Pro version offers a much better showcase for your work: the Movie→Present Movie command.

"Presenting" your movie is the best possible way to view a QuickTime movie on your screen. When you use this command (Figure 14-3), QuickTime Player blacks out the screen, automatically magnifies your monitor image (by choosing a lower resolution) so that the movie fills more of the screen, and devotes all the Mac's power to playing the movie smoothly. (To interrupt the movie, press ⌘-period.)

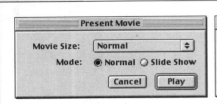 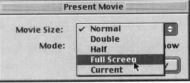

Figure 14-3:
The Present Movie command makes the movie fill your screen (although enlargement makes the movie grainier and coarser).

Manipulating Tracks

Using the commands in the Edit menu, you can view, turn on and off, add, or delete the individual *tracks* in a particular movie. (Most movies have nothing but a video track and a soundtrack. But a few specialized movies may also contain a text track, an animation track, alternate sound tracks, and so on.)

For example, it's useful to be able to delete the audio track from a movie you've exported from iMovie. (Old-timers may remember that this was the central move in overlaying new video over an existing audio track in iMovie 1.)

The key to understanding the multiple simultaneous tracks in a QuickTime movie is the set of three commands in the Edit menu:

• **Extract Tracks.** This command brings up the dialog box like the one shown at top in Figure 14-4, which shows you a list of all the tracks in your movie. "Extract" actually means *copy;* double-click the name of the track you want to copy into a new Player window. (If you double-click a soundtrack, it appears as nothing but a scroll bar with no picture.) At this point, you can copy some or all of the extracted track, in readiness to paste it into another movie.

• **Delete Tracks.** As the name implies, this command brings up a dialog box (Figure 14-4) in which you can double-click the name of a track that you want to remove from the movie. After experimenting to see which of several soundtracks you prefer, for example (as described next), you'll want to delete the rejected versions before you save the final movie.

- **Enable Tracks.** This fascinating command highlights an intriguing feature of QuickTime Player Pro—its ability to embed more than one audio or video track into a single movie. If you really wanted to, you could create a movie with six different soundtracks, all playing simultaneously—a useful tip to remember if the iMovie limit of three visible audio tracks is fencing you in.

As described on pages 331–332, the trick to inserting a new audio track is to press Option as you open the Edit menu. When you do so, the Paste command turns into the Add command. Choosing it inserts the new audio track into the selected portion of the movie. When you choose Edit→Enable Tracks, you'll see a list of all of the movie's tracks.

One useful application of this feature is to perform "A/B" tests of your audio tracks. Suppose you've created two different versions—one with background music, and one without. By choosing Edit→Enable Tracks and then clicking the On/Off buttons beside the track names (Figure 14-4), you can quickly and easily try watching your movie first with one soundtrack, then with the other.

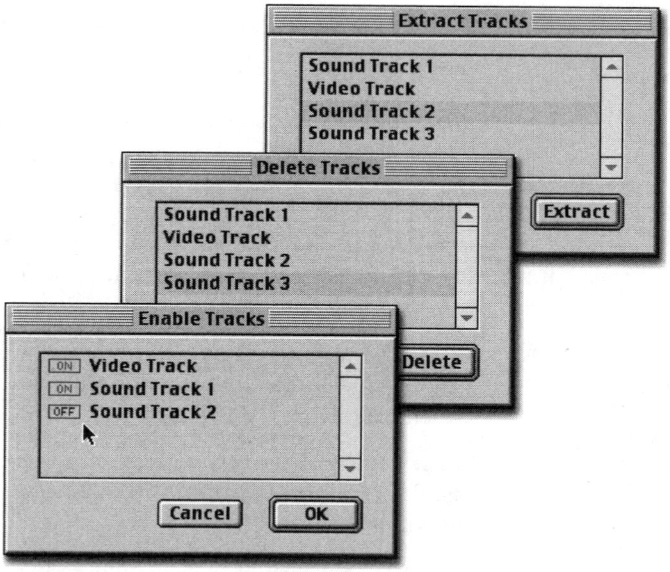

Figure 14-4:
From top: The Extract Tracks, Delete Tracks, and Enable Tracks dialog boxes. If you'd pasted some text into one of your QuickTime movies, you'd also see a Text Track listed in these dialog boxes, although iMovie is much better at handling text. As an iMovie fan, you'll probably find these boxes most useful when it comes to manipulating your audio tracks.

Turning QuickTime Files into iMovie Clips

Another indispensable tool in the QuickTime Player Pro toolbox is its ability to turn ordinary QuickTime movies into DV clips like the kind that iMovie uses. The process is described in detail on page 243. There you'll find out that the resulting file is enormous—3.6 MB per second, exactly like any other DV clip. But this feature can be a godsend if you want to incorporate footage from an existing QuickTime movie into your iMovie project.

Adding Special Effects

Thanks to the special effects described in Chapter 6, the special-effects tools in Quick-Time Player Pro aren't nearly as important to iMovie 2 work as they were to the original version of iMovie. QuickTime Player Pro lets you adjust the color, brightness, and sharpness of your clips—but so does iMovie 2.

Still, QuickTime Player offers a handful that aren't available within iMovie, including Lens Flare, Film Noise, and other very specialized effects. Here's how you can make them work for you:

1. **In QuickTime Player, choose File→Open. Navigate to the Media folder of your project, and open the captured iMovie clip you want to edit.**

   It opens on the screen in a very large window.

2. **Choose File→Export.**

   QuickTime Player's Save dialog box appears.

3. **From the Export pop-up menu, choose "Movie to QuickTime Movie." Click the Options button.**

   Now the Movie Settings dialog box appears.

4. **Click Filter.**

   The Choose Video Filter dialog box now appears (see Figure 14-5).

5. **After choosing the effect you want, click OK.**

   You return to the Movie Settings dialog box. Unfortunately, as noted earlier, QuickTime Player can't apply the special effects to DV clips (the kind that iMovie imports)—only to QuickTime movies.

   In the next steps, you'll convert this DV clip to a QuickTime movie. Unlike the usual DV-to-QuickTime conversions, however, this time you'll make all the settings in such a way that you minimize any loss of quality you might encounter when converting DV to pure QuickTime.

6. **Click Settings. Specify compression of None at 29.97 frames per second, in Thousands of Colors. Click OK. Click OK again. Save the resulting movie onto your desktop.**

   QuickTime Player takes a few minutes to convert the DV clip into a large-format QuickTime movie, applying the special effects in the process. (Note: *Large format* is putting it mildly. The resulting file requires a lot of disk space, so don't undertake this process if your hard drive is full.)

   As the final step, you must now convert the QuickTime movie *back* into a DV clip so that you can use it in iMovie.

7. **Choose File→Open. Navigate to your Desktop and open the movie you just exported. Then choose File→Export.**

Once again, the QuickTime Player-Save dialog box appears.

8. **From the Export pop-up menu, choose "Movie to DV Stream." Save the DV file to your hard drive.**

If you want to play it safe, save your exported clip under a *different* name (that is, leave the suffix on it).

9. **Import the DV clip into your iMovie project as described on page 242.**

The clip arrives at last on your Shelf. You'll see that the special effect has now been incorporated into the clip.

Figure 14-5:
In the Filter dialog box (top), QuickTime Player Pro offers special effects that let you adjust the color, brightness, or contrast of the footage; sharpen or blur it; add a phony "lens flare" (the bright star of light that sometimes appears when you take a picture facing the sun); or even add fake "Film Noise" like scratches and dust (shown here). The list of effects appears in the scrolling list at top left; a preview of the result appears in lower left. Use the controls on the right side of the dialog box to affect the intensity and other settings of the effect.

Using the Load and Save buttons, you can even save an effects configuration you've created onto your hard drive, so that you'll be able to apply exactly the same settings to another clip another time. (Unfortunately, you can apply only one effect at a time.)

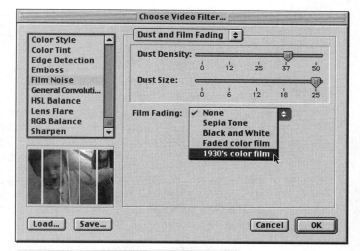

Editing Movies

By far the most powerful feature you gain in the Pro version is its ability to *edit* QuickTime movies. You can rearrange scenes, eliminate others, and save the result as a new movie with its own name.

All of this is perfectly possible within iMovie itself, of course, but sometimes you'll want to edit one of the QuickTime movies you've already exported from iMovie—to make it shorter for emailing, for example.

Tip: QuickTime Player can open DV clips, not just regular QuickTime movies. Therefore, it's perfectly capable of opening any of the files iMovie has captured into the Media folder of your project. This fact may come in handy if you want, for example, to snip just a few frames out of a captured clip, or combine two of these clips into one, or apply one of the QuickTime Player special effects to it even before beginning to edit the iMovie project.

Selecting footage

Before you can cut, copy, or paste footage, QuickTime Player needs to provide a way for you to specify *what* footage you want to manipulate. Its solution: the two tiny black triangles beneath the horizontal scroll bar, as shown in Figure 14-6. These are the "in" and "out" points, exactly like the crop handles in iMovie 2. By dragging these triangles, you're supposed to enclose the scene you want to cut or copy.

Tip: You can gain more precise control over the selection procedure shown in Figure 14-6 by clicking one of the black triangles and then pressing the right or left arrow key, exactly as when using the Scrubber bar under iMovie's Monitor window. Doing so expands or contracts the selected chunk of footage by one frame at a time.

You may also prefer to select a piece of footage by Shift-clicking the Play button. As long as you hold down the Shift key, you continue to select footage; when you release the Shift key, you stop the playback, and the selected passage appears in gray on the scroll bar.

Once you've highlighted a passage of footage, you can proceed as follows:

- Jump to the beginning or end of the selected footage by pressing Option-right or -left arrow key. (This doesn't work if one of the handles is highlighted.)

- Deselect the footage by dragging the two triangles together again.

- Play only the selected passage by choosing Movie→Play Selection Only. (The other Movie menu commands, such as Loop, apply only to the selection at this point.)

- Drag the movie picture out of the Player window and onto the desktop, where it becomes a *movie clipping* that you can double-click to view.

- Cut, copy, or clear the highlighted material using the commands in the Edit menu.

Tip: If you paste some copied text directly into QuickTime Player Pro, you get a two-second title (such as an opening credit) at the current frame, professionally displayed as white type against a black background. QuickTime Player automatically uses the font, size, and style of the text that was in the text clipping. You can paste a graphic image, too; once again, you get a two-second "slide" of that still image.

If you find it easier, you can also drag a text or picture *clipping file* directly from the desktop into the QuickTime Player window; once again, you get a two-second insert. To make the text or picture appear longer than two seconds, drag or paste it several times in a row.

In either case, you specify the fonts, sizes, and styles of your low-budget titling feature by formatting the text that way *before* you copy it from your word processor. (This feature requires a word processor that preserves such formatting on the Clipboard. Stickies, SimpleText, Word 98, AppleWorks, and America Online are all examples.)

Figure 14-6:
To select a particular scene, drag the tiny black triangles apart until they enclose the material you want. As you drag, QuickTime Player updates the movie picture to show you where you are. The material you select is represented by a gray strip of the scroll bar.

Pasting footage

After cutting or copying footage, you can move it elsewhere in the movie. Specify where you want the pasted material to go by first clicking or dragging in the horizontal scroll bar, so that the black Playhead marks the spot; then choose Edit→Paste. The selection triangles (and their accompanying gray scroll-bar section) show you where the new footage has appeared. (That makes it easy for you to promptly choose Edit→Cut, for example, if you change your mind.)

By pressing secret keys, moreover, you gain three clever variations of the Paste command. They work like this:

- If you highlight some footage before pasting, and then press Shift, you'll find that the Edit→Paste command has changed to become Edit→Replace. Whatever footage is on your Clipboard now *replaces* the selected stretch of movie.

- If you press Option, the Edit→Clear command changes to read Trim. It's like the Crop command in iMovie, in that it eliminates the outer parts of the movie—the pieces that *aren't* selected. All that remains is the part you first selected.

- If you highlight some footage, and then press Option, the Edit→Paste command changes to read Add. This command adds whatever's on the Clipboard so that it plays *simultaneously* with the selected footage—a feature that's especially useful when you're adding a *different kind* of material to the movie (see Figure 14-7).

- If you highlight some footage and then press Shift-Option, the Edit→Paste command changes to say Add Scaled. Whatever you're pasting gets stretched or compressed in time so that it fits the highlighted region, speeding up or slowing down both audio and video. The effect can be powerful, comical, or just weird.

Tip: You can edit sounds exactly as you edit movies, using precisely the same commands and shortcuts. Use the File→Open command in QuickTime Player Pro to locate a sound file you want to open. It opens exactly like a QuickTime movie, except with only a scroll bar–no picture.

Exporting Edited Movies

After you've finished working on a sound or movie, you can send it back out into the world in any of several ways.

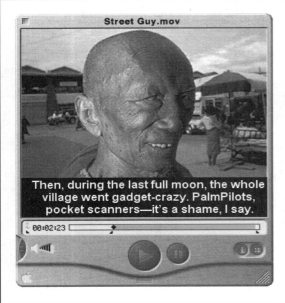

Figure 14-7:
iMovie may offer several different styles of subtitles (see Chapter 7), but QuickTime Player Pro's subtitling feature has charms of its own, including complete freedom of type style. Copy some formatted text from a word processor; highlight a slice of footage in Quick-Time Player; press Option; and choose Edit→Add. The copied text appears as a subtitle on a black band, beneath the picture, as shown here.

The "Save As" Command

If you choose Edit→Save As, you can specify a new name for your edited master-piece. You must also choose one of these two options:

- **Save normally.** The term "normally" is a red herring. You'll almost never want to use this option, which produces a very tiny file that contains no footage at all. Instead, it's something like an alias of the movie you edited: An edited file that you "save normally" works only as long as the original, unedited movie remains on your hard drive. If you try to email the newly saved file, your unhappy recipient won't see anything at all.

- **Make movie self-contained.** This option produces a new QuickTime movie— the one you've just finished editing. Although it consumes more disk space, it has none of the drawbacks of a "save normally" file.

The Export Command

Instead of using the File→Save As command, you can also use the File→Export command. The resulting dialog box offers two pop-up menus that can be very useful in tailoring your finished work for specific purposes:

- **Export.** Using this pop-up menu, you can convert your movie to AVI (Windows movie) format, DV Stream (for use with iMovie), Image Sequence (which produces a very large collection of individual graphics files, one per frame), and so

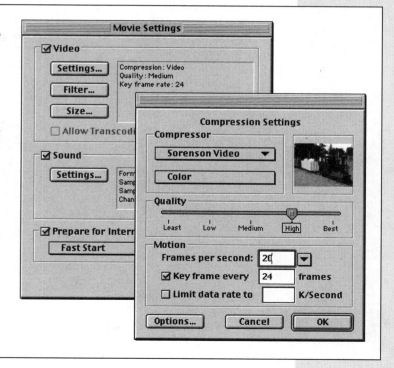

Figure 14-8:
If you're used to the Expert export options in iMovie, you may have wondered where QuickTime Player Pro hides its own compression settings. They're here, in the Export dialog box.

As Chapter 12 makes clear, for smooth playback from hard drive-based (but not Internet-based) movies, use fifteen frames per second or above; for best quality but small file size, use the Sorenson Video Compressor.

on. This pop-up menu also lets you convert a sound you've been working on to AIFF, System 7, or WAV (Windows) formats, for example.

- **Use.** This pop-up menu lets you establish your preferences for the export format you've just specified above. For a complete description of the various codecs and other compression options listed here, see page 291.

Compression and special effects

One of QuickTime Player's most powerful features is hidden in the Export dialog box, in a place where you might never find it. If none of the canned compression settings appeals to you, you can click the Options button in this dialog box. In the Settings dialog box that appears (see Figure 14-8), QuickTime Player Pro offers a staggering degree of control over the movie you're exporting.

When exporting a movie, here's where you can specify what codec you want to use (page 291), how many frames per second you want, and (by clicking Size) what dimensions you want the finished movie to have.

As a bonus, whenever you export as a QuickTime movie, you even get a Filter button that offers fourteen special video effects, as described earlier in this chapter.

Similarly, when you're exporting a sound file, the Options button lets you specify what sound quality you want, what compression method, and so on—all various ways of manipulating the tradeoff between file size and sound quality.

Tip: Once you're finished editing a QuickTime movie, rename it *startup movie* and put it into your System Folder. It plays automatically every time the computer starts up—alas, without its soundtrack.

Final Cut, Premiere, and EditDV

The history of digital-video editing software unfolded strangely, with the cart before the horse: The most expensive, extremely complex programs were in place *before* anyone wrote a simple, basic one. iMovie trickled down from the professional world to the amateur one, and it quickly became a hit with people who had no interest in spending their first filmmaking weekends just learning the software.

Simplicity plays a big part in iMovie's popularity. Apple designers examined the big-gun, high-priced editing programs, feature by feature, looked at each other, and said, "Nobody really needs that. Or that. That thing is way too complicated." Feature after feature was eliminated, until what we know as iMovie was all that was left.

The plan succeeded. The elegance, speed, stability, and simplicity of iMovie quickly made it the most-used DV editing program in the world. Thousands of people got to try their hands at video editing for the first time, with very little expense.

But the DV bug is hard to shake once you've been bitten. As much as you may love iMovie, you may be among that percentage of iMovie fans who begin to find the program *too* basic. Maybe you wish you had more control over transitions or titles. Maybe you wish you could superimpose clips to build more complex imagery. Or maybe you'd like to overlay video over audio without having to use the workaround described in Chapter 8.

This chapter offers a look at the world of DV editing software beyond iMovie. Stepping up to a more professional editing program is an expensive proposition, both in the cost of the software and in the time it will take to master, so choose carefully. On the Macintosh, the Big Three are EditDV, Premiere, and Final Cut Pro. Each offers a different assortment of features, requires a different amount of time to master, and *feels* different.

All three, however, include the essential features you've already learned in iMovie: a Monitor window, a shelf to hold clips, and a Movie Track that serves as a living storyboard for your movie in progress. (In iMovie 1's Movie Track, each clip was represented by a single square icon. iMovie 2 is much more like other editing programs in this regard; each clip is represented by a *strip* that indicates its length, as shown in Figures 15-1, 15-2, and 15-3.)

Intro to the Pro Leagues

There's a lot to like in pro-level editing programs. For example, all of them offer these advantages:

- Better organizational tools make it easier to work with *lots* of clips. In other words, folders within the Shelf.

- You can create multiple versions of the same project, which lets you try out several different ideas at the same time.

- You can import a wider range of multimedia files from a greater variety of sources.

- You can use more than one video and audio track, so that you can mix multiple images and soundtracks. You can manage these tracks individually or in groups.

- You can use hundreds of special effects features, such as changing certain colors, blurring the image, or even creating slow motion.

- You can create simple animations right there in the application.

- You've got far more advanced titling and text features, including completely free choice of font, size, style, color, placement, and animation style.

- Most of these programs offer *plug-in architecture,* so that you can buy new features in the form of add-on software modules.

- The Internet and local bookstore offer a huge and growing base of educational materials and technical help.

On the other hand, before you rush out to buy one of these programs, consider that with the added advantages come some distinct disadvantages:

- The programs are expensive. EditDV goes for $580; Premiere costs $590; and Final Cut Pro will set you back $1,000.

- These programs need a lot of computer horsepower. They may run on, say, an iMac, but all are much more effective on Macs with larger monitors (or *several* monitors), more memory, and more hard drive space.

- With their added complexity, these programs have a much steeper learning curve. (Their terse, written-for-professionals manuals don't help much.) These programs aren't designed for casual use. Once you've learned one of these programs, you have to *keep* using it, or you'll quickly forget how to use it.

- These programs assume that you already have a working knowledge of the technical aspects of digital video. If you're unfamiliar with this esoteric field, you may find yourself especially frustrated as you try to learn the software.

Meet the Players

Here's a quick look at each of the three most popular pro-level DV programs.

EditDV

EditDV (Digital Origin, *www.digitalorigin.com*) may be the easiest to learn of the Big Three (see Figure 15-1). Most people consider it a *prosumer* application—popular with people who are stepping up to more advanced capabilities, but who aren't subject to the demands of a full-time video-editing operation (although many professionals do use EditDV).

Another advantage: EditDV works on both Macintosh and Windows computers—a handy feature when several people are collaborating on a single project but who aren't necessarily using the same kind of computer.

Figure 15-1:
EditDV isn't the most difficult pro-editing program to learn, but that doesn't mean it's easy. Its windows are filled with cryptic icons you'll have to learn. Furthermore, EditDV is the only one of the Big Three editing programs whose timeline (the Sequencer window, shown at bottom) offers no indication as to what's in each video clip. (Final Cut and Premiere can show you at least a representative frame, as iMovie does.)

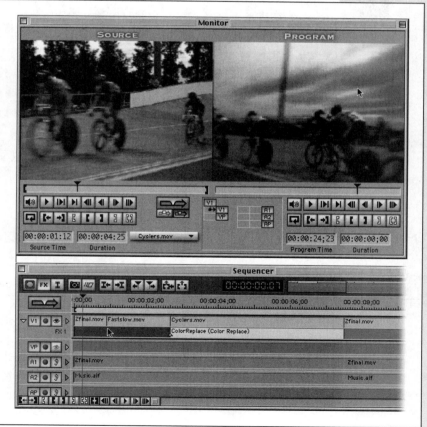

Premiere

Adobe Premiere (Adobe, *www.adobe.com*) has a large following for three reasons: It's been around for years, it comes with an extensive tool set, and it's the software that comes with a wide assortment of video capture cards (the expensive digitizing cards that people used to edit video on the Mac before the invention of the DV camcorder and FireWire). This program, too, is available for Macintosh or Windows (Figure 15-2).

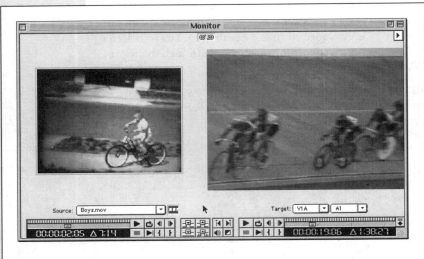

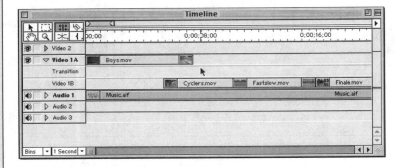

Figure 15-2:
In Premiere, as in iMovie 2, you can zoom the timeline window in or out. Here (bottom) you can see what your movie looks like at a scale where each tick mark on the "ruler" represents one second.

You can also see the multiple video tracks. To add transitions, you drag a transition icon onto the strip between the clips (indicated by the cursor) on these parallel tracks.

Final Cut Pro

Apple's Final Cut Pro is the newest kid on the block, having been released only in 1998. But for professional editors whose alternative is a hardware editing console costing tens of thousands of dollars, Final Cut Pro is rapidly becoming the system of choice. This program runs on Macs only.

Figure 15-3:
If you look closely at the Monitor window in Final Cut Pro (top), you'll discover something surprising: It's distinctly reminiscent of iMovie itself, right down to the curvy dip below the controls.

Bottom: FCP (as the insiders call it) has special commands that make it easy to repair the damage when your audio and video tracks get out of sync.

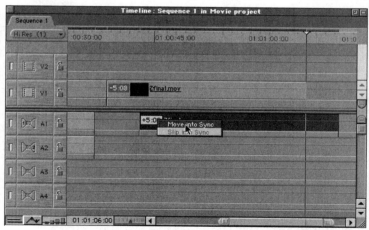

Working with Pro DV Software

Although each of these three programs has its own personality, they have certain things in common. For example, the sequence of steps you take—the workflow—is similar. It goes something like this:

Configure the Software

Before you actually begin to capture your video, it will take you some time just to configure the program. Each offers dozens of different parameters—what equipment you've got, what format you want the resulting movie to take, and so on. You have to fiddle with those parameters before you can get to work. Understanding what these settings represent is important, and requires knowledge of the technical aspects of video.

Capture Your Footage

When it's time to capture the video, you're treated to your first taste of a kind of efficiency not available in iMovie: *batch capturing* (see Figure 15-4). You start by watching your camcorder footage, controlling the camera using on-screen buttons, exactly as you would in iMovie. But when you see a scene you like, you don't actually capture it. Instead, you indicate where the desired scene begins, fast-forward to where you want it to stop, and then indicate where the scene ends. After you've logged all of the scenes that you want to import, you use a Batch Capture command. The software then automatically does whatever rewinding, playing, stopping, and recording is necessary to import all of the scenes you've marked into the Mac.

Figure 15-4:
Every high-end program offers a batch-capture dialog box like this one from EditDV. As you review your footage, you click icons at the left side to mark the beginnings and endings of shots you'll want transferred to the Mac. (You can use the fast-forward or rewind controls to make this process faster.) Then, later, you can tell the program to automate the capturing process based on the list of shots you've created.

Batch capturing saves you time during the *logging* process because you don't actually have to watch all of the footage; you can speed through it. And you save time during the capturing process because it's automated. You can do something else while the machine captures the footage.

Like iMovie, the professional programs let you import many different kinds of files, which you can then manipulate as though they're video clips. Like iMovie, Premiere and Final Cut Pro let you import Photoshop files. But in the more advanced programs, the Photoshop files come in with the *layers* intact. Each layer is treated as a separate clip. This feature is very useful for creating animations and title sequences, because you can store all of the elements in one file (on different transparent Photoshop layers).

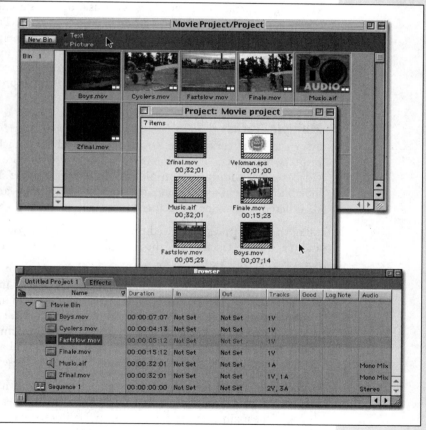

Figure 15-5:
From top: The bin windows of EditDV, Premiere, and Final Cut Pro.

You can name each bin window independently. For example, you might create a bin called "Graphics" to hold the still images you'll be using. You can also create bins within bins; there might be a Photos bin and an Illustrations bin inside of the Graphics bin, to help you further organize the clips.

The number of bins and clips that a project can have is limited only by the amount of storage (RAM and hard drive space) available on the computer. Like the iMovie Media folder, bin folders are stored on your desktop inside the project folder.

Clips in Bins

Once the footage is captured, you have to organize it. Long programs may have hundreds or even thousands of clips. Clearly, an iMovie-style Shelf with no means of grouping clips wouldn't quite be up to the task.

Instead, the pro programs let you hold your clips in *bins*—special windows that list your clips much like icons in a desktop window (Figure 15-5). Each can show either a list view or an icon view, just like Finder windows.

The Timeline Window

After capturing your clips, you set about arranging them into a sequence. You do this by dragging them into a Timeline window, which is exactly the same idea as the Movie Track in iMovie. Final Cut Pro even lets you create *multiple* Timeline windows, one for each sequence—a great convenience when you're creating a long show. Each sequence can represent a different part of the program (such as the sections between commercial breaks on a TV show).

In Final Cut Pro, you can even drag one sequence of clips into another sequence. The program treats the original sequence as though it's a single clip, making it very easy to apply the same effect to a group of clips all at once. (Premiere offers a similar feature called *virtual clips.*) You can also use this multiple-sequence feature to create different versions of the same movie, keeping all of them together so that you can easily jump back and forth between the versions. (Any video editor who's ever worked for clients who aren't quite sure what they want can appreciate the value of this feature!)

Multiple Tracks

iMovie lets you work with one track of video and three tracks of audio. For simple projects, that's plenty. But what if you want to superimpose some video over other video, such as adding kids-on-bicycles footage onto some sky background so they look like they're biking through the sky? Or what if you want to mix recordings of six different instruments together so that they sound like a band?

All of these examples require editing software that lets you set up multiple parallel audio and video tracks; all of the clips that are aligned vertically play back simultaneously (Figure 15-6).

With more video tracks, you can also superimpose several images on top of a background, such as people walking around in a still photograph. You can even create a multiple-panel effect like the one at the beginning of *The Brady Bunch*. Multiple parallel video tracks even lets you create a picture-in-picture effect, thanks to the ability to shrink one of the video clips to fit into a small area of the total image. EditDV, Final Cut Pro, and Premiere can handle all of these effects and more.

In the professional editing world, you'd be lost without having multiple parallel *audio* tracks, too. For example, in a hospital scene, you'd hear a lot more besides the dialog of the main characters. A good sound editor would add doctors being paged, phones ringing, background conversations, sirens outside, and so on (as a viewing of *ER* will quickly illustrate). Each one of those sounds would be on a separate audio track so they could be individually controlled. Final Cut Pro and Premiere can have up to 99 video and 99 audio tracks; EditDV offers an unlimited number.

Of course, with that many tracks to play with, figuring out where to *put* a particular clip becomes a real issue. Organization becomes critical. The track called Video 1 might be designated the main video track, with superimposed titles relegated to Video 2, picture-in-picture images on Video 3, and so on. You have to organize your audio tracks equally well. Tracks 1 and 2 might be dialogue tracks; 3 might be a voice-over or narration track; 4, 5, and 6 might be sound effects; and 7 and 8 could be music tracks.

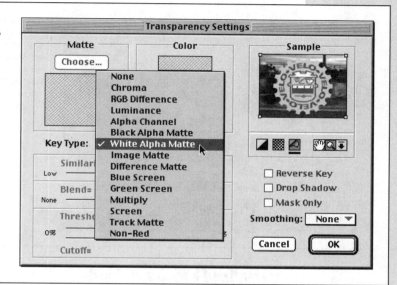

Figure 15-6:
Because you can set up multiple stacked video tracks in programs like Premiere (shown here), it's easy to create composite shots like this one. Here, a graphic image is superimposed on the moving video; you're telling Premiere to replace all white *areas of the graphic with the video picture.*

Editing Audio

Each of the three programs can also create an "audio waveform," a graph of the sound waves in an audio clip (Figure 15-7). This visual display is enormously valuable for editing sound; it lets you see the actual spoken words, pauses, music beats, and so on. These visual cues make it much easier to place your video cuts on specific sounds (or silences).

Split Edits

When you first capture a clip from the tape, the sound and picture are synchronized. When you shorten one, you shorten the other, and the audio and video remain synchronized.

Sometimes, however, you may want to create a movie where the audience hears the sound of the next clip *before* the picture appears—a very common technique in TV and movies. All three of the more advanced video editors let you create these effects, which are known as *split edits* (see page 219).

Similarly, all three programs make it extremely easy to overlay video over audio. That is, while a continuous audio track plays, cut from one video shot to another—a feature that finally appeared in iMovie 2 (see Chapter 8).

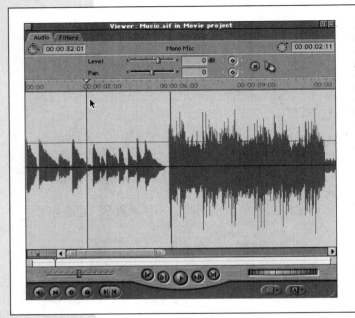

Figure 15-7:
In programs like Final Cut Pro, shown here, you can edit audio with extreme precision. The spikes in the audio graph indicate individual bursts of sound in a clip—individual words, chords, gurgles, and so on. You're free to chop them out, rearrange them, or perform other transformations. Being able to see the waveform makes it much easier to edit your video in sync, too.

Specialized Efficiency Tools

Professional programs give you more tools to accomplish specific tasks more easily and efficiently. For example, suppose you notice that if only you could shift the entire video track a fraction of a second, the cuts you've made would align nicely with the beats in the music track. Fortunately, all three of the professional programs offer a tool precisely for this purpose—creating a *rolling edit*.

All three programs also offer a Trim window that's split into two panes: One that shows the final frame of one clip, the other showing the first frame of the next one. (Figure 15-1 shows the effect.) This dual display lets you make transitions and cuts more precisely, because you can see both the outgoing and incoming frame simultaneously. The Trim windows also let you navigate easily, jumping from cut to cut, just by clicking a button. These tools make it easier to experiment, and to make your edits with the least amount of effort.

Other specialized tools let you:

- Select more than one clip (on a single track or on multiple tracks) simultaneously, so that you can apply an effect or editing maneuver to all of them at once.

- Trim a clip, making it shorter or longer, while automatically closing the gaps between clips.

- Draw lines that control the *signal strength* of a clip, giving you precise control over the rate of a cross dissolve from one clip into another, for example, or over the volume level of an audio clip along its length.

- Enlarge or reduce the scale of the Timeline. Reducing it makes it easier to see your entire movie at once and get the big picture; magnifying it makes it easy to see if two or more clips are synchronized perfectly or if they're a frame or two off.

- Adjust the In and Out points (beginning and ending frames) of a clip in tandem. Suppose you've got a 30-second clip, for example. You've cropped out the last 20 seconds. But now you decide that you want to crop out the *first* 20 seconds instead. Unlike iMovie, cropping in the advanced editing programs doesn't throw away the footage you've decided to "crop out." You're free to shift the In and Out points simultaneously, thus maintaining the overall duration—a useful trick when you like the timing of a clip, but want to use different frames from it.

The professional programs also offer many ways to do the same thing—menus, button icons, and keyboard shortcuts, for example. Video editors frequently keep one hand on the keyboard and the other on the mouse, so that they can point and click when necessary, but meanwhile use keystrokes when possible for better efficiency. (Final Cut Pro has the most complete set of icon buttons and keyboard shortcuts.)

Over time, you'll develop your own style—you may slowly graduate from using the menu commands to using keyboard shortcuts, for example. Unfortunately, all these duplicate ways to achieve the same commands contribute to these programs' reputations for being confusing and intimidating, especially for first-timers.

Special Effects

iMovie offers only a few special effects features along the liens of color-correcting video, blurring video, or adding echo to audio. The advanced video editing programs not only offer a huge range of effects, but they're also extendable. In other words, although many effects are programmed into the application, other programmers write and sell new effects that plug into your program. For example, Final Cut Pro can use many of the effects plug-ins developed for Adobe After Effects, a popular DV program for *compositing* (combining components of separate video clips) and animation.

What's especially useful is that you can *animate* the effects in these programs—that is, you can control the intensity over time (Figure 15-8), just as in iMovie 2.

Effects can even be stacked, too, by applying more than one effect to a particular clip. For example, you might direct one of the effects to make all of the green shades in a shot yellow, and then make the entire clip brighter. Furthermore, you can apply the same effect several times to the same clip, compounding the effect. For example, you can make a mirror image, then mirror the resulting image, then do it again, making your footage look as if it were shot through a kaleidoscope.

Titles and Text

Like iMovie, EditDV and Final Cut Pro have text-generating effects. In these programs, however, you can achieve fantastic effects, such as hollow lettering that you can *see through* to the live video picture underneath.

Premiere has a separate titling tool that gives you even more control over your typography and text. In Premiere, for example, it's easy to create rolling titles (although not quite as easy as in iMovie). Premiere's title tool also lets you add graphics and shapes to your titles (a semitransparent colored box behind the text, for example). Of the Big Three programs, Final Cut Pro has the weakest title tool.

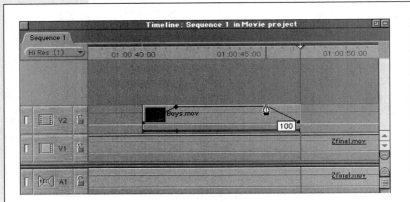

Figure 15-8:
You can control the intensity of a special effect over time. Here, the Pen tool is being used to make a video clip fade in and fade out; the higher the line, the stronger the image. You can use the same controls to affect image blur over a clip's length, to distort dialogue clips at different levels, and so on.

Animation

When movie fans talk about animation, they're usually thinking of drawn characters like Bugs Bunny and friends, and movies like *Toy Story* or *The Lion King*. But when professionals talk about animation, especially in the context of editing software, they refer to all kinds of elements that may change over time: shape, position on screen, color, and so on.

For example, a title can be animated so that it fades in, grows larger, moves from top left to bottom right, then gets blurry and fades out. Only its attributes are being animated—its opacity, scale (size), position, and blur.

Computers are wonderful for calculating these changes over a span of frames. In the old days, the animator might have had to hand-draw every frame; using software, you can focus on what something looks like when it *starts* to change and what it looks like when it *stops* changing. The computer can figure out all the in-between steps (the process animators call *tweening)* and draw the resulting frames.

Each of the Big Three programs can generate two-dimensional animation by making things change horizontally and vertically. Some examples:

• A logo that expands to fill the frame, then starts rotating clockwise as it shrinks back to the top right corner of the frame and finally fades out

- A picture-in-picture effect that changes position and size on screen (see Figure 15-9)

- A character's eyeballs moving (which you create by changing the position of two small black circles inside two larger white circles on either side of a vertical line)

- Motion graphics (like flying logos or opening title sequences)

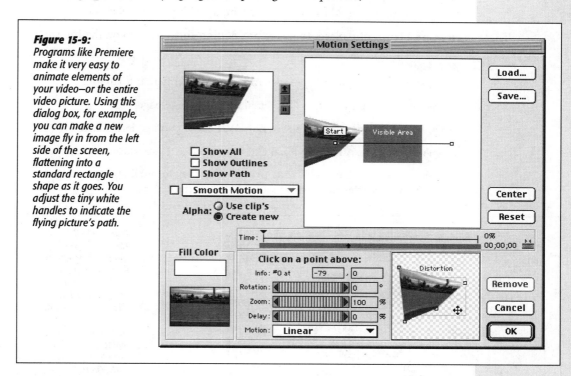

Figure 15-9:
Programs like Premiere make it very easy to animate elements of your video—or the entire video picture. Using this dialog box, for example, you can make a new image fly in from the left side of the screen, flattening into a standard rectangle shape as it goes. You adjust the tiny white handles to indicate the flying picture's path.

Multiple Platforms and Conversion

Once you've finished your DV masterpiece, you do exactly the same kinds of things that you do with a finished iMovie project: Send it back onto videotape for showing others, or save it as a QuickTime movie for posting on your Web site or on a CD-ROM. (See Figure 15-10.)

Before you can do so, however, you must *render* your entire movie, which usually involves a long wait as the software processes all of your special effects, titles, cross-fades, and so on. (The advanced programs don't automatically render each effect and title on the fly, as iMovie does.)

Exactly as with iMovie, you can render a certain project as many times as you like, using different settings each time. In other words, after editing a project once, you can make a few Export-command changes and send it to tape, the Web, a CD-ROM, and so on.

You Are Not Alone

As complicated as these pro programs are, you don't have to feel utterly at sea when using them. Even the most experienced editors started out not knowing anything, and there is a wonderful camaraderie in the digital video community. People are not only interested in sharing information, many are eager to do so. Web sites, Internet communities, and email lists are all popping up with great regularity.

Here are a few useful places to go for pro-editing-software help on the Internet:

Web Sites

- *www.adobe.com/products/premiere/main.html.* Premiere information.

- *www.apple.com/finalcutpro.* The Final Cut Pro home page.

- *www.digitalorigin.com.* All about EditDV. Lots of good general DV info.

- *www.2-pop.com.* A massive Final Cut Pro resource. Discussions, news, tips.

- *www.wwug.com.* The Worldwide Users Group may sound like a general Mac user group, but its offerings revolve around DV editing.

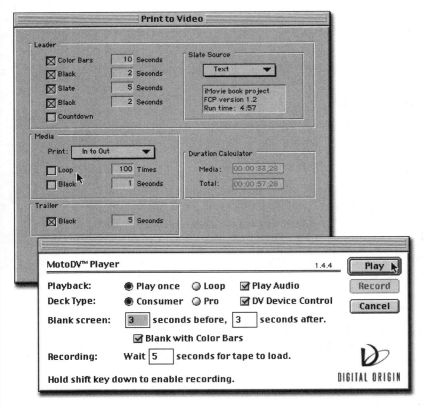

Figure 15-10:
The end of your video-editing efforts is exactly the same in the high-priced programs as it is in iMovie: a QuickTime movie or a videotape. These dialog boxes (Final Cut Pro, top, and EditDV) are the fancier versions of the iMovie Export dialog box. (The EditDV box doesn't let you send your movie back to the camcorder unless you press Shift as you click the Play button—a precaution against accidental recordings.)

- *www.postforum.com.* Macintosh DV resources. Articles, reviews, discussions, software.

- *www.dv.com.* Not Mac-specific, but DV-specific. How-to, reviews, case studies.

- *www.webcinema.org.* The home page of Webcinema, a nonprofit organization "dedicated to the independent filmmaker using Internet new-media technologies to finance, create, produce, distribute, and market independent film."

Newsgroups

Newsgroups are Internet bulletin boards; you can read them window, for example, Outlook Express. Two of them are filled with useful DV editing discussion: *rec.arts.video.production* and *rec.arvideo.desktop.*

Tip: You might be surprised at how many professional video editors have added iMovie to their toolkits. For capturing clips, iMovie is fast and efficient; its ability to begin a new clip with each new camcorder shot is a convenience not found in the pricier programs. Fortunately, the files iMovie creates when it captures footage are standard QuickTime DV clips that programs like Premiere and Final Cut Pro can import. iMovie gives professionals the best of both worlds: quick and automatic capturing, and big-gun software for editing.

ON LOCATION

iMovie in the Ad Agency

I'm an advertising art director. I have a "stack" reel of all the broadcast ads I've ever done. I thought I could use iMovie to edit my reel down to just the best ads, so I'd have it whenever someone asked to see my work.

My existing reel is in digital Beta format, so I took it to a postproduction house to get it dubbed to my Canon Elura.

Unfortunately, I didn't know at the time that I should have set my camera's audio to 16-bit instead of 12-bit. The sound in iMovie was badly distorted, apparently because of this 12-bit setting. My workaround was to reimport the audio separately, using the Elura's analog audio jack, and re-sync it with the video. It was time-consuming, but it worked.

Once I had my best spots in the order I wanted, I added identifying graphics at the beginning and end of my reel. Then I simply recorded the edited reel back to my Elura.

Now I can make my own dubs onto VHS, as many times and as often as I like, just by connecting my Elura to my VCR. Compared with having to spend tons of money to have a postproduction house prepare my reel, iMovie has proven to be a real value.

I was also able to export my iMovie reel as a QuickTime movie, so I could include my broadcast work on a CD. Now I've got a digital portfolio, a CD-ROM, that includes both my print work (in Acrobat format) and broadcast spots (in QuickTime).

Finally, just to get my feet wet in iMovie editing, I took four spots I'd done for Churchill Downs a few years ago and successfully edited a "new" single spot containing the best cuts.

I don't know if this is what everyone else does with iMovie, but for others in advertising, iMovie is a great way to prepare a broadcast reel.

—Richard Page
New Orleans, LA

Part Five:
Appendixes

5

iMovie 2, Menu by Menu

As you've certainly noticed by now, iMovie doesn't look like a standard Mac program. Part of its radical charm is that almost all of its functions are represented visually on screen—there aren't many menu commands. On the other hand, iMovie 2 uses menus more extensively than its predecessor, and you'll miss some great features if you don't venture to the top of the screen much.

Here's a rundown of the commands in iMovie's menus:

File Menu

As in any Mac program, the File menu serves as the program's interface to the rest of the Macintosh world. It lets you open and close movie projects, import or export still frames, import QuickTime movies and audio files, and quit the program.

New Project, Open Project

iMovie 2 features a File menu with no Close command. After you're finished working on a movie document (which iMovie calls a *project),* you can't close it. You can only take one of three paths:

- Begin a new, untitled movie project by choosing File→New Project. (If you haven't saved the changes to the one you've been working on, you'll be offered the opportunity to do so.)

- Open another existing project document. To do so, choose File→Open Project. The standard Open File dialog box appears. Navigate to, and double-click, the project document you want to open (it's inside a *folder* bearing the same name).

- Quit the program.

Save Project

This command preserves any changes you've made to your project, exactly as in a word processor or any other program.

iMovie saves such changes extremely quickly. It doesn't actually store any changes to the video clips you've captured; instead, it just makes a list of the changes you've made, which gets stored in the relatively tiny project document.

Tip: The File menu doesn't offer a Save As command, but it's easy enough to peel off a copy of your document-in-progress manually; see page 109.

Nor does iMovie have a Revert command. To achieve the same result and undo all the changes you've made to your files since the last time you saved it, simply quit iMovie. When you're asked if you want to save the changes, click Don't Save (or press the undocumented shortcut, ⌘-D). Then launch iMovie again. Your project will reappear as it was the last time you saved it.

Export Movie

This essential command is, in a way, the entire point of iMovie. It lets you send your finished movie out into the world in the search of an audience, the culmination of your video-editing adventure. You have two options:

- Export it back to the DV camcorder, and from there to a TV or VHS cassette.
- Convert it into a QuickTime movie for viewing on a computer.

Chapter 11 contains step-by-step instructions for transferring your opus to the camcorder; Chapter 12 guides you through creating QuickTime movies.

Save Frame As

Your digital camcorder is also a digital *still* camera, thanks to this command. As described on page 238, this command grabs whatever picture is visible in the Monitor window and opens the Save File dialog box, so that you can save the image to your hard drive as a graphics file. You can choose either PICT or JPEG format.

As Chapter 9 makes clear, the resulting images are nowhere near as sharp or as clear as the ones you get with an actual digital still camera. They're fairly low-resolution, for example, and the *interlacing* effect of the video signal makes it look like your image is composed of hundreds of thin horizontal lines—which it is. (You can escape this unpleasant side effect if your camcorder has a *progressive scanning* feature.)

Still, for creating images you plan to distribute electronically—by email or on the Web, for example—the iMovie-exported pictures may suffice. You can improve the image quality by shrinking the frame size in a graphics program, thereby condensing the component dots and sharpening the image, before you distribute it.

Import File

You can use this command to bring two kinds of multimedia files into iMovie:

- **Still images** (photographs, scans, graphic "title cards," and so on), as described in Chapter 9. The program accepts JPEG, GIF, PICT, BMP, and Photoshop files. A graphics file you import in such a way falls onto the Shelf and behaves like a video clip.

- **Audio files** that have been saved in AIFF format, as described in Chapter 8, for the benefit of your soundtrack. These files go automatically into your Audio Track.

- **DV Stream files**, which are movies that you've exported from QuickTime Player Pro, as described on page 243, or from iMovie itself. This option lets you "borrow" a DV clip from another iMovie project (by importing from its Media folder) with very little effort.

Clip Info

Opens the Clip Info dialog box for whichever clip is highlighted in the Movie Track or Shelf. (Unavailable if exactly one clip—audio, video, still, transition, or title—isn't highlighted.) The shortcut is simply double-clicking a clip.

Empty Trash

The Trash referred to by this command has nothing to do with the standard Macintosh Trash. Instead, it refers to the *project* Trash, the Trash-can icon on the iMovie screen. Every time you delete or crop some footage, iMovie pretends to put it into this Trash can. As described on page 120, however, you can't open this icon to view its contents or selectively rescue items inside it. Its only purpose is to keep you apprised of the *quantity* of footage you've deleted so far. It tells you that during your editing efforts, you've chopped out, say, 576 MB of footage.

Quit

This command closes iMovie after offering you the chance to save any changes you've made to your project file. The next time you open iMovie by double-clicking its icon, the program will reopen whatever project document you were working on.

Edit Menu

The Edit menu is especially useful in iMovie. It contains all of the editing commands described in Chapter 5. In fact, along with the various drag-and-drop editing techniques described in this book, the commands in the Edit menu are the only tools you need to build your movies.

Undo

In iMovie, you can take back not only the last editing maneuver, but the last *ten*. The ability to change your mind, or to recover from a particularly bad editing decision, is a considerable blessing.

The wording of this command changes to show you *which* editing step it's about to reverse. It might say Undo Import, Undo Move (after you've dragged a clip), Undo Split (after you've chopped a clip in half), and so on.

Keep in mind the pseudo-Revert (Quit and Don't Save) technique described on page 108. Between these two commands, you should find all the safety net you need in the event that you've really made a mess of your movie.

Tip: As noted earlier, emptying the project Trash command wipes out iMovie's memory of your last ten steps. You'll no longer be able to undo your previous editing actions.

Redo

We're only human, so it's entirely possible that sometimes you might want to *undo* your Undo.

For example, suppose that you've just used the Undo command a few times, retracing your steps back to a time when your movie was in better shape, and then decide that you've gone one step too far. That's when the Redo command is useful; it tells iMovie to undo your last Undo, so that you can step *forward* in time, redoing the steps that you just undid. (If you haven't just used the Undo command, then Redo is dimmed.)

Cut, Copy, Paste

You can use the Cut, Copy, and Paste commands in two different ways:

- **To move clips around** on the Shelf, on the Movie Track, or between the Shelf and the Movie Track. For example, you might click a clip in the Shelf, choose Edit→Copy, and then choose Edit→Paste. Doing so creates a duplicate of the clip. Now you're free to edit, crop, or chop up the original, confident that you've got a duplicate as a backup.

Tip: The beauty of copying clips in iMovie is that it doesn't really create new files on your hard drive, taking up more disk space. Although it looks like it has duplicated a physical clip, in fact, it has simply created a new *reference*—like an alias or pointer—to the original footage file.

- **To chop out some footage from a clip.** In other words, if you use the triangular handles under the Scrubber bar to highlight part of a clip (see Figure 5-3, for example), you can use the Cut command to delete that footage. The result is that you split the original clip into two clips—whatever was on either side of the part you excise. Now you can paste the cut material into the Shelf or Movie Track, where it becomes a new clip of its own. (You can use the Copy command in the same way, except that it doesn't split the original clip or remove any footage from it.)

The Paste command always deposits the cut or copied material onto the Movie Track, just *after* whatever clip is currently highlighted. If a clip in the Shelf is highlighted, iMovie puts the pasted clip there. And if no clip is selected anywhere, iMovie deposits the copied clip just after the clip containing the Playhead.

Cut, Copy, Paste, and Clear also work when you're editing *text,* such as the names of your clips or the text for your credits and other titles.

Tip: To get an interesting "instant replay" effect, try this trick. Copy a short bit of interesting video, such as your friend tripping over his shoelace and hitting the ground. Paste the snippet twice, so that you wind up with three copies of the same short snippet all in a row. Now select the middle copy and choose Advanced→ Reverse Clip Direction. Play through this sequence to see your friend fall down, bounce back up again (backwards!), and then fall down again, for hours of family entertainment. (Of course, there are many other ways to use this technique that aren't quite so reminiscent of *America's Funniest Home Videos.*)

Clear

The Clear command is identical to Cut except that it doesn't keep the deleted material on the invisible Clipboard. Instead, it simply removes the highlighted clip or selection without affecting what was already on the Clipboard. *Keyboard equivalent:* the Delete key.

Crop

Use the Crop command to trim excess ends off a clip after you've isolated a portion of it using the triangular handles under the Scrubber bar. The process is described and illustrated on page 126.

Split Clip at Playhead

It's often convenient to chop a clip in half; this command does the trick. The Playhead is the "scroll bar handle" under the Monitor window. Drag it, or press the right and left arrow keys, to position it precisely at the location where you want the split to be made. After you choose Edit→Split Clip at Playhead, you wind up with two clips. If the original clip was called "Great shot," iMovie names the resulting clips "Great shot" and "Great shot/1," for example.

Create Still Clip

This command adds, to your Shelf, a new still-image clip created from the frame in the Monitor window. See page 238 for more on this command.

Select All

This command highlights all of the clips in the Shelf, all of the footage in the Movie Track, or all of the text in the box, as described here:

- If any clip is highlighted, Select All highlights all of the clips in the same area (Movie Track or Shelf), as indicated by their bright yellow outlines. You might do this to select all the clips on the Shelf, for example, in readiness to drag all of them into the Movie Track at once. If audio clips are highlighted, Select All selects all the audio clips.

- If no clip is highlighted anywhere, Select All highlights all the clips in the Movie Track.

- If you're editing text, such as a title or the name of a clip, this command highlights all the text in the box. Now you can copy it using Edit→Copy or replace it by typing over it.

Select None

Memorizing this command (or better yet, its keyboard equivalent ⌘-D) is an excellent idea. It comes into play quite often; for example, every time you wrap up editing a particular clip and now want to watch your entire movie in progress. You can play back the entire movie only when no clip is selected.

Tip: You can also deselect all clips by clicking anywhere in the faint gray stripes of the iMovie background.

You can also use Select None after you've been fiddling with the crop handles under the Scrubber bar. Select None makes them disappear, so that none of the footage is highlighted.

Preferences

This command brings up the Preferences dialog box, as shown in Figure A-1. Here you're offered a smattering of useful options, arranged on several tabs:

Import tab

This tab offers three important controls:

- **Automatically start new clip at scene break.** iMovie, when importing footage from your camcorder, can automatically create a new clip every time it detects that the camcorder was turned off and on again during filming. In other words,

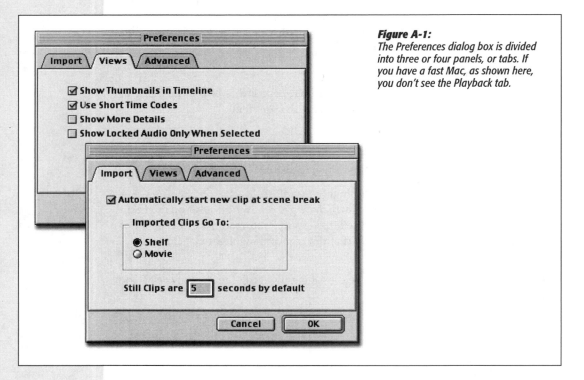

Figure A-1:
The Preferences dialog box is divided into three or four panels, or tabs. If you have a fast Mac, as shown here, you don't see the Playback tab.

every shot becomes its own clip—a useful and sophisticated feature not found in even the pro editing programs. (If this option is turned off, then you must use the Import button under the Monitor window to control when iMovie captures the footage the camcorder is playing.)

- **Imported Clips Go To: Shelf/Movie.** When you first install iMovie, it stashes each captured clip from the camcorder in the Shelf.

  If the scenes on your DV camcorder are roughly in the order you'll want them to be in the finished movie, however, you can save some dragging-from-the-Shelf steps by choosing to have iMovie stash them directly in the Movie Track as they're imported. Click the Movie option to make it so.

- **Still Clips are ___ seconds by default.** When you create or import a still picture, you can specify how long you'd like it to appear on the screen in movie time. If you're importing or creating a *lot* of stills, however, you'll appreciate this control, which is new in iMovie 2; it lets you change the default (proposed) time-on-the-screen for newly created still clips.

Playback tab

As noted on page 102, slower Macs aren't fast enough to display full-quality footage at full speed. When you view your movie in the Monitor window, therefore, you can choose between seeing smooth video with a slightly blurry picture (Smoother Motion) and slightly jerky video with a crisp picture (Better Image). You make that choice here by clicking either Smoother Motion or Better Image.

If your Mac is fairly fast—a Power Mac G4 running at 350 MHz or faster, for example—you don't have to make any such tradeoff. In fact, this tab doesn't even appear when you're running iMovie 2 on such a machine.

Views tab

This tab, new in iMovie 2, offers four checkboxes that govern what you see on the iMovie screen:

- Show Thumbnails in Timeline. "Thumbnails" refers to the tiny pictures that appear on each clip in the Timeline Viewer. Although these still images are helpful for identifying the clips, they also make scrolling much slower. By turning off this checkbox, you get sleek, pictureless bars in the Timeline Viewer (and therefore faster scrolling).

- **Use Short Time Codes.** When this checkbox is on, iMovie omits the minutes portion of its duration readout—"00:"—when the highlighted clip, selection, or movie is under one minute long.

  If you feel confused about whether you're seeing "minutes:seconds" or "seconds:frames," turn this box off. Now iMovie shows you the full three-segment time counter ("minutes:seconds:frames") wherever time codes appear.

- **Show More Details.** This option affects the Timeline Viewer only. When it's turned on, iMovie stamps the bars in the Timeline Viewer with the clips' names and durations—a great help in identifying the clips, especially if you've chosen to hide the thumbnail images. It also stamps each clip with a special symbol that indicates Reverse Motion, Slow Motion, Fast Motion, or a combination. (These symbols always appear on clips in the Clip Viewer or Shelf, but they're otherwise hidden in the Timeline Viewer.)

- **Show Locked Audio Only When Selected.** "Locked Audio" here means *pushpins*, of the sort shown on page 214—the tiny thumbtack icons that help you spot audio clips that you've pinned to video clips. If you find these symbols distracting, turn on this checkbox; now the pushpins show up in the Timeline Viewer only when you've actually *highlighted* an audio clip.

Advanced tab

These three options let you tweak iMovie 2's enhanced features:

- **Extract Audio in Paste Over.** In short, this option lets you paste video (without its audio) over existing audio tracks. See page 219 for details.

- **Filter Audio from Camera.** iMovie automatically screens out the beeps that indicate bad frames of audio recorded by the camera (see page 373). In iMovie 1, this filtering could occasionally *introduce* audio glitches instead of fixing them.

  Even though this problem was fixed in iMovie 2, the program offers this checkbox to control the filtering, just in case. Don't turn it off unless you're experiencing beeps in the imported audio, in which case turning this option off and re-importing the footage may help.

- **Video Play Through to Camera.** This is the on/off switch for iMovie 2's remarkable ability to show you your clips on your camcorder's LCD screen—or better still, a TV attached to the camcorder. See page 103 for details.

Advanced Menu

This menu, new to iMovie 2, holds the key to several of its juiciest new features. For example:

- **Extract Audio** splits the audio from a highlighted video clip into an independent audio clip in the Timeline Viewer, as described on page 220.

- **Paste Over at Playhead** lets you perform a video overlay. As described on page 219, that means pasting your most recently cut or copied video *on top of* (replacing) whatever video is now at the Playhead. (If you highlighted some footage before opening the Advanced menu, this command says Paste Over instead; iMovie, in this case, simply fills the highlighted stretch of time with whatever you've got on your Clipboard.)

- **Lock Audio Clip at Playhead** adds pushpins to the highlighted audio clip in the Timeline Viewer, as described on page 214, so that if the accompanying video clip shifts during editing, the audio moment will shift too, staying in sync with the moved video frame to which it was attached.

- **Reverse Clip Direction** makes the highlighted audio or video clip play backwards. (If several clips are highlighted, iMovie rearranges them, too, so that they play in backwards order as well.) Details on page 131.

- **Restore Clip Media.** As long as you haven't emptied the Project Trash, this command offers you the remarkable luxury of restoring a highlighted clip to its original condition, the way it was when first imported from the camcorder, no matter how much you've sliced or diced it in the meantime. See page 122 for more.

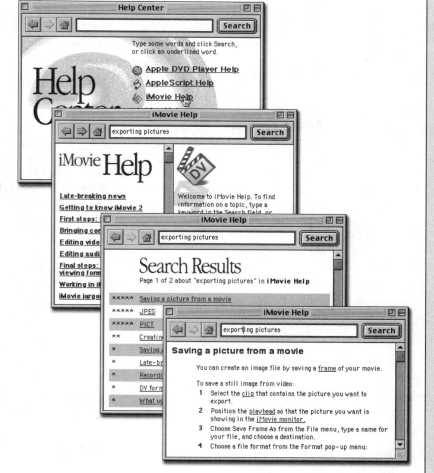

Figure A-2:
The Help Center shows all of the help-file modules that have been installed on your Mac by your various programs (at least, the help files in Apple Help Center format), as shown at top left. Type a phrase into the search blank and then click Search. You get a list of Help pages that it thinks might contain the information you want.

The asterisks indicate how confident the Help program is. A help page with more asterisks contains more occurrences of your search phrase relative to the rest of the text on it. Click one of the blue underlined text-page names to read the corresponding help page (bottom); click the left-arrow button at the top of the screen to return to the list of topics.

Help Menu

iMovie doesn't come with a manual—if it did, you wouldn't need this book. Instead, you're expected to learn its functions from the online help, whose commands are filed in this menu.

Help Center

The Help Center is nothing more than a list of all of the online help files that have been installed onto your Macintosh, as shown in Figure A-2. From here, you can click iMovie Help, if you like, but it's more direct to choose Help→iMovie Help to begin with.

Show Balloons

When you use this command, small cartoon balloons sprout from your cursor as you point to various objects on the iMovie screen. Each balloon tells you the button or window's name and provides a very short description. This feature—called Balloon Help—is a great way to learn what Apple has named the various gizmos on the iMovie screen.

To turn off Balloon Help, choose Help→Hide Balloons.

iMovie Tutorial

Many of the world's iMovie fans first learn how to use iMovie by taking this tutorial, which pops up in its own special Help window. (The downloaded version of iMovie 2 doesn't come with the tutorial; in that case, you don't have this command, either.) By switching back and forth between the tutorial window and iMovie itself, you can read about, and then perform, the steps necessary to put together a short movie about kids washing a dog.

iMovie Help

Choose this command to open the Macintosh Help window, where you'll see a list of iMovie help topics. You can use this Help program in either of two ways:

- Keep clicking blue underlined links, burrowing closer and closer to the help topic you want. You can backtrack by clicking the left arrow button at the top of the window, exactly as in a Web browser.

- Type a search phrase into the top window, such as *importing pictures,* and then click Search (or press Return), as shown in Figure A-2.

Either way, you'll probably find that the iMovie online help offers a helpful summary of the program's functions, but doesn't offer much in the way of "what it's for" information.

Troubleshooting iMovie 2

On the great spectrum of software complexity, iMovie falls pretty far to the left end, closer to SimpleText than to Microsoft Excel. It's a fairly small, fairly streamlined application that almost never crashes and only rarely leaves you scratching your head.

Chances are good, in fact, that any problems you encounter are related to FireWire, the computer itself, or your camcorder, not the iMovie software. Nonetheless, this appendix offers as complete a catalog of iMovie problems—and solutions—as has ever been assembled.

Tip: You'll note that the answer to many of these problems is, "Download the update." Apple has been quick to release new, updated versions of iMovie and its related extensions, with each update solving a wide range of problems. Therefore, before calling Apple's technical support hotline, or even before reading this appendix, consider visiting *www.apple.com/imovie* to download the very latest iMovie updater, QuickTime software, and FireWire extensions.

How iMovie Likes It

Processing video requires an enormous amount of computer concentration and effort. Years from now, we'll chuckle at the steps we had to take to give iMovie all the memory, disk space, and computing horsepower it requires. For now, however, here's what iMovie likes for smoothest operation:

• Don't run any other programs while you're working in iMovie.

• Don't change your monitor or sound settings while you're running iMovie.

- Don't hook up any FireWire gadgets to your Mac at the same time as the camcorder. (Actually, this arrangement works fine for most people, but Apple still advises against it. If you're having trouble, consider leaving only your camcorder hooked up.)

- Don't try to save an iMovie project onto anything but a hard drive attached to your Mac. That means no other drives on a network, Zip or Jaz drives, Orb drives, floppies, or other gizmos.

- If your Mac has more than 64 MB of RAM installed, turn off virtual memory (see page 374). If it has 64 MB or less, leave virtual memory turned on, *or* create an iMovie-only extensions set, as described on page 372. (Running only the extensions that iMovie needs generally releases enough free memory that you can afford to turn virtual memory off.)

- Connect and turn on your camcorder *before* launching iMovie (if you plan to capture video). Doing so lets iMovie identify what kind of camcorder it is—either NTSC (North American video) format or PAL (European video) format—and adjust its own settings accordingly.

Once you and the software are both comfortable, read on.

Starting Up and Capturing Video

Unfortunately for the eager beginner, one of the most frequent trouble spots of the iMovie experience comes right at the beginning, when you first try to launch the program and capture video from the camcorder.

"Navigation Services not installed"

The "Navigation Services not installed" error message is actually more descriptive than you might think: It appears if you've turned off the extension called Navigation Services. You may have done so using Extensions Manager (described on page 370). On the other hand, perhaps a piece of software, such as the popular shareware program Default Folder, disabled Navigation Services *for* you.

In any case, see the upcoming sidebar called "Restoring Specialized System Folder Items."

"Sound Lib not found"

The complete wording of this strange message appears in Figure B-1 at top. Once again, you or somebody you love has been playing hide-and-seek with important elements of your System Folder. In this case, someone has moved or deleted your Sound Manager extension.

See the "Restoring Specialized System Folder Items" sidebar for reinstallation instructions.

"Could not find the project"

Whenever you launch iMovie by double-clicking its icon, the program automatically reopens whatever project you are most recently working on. (How does it know? It stores the name of the project in a secret preferences file, as described at the end of this appendix.)

But if you move, rename, or delete that project, iMovie doesn't know what to open the next time you launch it. It throws its hands up and displays the message shown in Figure B-1, bottom.

Tip: iMovie is smart enough to notice (and not crash) if you delete the project you're actively working on *while you're still editing it in iMovie.* Why doesn't all software work like that?

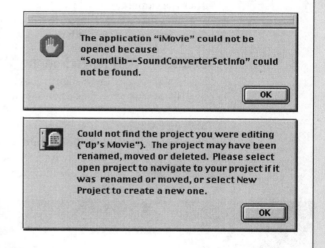

Figure B-1:
Top: When Apple made iMovie freely available on its Web site to all Mac users, all kinds of new glitches began to emerge, for the simple reason that the full range of Mac models offered a less controlled environment for iMovie to deal with than just the iMac DV. If your Mac is missing the Sound Manager extension, for example, you get the message shown at top.

Bottom: This is what happens if you move or rename a project behind iMovie's back.

Camcorder Control OK, but No Picture

Sometimes you can control the camera (make it rewind, stop, and so on) by clicking the buttons under the iMovie Monitor window, and yet no video picture appears on your Mac's screen. If this sounds familiar, unplug and reconnect the FireWire cable from the Mac. The video picture should return.

"Camera not connected"

If you get this message in the Monitor window when you click the Camera button, it probably means that:

• Your camcorder isn't plugged into the Mac with a FireWire cable.

• The camcorder isn't turned on.

- You're using a JVC camcorder or another one whose FireWire circuitry isn't completely compatible with the Macintosh.

- You haven't installed the latest FireWire software (version 2.5 or later), which is available from *http://asu.info.apple.com.*

- At some point, you installed EditDV, the professional DV editing program described in Chapter 15. The EditDV installer turns off the QuickTime FireWire extension, which prevents iMovie from working. Reinstate the QuickTime FireWire extension using Extensions Manager, as described in the sidebar box below.

If you get the "Camera not connected" message the very first time you try to connect a new camcorder to your Mac, and you've checked to make sure that the cable is connected properly and the camera is turned on, then you probably need to replace either the camera or the FireWire cable. (The occasional iMovie owner has become frustrated that a new camcorder doesn't work, but upon exchanging it for another of the same model, finds that it works beautifully.)

The Picture Isn't Perfect on the Mac

Slower Macs may show a slightly jerky or blurry picture in the Monitor window. See page 102 for more on this phenomenon and its simple solutions.

"Storage device is too slow"

The message is talking about your hard drive, and it's probably lying. Your hard drive is most likely perfectly fine; the software that controls it is the problem. This message generally appears only when the hard drive to which you're saving your

---

UP TO SPEED

Restoring Specialized System Folder Items

As you can read in this chapter, several intriguing error messages may appear if you've turned off or discarded certain System Folder elements that iMovie requires.

To restore them, start by choosing →Control Panels→Extensions Manager. As shown in Figure B-4, you get a list of every component of your Extensions and Control Panels folders. If the list contains the element that iMovie is complaining about, such as the Navigation Services extension or the Sound Manager extension, turn it back on and then click Restart.

If you *don't* see these items in the Extensions Manager window, choose File→Quit. Somebody has *thrown away* these important extensions, and it's your job to reinstall them.

Doing so requires the System Install CD-ROM that came with your Mac. Insert that disk into your CD-ROM drive. In the CD window that appears, double-click the Installer, which is usually the front-and-center icon in the CD's window.

On successive screens, click Continue; Select; Add/Remove. Finally, click the "flippy triangles" until you see the component you need. For example, you can find the Control Strip checkbox under the Control Panels heading.

Turn on the checkbox of the item you're missing, and then click OK. After the installation, your Mac restarts, and all is well.

---

movie data isn't an Apple hard drive. In that case, contact the manufacturer of the hard drive to request an updated set of driver software. (It's usually available at the hard-drive company's Web page.)

The message is talking about your hard drive. Some hard drives really aren't fast enough to handle digital video; technically speaking, they need a sustained throughput of at least 3.6 MB/second. Some drives, particularly those that are almost full or highly fragmented, can deliver data this fast, but not continuously without lagging. In either case, you'll see this message. (See page 368 for more on defragmenting.)

Some drivers, particularly FireWire drives, were shipped before anyone tried to use them with DV; if you see this message, it's always a good idea to contact the manufacturer of the hard drive to request an updated set of driver software. (It's usually available at the hard-drive company's Web page.)

Can't Pause when Scanning

This particular glitch is a quirk of some pre-2000 Canon DV camcorders. The symptom: When you're fast-forwarding or rewinding, clicking the Pause button under the iMovie Monitor window fails to stop the camcorder.

The solution is to click the Stop button instead.

Dropouts in the Video

A *dropout* is a glitch in the picture, as shown in Figure B-2. Dropouts are fairly rare in DV video; if you get one, it's probably in one of these three circumstances:

- You're using a very old cassette. Remember that even DV cassettes don't last forever. You may begin to see dropouts after re-recording the tape 50 times or so.

- You're playing back a cassette that was recorded in LP (long play) mode. If the cassette was recorded on a different camcorder, dropouts are especially likely.

- It's time to clean the heads on your camcorder—the electrical components that actually make contact with the tape and, over time, can become dirty. Your local electronics store sells head-cleaning kits just for this purpose. Whatever you do, clean the heads gently.

If you can spot the glitch at the same moment on the tape every time you play it, then the problem is on the tape itself. If it's there during one playback, but gone during the next, the problem more likely lies with the heads in your camcorder.

Tip: Different DV tape manufacturers use different lubricants on their tapes. As a result, mixing tapes from different manufacturers on the same camcorder can increase the likelihood of head clogs. It's a good idea, therefore, to stick with tapes from one manufacturer (Sony, Panasonic, or Maxell, for example) when possible.

Billions of Dropouts

If you're getting not just one dropout here and there, but a veritable snowfall (see Figure B-2), something more serious is at work. The likely problem is that the hard drive you're using to capture the footage is just not fast enough. A bad cable or out-of-date QuickTime and FireWire driver software could be to blame, too. Check Apple's Web pages or Internet help groups for suggestions about compatible systems and likely solutions.

Tearing

Dropouts

Figure B-2:
DV dropouts are always square or rectangular. They may be a blotch of the wrong color, or may be multicolored. They may appear every time you play a particular scene, or may appear at random. In severe circumstances, you may get lots of them, such as when you try to capture to a FireWire hard drive. Such a configuration may also cause tearing of the video picture, also shown here.

POWER USERS' CLINIC

Defragmenting the Hard Drive

If you seem to be experiencing a lot of audio or video dropouts, and it doesn't seem to be specific to your camcorder or a particular tape, it's remotely possible that the cause lies elsewhere. In a few rare cases, dropouts result because your hard drive needs to be *defragmented.*

If your hard drive is extremely full, the Mac is forced to chop up newly saved files into pieces that can fit into any little empty spaces it can find on the hard drive. The Mac keeps perfect track of the locations of these pieces, and reconstitutes them automatically when you try to open a file that's been segmented.

But when your Mac is recording digital video from the camcorder, it doesn't have a lot of time to hunt around for free space on your hard drive. Every fraction of a second counts. When you record video from your camcorder onto a nearly full hard drive, dropouts occur as the Mac struggles to search the drive for free storage space.

There are two ways to *defragment* a hard drive—that is, to reassemble all files that have been split apart, and to collect all the free space on the hard drive into one giant chunk. First, you can back up your entire hard drive, erase it (using the Drive Setup program that came with your Mac), and then copy all your files back onto it—a tedious but extremely inexpensive procedure. Second, you can use a software defragmenter, such as the one included with Norton Utilities *(www.symantec.com).*

Banding

Banding in the video picture is a relative of dropouts, but much less common. Once again, it may stem from dirt on either the tape itself or the heads in your camcorder. Most of the time, banding results when the tape was jammed or crinkled on an earlier journey through your camcorder. Now, as the tape plays, your camcorder heads encounter a creased portion of the tape, and then, until they can find any clean information to display, fill the screen with whatever the last usable video information was.

If the problem is with the tape itself, the banding disappears as soon as clean, smooth tape comes into contact with the playback heads. If you get banding when playing different cassettes, however, it's time to clean the heads of your camcorder.

Weird Font-Cropping Glitches

If the font iMovie uses for its clip names and timecodes doesn't look right (for example, the labels get chopped off), you probably have Microsoft Office, whose Curlz MT font conflicts with iMovie 2's font. To solve the proble, open your System Folde→Fonts folder and remove the Curlz icon, then restart iMovie.

Problems Editing Video

All right then: You've made it past the importing stage. You've successfully connected your camcorder, dumped the footage into the iMovie, settled back in your chair, comfortable and happy—and *then* the trouble begins.

The Frame Counter Is Off by One

When the Playhead is all the way to the right end of the Scrubber bar, you may think that it's misinforming you about the length of the selected clip. That is, the clip on the Shelf may indicate that the clip is 26:17 long (26 seconds, 17 frames), but the counter above the Playhead handle says 26:16.

Actually, there's no discrepancy at all. The Playhead identifies the "time code" of the frame it's on. When the Playhead is at the very beginning of the clip (frame 1, that is), its counter says 00:00. When it's at the beginning of frame 2, it says 00:01. And so on.

The "time code" displayed in the corner of a clip, on the other hand, measures the total *duration* of the clip—as measured to the *end* of the last frame, not the beginning of it.

Note: You'll probably notice this discrepancy only when examining clips in the Shelf. If you select a clip in the Movie Track instead, the Playhead time code identifies its place in the *entire* movie, not just in the clip itself, making this one-frame "difference" much less noticeable.

"No memory left"

If you're unlucky enough to see the "No memory left to finish this application" message, three things are probably true. First, you're probably trying to apply a transition or title to a movie with a very large number of clips in it, or a very large number of transitions and titles. Second, iMovie won't let you add another clip or transition—even after quitting the program or restarting the Mac. Third, you've probably never before entered the wild world of iMovie and memory.

When first installed, iMovie 2 is set to use 28.5 MB of RAM when launched. That may sound like a lot. But in the scheme of video and graphics software, that's peanuts. You should feel duly grateful that iMovie can do so much with so little memory.

It can't, however, do *everything* in that amount. As you've discovered, getting especially ambitious with the number of clips, titles, or transitions quickly exhausts the 28.5 MB that the Mac has set aside for iMovie.

Here's how to give iMovie more breathing room:

1. **Quit iMovie.**

   You can change a program's memory allotment only when it's not running.

2. **Open the iMovie folder on your hard drive. Highlight (click once) the iMovie icon inside that folder (Figure B-3).**

   This step frequently confuses beginners. The following steps won't work if you highlight the iMovie *folder*. They also won't work if you highlight an *alias* of the iMovie program—a duplicate of the icon, identifiable by its italicized file name.

3. **Choose File→Get Info→Memory.**

   The iMovie Info window appears, as shown in Figure B-3.

4. **Increase the number in the Preferred Size box by 10 MB or more, for example (if your Mac has it to spare).**

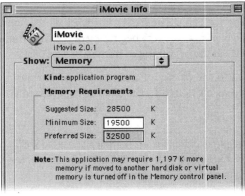

Figure B-3:
Highlight the iMovie application icon (left), not the alias, and not the folder. When you choose File→Get Info →Memory, you'll be shown three number boxes, two of which you can edit. iMovie may say that it "prefers" 28,500 K of memory, but it's just being modest. Lay it on thick; give it 35,000 or 40,000 K if your Mac has RAM to spare.

If your Mac has 128 MB of RAM, for example, then giving iMovie 40 MB wouldn't be out of line. It would certainly reduce the number of memory messages.

5. **Close the window.**

Using Extensions Manager to Maximize Memory

The previous steps are all well and good on a well-endowed Mac, one that's been blessed with a lot of RAM. If it has only 64 MB of RAM (the minimum for iMovie), however, more drastic steps may sometimes be required.

For example, if you were wondering how iMovie could possibly be running out of memory on a 64 MB machine even when you've allotted 30 MB to it, you wouldn't be the first. As it turns out, however, memory goes fast on the modern Macintosh. For example, Mac OS 9 itself scarfs down 20, 30, or even more MB for its own use the moment you turn on the computer. That leaves only half of your 64 MB for use by iMovie. Furthermore, any programs that are running at the same time as iMovie wolf down chunks of whatever memory is left.

Tip: Want to see where all your memory is going and how much your System software is using for itself? In the Finder, choose ****→About This Computer. The resulting graph shows you how much RAM each open program is using.

To give iMovie the benefit of whatever memory your Mac has, consider creating a special *extensions set* that you'll use when video editing. *Extensions,* the chunks of specialized software code whose icons parade across the bottom of your screen each time you turn on the computer, are responsible for consuming many megabytes of the memory that your System software seems to be hogging for itself. (They're also usually responsible for the very few iMovie software glitches you may encounter, like those described at the beginning of this appendix.) By turning off as many as possible, you can return a great deal of your Mac's memory to the pool from which iMovie drinks. You also make your Mac even more stable.

Here's how it works:

1. **Choose →Control Panels→Extensions Manager.**

   The Extension Manager program is the one that lets you turn your extensions on or off, as shown in Figure B-4.

2. **Note the name of the current set of extensions.**

   It's probably "My Settings," as identified by the Selected Set pop-up menu.

3. **Click Duplicate Set.**

   The "Name duplicate set" dialog box appears.

4. **Type a name for your new set of extensions (such as *iMovie Set),* and then click OK.**

Now "iMovie Set" appears at the top of the screen. Any changes you make now to the on/off status of your extensions will affect only this set.

5. **Choose Edit→All Off.**

The checkmarks disappear from all of the extensions and control panels listed. This shortcut saves you from having to click 95 times to turn off all of these extensions individually. You'll now turn *back on* only the handful that iMovie itself needs.

6. **In the Control Panels section, click the checkboxes to turn on Memory and QuickTime Settings. In the Extensions list, turn on anything containing the words** *ATI, Control Strip, QuickTime* **(but not** *QuickTime 3-D), FireWire,* **and** *Sound Manager.*

These are the System Folder items iMovie requires. You'll probably find seven QuickTime extensions, three FireWire ones, and five ATI drivers (for the standard Apple monitor).

Also turn on any extensions or control panels that you'll need when editing video. For example, if your keyboard or mouse requires special driver software (as the Microsoft IntelliMouse does), turn it on, too.

7. **Click Restart at the bottom of the window.**

The computer starts up again. You should notice immediately that the Mac starts up much faster than it did before. Once it "comes to," you'll also discover that it has a lot more free memory available (choose →About This Computer to see the result).

Finally, you'll discover that you can't do very much with your Mac. You can't connect to the Internet, hook up to the network, or scan; you may not even be

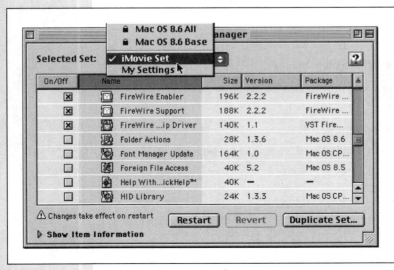

Figure B-4:
If you create a specialized set of extensions for iMovie, you gain several benefits, including the immediate disappearance of strange glitches caused by non-Apple software, along with better Mac stability and more available memory. You can open this window either by choosing →Control Panels→ Extensions Manager or by pressing the Space bar while the computer is starting up.

able to print. That's OK. The purpose of this exercise is to provide the ultimate *video editing* environment, and that's all. All those extra features got turned off when you turned off the corresponding extensions.

At this point, you may be able to give iMovie itself a larger memory allotment, as described in the previous section. You've stripped down your system software's own memory consumption by an enormous amount, making a lot more free for iMovie.

Note: After you're finished using iMovie, restoring your original, fully functional extensions set is easy. Restart the computer. As it's beginning to restart, press the Space bar continuously until the Extensions Manager window appears again. Choose My Settings (or whatever it said in step 2) from the Selected Set pop-up menu, and then click Continue. Your Mac continues to start up, this time with all its faculties intact.

In fact, this Space-bar-at-startup business will be useful from now on for switching both *from* your iMovie set and *to* it. Each time you start up the Mac, choose the corresponding set name from the Selected Set pop-up menu, and then click Continue.

Problems with Sound

Sound problems are especially frustrating when you're working with digital video, because they bear no resemblance to sound problems with more familiar equipment. In any other situation, if sound is too low or too loud, for example, you can adjust it with a knob. But what you do about random electronic beeps and buzzes that weren't there on the original tape?

Sound Is Too Soft

If the narration soundtrack or one particular clip is too soft, see page 209.

If, however, the entire movie soundtrack plays back too quietly, it's probable that iMovie has nothing to do with the problem. Instead, your overall Mac volume is probably too low. See Figure B-5 for the steps to the solution.

Random Electronic Beeps

When you transfer video from your camcorder into iMovie and then play the result on the screen, you may get the most frustrating of syndromes: random, high, loud, very short electronic-sounding beeps that weren't there in the original footage.

Just as there are video dropouts, as described in the beginning of this chapter, cheap tapes may sometimes give you *audio* dropouts. The problem is exactly the same: a tiny bit of dirt or a nonmagnetized particle on the tape. But this time, however, it affects the audio, not the video.

Unfortunately, there aren't any easy fixes for this problem. You'll never be able to recover the audio that would have been recorded during those fractions of a second. If the footage is extremely important, you can use Chapter 8 as your guide to replacing those beeps with short bursts of silence, following a procedure like this:

1. **Export your project as a QuickTime movie. Open it in QuickTime Player. Delete the video track and export the result as an AIFF file.**

   Chapter 8 contains instructions for performing similar maneuvers.

2. **Using a program like SndSampler, eliminate the beeps.**

   You can find this excellent sound-editing shareware program at *www. missingmanual.com,* among other places. It lets you highlight the specific sound waves that represent the beeps and change their volume, or replace them with pieces of sound you've copied from neighboring moments in the soundtrack.

3. **Export the result as an AIFF file, which you then reimport into your iMovie project. Once it has appeared on the Music Track, you can turn off the existing Camcorder audio track.**

   This procedure, too, appears at the end of Chapter 8.

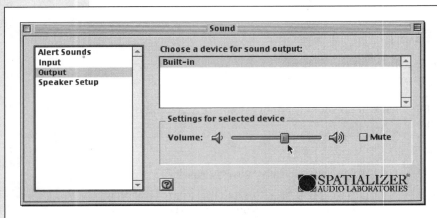

Figure B-5:
If you have Mac OS 9 or later, choose *→Control Panels→Sound. If you have Mac OS 8.6, choose* *→ Control Panels→ Monitors & Sound. Either way, click Output. Make sure that you've adjusted the volume slider to your eardrums' taste, especially if you find the iMovie overall volume too low.*

Distortion during Loud Parts

It's hard to imagine anything more frustrating than this: As you're listening to a clip in iMovie, or exporting footage to QuickTime or the camcorder, the sound turns into an electronic buzzing or crackling every time it reaches a certain volume.

Clearly, this problem has been on many minds, and its victims have come up with various solutions. Fortunately, almost everyone manages to solve it eventually by following one of these steps:

Turn off virtual memory

For many iMovie fans, turning off the Mac's *virtual memory* feature is an instant fix for the sound-buzzing problem. To do so, choose →Control Panels→Memory. Click the Virtual Memory Off button, close the window, and then restart the Mac.

Turning off virtual memory has a number of memory-related side effects. For example, you can't open as many programs simultaneously as you can when virtual memory is turned on. Furthermore, every program you run requires between 5 and 15 percent *more* memory than it did before. (iMovie itself, for example, requires about one megabyte more when virtual memory is turned off.)

Finally, if you have a Mac with "only" 64 MB of memory—an amount that only recently would have been considered an extremely generous amount—turning off virtual memory may make iMovie complain that not enough memory is available. To solve the problem, without causing the return of distortion, see "No memory left," earlier in this appendix.

Turn off your Mac's soundtrack

Having a Macintosh "soundtrack" turned on can also interfere with iMovie's soundtrack performance.

To see if you have one turned on, choose ⌘→Control Panels→Appearance. Click the Sound tab. Make sure that the "Sound track" pop-up menu says None. Then close the window.

Turning off audio filtering

If turning off virtual memory doesn't solve the buzzing problem, consider turning off the Audio Filtering feature of iMovie 2.

To do so, choose Edit→Preferences. Click the Advanced tab, and then turn off Filter Audio from Camera. Click OK.

You should find that any remaining sound-buzzing problems have disappeared. (Unfortunately, the buzzing may have been permanently embedded into the captured footage at this point. Turning off the iMovie audio filter affects only footage you capture from now on.)

Audio Dropouts when Exporting to Tape

If upon playing a movie you've exported back to tape (Chapter 11), you discover audio dropouts (such as random electronic beeps or other distortion), lower the volume of the clips in question (see page 209). When you export the movie back to the camcorder, you may find that the problem has disappeared.

Problems Exporting to Tape

Now suppose that you're able to capture the video successfully, and even edit it into a masterful work of video. The big moment arrives: You're ready to play the movie back onto the tape, so that you can then play it on a TV for friends and venture capitalists. Here are a few things that can go wrong.

You Live in Europe

If you bought your DV camcorder in Europe, it has probably been, as the Internet punsters say, "nEUtered." That is, it's been electronically rigged so that it *can't* record video from a FireWire cable.

Your PAL-format camcorder isn't broken. In fact, it's simply the victim of a European law, enacted under pressure from the motion-picture industry, that any camcorder that can accept a video input signal is, technically speaking, a video *recorder,* not a camera. Video recorders are subject to a huge additional tax. Camcorder manufacturers, in an attempt to keep their consumer product line inexpensive, responded by taking out the digital-input feature from the built-in software of *inexpensive* DV and Digital8 camcorders. (More expensive DV camcorders don't have this problem.)

If you're clever with electronics, you can surf the Web in a quest for black-market Web sites that explain how to *dis*-disable FireWire recording—a simple procedure involving a technician's remote-control unit. Video-repair shops in many European cities will perform this task for a small fee, too (but don't expect to see ads for this service). Otherwise, you have no choice but to limit your iMovie productions to QuickTime movies (instead of videotape), or to upgrade to a more expensive camcorder.

"Check DV input"

This particular glitch is limited to certain Panasonic and Sharp camcorders. When you try to export your iMovie project back to the camcorder, you get the "Check DV Input" message on the camcorder's LCD panel. The camcorder never actually records anything.

If it happens to you, stop the camcorder and cancel the iMovie export process. Try exporting to tape again, but this time, increase the amount of time in the "Wait __ Seconds for camera to get ready" blank of the Export Movie dialog box.

This time, before you export to the camcorder, watch its LCD panel. As soon as you see the blackness appear, as transmitted by iMovie, press the Still button on the VCR controls. This time, the camera begins recording.

Chopped-off Edges when Playing Back from Tape

The actual dimensions of a TV picture aren't what you'd expect. To avoid the risk that some oddball TV model might display a sliver of black empty space at a corner or edge of the glass, all NTSC television signals are *overscanned*—deliberately transmitted at a size *larger* than the TV screen. Sure, that means that the outer 5 percent of the picture at each edge doesn't even show up on your TV, because it's beyond the glass borders. But TV directors are aware of this phenomenon, and carefully avoid shooting anything that might get chopped off by the overscanning.

Unfortunately, iMovie has one foot in the world of video, and the other in the QuickTime world, where no overscanning is necessary. QuickTime movies always show *everything* in the picture, perfectly and precisely—nothing is ever lost beyond the borders of a QuickTime window. That's why some footage that looks spectacular and perfect in iMovie, or in an exported QuickTime movie, gets chopped off around the edges when viewed on a TV.

(This phenomenon explains the "QT Margins" checkbox in iMovie 2, described on page 174.)

Other "Can't export" Problems

This kind of problem could be anything. Maybe the exporting process cancels itself after only a few seconds. Or you can't export at all, even after reading the preceding sections.

In cases like these, Apple's latest FireWire software (version 2.5 or later) may solve the problem. Each release of the software (a set of extensions) makes camcorders and FireWire hard drives work better with your Mac.

To download this free software, visit *http://asu.info.apple.com* and search for *FireWire*. In the resulting list, download the FireWire software bearing the highest number.

The Secret Preferences Document

It's there, inside your System Folder→Preferences folder at this very minute: a secret icon called iMovie Preferences. It's nestled among the preference files of all the other programs on your Mac. But iMovie Preferences is not a normal preferences file. For example, if you move this file onto the desktop, and then drop it onto the System Folder icon, the Mac *doesn't* propose putting it into the Preferences folder automatically, as it would for a normal preferences file. Clearly, there's something funny going on with this file.

The iMovie Preferences document is, in fact, a plain text file that stores all of the iMovie settings as plain-English parameters *that you can edit* with any word processor (see Figure B-6). You can actually make changes in this document to affect the way iMovie works.

The Two Preference Categories

The settings available in the iMovie Preferences file fall into one of two categories:

- **Settings that duplicate iMovie settings.** Many of the settings in the iMovie Preferences document simply *reflect* the changes you've made from within iMovie (by choosing Edit→Preferences, for example). All that you gain by changing them in the secret Preferences document is the thrill of doing something sneaky.

- **Settings that you can't otherwise change.** This is where the iMovie Preferences file gets exciting. It contains settings that add flexibility to iMovie and have *no* corresponding controls within the program itself.

Making Changes to the Preferences Document

To open the iMovie Preferences document, first open your System Folder, then open the Preferences folder, and then double-click iMovie Preferences. As shown in Figure B-6, the file opens.

Most of the parameters here display either a 1 or a 0. That's the on/off switch for each feature: 1 means on, 0 means off. After editing these numbers, close the window, saving the changes. The next time you launch iMovie, your new preference settings will be in effect.

Tip: A message at the top of the iMovie Preferences document tells you, "Do not edit this unless you know what you're doing." Actually, however, that warning overstates the case somewhat.

It's true that if you plug random values into the settings, you might *confuse* iMovie. Under most circumstances, however, doing so can't *damage* iMovie or your video projects. (The exceptions are noted in the following pages.) If iMovie becomes confused by a change you've made in the iMovie Preferences file, no big deal; just throw the iMovie Preferences file away. The very next time you open iMovie, it will create a brand-new, perfect, untouched Preferences file in the same location.

Secret iMovie Preferences: a Catalog

Here's a line-by-line description of the items in the iMovie Preferences document.

- **PrefsFile Version.** This number tells iMovie the version of the Preferences file itself. This helps it decide when you have an old (or new) Preferences file that is incompatible with the currently running version of iMovie.

- **Volume.** This number identifies the hard drive upon which iMovie sits, using your Mac's internal reference number. Don't change this number.

- **Project.** When you open iMovie by double-clicking its icon, the program always opens whatever project you've most recently had open. And how does it remember? Simple—it takes notes. It records the name of the most recently used project on this line. (Don't change this entry.)

- **VideoStandard.** This parameter tells iMovie which kind of camcorder you've been using—the American (NTSC) format or the European (PAL) format.

  The video format affects numerous other iMovie parameters. For example, the PAL format shows 25 frames per second, not 30, so all of the counters and time codes in iMovie change to reflect this new counting system. A clip that's 1:15 long in the United States is 1:12 long in England. (It's 1.5 seconds long either way).

- **Option autoSceneDetect.** This line stores your preference for the "Automatically start new clip at scene break" setting (see page 105).

- **Option captureIntoMovie.** This line, too, reflects a setting you've made in the Edit→Preferences dialog box. The number 0 means that newly captured clips appear in the Shelf; 1 means that iMovie will put them directly into the Movie Track instead.

- **Option lowQualityPlayback.** Here's yet another preference setting that's reflected in the Edit→Preferences dialog box. The 0 refers to the Better Image setting; the 1 represents the Smoother Motion setting. (If your Mac is fast enough, as described on page 102, iMovie 2 ignores this setting.)

- **Option drawTimeCodesOnThumbs.** You can't make this setting at all from within iMovie—this is one of those delicious functions available *only* in the Preferences document. When this setting is 1, each clip on the Shelf or Movie Track displays a little time code stamp in the upper-left corner, which identifies its length. If you set this parameter to 0, that time-code stamp disappears, giving iMovie a cleaner look (but leaving you without any clue as to the durations of your clips).

- **Option drawPlayHeadOnThumbs.** Here's another Preference-file exclusive. When this setting is 0, the red inverted T cursor doesn't slide along the faces of the clips in the Movie Track during playback, as it does when this setting is 1. (You can see this cursor illustrated on page 138.)

- **Option filterAudio.** This option reflects the status of another Preferences setting—the one called Filter Audio from Camera.

- **Option swampThingSlowAudio.** This option does nothing. Like the Swamp Thing itself, it's vestigial.

The story: Before iMovie 2 shipped, it had a hidden preference setting that let you specify how you wanted the audio portion of slowed-down clips to play:

Figure B-6:
Some of the secret preferences are useful indeed; others are useless; a few are vestigial in iMovie 2. The important thing is to know that they are there, and how to change them when it serves your purpose to do so. Needless to say, the online iMovie help makes no reference to the existence of the secret SimpleText file. (Actually, this notion of an editable preference file isn't a bad idea. In fact, more software companies should adopt it.)

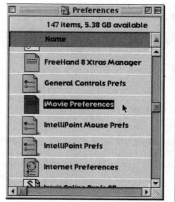
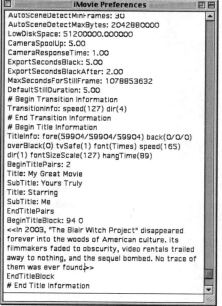

either low, gurgly, and pitch-shifted (which sounded like, yes, the Swamp Thing) or at original pitch, but drawn out (as in the final iMovie 2). Nobody at Apple liked the Swamp Thing audio, so the programmers disabled this preference; they left in the secret Preferences file just to confuse you.

- **Option singleFieldRender.** This option turns on/off the interlacing of video frames during playback (alternating sets of horizontal scan lines). There isn't much practical use for it, since you can't see the interlacing on the computer anyway.

- **Option multiTaskDuringCapture.** As you may have noticed, when you're capturing video from your camcorder, your Mac becomes remarkably single-minded. While the capturing is going on, it doesn't let you switch into any other program, or even do other work in iMovie. Instead, iMovie devotes all of its energies—and all the Mac's energies—to the video-capture process. That's the way it is when this parameter is set to 0.

Actually, however, iMovie 2 is perfectly capable of chugging along with your camcorder, importing away as you switch into some other program to get a little work done. If that other work is light—reading email or typing, for example—there's no downside to turning on iMovie's secret multitasking feature by setting this number to 1.

iMovie 2 comes with this option turned off, however, because if you do heavy work (Photoshop editing, say), you could conceivably experience dropouts in your capturing. (Even so, it's worth a moment of silence to thank iMovie's creators for the fact that you don't have to turn off AppleTalk, turn off Virtual Memory, and promise not to breathe when capturing video—a distinct improvement over its expensive rivals.)

- **Option multiTaskDuringPlayback.** This parameter is related to the previous item in that when it's set to 1, you're allowed to switch into other Mac programs while iMovie is playing your project back. It works fine on today's Mac models—but why would you want to play back your movie if you're not going to look at it?

- **Option multiTaskDuringExport.** Here's yet another variation of the same idea. If you set this option to 1, you can switch into other Mac programs to do other work while iMovie is exporting video back to your camcorder.

- **Option cameraPlaythrough, Option showThumbnailsInTimeline, Option useShortTimeCodes, Option showMoreDetails, Option smartPasteOver, Option showOnlySelectedAudioPins:** Not surprisingly, these items match up with the corresponding preference settings described on pages 358–360.

- **Remember dontConfirmSelectionMove.** If you try to move a clip that has a transition attached to it, iMovie warns you that it will have to eliminate the transition. If you turn on "Don't ask me again," the 0 in this Preference item turns into a 1, reminding iMovie not to bug you the next time the situation arises.

- **Remember dontShowManualCameraAlert.** If you have a converter box that lets you convert the signal to and from your analog camera (see page 113), iMovie 2 shows a warning box each time you hook it up. If you click "Don't ask me again" there, iMovie stores your answer here.

- **Remember dontAskAboutResolution.** When your monitor is set to 800 x 600 resolution, the very first time iMovie launches, a message appears on the screen that says, "iMovie prefers to run at a higher resolution." After that first run, however, iMovie no longer displays this message.

  If you set the "dontAskAboutResolution" parameter to 0, iMovie *forgets* that it has already shown you that message. The next time you run iMovie at 800 x 600 resolution, you'll get the message again.

- **Remember dontAskAboutReRender.** When you apply an effect, such as Brightness or Contrast, to a clip that you've already involved in a transition effect, an iMovie dialog box asks how you'd like to proceed. If you click OK, iMovie re-renders the transition so that it incorporates the effect you've applied. If you click Cancel, the transition stays as it was—and no effect is applied.

  And if you click "Don't Ask Again," the remaining option, iMovie changes this preference-document setting to 1, and doesn't bother asking permission to update the transition the next time the situation arises.

- **Remember timeLineAtLaunch.** Each time you launch iMovie, it remembers which panel of the Movie Track you were using—the Clip Viewer or the Timeline Viewer. If you were using the Timeline Viewer, this Preference setting says 1; if you were using the Clip Viewer, this setting says 0. (It's no use changing this setting, which *reflects* the current setting instead of *changing* it.)

- **AutoSceneDetectMinFrames.** As you may have read in Chapter 4, one of iMovie's neatest features is its ability, when capturing camcorder video, to create a new clip automatically each time a new shot begins on the tape. Below a certain shot length, however, this feature becomes more annoying than useful. For example, if iMovie were to create a new clip on your Shelf even for brief, blink-like, abandoned camcorder shots, your precious Shelf cubbyholes would quickly fill up.

  This number specifies the shortest clip the auto-detect feature is allowed to create. At 30 (frames), the factory setting, iMovie won't create a new clip unless it's longer than one second long.

- **AutoSceneDetectMaxBytes.** iMovie has a built-in clip limit: about 9½ minutes long, which corresponds to 2 GB of hard drive space. If you try to capture a clip longer than that, iMovie automatically ends the clip and begins a new one. The seam between the two clips is invisible upon playback.

  Unfortunately, you can't lift this limit simply by changing the number here; making iMovie take advantage of Mac OS 9's larger-than-2-GB-file-size limit involves a substantial programming effort. In fact, you can cause some serious problems within iMovie if you make this number higher than its default.

You can, however, *lower* this number, so that iMovie auto-creates clips that are *shorter* than 9½ minutes.

This number is expressed here in bytes, of which there are one billion per GB. To change the maximum clip limit to 1 GB (about four minutes per clip), the number here should be 1,073,741,824 (don't type the commas).

- **LowDiskSpace.** When you're about to run out of disk space while capturing video from the camcorder, iMovie displays a warning message. This statistic determines how low your free disk space should drop before the message appears. The proposed value is 51,200,000 bytes (50 MB, or about fifteen seconds of capturing). Change it to any other number of bytes you like.

- **CameraSpoolUp, ExportSecondsBlack, ExportSecondsAfterBlack.** These numbers, expressed in seconds, are the numbers iMovie proposes in its Export to Tape dialog box (see page 264). They correspond to the number of seconds iMovie waits for the camcorder electronics to prepare to record, and the number of seconds of blackness iMovie will record before and after the movie begins. (You're welcome to change these numbers here, of course, but you may find it simpler to change them in the dialog box itself. iMovie will remember the changes you make—by storing them in this preferences file—so that the same numbers will reappear the next time you export.)

- **MaxSecondsForStillFrame.** This parameter isn't used in iMovie 2.

- **DefaultStillDuration.** Here's another place where you can change the proposed duration for new still-image clips you import into, or create in, iMovie 2. (The easier place is the Preferences dialog box.)

- **#Begin Transition Information, #Begin Title Information.** These items aren't settings—they're headings that introduce the following items.

- **TransitionInfo: speed(0) dir(0).** These settings affect the default Speed and Direction settings for transitions, as described in Chapter 6.

- **TitleInfo.** These parameters, which govern the title feature described in Chapter 7, seem exciting enough. They appear to control the default font, speed, direction, TV-safe ("QT Margins"), speed and pause, background color, and foreground color settings of your title animations.

  However, iMovie sets many of them back to their factory-set values automatically (including Font). There are some exceptions, however. You may find it useful to edit the overBlack, tvSafe, speed, fontSizeScale and hangTime parameters; they set the defaults iMovie uses for the Over Black (0 or 1), QT Margins (1 or 0), Speed (on a scale of 0 to 255), font-size slider (0 to 255), and Pause (0 to 255) settings on the Title palette in iMovie.

- **BeginTitlePairs.** This number specifies how many slots you get for title/subtitle pairs, as described on page 171. Of course, it's easy enough to add or remove these slots right in iMovie; in fact, iMovie updates *this* number to reflect the number of pairs you've created in iMovie.

- **Title, Subtitle.** If "My Great Movie"... "Starring Me" isn't exactly your idea of terrific opening credits, you can change these iMovie proposals to anything you like. These lines of Preference-file information control the proposed title and subtitle for each of the title pairs (see page 171). (The number of pairs of text lines you see here corresponds to the BeginTitlePairs number described in the previous paragraph.)

  Of course, you can also make this change right in iMovie. Whatever you type *there* gets stored *here.*

- **BeginTitleBlock.** You don't gain much by changing these numbers. The first one simply counts how long your text block is (see the next paragraph), in characters. The second number has no effect; if you try to change it, iMovie resets it to 0 automatically.

- **<<paste or type a block>>.** The text here is the proposed text that you see when you select the Music Video or Scrolling Block title style (see the end of Chapter 7 for examples of these title styles). This parameter can actually be useful, if only because it's easier to word process in SimpleText (to prepare a long text block, for example) than in the tiny, scrollbar-less Title palette of iMovie itself.

Where to Get Help Online

You can get personal iMovie 2 help by calling Apple's help line at (800) 500-7078 for 90 days after you bought the program, or the Mac it came on. (Technically, you can call within the first 90 days of ownership, but the clock really doesn't start until your first call.) After 90 days, Apple is still delighted to help you over the phone—for $50 per call!

Beyond 90 days, however, consider consulting the Internet, which is filled with superb sources of fast, free technical help. Here are some of the best places to get your questions answered:

- **MacDV List.** This outstanding resource is a *mailing list,* which is like a public bulletin board, except that each message is emailed to everybody who has signed up for the list. To post a message yourself, you just email it to a central address. It's attended by both iMovie fans and Final Cut Pro users (see Chapter 15), but the group tolerates both beginner and advanced questions.

  You sign up for this free feature at *www.themacintoshguy.com.* Note that you can sign up either for the one-message-at-a-time membership, which sends about 20 messages a day to your email box, or for the Digest version, in which you get just one email each day containing all of the day's messages.

- **iMovie List.** Here's another mailing list, this one dedicated to iMovie and only iMovie. The level of technical discussion is much lower than the MacDV List—in other words, it's a perfect place to ask questions without embarrassing yourself. Sign up by visiting *www.egroups.com* and searching for *imovie*.

- **2-pop.com.** This Web site contains a lively and extremely informative iMovie discussion. There's nothing to the Web site. It's simply a list of questions from iMovie fans and replies from the Internet experts, but the information and enlightenment quotient is extremely high. And, of course, there's no charge. You can find it at *www.2-pop.com/cgi/boards/imovie/index.cgi*.

ON LOCATION

A Farewell Movie

My grandfather died three months short of his 107th birthday. He and I had been very close. So when my mom asked if I wanted to "do something" at the memorial service, I racked my brains. I wondered what I could do that would come close to expressing how great this guy was, how colorful his life had been, and how hilarious our times together had been, even during his final years.

For years, I've been unofficial family videographer, so I had a stack of videotapes from the last fifteen years of my grandfather's life. Nothing from before the invention of the camcorder, though.

So I got on the phone with my parents and my grandfather's friends from back home. They sent me all kinds of material. Mostly old photos, but a couple of movie reels.

I filmed the photos with the DV camcorder, transferred the older tapes into DV format via the analog inputs of my Sony TRV-9, and had a local service bureau convert the old reels into video. I spent a three-day weekend putting together a 12-minute movie that told, and showed, some of the highlights of my grandfather's life.

Only the videotapes had audio, so I quickly decided that this would be mostly a music-and-narration project. My sister and I took turns reading a script I wrote into the Mac's microphone. I don't mind admitting that I was crying, on and off, as I put this thing together. It was therapy, like a final farewell to a guy who had a great influence on my life.

We played it on a big-screen TV at the reception after the memorial service. The movie ended with a long hold on my grandfather's favorite photo of himself: in his mid-twenties, grinning devilishly, looking like a movie star in his leather World War I aviator helmet. As the music ended, the photo faded out very slowly. Everyone just sat there for a couple of minutes, quiet, sniffly, and pretty moved.

I felt good about it—not about choking everyone up, but that I'd been able to show them just a tiny glimpse of my grandfather the way I knew him. I don't know a lot about filmmaking or anything, but it didn't matter. The emotions pretty much told me what to do.

—*David Raney*
New York

Index

Colophon

Due to an annoying and permanent wrist ailment, the author wrote this book by voice, using Dragon Naturally Speaking on a generic Windows PC. To avoid further contamination, the Microsoft Word files were then transferred as quickly as possible to a Power Mac G4, where they were edited, illustrated, and transmitted to the book's editors and technical reviewers.

The screen images in this book were captured by Ambrosia Software's Snapz Pro 2 (*www.ambrosiasw.com*); DV footage frames were grabbed from the iMovie Monitor window or using PhotoDV (*www.digitalorigin.com*); Adobe Photoshop 5.5 (*www.adobe.com*) and Macromedia Freehand (*www.macromedia.com*) were called in as required for touching them up.

The book was designed and laid out in Adobe PageMaker 6.5 on a Power Mac 8500 and Power Mac G3. The fonts used include Formata (as the sans-serif family) and Minion (as the serif body face). To provide the and ⌘ symbols, a custom font was created using Macromedia Fontographer. The index was created using EZ Index, a Mac-only shareware indexing program by John Holder, which is available at *www.northcoast.com/~jvholder*. The book was then generated as an Adobe Acrobat PDF file for proofreading, indexing, and final transmission to the printing plant.

More Titles from Pogue Press/O'Reilly

The Missing Manuals

Mac OS 9: The Missing Manual

By David Pogue
1st Edition March 2000
472 pages, ISBN 1-56592-857-1

Mac OS 9: The Missing Manual is a warm, witty, jargon-free guide to the Macintosh platform's latest system software. Written with enough patience for the novice and enough depth for the power user, the book includes the shortcuts, surprises, and design touches that make the Mac the most passionately championed computer in the world.

AppleWorks 6: The Missing Manual

Jim Elferdink & David Reynolds
1st First Edition May 2000
450 pages, ISBN 1-56592-858-X

AppleWorks 6: The Missing Manual guides readers through both the basics and the hidden talents of the new version of AppleWorks, placing special emphasis on Version 6's enhanced word processing, Internet, and presentation features. With over 250 illustrations, a 2,000-entry index, and a menu-by-menu explanation of every command, *AppleWorks 6: The Missing Manual* is as smoothly put together as AppleWorks itself.

Windows 2000 Pro: The Missing Manual

By Sharon Crawford
1st Edition November 2000
450 pages, ISBN 0-596-00010-3

In *Windows 2000 Pro: The Missing Manual*, bestselling Windows NT author Sharon Crawford provides the friendly, authoritative book that should have been in the box. It's the ideal (and desperately needed) user's guide for the world's most popular corporate operating system.

Windows Me: The Missing Manual

By David Pogue
1st Edition September 2000
423 pages, ISBN 0-596-00009-X

In *Windows Me: The Missing Manual*, author David Pogue provides the friendly, authoritative book that should have been in the box. It's the ideal user's guide for the world's most popular operating system.

POGUE PRESS™
O'REILLY®

TO ORDER: **800-998-9938** • **order@oreilly.com** • **http://www.oreilly.com/**
OUR PRODUCTS ARE AVAILABLE AT A BOOKSTORE OR SOFTWARE STORE NEAR YOU.
FOR INFORMATION: **800-998-9938** • **707-829-0515** • **info@oreilly.com**

How to stay in touch with O'Reilly

1. Visit Our Award-Winning Web Site

http://www.oreilly.com/

★ "Top 100 Sites on the Web" —*PC Magazine*
★ "Top 5% Web sites" —*Point Communications*
★ "3-Star site" —*The McKinley Group*

Our web site contains a library of comprehensive product information (including book excerpts and tables of contents), downloadable software, background articles, interviews with technology leaders, links to relevant sites, book cover art, and more. File us in your Bookmarks or Hotlist!

2. Join Our Email Mailing Lists

New Product Releases
To receive automatic email with brief descriptions of all new O'Reilly products as they are released, send email to:
ora-news-subscribe@lists.oreilly.com
Put the following information in the first line of your message (*not* in the Subject field):
subscribe ora-news

O'Reilly Events
If you'd also like us to send information about trade show events, special promotions, and other O'Reilly events, send email to:
ora-news-subscribe@lists.oreilly.com
Put the following information in the first line of your message (*not* in the Subject field):
subscribe ora-events

3. Get Examples from Our Books via FTP

There are two ways to access an archive of example files from our books:

Regular FTP
- ftp to:
  ftp.oreilly.com
  (login: anonymous
  password: your email address)
- Point your web browser to:
  ftp://ftp.oreilly.com/

FTPMAIL
- Send an email message to:
  ftpmail@online.oreilly.com
  (Write "help" in the message body)

4. Contact Us via Email

order@oreilly.com
To place a book or software order online. Good for North American and international customers.

subscriptions@oreilly.com
To place an order for any of our newsletters or periodicals.

books@oreilly.com
General questions about any of our books.

software@oreilly.com
For general questions and product information about our software. Check out O'Reilly Software Online at **http://software.oreilly.com/** for software and technical support information. Registered O'Reilly software users send your questions to: **website-support@oreilly.com**

cs@oreilly.com
For answers to problems regarding your order or our products.

booktech@oreilly.com
For book content technical questions or corrections.

proposals@oreilly.com
To submit new book or software proposals to our editors and product managers.

international@oreilly.com
For information about our international distributors or translation queries. For a list of our distributors outside of North America check out:
http://www.oreilly.com/distributors.html

5. Work with Us

Check out our website for current employment opportunites:
http://jobs.oreilly.com/

O'Reilly & Associates, Inc.
101 Morris Street, Sebastopol, CA 95472 USA
TEL   707-829-0515 or 800-998-9938
       (6am to 5pm PST)
FAX   707-829-0104

O'REILLY®

TO ORDER: **800-998-9938** • *order@oreilly.com* • *http://www.oreilly.com/*
OUR PRODUCTS ARE AVAILABLE AT A BOOKSTORE OR SOFTWARE STORE NEAR YOU.
FOR INFORMATION: **800-998-9938** • **707-829-0515** • *info@oreilly.com*

Titles from O'Reilly

PROGRAMMING

C++: The Core Language
Practical C++ Programming
Practical C Programming, 3rd Ed.
High Performance Computing, 2nd Ed.
Programming Embedded Systems in
  C and C++
Mastering Algorithms in C
Advanced C++ Techniques
POSIX 4: Programming for the Real
  World
POSIX Programmer's Guide
Power Programming with RPC
UNIX Systems Programming for
  SVR4
Pthreads Programming
CVS Pocket Reference
Advanced Oracle PL/SQL
Oracle PL/SQL Guide to Oracle8i
  Features
Oracle PL/SQL Programming, 2nd Ed.
Oracle Built-in Packages
Oracle PL/SQL Developer's
  Workbook
Oracle Web Applications
Oracle PL/SQL Language Pocket
  Reference
Oracle PL/SQL Built-ins Pocket
  Reference
Oracle SQL*Plus: The Definitive
  Guide
Oracle SQL*Plus Pocket Reference
Oracle Essentials
Oracle Database Administration
Oracle Internal Services
Oracle SAP
Guide to Writing DCE Applications
Understanding DCE
Visual Basic Shell Programming
VB/VBA in a Nutshell: The Language
Access Database Design &
  Programming, 2nd Ed.
Writing Word Macros
Applying RCS and SCCS
Checking C Programs with Lint
VB Controls in a Nutshell
Developing Asp Components, 2nd Ed.
Learning WML & WMLScript
Writing Excel Macros
Windows 32 API Programming with
  Visual Basic
ADO: The Definitive Guide

USING THE INTERNET

Internet in a Nutshell
Smileys
Managing Mailing Lists

SOFTWARE

WebSite Professional™ 2.0
Polyform™
WebBoard™ 4.0

WEB

Apache: The Definitive Guide,
  2nd Ed.
Apache Pocket Reference
ASP in a Nutshell, 2nd Ed.
Cascading Style Sheets
Designing Web Audio
Designing with JavaScript, 2nd Ed.
DocBook: The Definitive Guide
Dynamic HTML: The Definitive
  Reference
HTML Pocket Reference
Information Architecture for the
  WWW
JavaScript: The Definitive Guide,
  3rd Ed.
Java and XML
JavaScript Application Cookbook
JavaScript Pocket Reference
Practical Internet Groupware
PHP Pocket Reference
Programming Coldfusion
Photoshop for the Web, 2nd Ed.
Web Design in a Nutshell
Webmaster in a Nutshell, 2nd Ed.
Web Navigation: Designing the
  User Experience
Web Performance Tuning
Web Security & Commerce
Writing Apache Modules with
  Perl and C

UNIX

SCO UNIX in a Nutshell
Tcl/Tk in a Nutshell
The Unix CD Bookshelf, 2nd Ed.
UNIX in a Nutshell, System V Edition,
  3rd Ed.
Learning the Unix Operating System,
  4th Ed.
Learning vi, 6th Ed.
Learning the Korn Shell
Learning GNU Emacs, 2nd Ed.
Using csh & tcsh
Learning the bash Shell, 2nd Ed.
GNU Emacs Pocket Reference
Exploring Expect
TCL/TK Tools
TCL/TK in a Nutshell
Python Pocket Reference

USING WINDOWS

Windows Millenium: The Missing
  Manual
PC Hardware in a Nutshell
Optimizing Windows for Games,
  Graphics, and Multimedia
Outlook 2000 in a Nutshell
Word 2000 in a Nutshell
Excel 2000 in a Nutshell
Paint Shop Pro 7 in a Nutshell
Windows 2000 Pro: The Missing
  Manual

JAVA SERIES

Developing Java Beans
Creating Effective JavaHelp
Enterprise Java Beans, 2nd Ed.
Java Cryptography
Java Distributed Computing
Java Enterprise in a Nutshell
Java Examples in a Nutshell,
  2nd Ed.
Java Foundation Classes in a
  Nutshell
Java in a Nutshell, 3rd Ed.
Java Internationalization
Java I/O
Java Native Methods
Java Network Programming,
  2nd Ed.
Java Performance Tuning
Java Security
Java Servlet Programming
Java ServerPages
Java Threads, 2nd Ed.
Jini in a Nutshell
Learning Java

GRAPHICS & MULTIMEDIA

MP3: The Definitive Guide
Photoshop 6 in a Nutshell, 3rd Ed.
Director in a Nutshell
Lingo in a Nutshell
FrontPage 2000 in a Nutshell

X WINDOW

Vol. 1: Xlib Programming Manual
Vol. 2: Xlib Reference Manual
Vol. 4M: X Toolkit Intrinsics
  Programming Manual, Motif Ed.
Vol. 5: X Toolkit Intrinsics Reference
  Manual
Vol. 6A: Motif Programming Manual
Vol. 6B: Motif Reference Manual, 2nd
  Ed.

PERL

Advanced Perl Programming
CGI Programming with Perl,
  2nd Ed.
Learning Perl, 2nd Ed.
Learning Perl for Win32 Systems
Learning Perl/Tk
Mastering Algorithms with Perl
Mastering Regular Expressions
Perl Cookbook
Perl in a Nutshell
Programming Perl, 3rd Ed.
Perl CD Bookshelf
Perl Resource Kit — Win32 Ed.
Perl/TK Pocket Reference
Perl 5 Pocket Reference,
  3rd Ed.

MAC

AppleScript in a Nutshell
AppleWorks 6: The Missing Manual
Crossing Platforms
iMovie: The Missing Manual
Mac OS in a Nutshell
Mac OS 9: The Missing Manual
Photoshop Cookbook
REALbasic: The Definitive Guide

LINUX

Building Linux Clusters
Learning Debian GNU/Linux
Learning Red Hat Linux
Linux Device Drivers
Linux Network Administrator's
  Guide, 2nd Ed.
Running Linux, 3rd Ed.
Linux in a Nutshell, 3rd Ed.
Linux Multimedia Guide

SYSTEM ADMINISTRATION

Practical UNIX & Internet Security,
  2nd Ed.
Building Internet Firewalls, 2nd Ed.
PGP: Pretty Good Privacy
SSH, The Secure Shell: The
  Definitive Guide
DNS and Bind, 3rd Ed.
The Networking CD Bookshelf
Virtual Private Networks, 2nd Ed.
TCP/IP Network Administration,
  2nd Ed.
sendmail Desktop Reference
Managing Usenet
Using & Managing PPP
Managing IP Networks with Cisco
  Routers
Networking Personal Computers
  with TCP/IP
Unix Backup & Recovery
Essential System Administration,
  2nd Ed.
Perl for System Administration
Managing NFS and NIS
Volume 8: X Window System
  Administrator's Guide
Using Samba
Unix Power Tools, 2nd Ed.
DNS on Windows NT
Windows NT TCP/IP Network
  Administration
DHCP for Windows 2000
Essential Windows NT System
  Administration
Managing Windows NT Logons
Managing the Windows 2000
  Registry

OTHER TITLES

PalmPilot: The Ultimate Guide, 2nd Ed.
Palm Programming:
  The Developer's Guide

POGUE PRESS™
O'REILLY®

TO ORDER: **800-998-9938** • **order@oreilly.com** • **http://www.oreilly.com/**
OUR PRODUCTS ARE AVAILABLE AT A BOOKSTORE OR SOFTWARE STORE NEAR YOU.
FOR INFORMATION: **800-998-9938** • **707-829-0515** • **info@oreilly.com**

International Distributors

UK, EUROPE, MIDDLE EAST AND AFRICA (EXCEPT FRANCE, GERMANY, AUSTRIA, SWITZERLAND, LUXEMBOURG, AND LIECHTENSTEIN)

INQUIRIES
O'Reilly UK Limited
4 Castle Street
Farnham
Surrey, GU9 7HS
United Kingdom
Telephone: 44-1252-711776
Fax: 44-1252-734211
Email: information@oreilly.co.uk

ORDERS
Wiley Distribution Services Ltd.
1 Oldlands Way
Bognor Regis
West Sussex PO22 9SA
United Kingdom
Telephone: 44-1243-843294
UK Freephone: 0800-243207
Fax: 44-1243-843302 (Europe/EU orders)
or 44-1243-843274 (Middle East/Africa)
Email: cs-books@wiley.co.uk

FRANCE

INQUIRIES & ORDERS
Éditions O'Reilly
18 rue Séguier
75006 Paris, France
Tel: 33-1-40-51-52-30
Fax: 33-1-40-51-52-31
Email: france@oreilly.fr

GERMANY, SWITZERLAND, AUSTRIA, LUXEMBOURG, AND LIECHTENSTEIN

INQUIRIES & ORDERS
O'Reilly Verlag
Balthasarstr. 81
D-50670 Köln, Germany
Telephone: 49-221-973160-91
Fax: 49-221-973160-8
Email: anfragen@oreilly.de (inquiries)
Email: order@oreilly.de (orders)

CANADA (FRENCH LANGUAGE BOOKS)

Les Éditions Flammarion ltée
375, Avenue Laurier Ouest
Montréal (Québec) H2V 2K3
Tel: 00-1-514-277-8807
Fax: 00-1-514-278-2085
Email: info@flammarion.qc.ca

HONG KONG

City Discount Subscription Service, Ltd.
Unit A, 6th Floor, Yan's Tower
27 Wong Chuk Hang Road
Aberdeen, Hong Kong
Tel: 852-2580-3539
Fax: 852-2580-6463
Email: citydis@ppn.com.hk

KOREA

Hanbit Media, Inc.
Chungmu Bldg. 210
Yonnam-dong 568-33
Mapo-gu
Seoul, Korea
Tel: 822-325-0397
Fax: 822-325-9697
Email: hant93@chollian.dacom.co.kr

PHILIPPINES

Global Publishing
G/F Benavides Garden
1186 Benavides Street
Manila, Philippines
Tel: 632-254-8949/632-252-2582
Fax: 632-734-5060/632-252-2733
Email: globalp@pacific.net.ph

TAIWAN

O'Reilly Taiwan
1st Floor, No. 21, Lane 295
Section 1, Fu-Shing South Road
Taipei, 106 Taiwan
Tel: 886-2-27099669
Fax: 886-2-27038802
Email: mori@oreilly.com

INDIA

Shroff Publishers & Distributors Pvt. Ltd.
12, "Roseland", 2nd Floor
180, Waterfield Road, Bandra (West)
Mumbai 400 050
Tel: 91-22-641-1800/643-9910
Fax: 91-22-643-2422
Email: spd@vsnl.com

CHINA

O'Reilly Beijing
SIGMA Building, Suite B809
No. 49 Zhichun Road
Haidian District
Beijing, China PR 100080
Tel: 86-10-8809-7475
Fax: 86-10-8809-7463
Email: beijing@oreilly.com

JAPAN

O'Reilly Japan, Inc.
Yotsuya Y's Building
7 Banch 6, Honshio-cho
Shinjuku-ku
Tokyo 160-0003 Japan
Tel: 81-3-3356-5227
Fax: 81-3-3356-5261
Email: japan@oreilly.com

THAILAND

TransQuest Publishers (Thailand)
535/49 Kasemsuk Yaek 5
Soi Pracharat-Bampen 15
Huay Kwang, Bangkok
Thailand 10310
Tel: 662-6910421 or 6910638
Fax: 662-6902235
Email: puripat@.inet.co.th

ALL OTHER ASIAN COUNTRIES

O'Reilly & Associates, Inc.
101 Morris Street
Sebastopol, CA 95472 USA
Tel: 707-829-0515
Fax: 707-829-0104
Email: order@oreilly.com

AUSTRALIA

Woodslane Pty., Ltd.
7/5 Vuko Place
Warriewood NSW 2102
Australia
Tel: 61-2-9970-5111
Fax: 61-2-9970-5002
Email: info@woodslane.com.au

NEW ZEALAND

Woodslane New Zealand, Ltd.
21 Cooks Street (P.O. Box 575)
Waganui, New Zealand
Tel: 64-6-347-6543
Fax: 64-6-345-4840
Email: info@woodslane.com.au

ARGENTINA

Distribuidora Cuspide
Suipacha 764
1008 Buenos Aires
Argentina
Phone: 5411-4322-8868
Fax: 5411-4322-3456
Email: libros@cuspide.com

POGUE PRESS™
O'REILLY®